THE GEOMETRY OF MODERNISM

Literary Modernism Series
Thomas F. Staley, Editor

MIRANDA B. HICKMAN

THE GEOMETRY

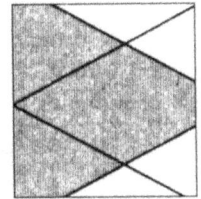

OF MODERNISM

The Vorticist Idiom

in Lewis, Pound,

H.D., and Yeats

University of Texas Press, Austin

Copyright © 2005 by the University of Texas Press
All rights reserved
Printed in the United States of America
First edition, 2005

Requests for permission to reproduce material from this work should be sent to Permissions, University of Texas Press, P.O. Box 7819, Austin, TX 78713-7819.

www.utexas.edu/utpress/about/bpermission.html

♾ The paper used in this book meets the minimum requirements of ANSI/NISO Z39.48-1992 (R1997) (Permanence of Paper).

LIBRARY OF CONGRESS CATALOGING-IN-PUBLICATION DATA

Hickman, Miranda B., date.
  The geometry of modernism : the vorticist idiom in Lewis, Pound, H.D., and Yeats / Miranda B. Hickman.—1st ed.
    p.   cm. —(Literary modernism series)
Includes bibliographical references and index.
ISBN: -0-292-72227-3
  1. English literature—20th century—History and criticism. 2. Modernism (Literature)—English-speaking countries. 3. Yeats, W. B. (William Butler), 1865–1939—Criticism and interpretation. 4. H.D. (Hilda Doolittle), 1886–1961—Criticism and interpretation. 5. Lewis, Wyndham, 1882–1957—Criticism and interpretation. 6. American literature—20th century—History and criticism. 7. Pound, Ezra, 1885–1972—Criticism and interpretation. 8. Fascism and literature—English-speaking countries. 9. Vorticism—English-speaking countries. 10. Geometry in literature. I. Title. II. Series.
PR478.M6H53 2005
820.9'112—dc22   2005007255

Then nothing is surer, said I, than that we must require that the men of your fair city shall never neglect geometry, for even the byproducts of such study are not slight.

PLATO, *Republic:* VII

it is geometry on the wing

H.D., "THE FLOWERING OF THE ROD," *Trilogy*

Illustrations ix

Abbreviations xi

Preface xiii

Acknowledgments xxi

Permissions and Sources xxiii

Introduction 1

 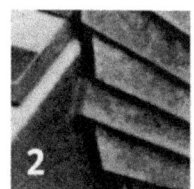  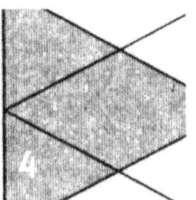

Wyndham Lewis, Vorticism, and the Campaign against Wildean Effeminacy

27

A Vorticist Renaissance? Ezra Pound, the Geometric "Clean Line," and Facist Italy

89

"Embodied . . . in Square and Cube and Rectangle": H.D. and the Vorticist Body

133

"Mystic Geometry": The Visionary Texts of Yeats and H.D.

187

Epilogue 245

Notes 255

Bibliography 305

Index 319

Illustrations

Cover of *Blast 1* (1914) 30

Aubrey Beardsley, cover of prospectus for *The Yellow Book* (1894) 38

Advertisement for *The Yellow Book* in *Blast 1* 39

"Bless the Hairdresser," from manifestoes of *Blast 1* 59

Monument by Jacob Epstein, tomb of Oscar Wilde in Père Lachaise Cemetery, Paris 64

Wyndham Lewis, *Timon of Athens* (from *Blast 1*) 67

First lines of "The Fourth Canto" (initial by Henry Strater), Ezra Pound, *A Draft of xvi. Cantos* (Paris: Three Mountains Press, 1925) 90

First lines of "Canto I" (initial by Dorothy Shakespear), Ezra Pound, *A Draft of xxx Cantos* (Paris: Hours Press, 1930) 90

First lines of "The Twenty Fourth Canto" (initial by Gladys Hynes), Ezra Pound, *A Draft of the Cantos 17–27* (London: John Rodker, 1928) 91

First lines of "Canto VIII" (initial by Dorothy Shakespear), Ezra Pound, *A Draft of xxx Cantos* (Paris: Hours Press, 1930) 91

Images from the 1932 Mostra della Rivoluzione Fascista (Exhibit of the Fascist Revolution) exhibition catalogue 106

Images from the 1932 Mostra (MRF catalogue) 107

Photograph of Kenwin (residence of H.D.), Switzerland 134

Diagrams from Yeats, *A Vision* (1937; p. 75) 202

Diagrams from Yeats, *A Vision* (p. 266) 203

Abbreviations

AVB	William Butler Yeats, *A Vision* (1937)
B1	Wyndham Lewis, ed., *Blast 1*
B2	Lewis, ed., *Blast 2*
C	Pound, *The Cantos*
G-B	Pound, *Gaudier-Brzeska*
GK	Pound, *Guide to Kulchur*
J/M	Pound, *Jefferson and/or Mussolini*
LEP	Pound, *Letters of Ezra Pound*
LWBY	W. B. Yeats, *Letters of W. B. Yeats*
LE	Pound, *Literary Essays of Ezra Pound*
P/L	Materer, ed., *Pound/Lewis: Letters of Ezra Pound and Wyndham Lewis*
P&P	Pound, *Ezra Pound's Poetry and Prose: Contributions to Periodicals*
SP	Pound, *Selected Prose*
TF	H.D., *Tribute to Freud*
WLOA	Lewis, *Wyndham Lewis on Art*

Preface

In his 1993 play *Arcadia*, Tom Stoppard features the concept of geometry in two conspicuously different lights: at moments, it is construed as the discipline that illuminates the elegant patterns underlying chaotic human life—and at other times, as a figure for all the deterministic schemes invoked in the play that humans like to believe their passions elude, the categories and formulae that can never quite accommodate the splendid errantry of human conduct. An ancient science of measurement, associated by Plato with eternal forms, geometry is typically read as thus Janus-faced—a symbol both for the pleasures and inadequacies of orderly pattern. In Stoppard's play, geometry is linked with Euclid, Hobbes, the Enlightenment, and the carefully arranged European gardens of periods before Capability Brown challenged their symmetries in mid-eighteenth-century England with his picturesque aesthetic. As Stoppard suggests, the allure of geometry has spanned the centuries—and the uses to which it has been put, the meanings it has been assigned, are clearly myriad. This book addresses how a fascination with geometric forms played a significant role in the development of Anglo-American modernism—and provided many modern writers with a language through which to imagine and articulate their ideals: a language, in Ezra Pound's words, both to "think in" and to "use" (*LE* 194).

Addressing both the literature and the visual arts of Anglo-American modernism, this project concentrates on the widespread, generative preoccupation among modernist writers with geometric forms—a preoccupation that manifests itself variously in their work as geometric metaphors, images, and diagrams. In the context of modernism, geometry came to bear significances far removed from those with which it has traditionally been associated. In *Arcadia*, the precocious Thomasina, dismissing both Euclid and her tutor's counsel, announces, "There is another geometry which I am engaged in discovering" (84): the moderns, likewise, discovered "another" geometry, a geometric language distinctive to the early twentieth century, conditioned by their environment and suitable to their own aims and desires. This study contends that crucial to the way modernist writers Ezra Pound, H.D., and William Butler Yeats employed geometric figures in their work is how the language of geometry accrued significance within the early modernist movement of Vorticism, emergent in London just before the First World War.[1] The book enlists historicist recovery, archival research, close reading, and contemporary textual scholarship to illuminate how Vorticist geometrics play out in the work of late modernism, as appropriated by Pound, H.D., and Yeats.[2] Between the wars, these writers used the language of Vorticist geometric forms to conceptualize and articulate their aesthetic, cultural, and philosophical ideals.

Currently, modernist studies is undergoing significant revival and change as new materials about the work of writers associated with modernism continue to surface from the archives, valuably dislodging commonplace understandings of what modernism was and uncovering ways of reading it in future.[3] This study joins the contemporary effort to enrich and revise our concepts of modernism by offering new material for the historical record, obtained by way of archival research, reading modernist texts through the lens of contemporary textual scholarship, and directing attention to hitherto understudied modernist work.

Geometry, as its name implies, is an ancient science of measurement, practiced by the Babylonians, the Egyptians, and the Greeks, appropriated and transformed over the centuries in countless ways. As Yeats and Pound note, we associate it with names from ancient Greece such as Pythagoras, Euclid, Empedocles, and Plato; and figures from later days such as Dante, Descartes, and Blake. As the "science which investigates the properties and relations of magnitudes in space, as lines, surface, solids," geometry summons to mind structure, clean lines, and the representation of spatial relationships among objects.[4] In view of Plato's famous association of geometry in the *Republic* with ideal patterns, "essence," "pure knowledge," and the "eternally existent" (759), geometry has also long suggested the notion of the eternal form, the archetypal pattern. The ways the modern writers addressed by this study used geometry, however, while somewhat indebted to this host of traditional meanings, also diverge from them significantly. Again, the principal influence on how these modernist writers came to enlist geometry was how geometric forms accumulated significance in the context of the early modernist movement of Vorticism.

The Vorticist movement was inaugurated by painter and writer Wyndham Lewis in London, just before the First World War, with the magazine-*cum*-manifesto *Blast* (1914–1915). Intended to bring together branches of the arts, Vorticism included a range of painters, sculptors, and writers. Vorticism *per se* did not last long; after two years, the force of the Great War sabotaged its momentum. But in the early 1930s, nearly twenty years after Vorticism had supposedly disappeared from the avant-garde scene, H.D., Pound, and Yeats began conspicuously to draw upon the language of geometric figures, as forged within Vorticism, in their late modernist texts. Although a geometric idiom was of course widely used in the visual arts before the First World War as part of a drive toward nonrepresentational abstraction, it was the constellation of meanings with which geometry came to be freighted within Vorticism that significantly governed the late modernist geometric work of Pound, H.D., and Yeats. The Vorticist geometric idiom provided a vital conceptual and lexical resource as these writers responded to crises—both personal and public—during the years between the wars. In the 1937 version of his occult text *A Vision* (cited as AVB), Yeats refers to Wyndham Lewis's Vorticist "cubes" to explain the "stylistic arrangements of experience" in his own book (AVB 25); Pound invokes Vorticist notions of the geometric line to praise Mussolini's Italy; in prose fiction of the late 1930s, H.D. imagines bodily conditions conducive to visionary states of consciousness by drawing upon the kinds of geometric figures that she has linked with Vorticism. It is this late modernist turn back to Vorticism, prompted by the conditions of the years between the wars, that the present study documents and explores.

The preoccupation with geometric patterns, as defined in this study, appears chiefly not in the formal structures of the texts of these modern writers, nor in their descriptions of relationships among elements of a system, nor even in how they describe the dynamics and ties among individuals—but rather in the vocabulary with which they imagine and figure ideal cultural conditions, bodily states, philosophical attitudes, and epistemological methods. As I will argue, a geometric idiom became especially vital to the instructive and reformative modes of their work of the 1930s and early 1940s, as they confronted public and personal crises during the years leading up to the Second World War.

As Renato Poggioli suggests, to do justice to avant-garde work of the early twentieth century, we need to consider how the pervasive "concept of a movement" influenced the thought and work of the time (*Theory of the Avant-Garde* 16). To do so, we need not only to document the history of early twentieth-century movements in the arts, but also to consider the effects such movements as Vorticism had on the modernist writers themselves—how the lived experience of such movements informed their work. In the case of Vorticism, that lived experience often entailed retaining a powerful memory of the movement's signature geometric language, along with the values that endowed that language with significance in the Vorticist context. Long after the Vorticists had disbanded, ideas associated with Vorticism remained in the minds of these writers, sustaining their work and thought. Vorticism's celebration of a range of values falling within the semantic categories, intertwined within Vorticism, of precision and dynamism—as I will explain in Chapter 1, initially part of Vorticism's phobic response to "effeminacy"—came to be adapted to serve different projects in late modernist work by Pound, H.D., and Yeats.

One of the concomitant goals of this study will be to shed light on several of the more disturbing and enigmatic texts of late modernism, as it is in these that the geometric idiom appears most prominently. Specifically, geometric language tends to mark texts that belong among the late modernist pedagogical-polemical work of H.D., Pound, and Yeats—reformative work, both explicitly manifestic and otherwise, that articulates ideals toward cultural and philosophical analysis and transformation. Although the geometric "arrangements" of their work can sometimes be found in their verse, it is their prose—and specifically the prose that responds to the cultural climate of crisis between the wars—that forms the chief locus for the geometric idiom. Accordingly, texts taken up in detail here include Pound's *Jefferson and/or Mussolini* (1935), in which Pound justifies his growing admiration for Italian Fascism; H.D.'s *Nights* (1935), a novella about a writer's suicidal quest for perfection; H.D.'s *Tribute to Freud*, written in the 1940s, in which she reflects upon her sessions with Sigmund Freud in Vienna 1933–1934 and details her ambivalent attitude toward the man she called "the Master"; and Yeats's occult text *A Vision* (1937), in which he enlists wisdom from spiritual "Instructors" to chart the cycles of individual lives and Western history. Also addressed here are other texts relevant to the development and permutation of the geometric idiom: H.D.'s *Notes on Thought and Vision* (1982; written 1919) and *HERmione* (1981; written c. 1927), Pound's *Guide to Kulchur* (1938), and Lewis's *Enemy of the Stars* (1914) and *Tarr* (1918).

More generally, this study illuminates several cruxes integral to the evolution of Anglo-American modernism that demand further attention. First, it explores the struggle with the category of "effeminacy," pivotal to much modernist work, as it influences the significances with which Vorticist geometrics initially come to be endowed. Through an exploration of Ezra Pound's increasing infatuation with Italian Fascism in the 1930s, it addresses more broadly the ways in which many modernist writers responded to the problem of what Auden termed the "failure of liberal capitalist democracy" by turning to the possibility of fascism. Here I join the work on modernism and fascism by such scholars as Chace (*The Political Identities of Ezra Pound and T. S. Eliot*), Craig (*Yeats, Eliot, Pound, and the Politics of Poetry*), Cullingford (*Yeats, Ireland, and Fascism*), North (*The Political Aesthetic of Yeats, Eliot, and Pound*), Redman (*Ezra Pound and Italian Fas-*

cism), and Sherry (*Ezra Pound, Wyndham Lewis, and Radical Modernism*). In my method, I take a cue from Lawrence Rainey's call for specific studies of individuals' lived experiences of fascism—in this case, I trace the role of geometry in the formation of Pound's allegiance to Mussolini's Italy—in order to enrich theoretical claims about the nexus between modernism and fascism (*Ezra Pound and the Monument of Culture* 3). Through its discussion of a little-known novella by H.D., *Nights*, whose protagonist meditates frequently, even obsessively, on geometric figures, the book explores modernism's debates about bodily sanity. Finally, through analysis of how Yeats and H.D. use a geometric lexicon to record the experience of mystical knowledge, as well as of how their geometric vocabulary comes to register their attitudes toward mystical epistemology, the book contributes to a growing body of scholarship on modernism's relationship to the occult—including recent work by Materer (*Modernist Alchemy*), Surette (*The Birth of Modernism*), Sword (*Engendering Inspiration*), and Tryphonopoulos (*The Celestial Tradition*).

Major chronicles of Anglo-American modernism such as Kenner's classic *The Pound Era* (1971), Levenson's *Genealogy of Modernism* (1984), and Nicholls's *Modernisms* (1995) have recognized Vorticism as one of the vital early projects of Anglo-American modernist practice. Although even one of the movement's major chroniclers, Richard Cork, has acknowledged Vorticism's tepid critical reception throughout the decades of the twentieth century, the scholarly attention Vorticism continues to draw suggests that it is still a topic that merits debate, especially as traditional accounts of modernism's development undergo reconsideration. I argue, in fact, that understanding the way Vorticism has been appropriated within the chronicles of modernism's history can tell us much about the assumptions and desires guiding our modernist mythmaking.

Germinal books on the movement include William Wees's *Vorticism and the English Avant-Garde* (1972) and Cork's own massive *Vorticism and Abstract Art in the First Machine Age* (1976). Subsequent studies by Materer (*Vortex: Pound, Eliot, and Lewis*, 1979) and Dasenbrock (*The Literary Vorticism of Ezra Pound and Wyndham Lewis*, 1984), like the present one, explore the impact of Vorticism on literary practice. A major exhibit in German museums in 1996–1997, which attests to a continuing interest in Vorticism, has given rise to a substantive collection of new articles on the movement. Other recent work has focused on Vorticism's "aesthetic turbulence" (Graver, "Vorticist Performance," 1992), its construction of a nationalist avant-garde program in the context of the Great War (Peppis, "Surrounded by a Multitude of Other Blasts," 1997), and its use of promotional tactics inspired by British advertising culture (Reynolds, "'Chaos Invading Concept,'" 2000).

In most accounts, however, Vorticism is presented as merely a short-lived movement whose consequences were limited, its promise cut off by the arrival of the Great War. The present study counters this interpretation by tracing Vorticism's continuing influence on late modernist literary practice. Like this book, Reed Way Dasenbrock's *Literary Vorticism of Ezra Pound and Wyndham Lewis* (1985) recognizes the effects of Vorticism on late modernist literature. However, while my study owes a great deal to Dasenbrock's extensive and insightful analysis, here I offer an account of Vorticism's genesis that differs from his: I argue that Vorticism at once sustains many of the central aesthetic and philosophical tenets of British *fin-de-siècle* Aestheticism and moves defensively away from the "effeminacy" that, by the early twentieth century, Aestheticism had come to connote. Unquestionably, Vorticism formulated its geometric vocabulary partly in response to contemporary movements such as Cubism and Futurism; as Chapter 1 addresses, the Vorticists were constantly reacting to, often defining themselves defensively against, the examples of their contemporaries, in a process of what Janet Lyon rightly calls "incremental self-differentiation" ("Militant Discourse" 105). But what both the rhetoric of Vorticism and its canny position-taking indicate is that the movement's formation was decisively guided by its intimate and ambivalent response to its Aestheticist predecessors; and, accordingly, that its geometric gestures were enlisted in a phobic project of countering the kind of "effeminacy" that had come to be linked in the public mind with Aestheticism. The campaign against effeminacy, pervasive and widely discussed in chronicles of modernism's history, is fundamental to the evolution of both Vorticism and its geometrics: it governed the qualities that geometric language—in the form of metaphor, visual diagram, and verbal image—came to assume within Vorticism, the signals that its geometric idiom was intended to send.

This study addresses, first, an audience of modernist scholars seeking new perspectives on ostensibly well-travelled territory—Anglo-American avant-garde practices of the years before the First World War and their effects on later modernist work. Through historicist recovery, it seeks to play out in a new modality Marjorie Perloff's contention that this early "Futurist Moment" cast a long shadow over the modernist years (*Futurist Moment* xx). Its discussions of Pound's relationship to Italian Fascism (and especially his responses to the 1932 Mostra della Rivoluzione Fascista, which remain underexamined) are intended for a broader scholarly audience interested in the perennial question of how to interpret what Frank Kermode famously called the "correlation between early modernist literature and authoritarian politics" (*The Sense of an Ending* 108). Its exploration of H.D.'s novels and memoirs, meanwhile—taken up at a moment when H.D.'s prose, more widely available than ever before, attracts as much attention as her poetry—is aimed at scholars considering the new directions feminist scholarship in literary studies might take, and the pitfalls it might avoid, in the twenty-first century. And the book's treatment of Yeats's and H.D.'s conflicted relationship to mystical epistemology is directed at scholars concerned with the impact of occult thought on the development of modernism.

Ultimately, this project seeks to join the larger current effort within modernist studies to reevaluate our concepts of modernism with the hindsight available to us as we leave the century of modernism's emergence. To revisit Vorticism is to return to a milieu regarded as both cradle and crucible of Anglo-American modernism. Accordingly, through its reexamination of Vorticism and its aftermath, this study interrogates the narratives of modernism's origins and development that have come to dominate our chronicles. By reassessing the critical treatment accorded to Vorticism and its geometrics, as well as how we have incorporated these into our stories about modernism, we can better understand the investments that have shaped our ideas of modernism thus far—and this understanding, in turn, can help us to decide the ideas that will serve best in years to come.

Acknowledgments I still remember the first time I encountered Jerome McGann's persuasive argument that textual production was an inherently social and collaborative process. Although this book has largely been a solo endeavor, I know, in hindsight, that I owe profound thanks to all the colleagues, mentors, students, family members, and friends who have directly or indirectly supported the project and have given me the wherewithal and presence of mind to complete it.

Thanks are due, first, to John Whittier-Ferguson, who long ago saw promise in an unusual idea—and encouraged me through the laborious stages of bringing the project into its first full draft. His thoughtful, generous, energetic approach to supervision has remained in my mind as exemplifying some of the best teaching this field has to offer. George Bornstein's inspiring lessons about textual scholarship provided the analytical and theoretical resources for much of my work with both Ezra Pound and Wyndham Lewis. To Martha Vicinus's expertise in the Victorian period, I owe key insights about Oscar Wilde and the *fin de siècle*, and it was her offhand remark about my work on H.D. that gave me the courage to work it up into a more full-fledged project.

I am also indebted to Janice Koistinen-Harris, Maren Linett, Michael Sharp, and Bill Wees for incisive feedback on portions of this project while it was in formation. Vincent Sherry, Omar Pound, Philip Grover, Richard Cork, Brigid Peppin, and Cy Fox also offered crucial guidance at key points. And Caroline Duroselle-Melish of Harvard's Houghton Library supplied invaluable counsel about how to understand books as physical artifacts.

I owe thanks, too, to the staff at several archives: Yale University's Beinecke Rare Book and Manuscript Library, where Patricia Willis has often provided crucial information; the Harry Ransom Humanities Research Center, where Cathy Henderson and Willard Goodwin assisted in various quests; and Cornell University's Rare and Manuscript Collections at the Carl A. Kroch Library, where Lorna Knight responded helpfully to my queries. My study of the Wyndham Lewis Papers at the University of Buffalo, although never directly incorporated into the project, greatly enriched my understanding of Lewis's early work. My thanks to Robert J. Bertholf and Michael Basinski for all their hospitality while I was there. The same kind of gratitude goes to Lori Curtis, curator of the Special Collections Library at the University of Tulsa; while Tulsa's holdings never made their way directly into my work, Curtis's passion for archival work remains an inspiration to me and continues to inform my conduct in the archives.

Many thanks are due also to the English Department of McGill University, and especially to its chair, Maggie Kilgour, for the semester's leave that made it possible for me to complete the book. To my students at McGill, especially those in my graduate and undergraduate courses on modernism, I owe the excitement about modernism and its eccentricities that allowed me to complete the book with renewed vigor. It is no exaggeration to say that their enthusiasm for the surprises and hideaways of modernist literature has given me the energy to go on.

The deepest personal thanks go to Bill, my father, and to Dave Gardner, for the support it took to see this through. I dedicate the book to them and to three people who are no longer living but who remain with me through everything: my grandparents from Friuli-Venezia Giulia, Fulvio Antonio and Silla Rosa Brun—and my mother, Fulvia, who loved English literature.

Permissions and Sources

Material from *The Cantos* by Ezra Pound (copyright © 1930, 1934 by Ezra Pound) and correspondence by Ezra Pound (copyright © 2005 by Omar S. Pound and Mary de Rachewiltz) is reprinted with the permission of New Directions Publishing Corporation.

Quotations from *Nights* by H.D. (copyright © 1986 by Perdita Schaffner) are also reprinted with the permission of New Directions Publishing Corporation.

Material from Wyndham Lewis (© Wyndham Lewis and the estate of the late Mrs. G. A. Wyndham Lewis) is reprinted with the kind permission of the Wyndham Lewis Memorial Trust (a registered charity).

Material from the Wyndham Lewis Collection, 1877–1974, Number 4612, housed in the Carl A. Kroch Library, Cornell University, is quoted courtesy of the Division of Rare and Manuscript Collections, Cornell University Library.

Material from *A Vision* by W. B. Yeats (© 1937 by W. B. Yeats, © renewed 1965 by Bertha Georgie Yeats and Anne Butler Yeats) is reprinted in the United States with the permission of Scribner, an imprint of the Simon & Schuster Adult Publishing Group.

Material from *A Vision* by W. B. Yeats is reprinted outside the United States by permission of A. P. Watt Ltd. on behalf of Michael B. Yeats.

The source for the photograph of Kenwin; for images from Ezra Pound's *Draft of xvi. Cantos, A Draft of the Cantos*

17–27, and *A Draft of xxx Cantos*; and for quotations from hitherto unpublished material by Ezra Pound and H.D. is the Yale Collection of American Literature, Beinecke Rare Book and Manuscript Library.

Images from *Blast 1* (1914) are from the copy of *Blast* housed at the Cutter Collection at the Rare Books and Special Collections Division of McGill University Libraries, Montréal, Québec.

Permissions and Sources A quotation from a letter by Nancy Cunard is reprinted by permission of A. R. A. Hobson, literary executor representing the heirs of Nancy Cunard.

The photograph by Maggie Kilgour of Jacob Epstein's monument for Oscar Wilde's tomb, Père Lachaise Cemetery, Paris, is reprinted with the permission of the photographer.

THE GEOMETRY OF MODERNISM

Introduction

A famous injunction, engraved on the front of the Pythagorean Academy and reiterated by Plato, dissuaded any from entering the academy who were "ignorant of Geometry." Although knowledge of geometry was not quite a prerequisite for entrance into the groves of modernist art, the language of geometric figures was so widely discussed in avant-garde circles of the early twentieth century that few of the moderns could long have remained ignorant of it. The present study explores the role of geometric forms—and more precisely, a generative preoccupation with using an idiom composed of geometric forms as a means for imagining and articulating desired attitudes and conditions of existence—in the work and thought of four major Anglo-American modernist writers: Wyndham Lewis, Ezra Pound, H.D., and W. B. Yeats.

"What the analytical geometer does for space and form," Pound noted in 1912, "the poet does for the states of consciousness" (*SP* 362).[1] Two years later, in his essay "Vorticism," he would echo the analogy, enlarging his scope to include art more generally: "The difference between art and analytical geometry is the difference of subject-matter only" (*G-B* 91).[2] By invoking geometry to define the task of the artist, Pound was in fact participating in a practice that would become widespread among Anglo-American modernist writers. Though little discussed in modernist criticism, geometric language pervades the writing and thought of Pound, H.D., Lewis, and Yeats.[3] Elsewhere, Pound used not only such comparisons, but even actual geometric formulae to depict the work of the artist; Lewis punctuated his artistic manifestoes with geometric vortices; H.D. employed verbal descriptions of geometric figures—"square and cube and rectangle"—to imagine ideal bodily states conducive to artistic vision and transcendent awareness; and Yeats diagrammed the cycles of Western civilization with geometric gyres.

Invoked and handled in a variety of ways, geometric terms provided a crucial conceptual and lexical resource for the moderns as they conceived and articulated their convictions—convictions registered in manifestoes, critical essays, and reflective moments in their poetry or fiction.[4] As Gail McDonald notes, alluding to Hugh Kenner's phrase, the moderns often stood "at the blackboard," forming schools and launching movements; developing aesthetic, philosophical, and cultural theories; and making pronouncements (*Learning to Be Modern* vii)—and geometric vocabulary played a significant role in the development and enunciation of this pedagogical-polemical dimension of their work.[5] Their shared investment in geometric figures, as defined in this study, appears chiefly not in the formal structures of their writing, nor in their descriptions of relationships among elements of systems they address, but rather in how they imagine and figure ideals—with regard to social conditions, philosophical attitudes, artistic stances, and epistemological methods. As I will argue, a geometric idiom became especially vital to the instructive and reformative mode of their work of the 1930s and early 1940s—as they faced, and strove to respond adequately to, the public and personal crises of the years leading up to the Second World War.

By 1925, when Le Corbusier announced in *Urbanisme* that "modern art and thought" were tending in the "direction of geometry" and that "the age" was "essentially a geometrical one" (*City of Tomorrow* xxi–xxii), he was advancing claims that had become so uncontroversial as to be commonplace: in the first two and a half decades of the twentieth century, the geometric shape was increasingly used as a vehicle for the nonrepresentational impulse in the visual arts and was pervading visual culture more generally. Britain, continental Europe, Russia, and slightly later, North America had been swept by the abstract geometric art of the Cubists, Expressionists, Futurists, Suprematists, and Constructivists, as well as by the geometric architecture and design of Walter Gropius's Bauhaus and of Le Corbusier himself, whose white Purist villas were earning him a reputation as a visionary. By 1924, Roger Fry's landmark Post-Impressionist exhibits of 1910 and 1912 in London and their New York counterpart, the Armory Show of 1913, were more than a decade past. Audiences acquainted with the avant-garde were accustomed to a proliferation of geometric work by such artists as Delaunay, Picabia, Duchamp, and Kandinsky; declarations such as Le Corbusier's; and even internal divisions among the artists associated with a geometric idiom. By 1927, when Virginia Woolf had a puzzled Mr. Bankes in her novel *To the Lighthouse* tap painter Lily Briscoe's canvas with his penknife and ask her to explain the "triangular purple shape—just there," she was clearly using this inquisitive gesture to evoke a moment twenty years before.

But while the shock of the new produced by geometric abstraction may have abated by the mid-1920s, there was still widespread debate about the artistic and philosophical goals associated with such abstraction, its significance, and the extent to which it should be cultivated for the most successful art.[6] Of course, the polyvalence of the geometric signifier remains today, along with the multiplicity of ends toward which it can be enlisted. Accordingly, I begin this study by narrowing in more specifically on how the modernist writers addressed here interpreted and appropriated the language of geometry in their historical context.

In 1929, Le Corbusier's *Urbanisme* appeared for the first time in an English edition—under the title *The City of To-Morrow and Its Planning*. The translator was painter Frederick Etchells, who had also translated Le Corbusier's widely influential *Vers une Architecture* (1923) as *Towards a New Architecture* (1927). It is fitting that Etchells should bring to an anglophone readership an ardent paean to the expressive and generative power of geometry: fifteen years before, Etchells had cut a profile in London with one of the avant-garde movements in London recognized for its geometric forms, though less well known than those catalogued above: Vorticism. Inaugurated by painter and writer Wyndham Lewis in 1913–1914, Vorticism was launched with the express intention of linking several of the arts while respecting the distinctness of each.[7] During its brief life span (most commentaries read it as closing entirely by 1919), its adherents included painters such as Etchells, Edward Wadsworth, Cuthbert Hamilton, Helen Saunders, Jessica Dismorr, David Bomberg, and William Roberts, sculptors such as Henri Gaudier-Brzeska and Jacob Epstein, photographers such as Alvin Coburn and Malcolm Arbuthnot, and poets such as Ezra Pound.[8] The cluster of different arts associated with it notwithstanding, its principal achievements were in painting and sculpture. Its major theoretical statements appeared through the periodical-*cum*-manifesto, *Blast*, which debuted in 1914; the second, and final, issue of *Blast* appeared in 1915—as a "War Number" issued from the midst of the First World War.

Despite the aggressive, often bombastic, artistic pronouncements for which the Vorticists came to be known, the aesthetic program with which they began was neither coherent nor precisely articulated—but from the outset, they were consistently recognized, and often caricatured, for their signature geometric idiom. In a 1914 catalogue introduction designed to advance the ideas that would presently be regarded as those distinctive to Vorticism, Wyndham Lewis noted that the work of his cohort "underline[d]" the "geometric bases and structure of life" ("Cubist Room" 9). Writing about the work of this group in the *New Age*, critic and philosopher T. E. Hulme maintained that he was describing a "new constructive geometric art," whose "geometrical" character he repeatedly underscored ("Modern Art—I" 341).⁹ In a contemporary review of March 1914, Lewis, exhibiting with the painters who would soon be recognized as Vorticists, was rebuked by critic Paul Konody for "geometrical obfuscation."¹⁰

The nucleus of the Vorticists—consisting of Lewis, Etchells, Wadsworth, and Hamilton—initially issued out of a schism with the Omega Workshops in London, an atelier led by Bloomsbury critic and painter Roger Fry, for which they worked for a time. When with the Workshops, they shared with the Bloomsbury artists an interest in "pure form"—theorized by critic Clive Bell in *Art* (1914) as "significant form" and often played out formally in geometric terms. With the concept of "significant form," Bell provided one of the most durable early twentieth-century crystallizations of the assumption, animating the work of many contemporary artists, that "lines and colours combined in a particular way, certain forms and relations of forms, stir our aesthetic emotions," independent of any relationship they might have to referents in the external world (8). While not precluding geometric forms from serving in some representational capacity, this would nonetheless mean that the shapes and lines and colors themselves, apart from things in the world to which they pointed, would bear significance in their own right. In an essay of the same year, Pound reflected the currency and influence of this idea, invoking (and misquoting) Whistler to underwrite a similar claim: "Whistler said somewhere in *The Gentle Art*, 'The picture is interesting not because it is Trotty Veg [Veck], but because it is an arrangement in colour'" (*G-B* 85).¹¹ He paraphrases in the same spirit in *Blast 1*, crediting Whistler with the sentiment: "You are interested in a certain painting because it is an arrangement of lines and colours" (*B1* 154). Or as Lewis notes in *Blast 2*,

> A Vorticist, lately, painted a picture in which a crowd of squarish shapes, at once suggesting windows, occurred. A sympathiser with the movement asked him, horror-struck, "are not those windows?" "Why not?" the Vorticist replied. "A window for you is actually a window: for me it is a space, bounded by a square or oblong frame, by four bands or lines, merely." (44)

According to Lewis's account, then, the Vorticist is most interested in the shape created, and what it suggests in itself, "the value of color and form as such independently of what recognisable form it covers or encloses" ("Cubist Room" 9), though it may retain representational meaning for other viewers. In their work for the Omega Workshops, Lewis, Hamilton, Wadsworth, and Etchells emphasized nonrepresentational geometrics more intensely than did their compatriots; once divided from the Omega group, they heightened their geometric abstraction still further. Walter Michel notes that Vorticist art typically featured "jagged" forms and "compositional elements" that were "sharply bounded by straight-lines or geometric arcs" ("Vorticism and the Early Wyndham Lewis," 6). And they began to endow their geometrics with qualities and significances other than those they bore within the Omega context.

Specifically, the geometric forms that came to be characteristic of Vorticism were, on the one hand, sharply delineated, and on the other, constructed and arranged so as to suggest driving, rushing, forceful motion. In his survey of the development of the Vorticist aesthetic, Reed Way Dasenbrock explains this aspect of Vorticist geometrics by addressing Vorticism's much-rehearsed debt to both Cubism and Italian Futurism (albeit one often strategically erased by Lewis so as to heighten the impression of Vorticism's independence and originality), as well as its important differences from both. Dasenbrock rightly refutes the charge of derivativeness often levelled against Vorticism by highlighting the Vorticists' fusion—what Lewis called their "new synthesis" (*B2* 42)—of what they regarded as the best elements of both Cubism and Futurism: in fact, their deliberate appropriation of Futurist maneuvers to "correct" (*B2* 41) what they presented as the shortcomings of Cubism and vice versa. And although Cubism and Futurism indeed dominate Vorticist rhetoric as the coordinates by which Vorticism plots its location, in "A Review of Contemporary Art" in *Blast 2*, Lewis adds Wassily Kandinsky's Expressionism as a third "point of the compass" (39)—as another idiom to criticize and oppose in the service of self-definition. From Cubism, the Vorticists drew a commitment to a vocabulary of exactly delineated, geometric forms, as well as a concomitant refusal of the "fluid and imprecise" (Dasenbrock, *Literary Vorticism*, 32) approach they saw as characteristic of much Futurist work; from Futurism, a dedication to suggesting dynamic motion—which, according to Vorticist rhetoric, Cubist work lacked (*B2* 38). Steering its course so as to avoid the errors of its contemporaries, Vorticism shunned what it read as the "deadness" (38) of Cubism, the unbridled "vivacity" (41) of the Futurists, and Kandinsky's Expressionism, which, Lewis noted, exhibited much the same passivity as Cubism and much the same indefiniteness as Futurism (40). Dasenbrock coins the term "dynamic formism" to encapsulate the aesthetic with which the Vorticists emerged (*Literary Vorticism*, 41). Lewis, meanwhile, deems this desired Vorticist condition a "mastered, vivid vitality" (*B2* 38)—"mastered" in that, unlike Futurist work, it is controlled and exact, "vivid" and "vital" in that, unlike Cubist work, it is also intensely and aggressively energetic.

Scholars of Vorticism agree that this combination of precise form and dynamism characterizes Vorticist art. Cork notes that Vorticist art stands "poised half-way between the kinetic dynamics of Futurism and the static monumentality of Cubism"—such that "a typical Vorticist design shoots outward in iconoclastic shafts, zig-zags, or diagonally oriented fragments, and at the same time asserts the need for a solidly impacted, almost sculptural order" (*Vorticism and Its Allies* 22). William Wees's description of the experience of Vorticist work at London's Tate Gallery in the late 1960s likewise captures the union of dynamic motion and stark, crisply delineated geometric forms that fosters the effect of the characteristic Vorticist canvas:

> White and blue angular forms seem almost suspended over a large red rectangle. Three triangular areas of mustard brown lie outside the rectangle, and a brown and black shaft cuts across it from top to bottom. The painting is David Bomberg's *Mud Bath* (1914) . . . and it shares the wall with two other Bomberg paintings . . . . In both, Bomberg experimented with an unusual grid pattern made from vertical and horizontal lines regularly spaced and intersected by diagonal lines. Both pictures begin with figures in action . . . and then transform them into nearly unrecognizable fragments within the overall pattern of triangles-within-squares.
>
> (VORTICISM AND THE
> ENGLISH AVANT-GARDE 3–4)

It is the signature geometric idiom of Vorticism—that both presents exact "pattern[s]" and nonetheless suggests "figures in action"—that the present study takes as its point of departure, as it was Vorticism that imbued the geometric idiom with the cluster of significances with which many modernist writers would associate it—and upon which they would draw in later years.

The late Hugh Kenner's landmark study of modernism, *The Pound Era* (1971), famously assigns Vorticism a central position in the development of modernism: his book remains, in fact, the best-known critical tribute to Vorticism. Much criticism since the 1970s has regretted Kenner's androcentric view, and in today's climate, his deliberately heroic narrative of the men of 1914 is increasingly invoked as emblematic of an era in modernist studies now past.[12] Nonetheless, the wealth of scholarly attention that Vorticism has drawn since the 1970s — from such critics as Cork, Wees, Materer, Dasenbrock, and more recently Peppis, Graver, and Reynolds (see Preface) — suggests that, even if *The Pound Era* has been superseded, the Vorticist movement it salutes remains a topic to be reckoned with. Given the clear signs of ongoing interest in Vorticism, we need to continue to reassess our understanding of the movement and its place within the development of what we have come to think of as Anglo-American literary modernism — which of course is currently undergoing its own extensive reassessment.

I am certainly not prepared to argue that, contrary to popular belief, Vorticism was a weighty, thoughtful, groundbreaking movement of great import. Evidence indeed suggests that it ascended and declined rapidly, generally met with unfavorable reviews, and contributed only one among many equally important isms to its feverishly active London avant-garde milieu.[13] It was mischievous, prankish, lobbed to the public with a broad sense of absurdity, formed in defiant and defensive reaction to its contemporaries, filled with the kinds of exaggerated pronouncements that aimed to make noise and gain an audience rather than with legible, durable philosophical and aesthetic commitments. Contemporaries such as A. R. Orage were announcing its death just a few months after the first appearance of *Blast*; and even its founder, Lewis, reminisced about it later in his career as a brief movement, "snuffed out by the Great War," that he outgrew.[14]

Nonetheless, Vorticism has subsequently come to play a crucial role in the development of historical narratives about the birth of Anglo-American literary modernism, one whose consequences we would do well to interrogate. Moreover, and for this study more importantly, its use of a geometric mode influenced considerably the course of much later work by Anglo-American modernist writers. Although I certainly would not suggest, as Shari Benstock characterizes the view she attributes to Hugh Kenner, that "the literary practice of Modernism is that defined by Pound as Vorticism" (*Women of the Left Bank*, 24), with Kenner and Dasenbrock, I do regard Vorticism as a "key locus of innovation" (Dasenbrock, *Literary Vorticism* 150) that keenly affected later modernist work as well as, I would add, stories of modernism's origins.

Accordingly, as Paul Peppis suggests, the received ideas with which Vorticism has become associated stand in need of further scrutiny and revision.[15] As I will argue in Chapter 1, at this moment in modernist studies, a time ripe for the reevaluation of modernism, we would benefit from revisiting Vorticism: as Leon Surette notes, having left the twentieth century during which modernism came of age, we can now begin to do justice to its history (*Birth of Modernism* 1). We especially need to reconsider how Vorticism has been deployed in our narratives about modernism, in which, in an apparent contradiction, it has often been figured as both a crucial site of origin and a negligible flash in the pan. A movement, of course, can both be short-lived, extinguished before it has chance to fulfill its promise, and at the same time a cultural matrix from which unfold many other developments. But as I will suggest, modernist historiography has yet to confront responsibly the incongruity between the way Vorticism is dismissed as lightweight and yet frequently invoked as vital to our understanding of modernism's formation.

Furthermore, we need to query even the received ideas about Vorticism as merely ephemeral, its "blast" drowned out by the roar of the First World War, its consequences limited.[16] Significances taken on by geometric forms in the context of the Vorticist movement remained attached to them in the minds of many modernist writers—and while, in later years, Vorticist geometric forms were no longer used as part of Vorticist projects, the meanings they had acquired from those projects remained, to be directed in the service of other ends.

Vorticist geometry exerted an influence on the imaginations of not only the writers associated with the Vorticist circle of 1914, but also Yeats and H.D., who certainly had personal links with members of the Vorticist movement but never participated in it directly. Yeats and H.D. encountered the movement by virtue of their proximity to Pound and their involvement in the London scene of the *avant-guerre*. In 1913, H.D. had just arrived back in London and was living across the street from Pound as various soon-to-be Vorticists entered and left his apartment. Shortly before this, she had witnessed proto-Vorticist work at Frida Strindberg's club, the Cave of the Golden Calf (Guest, *Herself Defined* 60). She had attended "evenings" at which Wyndham Lewis was present (57). Guest suggests that, at this point, H.D. may even have felt displaced from Pound's attention by his devotion to the new movement (60–65). A few years later, in a review of Yeats's *Responsibilities*, H.D. would register her response to Vorticism by positioning it as exemplary of the philosophical currents, albeit destructive ones, of her generation.[17]

Yeats, meanwhile, was collaborating closely with Pound just before Vorticism coalesced: in the winter of 1913, the year before the appearance of *Blast*, the two poets were working together closely at Stone Cottage in Sussex. James Longenbach notes Yeats's influence, as a result, on Pound's contributions to Vorticist projects, suggesting that the "lessons" about elite standards Pound gleaned from Yeats at Stone Cottage "stand behind his Vorticist pronouncements" (*Stone Cottage* 73) and that Pound's contact with Yeats's esoteric reading in 1914 also guided his conceptualization of the Vorticist aesthetic. Yeats, in turn, was aware of Vorticist doings: attending exhibits of Vorticist work—as Pound notes in "Canto 80," Yeats was accosted at a "vorticist picture-show" (*c* 518)—remaining closely involved with Pound as Pound became central to the development of Vorticism, and reading *Blast*.

Years later, in his famous 1928 introduction to *A Vision* (1937), Yeats would identify Wyndham Lewis with geometric "cubes" and "stylistic arrangements of experience," and as it was only Lewis's early Vorticist work that was connected with either, Yeats had clearly retained the geometrics of Vorticism as part of his lexicon for understanding and describing philosophic and artistic endeavor. Both H.D. and Yeats, then, though not members of the Vorticist movement, certainly encountered it, responded to it, and maintained its signature geometric language as part of their aesthetic and philosophical vocabulary, such that the values associated with that language conditioned their later textual invocations of geometry.

Inspired by geometric forms and their Vorticist significances, these modernist writers later came to enlist a geometric idiom in the interpretation of their environments, the construction of their desires and convictions, and the articulation of their ideals for social and philosophical transformation. In part, they did so influenced by Vorticism; contributing to their effort also was their search for new forms of expression, now considered characteristically modernist, that would allow them to supersede what many moderns famously regarded as the limitations of conventional verbal language. As Pound put it, "Any mind that is worth calling a mind must have needs beyond the existing categories of language" (*G-B* 88); later, in a memoir, he would reminisce about his early effort to "make" a language not only to "use" but also to "think in" (*LE* 194). And as H.D. wrote, "I must find new words . . . to explain certain as yet unrecorded states of mind or being" (*TF* 145). Together, such comments delineate the contour of a communal attempt to redress what these writers perceived as the impoverishment of existing vocabularies—an impulse that played out, in part, in their attraction to the geometric idiom, which, insofar as it was pictorial, provided a welcome alternative to what they regarded as an untrustworthy and insufficient verbal medium.

Their most pronounced use of the Vorticist geometric idiom dates from the 1930s and early 1940s. This late turn of modernist writers to a Vorticist geometric language, then, is associated with a specific historical moment of markedly intense political and cultural pressure: confronted by the crises riving Europe during the years between the economic depression and the Second World War, feeling impelled to respond to them with commentary and counsel, Pound, H.D., and Yeats reached to a geometric lexicon to explain themselves—which, for them, remained linked to values developed within the context of Vorticism.

Again, within Vorticism, geometric forms had come to accrue connotations of, on the one hand, precision, rigor, and analytical detachment (expressing Vorticism's accord with the Cubist insistence on clearly delineated "form" and valorization of the frame of mind capable of producing such exact form); and on the other, force, aggression, and action (here expressing Vorticism's emulation of the Futurist commitment to dynamism). Arguably, although the Vorticists would not have acknowledged this publicly, the example of Futurism alone suggested the combination of precision and force. Largely in the name of identity construction, the Vorticists constantly faulted the Futurists for their lack of precision and bounding lines; but in his manifestoes, Futurist leader F. T. Marinetti in fact demanded both "*de la violence et de la précision.*"[18] The phrase is particularly apt for describing Vorticist tenets: as coded within a Vorticist context, geometric *précision* in fact comes to connote violent motion, the dynamic force of *violence*—and in the Vorticist view, aggression will not transmit sufficient force unless it involves precision.

Framed by the rhetoric of Vorticism and employed in Vorticist paintings, Vorticist geometry thus came to suggest a disciplined condition of both maximum intensity and dynamic force. As a result, Vorticist geometry often implied a certain posture toward the world: one that combined active engagement—entailing the desire to act upon, interpret, respond vigilantly to, and even transform, the elements of one's environment—with an attitude of detachment that allowed for control.[19] As the discussion of Chapter 1 will clarify, these two stances, analytical detachment and active, forceful responsiveness, although apparently at odds, in fact cooperate within the Vorticist project through their common cause of combating the perceived dangers of effeminacy. As indicated by its geometrics, Vorticism celebrates "a mode of approach" to the world (to use H.D.'s phrase from *Notes on Thought and Vision*)—as well as qualities that imply that mode, which may be found in an observed object. For Pound, for instance, the laudable "form-sense" (*GK* 134) that he associated with Vorticist geometrics could be expressed both in an artist's ability to address the surrounding world with an attitude uniting detachment, vigilant attention, and active responsiveness—and in the art produced by the artist who had achieved this attitude. Reminiscing about Vorticism in 1939, Lewis would note that it had involved

> the sternness and severity of mind that is appropriate to the man who does the stuff ... especially when that stuff is a harsh, reverberative, and indeed rather terrible material.... It was ... *professional*. (Lewis's italics)
>
> (WLOA 342)

This is colloquially put, but illuminating nonetheless: the attitude described is the controlled "sternness" and "severity of mind" that accompanies, and enables, action ("appropriate to the man who *does* the stuff" [my italics])—action that is in turn both forceful (it can work with "*harsh*" material [my italics]) and efficient and unsentimental ("*professional*"). This, then, is the condition of mind and the attendant capacity for action that Pound, H.D., and Yeats all later come to associate with geometrics. As Chapters 1 and 2 explain at greater length, given Vorticism's double desire for precision and vigorous force, the image of precise lines, in a Vorticist context, in fact comes to "imply force and action" (*B2* 44). In 1910, Pound forecasts what will become the Vorticist linkage between clean lines and forceful action when he notes that a line "marks the passage of a force." "All our ideas of beauty of line," he observes, "are in some way connected with our ideas of swiftness or easy power of motion" (*Translations* 23). Within Vorticism, geometric lines, conspicuously exact, come to be intimately connected both with "motion" and "force."

This study thus addresses a group of late modernist texts, appearing approximately twenty years after Vorticism's first efflorescence, in which resurface Vorticism's linked commitments to both action and "sternness and severity of mind," as well as the geometric forms attendant upon these commitments. Reckoning with a range of crises, personal and political, arising from the 1930s and early 1940s, the writers considered here returned to Vorticist ideals of rigor, precision, intensity, and dynamism—and expressed their adherence to these ideals through a geometric idiom. At this point, Lewis, the self-styled Vorticist leader, was himself revisiting Vorticism, publishing retrospective articles about the movement and issuing new, revised editions of both *Tarr*, his Vorticist novel written about 1915, and *Enemy of the Stars*, the 1914 play in *Blast 1* that he had intended as an exemplar of literary Vorticism. But it is not Lewis's kind of commemorative project, devoted to returning to and revising existing Vorticist texts, that I document here. Rather, this book concentrates on how Pound, H.D., and Yeats revived Vorticist geometrics between the wars—and redirected the geometric idiom in the service of new projects responsive to the era's political and philosophical crises.

Pound, engaged in the typical 1930s effort to reply to what Auden famously called "the failure of liberal capitalist democracy,"[20] immersed in the study of economics and infatuated with Mussolini, strove to awaken Vorticist precision and dynamism in Italy in a way that would both accord with and contribute to what he believed to be the salvific projects of the Fascist regime. During a period of especially intense introspection in the 1930s, heightened by her psychoanalytic work with Freud and fears about the escalating political tensions in Europe, H.D. developed a fantasy of a geometric body, streamlined and charged with electric force, that reflects Vorticist values and indicates a wish for invulnerability in a climate of risk. And prompted especially by the political turbulence of the 1930s, H.D. and Yeats both produced visionary writing, chronicling their contact with occult wisdom, whose pages are dominated by geometric images—and whose development, I argue, was shaped by a Vorticist distrust of the passivity of mystical epistemology (what Lewis called, invoking the leader of the occultist Theosophical movement, "the Blavatskyish" attitude [*B2* 43]).

Taken together, these examples illuminate what I call a late modernist tendency toward geometric "arrangements" (Yeats called his geometric figures "stylistic arrangements") within modernism: one might regard them as the "arrangements" of James McNeill Whistler transmuted in the crucible of Vorticism, then again transformed in the climate of the crises, both public and private, experienced by these writers between the wars. These geometric arrangements became crucial to these writers' late modernist efforts to develop and enunciate ideals—aesthetic, social, and philosophical—to respond to the various forms of turmoil, public and personal, that they confronted in the 1930s and early 1940s. In some cases, Pound, H.D., and Yeats use geometric language to figure the ideal stance that they both themselves seek to adopt toward their fraught environment and recommend to others; and in other cases, to figure the ideal conditions toward which they wish their current environments to transform.

The texts addressed in this book clearly belong among the most provocative of modernist work. Modernist work in general, of course, is fabled for its knottiness, as Leonard Diepeveen's incisive recent study, *The Difficulties of Modernism*, rightly notes. But the texts featured here, which enlist the geometric idiom, belong among those that continue to elicit the most critical uneasiness. Pound's *Jefferson and/or Mussolini* provokes discomfort and incredulity with its driving conviction that despite their differences—which Pound dismisses as merely superficial "top dressing" (*J/M* 11)—Thomas Jefferson and *il Duce* were essentially kindred. H.D.'s novella *Nights* continues to disturb with its apparently sympathetic portrait of sadomasochistic fantasy and suicide. H.D.'s *Tribute to Freud*, the memoir of H.D.'s work with Freud, can still thwart readerly expectations with the reverence it directs, albeit amid a mixture of homage and critique, toward Sigmund Freud himself, whom H.D. at times referred to as "The Master." And Yeats's *Vision* continues to baffle and madden many critics of Yeats, leaving them unready to admit this knotty occult text into either his canon or those of modernism. Addressing the role of geometry within modernist literature can thus shed valuable light on late modernist texts that seem to remain among the most resistant to our accounts, many of them wishful, about modernism's achievements.

While in part, then, I address these texts because they most usefully illuminate the geometric work I seek to limn here, I also feature such texts as *Jefferson and/or Mussolini*, *A Vision*, and *Tribute to Freud* to direct attention to texts by authors regarded as major modernists that merit richer study, whose thorns have prevented their receiving the attention they deserve. I do so also to continue the effort to regard these texts as more than merely nonfictional "prose backing" of modernist poetry and fiction (*LWBY* 625). Though they unquestionably provide material useful for understanding the poetry or fiction of H.D., Pound, and Yeats, these texts also deserve consideration independent of this role: in fact, they belong to a distinct genre within Anglo-American literary modernism, separate from its poetry and prose fiction—one devoted to cultural and philosophical commentary and the articulation of cultural and philosophical ideals.

■

Before proceeding further, I'd like to sound a note of caution about the temptation to rush to judgment about the significance of the geometry used by these artists and writers. Within Western culture, geometric forms have accumulated such a wealth of associations that it is all too easy to draw rapid conclusions about their meanings that may not pertain to the situation at hand. Historian Zygmunt Bauman, for instance, provides a pithy formulation of one common understanding of geometry's significance when he describes it as "the archetype of modern mind" that epitomizes the modern devotion to "taxonomy, classification, inventory" and "catalogue" (*Modernity and Ambivalence* 15)—the modern "quest for order" (1). Certainly his claims resonate with those of Le Corbusier, who celebrated geometry precisely because it could both suggest and promote order. "Modern mastery," Bauman remarks,

> is the power to divide, classify and allocate
> .... Paradoxically, it is for this reason that ambivalence is the main affliction of modernity
> .... Geometry shows what the world would

be like were it geometrical. But the world is not geometrical. It cannot be squeezed into geometrically inspired grids. (15)

Invoking "classification," "inventory," and "catalogue," Bauman rightly indicates a series of concepts with which we conventionally link geometry when we remove it from the province of mathematics—as did the Vorticists—and enlist it to suggest other concepts and processes.[21] Its name deriving from Greek etyma having to do with measurement and the earth, geometry is an ancient science of measurement, practiced by the Babylonians, the Egyptians, and the Greeks, appropriated and transformed over the centuries in myriad ways. As the "science which investigates the properties and relations of magnitudes in space, as lines, surface, and solids," geometry suggests to us structure, clean lines, the representation of spatial relationships among objects.[22] Further, given Plato's well-known invocations of geometry—as in the *Republic*, where he presents the study of geometry as having the capacity, when used well to transcend earthly matters, to facilitate understanding of the "idea of good," "essence," and "knowledge of the eternally existent"[23]—geometry has also long suggested the notion of the pure form, the archetypal pattern susceptible of repetition and instantiation in various local particulars. Thus when Bauman employs geometry to figure the activities of taxonomy, inventory, and catalogue, his usage unquestionably resonates with longstanding assumptions about the valences that the geometric figure suggests.

But the persuasiveness of Bauman's description notwithstanding, it does not adequately capture the significance of geometry for these four modernist artists working in a specific early twentieth-century context. Some artists in their climate were indeed understanding geometry according to Platonic notions. As Rajeev Patke notes, when Cézanne remarked to Émile Bernard in April 1904: "*traitez la nature par le cylindre, la sphère, le cône*" (Cézanne 300), he was advocating that the artist use geometric forms to plumb to the essence of perceived objects in nature, and "reach[ing] as far back in the history of Western aesthetics as the Socrates of Plato's *Philebus*, for whom shapes, lines, and curves possessed an intrinsic beauty."[24] At times, even the Vorticists themselves suggested that they were using such Platonic forms—as Dasenbrock suggests (*Literary Vorticism* 71)—diagramming through geometry the "essence" of the objects they depicted (*B2* 45). But as I will explain in Chapter 1, predominant in the Vorticist lexicon was another set of meanings for geometry, meanings that arose from the effort to stave off the threat of effeminacy associated with *fin-de-siècle* Aestheticism.

For initial indications about the specific significances with which geometry came to be freighted in the arts at this time, we need to turn, first, to the work of British philosopher and critic T. E. Hulme—one of the Vorticists' major exponents. In January 1914, as the Vorticists were still six months from officially launching themselves, Hulme delivered his now well-known address to London's Quest Society, "Modern Art and Its Philosophy," in which he singled out for special praise the work of artists soon to be associated with Vorticism. Both Ezra Pound and Wyndham Lewis, also giving lectures that day, sat among his audience.[25] The premise of Hulme's lecture was that much early twentieth-century art was clearly evincing a "geometrical character" that allied it with the art of Egypt and Byzantium and set it apart as "absolutely distinct in kind" from Renaissance humanist representational art (77).[26] Establishing a binary opposition between the "geometrical" and the "vital," Hulme placed the "new geometrical art" as abstract and therefore at odds with "vital," realistic, representational art. Hulme further recognized this contemporary geometric art, with its "tendency to abstraction," as the most advanced and promising work of the day. Indicating at the close of the lecture his "enthusiasm" for the new art (109), he also signaled his own allegiance to the "clean" lines and "geometrical" curves of the new art by way of phrases he used to describe the maneuvers of his lecture: he wanted, he said, to follow "the contours" of modern art (76) and to give his argument "more shape" (77). In the *New Age* that spring, Hulme would continue to spin out his ideas about the "new constructive geometric art" in a series of articles on "Modern Art."[27]

Hulme's lecture both reflects and forms part of a general colloquy about geometry underway in European intellectual discourse at this moment: geometric abstraction in art was also being theorized by German aesthetician Wilhelm Worringer, whose 1908 dissertation *Abstraction and Empathy* (*Abstraktion und Einfühlung*) had addressed the psychological drives behind an abstract geometric style; as well as by philosopher José Ortega y Gasset, who had studied in Berlin as Worringer's thought dominated the aesthetic scene.[28] In his lecture, Hulme made particularly explicit his debt to Worringer, whose disciple he styled himself,[29] and whereas commentators such as Wees and Dasenbrock have emphasized the degree to which Hulme transformed Worringer's views in his account (at times at the expense of their subtleties), Hulme certainly positioned himself in the role of transmitting Worringer's ideas to an anglophone audience. The notion of a "geometrical style" was Worringer's, as was the dichotomy that formed the basis for Hulme's arguments: the distinction between a "vital" art, grounded in an empathic attitude toward the world, and a "geometrical" abstract art, emerging from an attitude of estrangement from the world.[30]

Clearly, however, whatever derivativeness or reductiveness we might ascribe to Hulme's work, he was more than merely conveying Worringer's ideas: he was acting as their emissary in the realm of modern art, which Worringer's treatise does not broach, ushering them into a new avant-garde context in which they were highly apropos. Positioned amid the *avant-guerre* London ferment in the arts, Hulme had been surrounded by examples of geometric abstraction. By the time of his lecture to the Quest Society, he had been for several years closely engaged with such artists as Lewis, Pound, and Jacob Epstein—and it is generally agreed that the work of these proto-Vorticists acted as the most immediate inspiration for his comments, as well as his source of aesthetic values.

But he had also encountered much other geometrically accented art emerging from London avant-garde circles of this time. Bloomsbury's Post-Impressionists were experimenting with "significant form." The Post-Impressionist exhibits organized by Bloomsbury critic Roger Fry—the landmark show of 1910 and its sequel in 1912—had brought before Londoners a wealth of work exhibiting geometric abstraction by Matisse, Derain, Gaugin, and Cézanne. And as *Blast* attests, London artists at the time were responding especially to the examples of the Cubists, the Italian Futurists, and Kandinsky, whose treatise *Über das Geistige in der Kunst* (1912) meditated on the spiritual significance and "inner content" of abstract form. In 1914, Kandinsky's text was first translated into English in the pages of *Blast*; in his 1914 essay "Vorticism," Pound recognized its ideas as akin to those of the Vorticists (*G-B* 86–87). As quoted and translated in *Blast*, Kandinsky's claims read: "Form alone, even if it is quite abstract and geometrical . . . is a spiritual entity with qualities that are identical with this form: a triangle (whether it be acute-angled, obtuse-angled or equilateral) is an entity of this sort with a spiritual perfume proper to itself alone" (*B1* 121).[31] Despite what Kandinsky's phrasing suggests, "abstract and geometrical" form was not, in this milieu, the exception, but rather the major symbol for pure form whose significance and worth derived solely from itself. At this moment, such pure form, expressed in geometric terms, constituted the distinctive mark of avant-garde visual art.

While Worringer's thought guided Hulme's arguments, then, what occasioned and directed his commentary was the profusion in his climate of both geometric work and discourse about the geometric. Hulme's work registers the considerable investment by many artists in geometric abstraction in the years just before the Great War—as well the abundance of speculation about what the new prominence of the geometric might betoken. His lecture in fact explicitly distinguishes the "new complex geometrical art" he wants to isolate from work by the Futurists, by Post-Impressionists such as Cézanne, Gaugin, Maillol, and Brancusi, and by Cubists such as Metzinger: emphasizing the particular kind of geometric art he addresses, differentiating it from others, he thereby acknowledges the wealth and diversity of abstract art in his environment (*Speculations* 94).

At this moment, then, the concept of "the geometrical" was assuming a wide variety of slightly different significances in avant-garde circles. This study, however, focuses on the valences that geometric forms came to accrue within the force field of the Vorticist movement in particular—which most directly catalyzed Hulme's remarks and inspired his appreciation. In his lecture, Hulme makes clear the distinctiveness of the work that will become associated with the Vorticists: separating out the "complex geometrical art" he favors, he reserves approval for Wyndham Lewis and Jacob Epstein—whose full-fledged geometric work, which he codes as progressive and "constructive," surpasses the comparatively "embryonic" work of painters such as Metzinger.[32] In his articles of that spring, likewise, he positions Post-Impressionist and Cubist art as "transitional" work paving the way for the geometric art he prefers (associated with not only Lewis and Epstein, but also Wadsworth, Hamilton, Nevinson, Roberts, Gaudier-Brzeska, Bomberg, and Etchells), which is the only kind "containing possibilities of development" ("Modern Art—I" 341). Even this work, however, still lacks "cohesion and unity": it only interests him insofar as it is "on the way to something else" ("Modern Art—III" 661). Hulme reads the work of the proto-Vorticists with cautious "enthusiasm," as harbinger of a "much wider"—and for him, welcome—"change in philosophy and general outlook on the world" (*Speculations* 109), one that involves an "intensity" he admires ("Modern Art—II" 467).

Cued by Worringer's work, Hulme also interprets the "re-emergence of geometrical art" (*Speculations* 78) as driven by impulses that have animated kindred geometric art throughout the centuries, revealing what he quotes Worringer as calling a transhistorical "*tendency to abstraction*" (85; Hulme's italics).[33] In the past, he maintains, people whose art was geometric felt estranged from their environment, believing themselves incompatible with and inadequate to it. Often, communities given to abstract art feared their environment and felt impelled to take "refuge" from it: they sought sanctuary particularly from the "flux and impermanence of outside nature" (86). Of these people, Hulme notes,

> [P]ure geometrical regularity gives a certain pleasure to men troubled by the obscurity of outside appearance. The geometrical line is something absolutely distinct from the messiness, the confusion, and the accidental details of existing things. (87)

Hulme concedes that the contemporary surge in geometric art does not necessarily signify a return of this attitude of "spiritual 'space-shyness'" (86). It does, however, most likely signal something about the "disharmony or separation between man and nature" (87), which artists might register without being fully conscious thereof. And while Hulme acknowledges that machines in the contemporary twentieth-century environment will influence the way artists handle geometric forms—such that the impact of machinery will differentiate the nature of this geometric art from that of centuries past—he denies that the contemporary "environment of machinery" actually produces the new geometrical art (108): rejecting such directly "materialist" explanations of the trends in the visual arts, he prefers to maintain instead that modern art emerges from a "condition of mind" (85) expressed in geometric form, which may be inflected, in unpredictable ways, by the example of machine forms. In his vigorously antimaterialist method of interpretation of the evolution of art, Hulme is clearly influenced by Alois Riegl, whom Worringer credits with the concept of "artistic volition": the notion that works of art bring to objective existence a will to form, and that their style is to be accounted for not by the available materials, techniques, or needs of the artist's immediate environment, but rather by an artistic "volition"—a psychological urge—as conditioned by environmental factors.

Ultimately, Hulme stops short of a full interpretation of the significance of the "new complex geometrical art," neither willing to draw definitive conclusions nor offer unqualified endorsement. Relevant here for the Vorticists, however, are his founding assumptions: they follow his lead in using style (in this case, geometric style) as both correlative and index to a "condition of mind" (85) and its attendant "general world outlook" (88), approach to external conditions, and values. Here, like Hulme and Riegl, they assume that the style of a work of art manifests a certain "volition" (Worringer, *Abstraction and Empathy* 9). And they also concur, of course, with his assumption that the new geometric art, as distinct from Futurism, Post-Impressionism, and Cubism, points in the most live and promising new direction.

Within the context of Vorticism's projects and principles—as Vorticist William Roberts once put it, "the Art atmosphere of the period, which we all breathed" (Wees, *Vorticism and the English Avant-Garde* 152)—the geometric signifier assumed the distinctive significances it bears in the work of the four writers featured here. Specifically, it came to indicate a generative anxiety—one forcefully, though neither originally nor exclusively, displayed through Vorticist work—about a threat of "effeminacy," which I will detail in Chapter 1. For the Vorticists, the category of "effeminacy" included qualities of languor and laxity; that which was "wandering," "slovenly" (*B2* 43), "passive," and "slack" (40).

Accordingly, Vorticist work pitches against the "effeminacy" it takes as its enemy an effort toward conditions of mind and being capable of countering such effeminacy, conditions which their geometric figures come to encode. Such geometric figures signal desires for that which is instead "tense and angular" (*B2* 43), severe, "austere, mechanical, clear cut, and bare" (Hulme, *Speculations* 96), active, and even "violent" (*B1* 144). Within Vorticism, the geometric idiom comes to express a value system that privileges tension, intensity, precision, activity, and force — all in the name of combating that which, in the Vorticist view, falls within the domain of effeminacy.

As I will address in Chapter 1, the battle against the "wandering and slack" out of which Vorticism was initially forged emerged from a phobic reaction to effeminacy of a kind linked in the public mind at this juncture with the Aestheticism of the *fin de siècle* just past. Accordingly, from the perspective of the Vorticists, the qualities against which they militated were located in the figure of the male Aesthete as epitomized by Oscar Wilde. For them, Wilde exemplified the languor, passivity, weakness, and effeteness they resisted. For my understanding of effeminacy here, I am indebted to Alan Sinfield's *Wilde Century*, which traces the uses of the category of effeminacy over the centuries, addressing how, in the late nineteenth century, effeminacy came to be assumed to correlate with male homosexuality and, more specifically, with the figure of the male Aesthete. As the trials of Oscar Wilde brought both his perceived effeminacy and homosexuality before the public eye, marking them as scandalous, effeminacy came to be increasingly vilified, and the male Aesthete, a chief target for that vilification.

Accordingly, in the aftermath of the Wilde trials, and swayed by their example, the Vorticists identified the qualities they condemned chiefly within the figure of the male Aesthete. The constellation of qualities the Vorticists celebrated, such as severity of attitude, spareness of outline, and vigorous force, are not altogether strange bedfellows — they all belong to a common realm of "austerity" or "intensity" — but neither are they entirely continuous with one another. It was Vorticism's anxious, reactive effort to battle the qualities associated with the category of effeminacy that brought together this coalition of desiderata: what Vorticism prized, then, was the obverse of effeminacy — or, to put it another way, the inverse of what was at the time regarded as the province of the male invert. Because the laxity of effeminacy was denigrated, Vorticism celebrated continence, precision, and discipline; because passivity and weakness were disparaged, Vorticism valorized activity and strength. Vorticism constructed its program, and enlisted its geometry, to exorcise the spectral effeminate Wildean Aesthete.[34]

Of course, the qualities heralded by Vorticism are those conventionally linked to forms of masculinity, which traditionally have been predicated upon an abjection of effeminacy. I will take up Vorticism's fraught relationship with masculinity in Chapter 1. For now, I would offer that, especially as the qualities Vorticism endorses, traditionally associated with the masculine, begin to travel into later modernist work, their connection with the domain of masculinity weakens. Although activity and strength, severity and intensity have certainly often been connected with masculinity, they need not be: in later modernist projects associated with these Vorticist values, the importance of their link to masculinity recedes. In the late modernist years, as the values of Vorticism are transposed into the distinctive keys of different writers and other historical circumstances, Vorticism's primary struggle against effeminacy is displaced into various other projects, transformed under the pressure of new needs, redirected toward different adversaries.

Originally, then, the campaign at the root of Vorticism was fundamentally a campaign against effeminacy and the male Aesthete qua homosexual thought to be its locus classicus; later, the qualities celebrated by writers enlisting Vorticist values came to be detached from both the male Aesthete and effeminacy. In later work by Pound, H.D., and Yeats, the Vorticist attack on qualities such as languor, imprecision, laxity, passivity, and weakness continues, but the projects served by these critiques change considerably, as do the examples that give body to the qualities considered objectionable. In Pound's work of the 1930s, the qualities under critique are epitomized by "thick" lines in the material forms of a culture, such as the "bulbous" forms of furniture and ornamentation at the Schönbrunn palace in Vienna. For H.D., the undesirable qualities are often exemplified by a heavy body, especially a childbearing female body; and for both H.D. and Yeats, these characteristics are exhibited in the condition of the "passive" and "medium-like" visionary figure.

■

So far, I have focused on the significances with which geometry came to be endowed within the context of Vorticist desires and values, and on the way that H.D., Pound, and Yeats came to be guided by these Vorticist significances—as they continued, in residual form, to be associated with a geometric idiom—in their later works. I should take a moment here to point to other cultural factors that also guided uses of the geometric idiom.

Worringer's theories aside, and beyond the immediate example of geometric abstraction in the visual arts, the artists addressed here were at times drawn to geometric images by the geometric machine forms that pervaded the early twentieth-century urban landscape. In "Modern Art," Hulme notes the ways in which machine forms inspired (though he insisted that they did not directly cause) the use of geometric forms:

> [T]he new 'tendency towards abstraction' will culminate, not so much in the simple geometrical forms found in archaic art, but in the more complicated ones associated in our minds with the idea of machinery. In this association with machinery will probably be found the specific differentiating quality of the new art.
>
> (*SPECULATIONS* 104)

In 1914, filling the pages of *Blast* with geometric forms, Wyndham Lewis explicitly announced the Vorticist embrace of machines: "Machinery is the greatest Earth-medium . . . . [I]t sweeps away the doctrines of a narrow and pedantic Realism at one stroke" (*B1* 39). The same manifestic gesture celebrates England for its "Machinery, trains, steam-ships" (39). In a later piece of 1919, *The Caliph's Design*, Lewis again maintained the importance of machine forms to his kind of art, insistently differentiating between the Futurists' uncritical worship of machines and the more unsentimental use of them that he endorsed: "Machinery should be regarded as a new pictorial resource, as with a new mineral or oil, there to be exploited" (*WLOA* 150).[35]

The writers featured in this study were also impelled toward geometry by developments in science. H.D. grew up with a grandfather, father, and brother steeped in mathematical and scientific work—work which she emblematized in her texts through geometric images and figures. In her autobiographical roman à clef *HERmione*, H.D.'s main character, whose brother and father are likewise scientists, uses the phrase "conic sections" to capture the nature of their work (5). H.D. has her protagonist Hermione name both "triangles" and "molecules" in the same breath, suggesting the affinity she perceives between the realm of geometric figures and the biological phenomena of the world that scientific inquiry takes as objects of study (51). In *Tribute to Freud*, H.D. continues this linkage, foregrounding the personal reference that leads her to associate scientific work with geometric shapes. On her father's desk, she reports, in the study in which he devoted himself to scientific pursuits, there was a paperweight that especially compelled her attention: one that featured "a set of prismatic triangles, placed on another set of triangles" (24). Slightly later in the text, she repeats this image, attesting to the fastness of the connection in her mind between her father's scientific work, marked by his abundance of books, and the geometric images of this paperweight. Her father, she notes, "has more books even than our grandfather and he has that triangle paper-weight that shows the things in the room repeated in various dimensions" (34).

Lewis, meanwhile, according to Jeffrey Meyers, read widely in the British Museum about new developments in science during the formative years of his art (*Wyndham Lewis* 103); Michael Wutz infers from this that Lewis's use of the vortex, in both his paintings and writing, was informed by his understanding of new developments in electrical field theory ("Energetics of *Tarr*" 848).[36] Pound also showed himself influenced by the discourse of electromagnetism, his familiarity with which may have influenced his notion of the vortex. Furthermore, as Ian Bell suggests, Pound may have been moved toward considering the "poet as geometer" out of his readings of Whistler, who argued that art, at its best, achieved a scientific precision of methods and results. Ian Bell also notes that Pound's thought on analytic geometry accorded closely with Sir Oliver Lodge's account of the achievement of Descartes—which addressed both his theory of vortices and his system of analytical geometry—in Lodge's popular, widely circulated science textbook of 1893, *Pioneers of Science*. Bell does not have the evidence to conclude that Pound actually drew his ideas from Lodge's discussion, but he notes that Lodge's book was reprinted in 1913, just as Pound began engaging with the Vorticists (Bell, *Critic as Scientist* 12–15).

Finally, a third important source of geometric forms for writers of this period was the study of the occult. As Timothy Materer notes, Pound's theory of poetry—which involves the use of geometric form—was "as mystical" as it was "scientific" (*Modernist Alchemy* 34). In part, Pound was steered toward the geometric image of the vortex by his early reading of commentary on "yogi philosophy" and "occultism" by one Yogi Ramacharaka (33). Pound and Yeats both were also affected by the occultist movement of Theosophy—Yeats directly, as a member of London's Theosophical Society, Pound more indirectly, through contact with Yeats and members of the Theosophical Quest Society—which often featured a mixture of scientific and mystical thought, and which, more importantly, accented geometric patterns in its work. Helena Blavatsky, leader of the Theosophists, addressed geometric vortices in her pivotal study, *The Secret Doctrine* (1888), noting that ancient discussions of "the law of vortical movement of primary matter" derived from Greek, Egyptian, Chaldean, and Indian sources and predated Descartes's and Swedenborg's treatments of vortices by two thousand years (117). And Theosophists such as Annie Besant and C. W. Leadbeater used geometric figures to diagram what they believed to be "thought forms" that were inscribed in the "etheric matter" in response to certain thoughts and emotions

(Materer, *Modernist Alchemy* 32–34). As Chapter 4 will address, Yeats and H.D. were also drawn toward geometric forms by their study of occult thought apart from Theosophy per se.

The realms of machinery, science, and the occult, then, primed these writers to reach for a Vorticist geometric vocabulary, and paved the way for the significances that geometry would accrue within a Vorticist context—significances initially theorized by Lewis and Pound, Lewis taking the lead, and later accepted and permuted by Yeats and H.D. Perhaps in part because artists and writers of this milieu were often responding to machine forms in their environment, along with diagrams of physical forces and electrical current, the geometric figure within Vorticism came to signify not so much through its traditional ability to represent pure Platonic form and to diagram relations among elements of a system—but rather through its capacity to suggest the hard-edged forms and surging currents, electric and otherwise, of modern urban life. This was geometry with a distinctive early twentieth-century spin.

Accordingly, within the Vorticist context, the geometric line came to suggest a wire stretched taut between two points and thus to connote tension, intensity, and attention; it implied the trajectory that such a wire makes possible—and thus connoted unimpeded, rapid, and efficient motion. The lines of geometric shapes suggested vigor and power, even aggression. And it was this conceptual equation between geometric figures and lines of force, exemplified in the Vorticist visual vocabulary, that continued to mark the late modernist work of Pound, H.D., and Yeats.

■

This Vorticist effort toward a combination of precision and dynamism clearly resonates with a much larger modernist aesthetic impulse often recognized in critical studies: a movement toward hardness, clarity, condensation, and paring down. This effort has been variously characterized—as, for instance, the drive toward "hardness" or toward "phallic, anorexic bodies"; or as a "masculinist" and "misogynist" flight from the Romantic and the Decadent.[37] What this study adds to this discussion in modernist studies is fourfold. First, it examines the way this drive plays out through a collection of geometric rhetorical strategies within modernism, no thorough study of which exists. Second, it focuses on how this trend is expressed specifically within Vorticism, in the distinctively Vorticist desires that emerge from a fear of Aestheticist effeminacy: desire for a combination of precision and dynamism arrived at through the tautening of posture and material bodies. Third, whereas most accounts refer to the Vorticist project as just one among many salient examples of the effort toward modernist "hardness," this study concentrates on Vorticism, arguing that Vorticism exemplifies a set of values that in its own right comes significantly to influence later modernist literature, independent of other such trends. Finally, this book addresses Yeats and H.D. in ways that interrogate our current understanding of their places within the landscape of modernism, as well as our current understanding of Vorticism.

Through the inclusion of Yeats and H.D., I hope to complicate not only our understanding of what texts, values, and writers might properly, and valuably, be associated with Vorticism, but also our understanding of the gender of Vorticism. Yeats, albeit sometimes linked with the quest for hardness in "male modernism,"[38] is usually not understood as participating in Vorticist strategies per se; recognition of the ways in which his work and values intersect with Vorticism can illuminate new dimensions of his work as well as the distinctive characteristics of the Vorticist strain within modernism. And by including H.D., this study interrogates the commonplace alignment of the Vorticist aesthetic with masculinism and misogyny.

Understandably, Vorticism has traditionally been linked with the narrative of the "men of 1914" within modernist studies and, accordingly, with the kind of "male modernism" that recent work in modernist studies has recognized as an integral, albeit in some respects unfortunate, part of the development of early modernist work. Unquestionably, many of the writers who contributed to early modernist projects were male, many of them both masculinist and misogynistic — and given to inscribing their masculinism and misogyny in their work. As Chapter 1 notes, many of them were responding defensively to what Lisa Tickner identifies in "Men's Work?" as a late nineteenth- and early twentieth-century crisis in masculinity. And of the early modernist movements, Vorticism was doubtless the most overtly masculinist: unabashedly he-man in its antics, inclined, like Italian Futurism, to announce loudly its "scorn for woman" (Apollonio, *Futurist Manifestos* 22).

But as I intend the discussion of H.D. to show, not all Vorticist ideals need be read as inherently masculinist or misogynistic. Nor does H.D. always evince in her work the significant departures from her male comrades that much recent criticism would suggest that, because she is feminist, she does. Often, H.D. is read as employing strategies associated with her male compatriots only early in her career while still in the thrall of male mentors and their patriarchal standards; once closer to mature self-actualization, as Susan Friedman has suggested, she is generally portrayed as breaking free of these.[39] Even late in her career, however, H.D.'s values did, in fact, sometimes coincide with those of her male comrades; her values sometimes stemmed from the same Vorticist sources as theirs; and her relationship to the Vorticist effort, albeit ambivalent, was no more ambivalent, though differently ambivalent, than Lewis's, Pound's, and Yeats's. Furthermore, whatever differences from her male comrades she displayed, I am not willing to attribute solely to her status as a woman. Much recent criticism, fortunately, has now deplored the tendency to assign the male and female moderns to different camps and ascribe to them differences that supposedly issue from their difference in gender (I think especially of statements by Marjorie Perloff in "Modernist Studies" and by Michael Kaufmann in "Gendering Modernism"). But given the persistence of the assumption within H.D. studies that her approach differed from those of her male colleagues because she was a woman, we need to continue to take seriously the possibility that a woman modernist can use techniques usually associated with "male moderns," and we need to do so without presuming that her use of them is necessarily either, on the one hand, unfortunately complicit, or, on the other, subversively imitative. Although H.D.'s geometric gestures may indeed sometimes constitute subversive reappropriations of the geometric idiom, her defiance is not always necessarily directed toward her male modernist contemporaries.

■

Each chapter of this study addresses a different way in which geometry is enlisted as part of a Vorticist project to correct a condition of laxity and passivity—and to promote instead streamlining and vigorous force. Chapter 1 treats the semiosis by which geometry is initially appropriated and coded within Vorticism to combat effeminacy, exploring Vorticism's fundamental, and fundamentally phobic and ambivalent, relationship to its Aestheticist predecessors.

Chapter 2 addresses how Pound's Vorticist investment in the geometrically "clean line," which remains with him long after the Vorticist movement has faded from the avant-garde scene, later informs his arguments in the 1930s for Mussolini's Italy. His sympathy for Fascist Italy, I argue, is significantly guided by his desire to resurrect the Vorticist project in an overtly political context. His preoccupation with the geometrically "clean line" shows itself both in the way that he campaigns for the production of such clean lines in the architecture and artifacts of the new Italy, as well as in the way he celebrates Mussolini's regime on the basis of the desirably clean lines that it has already fostered.

Chapter 3 focuses on H.D.'s effort, through the use of geometric terms, to advance the ideal of an erotically aroused, charged, rarefied body that fosters visionary states of consciousness. She calls for a transfiguration—an attenuation—of the ordinary corporeal body through subjection to forms of severity and, conversely, an effort away from the heavy, fleshy state epitomized by the female childbearing body. As I will show, the values animating this project resonate significantly with those of Vorticism.

Chapter 4 explores another dimension of H.D.'s use of geometry—by examining how, both in her visionary texts and in those of Yeats, geometry marks their ambivalent relationship to visionary epistemology. This ambivalence, I argue, is in large part born out of their response to the intellectual standards set for H.D. and Yeats by their fathers, whose influence they still felt long after their fathers' deaths. The way they employ geometry in their accounts of visionary experience—in, I argue, a Vorticist manner—registers a desire to defend themselves against charges of being too "passive and medium-like" in their relationship to visionary experience.

In 1913–1914, then, each of these writers encountered the movement of Vorticism, directly or indirectly, and carried away an impression of it that stayed with them and reappeared in their later work. After the era of *Blast*, these writers remained haunted by Vorticism—imprinted in their memories, in shorthand, through geometric forms—that would resurface in later projects as they sought a vocabulary adequate both to articulating their aesthetic, philosophical, and cultural ideals and to responding to the crises, public and personal, of their milieux. Pound, maintaining his admiration for Vorticist ideals, sought to involve what he termed the Vorticist "form-sense" in his arguments of the 1930s for Fascist Italy. H.D. retained in her memory a connection among geometry, Vorticism, and violence—and informed later texts with this semantic linkage. Yeats, impressed by Vorticism from a remove, drew upon his recollections of it to gain vocabulary and legitimacy for his own later projects.

Although each of these writers maintained subtly different memories of Vorticism, their geometric gestures all likewise indicated a Vorticist desire for streamlining, for a rejection of the "wandering and slack," and for a celebration of the "tense and angular," the "violent and geometric." This study addresses, then, the transmission, translation, and transformation of Vorticist geometrics from a point of, if not origin, at least conspicuous crystallization, in 1914. Specifically, it considers how Vorticist geometry is carried to moments in the 1930s and early 1940s—when circumstances, for different reasons in the case of each writer, warranted a resurrection of Vorticist values.

> *I have been portraying to the best of my ability the heir to the aesthete of the Wilde period.*
>
> WYNDHAM LEWIS, "The Caliph's Design" (1919), *Wyndham Lewis on Art*

> *Balla . . . is a rather violent and geometric sort of Expressionist. Cannot Marinetti . . . be induced to . . . follow his friend Balla into a purer region of art?*
>
> WYNDHAM LEWIS, *Blast 1*

Wyndham Lewis, Vorticism, and the Campaign against Wildean Effeminacy

In 1915, Wyndham Lewis characterized *Blast*, the British little magazine of which he was editor, as a "history book." In his prefatory remarks to the latter-day reprint of the magazine by the Black Sparrow Press, Bradford Morrow underscores Lewis's use of this phrase to describe *Blast*—so it has become familiar to all those using the journal in its contemporary edition. I would like to open this chapter on *Blast* and Wyndham Lewis by pressing this phrase for significance.

In 1914, Lewis—painter, writer, polemicist—launched *Blast* in London to promote the new movement in the arts, Vorticism, whose emergence he had directed. The phrase "history book," which appears in Lewis's letter to his friend and fellow painter Augustus John, captures the way that Lewis positioned the project of *Blast* historically—as a reaction against the *fin de siècle*, which Lewis represents as a "stagnant time after the full blast of Victorianism—surely one of the most hideous periods ever recorded" (*Letters of Wyndham Lewis* 70), lamentably not even as vigorous as the "Victorianism" that Lewis also deplored. In other words, Lewis's avant-garde journal *Blast*, bristling with bold paintings, poems, manifestoes, and essays, was from the outset advanced as a *counter-blast*,[1] principally against the *fin de siècle*: it merited the title of "history book" because it was a "book" responding to "history," its gestures taking on significance by virtue of their placement in history. The contents of *Blast* suggest that Lewis also conceived of the periodical as a "history book" because it would both *document* history—by bearing witness to the vital events and currents of its cultural environment—and *make* history by reinvigorating moribund artistic practice in England. According to Lewis's vision, *Blast* would contribute to the effort to "blast" away from the London art scene the residual traces of both the "blast" of Victorianism and what he perceived as the ensuing *fin-de-siècle* lapse.

A century later, as we retrospect about the time to which Lewis refers, the efforts he describes may seem quaint and far away, at times amusingly antic; and *Blast* itself, now a commonplace in modernist criticism, may seem a once fiery statement turned souvenir, even gimcrack, its revolutionary luster faded to a pale indicator of what once was.[2] I would advocate, however, that we guard against regarding in this way either the journal itself or the moment to which it points. For us, *Blast* has indeed become a "history book," and a valuable one at that: a document that registers sensitively both a crucial early moment in the development of Anglo-American modernism and a milieu that became a cradle for later modernist literature and visual art.

It is a document that merits revisiting today not only for what it can teach us about that time past, but also for the way it can help us to reassess "modernism" more generally. The cultural phenomenon of modernism in the arts, though endlessly examined and redefined over the decades—disparaged as misogynistic, homophobic, politically reactionary; at times dismissed as obsolete; reread; rehabilitated—nonetheless continues to hold a dominant position in scholarly discourse.[3] As we enter the new millennium, Anglo-American literary modernism remains an inescapable category of understanding in discussions of early twentieth-century literature.

What modernism "was," however, even after many decades of debate, remains elusive.[4] Scholars usually at least agree that it "designates an experimental trend in English-language literature that flourished from about 1890 to about 1945" (Witemeyer, *Future of Modernism*, 1).[5] The recommendation currently ascendant is that we conceptualize what has been called "modernism" not as one monolithic entity, but rather as a host of loosely affiliated trends, movements, texts, and desires better termed "modernisms," which cluster into a group of related canons.[6] As indicated by the vibrancy of the new Modernist Studies Association, which has gained force steadily since its founding in 1999, modernist studies is now widely regarded as having entered a revitalized era—even, as Robert Spoo suggests, a newly "emergent phase" ("H.D. Prosed" 201).

The question of what qualifies as "modernist," however, is still actively contested, as is the problem of how we should regard modernist work today. *Blast*, I would argue, can help us to reevaluate what the concept of modernism[7] has been to us, what it is now, how we have used it, and how we might use it in future. By considering the critical investments conditioning critical treatment of *Blast* over time, we can better understand investments in this fiction of "modernism" that, as it continues to provoke controversy, continues also to exert a powerful fascination.

In critical narratives about the development of modernist literature, when one encounters mention of *Blast*, the language used to describe this "little" magazine certainly connotes anything but "littleness." Accounts of the magazine often suggest giants and tall tales, a world much larger than life. *Blast* was in fact just one of a host of comparable avant-garde periodicals published in Anglo-American artistic circles in the years neighboring the Great War, but the journal is usually depicted through exaggerated rhetoric that makes it seem both impressive and exceptional. Like a beast of legendary proportions, *Blast* is frequently heralded for its formidable size and fearsome appearance. Most portrayals emphasize that it was nearly a foot tall; its color is termed "puce," "magenta," "cerise," or "violent pink."[8] It has been called a "monster," its bright exterior referred to by Ezra Pound as creaturely "plumage."[9] Descriptions often note that the thick black letters on its front cover were three inches high, striding in diagonal procession across the page. A reviewer in *Poetry* constructed *Blast* as possessing a physical body by suggesting that a cover in such "bright cerise" made one feel that "the outer cuticle had been removed"—presumably, the outermost skin of the magazine itself.[10]

Hugh Kenner's well-known elegiac remarks on *Blast* in *The Pound Era* exemplify this hyperbolic rhetorical tendency: as he recounts the magazine's eventual demise, Kenner's simple diction and syntax, evocative of a mythic realm, as well as his strikingly metonymic descriptive technique, imply that we are receiving the legend of the fall of *Blast*.

> A new copy of *Blast*, puce, the size of a telephone directory lettered from corner to corner, lay on an aristocratic garden table. The summer day darkened. The rains commenced to fall. No one rescued it. Through

> a spattered pane wide aristocratic eyes saw in a sudden blazing lightning-flash the shocking pink color start forth, the five fierce black letters, B L A S T. Darkness recomposed. The dull rain fell and fell. (246)

Of course Kenner, doyen of modernist scholarship, is known for his deliberately maverick critical idiom—so that there should be a paragraph of this kind in his 1971 study, with its hagiographic portrait of the group Lewis called the "men of 1914," is not surprising.[11] But *Blast* has inspired heightened rhetoric in many other commemorations as well. Again, most conspicuous in descriptions of the journal has been an emphasis on its physical features—elements of what contemporary editorial theorist Jerome McGann theorizes as its "bibliographic code"[12]—and its status as a remarkably substantial physical artifact. Many remarks focus on what Kenner calls its "poster-like" visual conventions (*Wyndham Lewis* 17), accentuating its "inch-high letters on a 9 x 12 page" (17–20).

In *Vorticism and the English Avant-Garde*, for instance, the pioneering schol-

Cover of
Blast 1 *(1914)*

arly monograph on the Vorticist movement, William Wees begins his commentary on *Blast* with a blazon of visually arresting qualities:

> In keeping with the avant-garde spirit of the day, *Blast* intended to shock. Not only its name, but its cover, size, and typography worked to that end. Variously described as "violent pink," "puce," [and] "purple" ... *Blast*'s cover was a broad expanse of pinkish purple crossed diagonally by the single word BLAST in three-inch high block letters. (165)

Wees underscores that *Blast* exerted its impact through appearance—its "cover, size, and typography"—asserting its significance by way of its physical difference from other similar projects:

> Compared to other smaller, thinner, and more decorous avant-garde magazines of that time, such as *Rhythm* and *Blue Review* (with their conservative blue covers), *Poetry* (with even more conservative grey), and the *Little Review* (with muddy brown), *Blast* seemed exceedingly brash.... There was a certain barbaric aggressiveness, not only in the sheer bulk of the magazine, but also in Lewis' manipulation of the attention-grabbing devices of newspaper headlines and advertising posters. (165)

Here again, the emphasis is on size, color, and letters "three inches high"—and moreover, on the magazine's impressiveness as physical object: we hear of its "sheer bulk" and "unusually heavy paper" (165). Richard Cork's lavish study of Vorticism (1976) likewise begins its section on *Blast* with an acknowledgment of the "thick black capitals of *Blast No. 1*'s opening manifesto," its "brazen pink covers," its "title in giant letters stamped diagonally across them like lightning," and its "freewheeling and exclamatory typography" (*Vorticism and Abstract Art* 239). Cork even pays implicit tribute to the size of *Blast* by issuing the two volumes of his own book in a comparable folio size. Marjorie Perloff's *Futur-*

ist Moment (1986), meanwhile, which opens its chapter on Pound with a nod to *Blast*, follows suit with commentary on the magazine's ability to startle by virtue of color and size: it was "a large (nearly a foot high) folio, whose shocking-pink cover bore, in three-inch block letters arranged diagonally top to bottom, the title BLAST" (163). Perloff borrows Kenner's phrase here, "shocking pink," and, like both Kenner and Wees, describes the length of the folio as "height," conjuring an image of the magazine as a kind of freestanding entity—a building, perhaps, towering above neighboring edifices. In *The Public Face of Modernism*, a study of modernist little magazines published thirty years after Kenner's *Pound Era*, Mark Morrisson rehearses many of these same rhetorical gestures: he calls *Blast* "flamboyant" (116), notes the magazine's "glaring puce cover and oversized diagonal block letters" (117), and invokes Lewis's sobriquet for the magazine from 1914: "puce monster" (quoted in Norman, *Ezra Pound* 150).

As this phrase from Lewis indicates, in addition to the rhetoric of substantial physicality, the rhetoric of "monstrosity" also comes to the fore in scholarship on *Blast*—a monstrosity primarily of neither freakishness nor deformity (although both qualities have been associated with *Blast* by its detractors), but rather of gigantic scale and redoubtable strength—and this, in turn, indicates the historical role in which the magazine has been cast. Cork invokes Lewis's "puce monster" as well; Wees goes further when he observes that *Blast* sought to create a "new civilization" according to a Nietzschean declaration: "The universe is a monster of energy" (*Vorticism and the English Avant-Garde* 165). In view of the rhetorical pattern created by scholarly accounts of *Blast*, Wees's syntax invites an act of rhetorical hypallage: his description suggests that here it is *Blast*, and not just the "universe," that deserves recognition as a "monster" of "energy."

Blast has been often been represented as a "monster," I would offer, not only because Lewis called it that and because it was both deliberately strident and formidably large: more importantly, it has been constructed as a Grendel-like "monster" because of a critical stake in regarding the magazine as possessing mythic proportions and gargantuan stature. Throughout the twentieth century, especially since the end of the first wave of modernist work between the wars, the critical commitment at work here in discussions of *Blast* has been twofold: on the one hand, to commemorate *Blast* and keep it before the historiographical eye, and on the other, to preserve for *Blast* a reputation of ferocity and strength.

This tenacious image of the magazine's bulk, aggression, and importance stands in pronounced contrast to the slightness of its actual impact. *Blast* shared with many other little magazines of its cultural climate a markedly abbreviated life span: only two issues appeared in 1914 and 1915 before the venture was interrupted by both financial instability and the war.[13] Lewis's occasionally expressed plans to resume the magazine during and after the war never came to fruition. Those who read *Blast*, though Lewis boasted subscribers as far away as "Santa Fe" and the "Khyber Pass" (*B2* 7), composed only a tiny elite. Furthermore, *Blast*'s two issues were not generally well received: although the magazine did earn some praise, those who commended it often had personal connections to the magazine that compromised the credibility of their commentary. (Ford Madox Ford and Richard Aldington, for instance, who both publicly praised the magazine, numbered among Pound's circle of associates—and Ford had published in *Blast*.)

Moreover, such praise was scarce: the magazine more often met with derisive reviews. Some of the most scathing appeared in the *New Age*, where C. E. Bechhöfer offered detailed parodies of sections of the magazine, and A. R. Orage, writing as "R.H.C.," first damned it with faint praise through litotes as "not unintelligible," then finished the job by saying that it was nonetheless "not worth the understanding" (July 9, 1914, 229). At least here, albeit acerbically, Orage engaged with specifics of the project, thereby lending it some dignity by implying that, its failure notwithstanding, it was worth an expenditure of critical energy. He even went so far as to applaud Lewis's *Enemy of the Stars* as an "extraordinary piece of work" (July 16, 1914, 253). Bechhöfer's skillful parodies, meanwhile, attest that he had taken equally careful note of *Blast*'s particulars. Often, however, as Lawrence Rainey observes, *Blast* was not even so fortunate as to have such attentive critics as these; many merely found the journal wearisome: "[C]ontrary to what later critics have suggested, contemporary critics were neither angered nor provoked by *Blast*. They were simply bored" ("Creation of the Avant-Garde" 210).[14] Certainly this was the note sounded in the review in *Poetry*, whose editors read the journal's bombast as belated and derivative: using a reference to the American Independence Day to capture both the magazine's noise and effort to foment revolution, they described it as generating only "the wan excitement of Fourth of July Fireworks on the day after the Fourth" ("Our Contemporaries" 44).[15]

But despite its brief run and its lukewarm reception before the war, *Blast* now unquestionably stands as a prominent landmark of early Anglo-American literary modernism. Again, the devotion of critical energy to it is unmistakable: evident is not only the insistence on the magazine's "commanding dimensions" (Morrow, "Blueprint to the Vortex" vi) but also, more generally, the regularity with which *Blast* is invoked.[16] Its frequent appearance in chronicles of modernism's development, along with the reprints of its two installments issued during the 1980s and 1990s by the Black Sparrow Press, have ensured its continued visibility and perpetuated the myth of its mission to galvanize the art world. Images of *Blast* are often reproduced in scholarly accounts of modernism: Hugh Kenner exhibits visuals from the magazine in both *Wyndham Lewis* and *The Pound Era*; Timothy Materer's *Vortex* includes one of *Blast*'s pages; Marjorie Perloff features a color plate of its cover in *The Futurist Moment*; and Mark Morrisson displays pages of *Blast* in his recent study of modernist little magazines. Taken together, these many references clearly indicate that criticism has needed *Blast*—and needed to maintain its prominence. Critical discussions of *Blast* have inscribed in readers' minds not only the "poster-like" features of *Blast* (Kenner, *Wyndham Lewis* 17), but also ideas about Vorticism, the movement for which the magazine served as official organ.

In part as a result of these accounts, and in part as a consequence of the forces that engendered them, *Blast* has come to serve as a convenient symbol for the efforts of the early twentieth-century avant-garde context that we now read as a matrix for Anglo-American literary modernism. At the turn of a new century, as scholars revisit the development of modernism over the past hundred years, we need to examine the place of *Blast* within our constructions of modernism, paying particular attention to why, despite its rather unimpressive showing in 1914–1915, this little magazine continues to have such a big reputation—and to spur such lively scholarly interest. And as we do so, we also need to reconsider the influence of Vorticism, the movement that *Blast* announced, on both modernist work and on our concepts of modernism. This study argues that Vorticism, despite the wealth of existing commentaries on its rise and decline, has not yet been given its due.

BLAST AND MYTHS OF ORIGIN

How might we account for the historiographical emphasis on *Blast*? Its attractiveness as an exhibit in narratives about modernism certainly cannot stem from the literature it featured: most critics agree that the contributions of the writers involved—most notably, Pound—were negligible.[17] Furthermore, many other little magazines of the time, usually accorded less attention than *Blast* in standard chronicles of modernism, included many more texts than did *Blast* that were later canonized as classics of modernism.[18] The visual artwork exhibited in *Blast*, mostly that of Lewis and other Vorticists such as Wadsworth and Etchells, is too little known these days to generate much excitement on its own.[19]

In order to explain the power of the myth of *Blast*, we need to turn elsewhere. Contributing to *Blast*'s high profile today, I would offer, is that, first, those makers of modernism on whom latter-day scholars have relied for authoritative accounts of the period's activities tended to credit the journal with great significance. Ezra Pound, for instance—clearly among those most responsible for the stories of modernism we have inherited—continued to wax nostalgic about the import of *Blast* long after his participation in the artistic ferment of 1914. In 1924 he wrote to Wyndham Lewis, "I have just, ten years an [sic] a bit after its appearance ... taken out a copy of the great MAGENTA cover'd opusculus. We were hefty guys in them days" (P/L 138). In 1936 Pound reported to Lewis that he was once again looking at a copy of *Blast* and, at this juncture, not only reminiscing fondly about the magazine but in fact hoping to reawaken and continue its regenerative project (P/L 189); he even issued a new manifesto at this point to pick up where *Blast* had left off (Stock, *Life of Pound* 340–341). In 1938 Harriet Monroe, editor of *Poetry*—by the late 1930s widely recognized as a significant cultural arbiter whose work had shaped the course of modernism—was likewise elevating *Blast* in her memoir as a "huge" and "cyclonic" wonder. She, too, heralded the power of the "thick black capitals half an inch high" and the "twelve-by-nine pages" (*Poet's Life* 355).[20]

Monroe's and Pound's similar emphases here set the tone for later criticism—like the many other latter-day critics noted above, they accent both *Blast*'s bold physical features and its impressive stature—and point to the further reason for *Blast*'s remarkable staying power. Again, in invocations of *Blast*, usually foregrounded are its "blinding covers" and "commanding dimensions"[21] as well as its attendant ability to draw notice. Of course, in part these features are underscored because, like those of an enormous building, one can hardly miss them. But there is also at work here a deeper interest in these features, for it is they that render *Blast* susceptible to incorporation in many narratives of modernism's development.

In other words, not only is *Blast* commemorated *by way* of its exaggerated typography, bright color, audacious rhetoric, size, and weight, but in fact often *because* of these characteristics. Its exaggerated features are valued, first, because they are easily recalled and replicated; second, because in 1914–1915, they were clearly enlisted in the service of a call for revolution that, in retrospect, we now associate with modernism's beginnings and that helps us make sense of those beginnings ("in them days," as Pound says); and third, because they suggest that the activities with which *Blast* was associated were vitally important (Pound moves from noting the magazine's physical bulk to commenting that Lewis and he, in their work, were likewise "hefty"; in his description, as in many others, physical stature is conceptually linked with and used to connote the "stature" of eminence). More than just riveting attention by virtue of scale and splash, then, these physical characteristics are attractive because, in bold, comprehensible strokes, they paint what critics have often wanted to understand as the story of modernism's beginnings: they appear to mark a desirably legible origin to the modernist call for revolution. Equally appealing is that the ferocity of *Blast*'s pronouncements suggests that the movement for which it stood was imbued with forceful revolutionary energy, thus in turn implying the significance of scholarship devoted to such valuably subversive work.

Ultimately, then, it is *Blast*'s combination of memorable attributes, ability to suggest an easily accessible narrative of origins, and capacity to connote the importance of both modernist work and scholarship dedicated to it—all this enabled by its "commanding" physical "dimensions"—that, on the one hand, makes *Blast* a "history book," and, on the other, assures it a place in what Lewis called (in the same 1915 letter to Augustus John) the "history books."

Blast also enters the "history books" of modernism by way of its alignment with similar projects of the European avant-garde of the time. In 1914 as Lewis and the other members of the coalescing Vorticist group developed *Blast*, they drew upon examples from contemporary reform-minded movements in the arts—continuing and permuting, sometimes parodically, practices of continental avant-garde figures such as F. T. Marinetti, Guillaume Apollinaire, and the Russian Futurists.[22] As Paige Reynolds notes, the Vorticists appropriated the techniques of these avant-garde contemporaries, along with those of British promotional culture of their time, with a nationalist imperative in mind—in the name of creating a native English art.[23] They hoped to make themselves legible as pioneers who both shared and superseded the spirit of revolution expressed by like-minded Continental comrades, and directed it toward a specifically British project. Although their strategies for securing literary fame, which replicated and pointed to similar gambits used in other movements, were only mildly successful in 1914 (again, seeming to many commentators merely derivative[24]), they have clearly had much greater impact in the long term.

BLAST AND THE FIN DE SIÈCLE

If *Blast*'s continued stature within modernist accounts has been assured, however, so too has been the confinement of its image to a neat, easily transmissible caricature that obscures both other important aspects of the magazine and less evident, although integral, dimensions of Vorticism. If we are to reconsider the role of *Blast* in sculpting our current concepts of modernism, we need to reexamine it with an eye toward enriching our currently limited views of both the magazine and the Vorticist movement it announced and advanced.

The journal's self-conscious flamboyance, of course, invites reductive images of its venture. Both *Blast* and Vorticism are remembered for their bombast, their ostensibly uncompromising repudiation of preceding eras, and for all the elements of the journal that seem to suggest those qualities by metonymy—not only the much-discussed stark typography and large scale, but also the angular geometric figures that, within the context of Vorticism, likewise came to signify severity and aggressive action. Indeed, if *Blast* tends to be represented by its bold features such as typeface and color, analogously, Vorticism has often been represented synecdochically by its geometric shapes—what Lewis in later years would term its "geometrics" (*Rude Assignment* 129).

At this point in modernist scholarship, as we interrogate modernism's myths of origin, we need to look not only at these oft-rehearsed signature characteristics of *Blast* and Vorticism, but also at their less apparent features—to discover other facets of the magazine and the movement for which it stood, as well as to better understand the best-known and most visible aspects of both. Specifically, we need to examine the attributes of *Blast* that reveal Vorticism's relationship to its nineteenth-century Aestheticist predecessors, a relationship actively obscured by the magazine's rhetoric. Careful tracing of the contours of *Blast*'s relationship with its Aestheticist precursors can deepen understanding of Vorticism—and, specifically, of the impetus behind what I will be calling its characteristic "geometric gestures." Not only have these geometric gestures become a kind of shorthand for the movement's work, but they have also become inescapably involved in our image of the cultural environment from which the movement emerged.

In a move typical of artistic positioning of the time, the Vorticists themselves denied not only their debt to *fin-de-siècle* Aestheticism—which they claimed to repudiate—but also their relationship to their cultural context: the attitude predominant in the pages of *Blast 1* is that "the moment a man feels or realizes himself as an artist, he ceases to belong to any milieu or time" (*B1* 7). Janet Lyon in fact suggests that the very genre of the modernist manifesto, especially as employed in *Blast* to "narrate" Vorticism's "originary moment," tends misleadingly to suggest that a movement has emerged ex nihilo, occluding its dialogic relations with other movements and events of its moment ("Militant Discourse" 101). *Blast*, however, of course inescapably "belongs" to its "milieu"; considering attentively the nature of its relationship to that milieu will help to enhance understanding of not only Vorticism, but also the legacy of Vorticism in the twentieth century—a legacy on which this study concentrates.[25] It can also shed light more generally on the imprint left by the *fin de siècle* on avant-garde movements of the early twentieth century.

All this, then, is not to say that that we need avert our gaze from the magazine's now overplayed size, bright cover, and stark typography, or from the aggressive geometric figures of its pages thought to emblematize the work of Vorticism. On the contrary, we need to pay better attention to these characteristics, considering them not in isolation, but rather as they signify in concert with a constellation of other elements within *Blast* to suggest the nature of Vorticism's relationship to Aestheticism.

Prospectus for first issue of The Yellow Book (1894)

> *THE YELLOW BOOK*
>
> IN COMPLETE SETS OF THIRTEEN VOLUMES
>
> £3 5s. net
>
> PRINCIPAL CONTRIBUTORS
>
> *LITERARY*
>
> BARING, HON. MAURICE
> BENSON, A. C.
> BEERBOHM, MAX
> BUCHAN, JOHN
> CORVO, FREDERICK BARON
> CRACKANTHORPE, HUBERT
> CROSSE, VICTORIA
> CUSTANCE, OLIVE
> D'ARCY, ELLA
> DAVIDSON, JOHN
> DOBSON, AUSTIN
> DOWIE, MENIE MURIEL
> DOWSON, ERNEST
> EGERTON, GEORGE
> FRANCE, ANATOLE
> FREDERIC, HAROLD
> FULLERTON, MERTON
> GALE, NORMAN
> GARNETT, RICHARD
> GILCHRIST R. MURRAY
> GISSING, GEORGE
> GOSSE, EDMUND
>
> GRAHAM, MRS. CUNNINGHAME
> GRAHAME, KENNETH
> GREENWOOD, FREDERICK
> HAMERTON, PHILIP GILBERT
> HAPGOOD, NORMAN
> HARLAND, HENRY
> HOBBES, JOHN OLIVER
> HOPPER, NORA
> JAMES, HENRY
> JOHNSON, LIONEL
> LEE, VERNON
> LE GALLIENNE, RICHARD
> LEVERSON, MRS. ERNEST
> McCHESNEY, DORA GREENWELL
> MIALL, A. BERNARD
> COUTTS, F. B. MONEY
> MOORE, GEORGE
> NESBIT, E.
> NEVINSON, HENRY W.
> PHILLIPS, STEPHEN
>
> PRESTAGE, EDGAR
> PREVOST, FRANCIS
> RADFORD, DOLLY
> RALEIGH, WALTER
> RISLEY, R. V.
> ROBERTS, CHARLES G. D.
> ROBERTSON, JOHN M.
> RUSSELL, T. BARON
> SALT, H. S.
> SHARP, EVELYN
> STREET, G. S.
> STRETTELL, ALMA
> SWETTENHAM, SIR FRANK
> SYMONS, ARTHUR
> TADEMA, LAURENCE ALMA
> TOMSON, GRAHAM R.
> TRAILL, H. D.
> WATSON, ROSAMUND MARRIOTT
> WATSON, WILLIAM
> WATT, FRANCIS
> WATTS, THEODORE
> WELLS, H. G.
> YEATS, W. B.
>
> *ARTISTIC*
>
> BALL, WILFRID
> BELL, R. ANNING
> BEARDSLEY, AUBREY
> BEERBOHM, MAX
> BRAMLEY, FRANK, A.R.A.
> CONDER, CHARLES
> CAMERON, D. Y.
> CAMERON, KATHARINE
> CHRISTIE, J. E.
> COTMAN, F. G.
> CRANE, WALTER
> CRAWHALL, J.
> DEARMER, MABEL
> DRAPER, H. J.
> EDEN, SIR WILLIAM (BART.)
> FORBES, ELIZABETH STANHOPE
> FORBES, STANHOPE, A.R.A.
>
> FURSE, CHARLES W.
> GASKIN, A. J.
> GASKIN, MRS. A. J.
> GOTCH, CAROLINE
> GOTCH, T. C.
> GUTHRIE, JAMES
> HAMMOND, GERTRUDE D.
> HARTRICK, H. S.
> HENRY, GEORGE, A.R.A.
> HORNEL, E.
> HOUSMAN, LAURENCE
> HOWARD, FRANCIS
> HYDE, WILLIAM
> LAVERY, JOHN, A.R.A.
> LEIGHTON, LORD
> MACDONALD, FRANCES
> MACDONALD, MARGARET
> MACDOUGALL, W. BROWN
> McNAIR, J. HERBERT
>
> NETTLESHIP, J. T.
> NEW, E. H.
> PENNELL, JOSEPH
> PIMLOTT, E. PHILIP
> PRIDEAUX-BRUNE, GERTRUDE
> REED, ETHEL
> ROBINSON, CHARLES
> ROCHE, A.
> ROTHENSTEIN, WILL
> RUSSELL, W. W.
> SICKERT, WALTER
> STEER, P. WILSON
> STEVENSON, R. M.
> STRANG, WILLIAM, A.R.A.
> SULLIVAN, E. J.
> THORNTON, ALFRED
> VALLANCE, AYMER
> WALTON, E. A.
> WILSON, PATTEN
>
> JOHN LANE, THE BODLEY HEAD, VIGO ST., LONDON & NEW YORK

Advertisement for copies of The Yellow Book *in* Blast 1

Far less conspicuous within *Blast*'s pages than its bold manifestic pronouncements and geometric figures, these other elements can help to situate *Blast* in the historical context with which the Vorticists were initially reluctant to acknowledge their connection—and enrich understanding of the significance of the journal's more evident gestures.

In the two issues of *Blast*, for example, the name of the magazine's publisher, John Lane, appears on both its title page and in several places in the advertisement lists at the back, which feature Lane's latest publications. In the last pages of *Blast 1*, one also finds advertisements for the well-known magazine of the 1890s, *The Yellow Book*, likewise published by Lane. In fact, the back pages of *Blast 2*, which provide "press opinions" about *Blast 1*, draw parallels between *The Yellow Book* and *Blast*: London's *Sunday Times* is quoted as claiming that "what the yellow book [sic] did for the artistic movement of its decade 'BLAST' aims at doing for the arts and literature of to-day" (*B2* 104). These signals, especially the explicit comparison between *The Yellow Book* and *Blast*, direct us to Vorticism's *fin-de-siècle* antecedents. Responding to such signals in 1914, A. R. Orage noted in the *New Age* that *Blast* had been "announced as the successor of the 'Yellow Book.'"[26]

In the 1890s *The Yellow Book*—the avant-garde journal that, for many, epitomized the Decadent-Aestheticist sensibility of the 1890s—gained an indelible reputation as a succès de scandale. Much like *Blast*, it was hailed by derisive reviewers as a "monster"—"jaundiced-looking" and "indigestible," "half-book, half-magazine."[27] Although it promoted no particular movement or project, its unifying mission, akin to *Blast*'s, was to shock. Just few months into its run, the magazine had already come to be figured in the public imagination by the mischievous drawings of wunderkind Aubrey Beardsley, which much of the public found unsettling, even disturbing.

Two decades later, as the Vorticists were likewise positioning themselves as scandalous, readers of *Blast* would likely have agreed with claims about parallels between *Blast* and *The Yellow Book*. Mark Morrisson has suggested that the references to *The Yellow Book* in *Blast* indicate the debt of the work of early modernism to the 1890s (*Public Face of Modernism* 124). I would go further to underscore the structural homology between the cultural niche occupied by *The Yellow Book* in the 1890s and that inhabited by *Blast* in the 1910s, as well as between the cultural work performed by the two magazines during their respective decades. Notice that the *Sunday Times* captures the relationship with the phrase "What the yellow book *did* for the artistic movement of its decade" (my italics), thus emphasizing the likeness between the magazines' cultural functions. Encountered by readers of the time, the name of publisher John Lane, under whose aegis both magazines appeared, would have reinforced the impression that *Blast* served to transpose *Yellow Book*'s project into a twentieth-century idiom. And I would suggest that this was an impression that the Vorticists deliberately courted: as signals in *Blast* attest, the Vorticists sought to place *Blast* as successor to both the *Yellow Book*'s controversial status and its brand of satire, and thereby also to its cultural role.

However, any accurate characterization of Vorticism's relationship to *The Yellow Book* and the *fin-de-siècle* Aestheticism it was thought to exemplify requires that this claim be qualified with another: although the Vorticists sought propinquity to some features of *The Yellow Book*, they also distanced themselves carefully from other aspects of the magazine's reputation, fearing the consequences of too close a linkage. In other words, though desiring the notoriety of the 1890s periodical, the Vorticists simultaneously shied from advertising themselves as altogether the inheritors of what they regarded as its—and, more generally, Aestheticism's—flaws, which were often described by them and others in their cultural climate as diseases of the *fin de siècle* that they might risk contracting were they to draw too near to its projects and values.[28] Thus even as much of what they did placed them as heirs to *The Yellow Book*'s impish, intelligent, counterhegemonic antics, they strove to disavow many of the implications of this lineage.

As critical accounts such as Materer's and Morrisson's have suggested, what troubled the Vorticists chiefly was Aestheticism's cultural association with various forms of "effeminacy." Andreas Huyssen has famously maintained that modernism was centrally driven by its need to resist the feminized Other of mass culture;[29] Cassandra Laity, meanwhile, advances a related and structurally analogous argument by suggesting that early forms of modernism were also often fueled by a homophobic need to stave off the threat of another feminized Other: the figure of an Aesthete who is not only feminized, but more precisely, *effeminate* in a way that, during the years immediately preceding World War I, summoned the idea of the male homosexual.[30] Laity's argument certainly pertains to Vorticism: it is Vorticism's radical preoccupation with this "effeminate" figure of the male Aesthete, its relationship with which is both antagonistic and symbiotic, that crucially conditioned the development of the Vorticist movement.

I would suggest, in fact, that the larger-than-life features of *Blast* with which this discussion began—the bright "puce" cover, the ferocious diction, and the proliferation of angular, geometric images now regarded as representative of Vorticism—emerged from the Vorticists' anxiety about allying themselves too closely with the kind of the Aestheticist effeminacy *The Yellow Book* had come to represent. These exaggerated features, in other words, enact the Vorticists' effort to evict the specter of the male Aesthete qua homosexual from their midst—so as, from the homophobic Vorticist perspective, to allow proximity to Aestheticism without risk of contamination from it.

We are back, then, to the "commanding dimensions" and "blinding covers" of the magazine's first issue. I have suggested reasons for their prominent placement in critical narratives about *Blast* and modernism. I would submit further that Vorticism itself invested deeply in these features: they encode the foundational Vorticist desire to engage in an active rewriting of the flamboyance of the Aestheticist 1890s, to replace it with a different flamboyance, so as symbolically to assert a new form of Aestheticism expunged of effeminacy.

For greater understanding of this desire, at once phobic and fertile, we need to turn to Vorticism's well-known "geometric bias."[31] Within the term "geometric," admittedly a commodious one, I include not only Vorticism's overtly geometric visual images—its signature—conspicuously displayed in *Blast*, but also the diction and themes of *Blast*'s prose, as well as the characteristics I have noted above, such as typography, layout, and size. These latter characteristics resonate with the more strictly geometric images because they trace semiotic trajectories similar to theirs. Together with the geometric images, they participate in the magazine's project of exorcism: within the pages of *Blast*, in other words, I subsume under the rubric of the magazine's "geometric gestures" everything harnessed to purge Vorticism of what the Vorticists regarded as the sins of Aestheticism.

This chapter addresses how Vorticism's well-known "geometric bias" encodes its fundamentally, and generatively, ambivalent relationship to 1890s Aestheticism. The relationship is an admixture of attraction and repulsion, affinity and difference, such that Vorticism's forceful efforts at exorcism are in fact necessitated by its own undeniable nearness to *fin-de-siècle* Aestheticism. When the Vorticists conspicuously try to "correct" (*B2* 41) what they perceive as the effeminate waywardness of Aestheticism, then, this is in part because they have a stake in drawing upon other qualities of Aestheticism. Moreover, as this chapter will explore, at times Vorticism needs to engage in such public "corrections" because it covertly draws upon the very values of Aestheticism that it apparently refuses.

One of the best indices for understanding Vorticism's anxious, productive nexus with Aestheticism is *Blast*'s evocation of a figure closely linked to both 1890s Aestheticism and the reputation of *The Yellow Book*: Oscar Wilde. It is in fact appearances of the category of the "Wildean" within *Blast*, along with a collection of other signifiers metonymically related to Wilde, that best illuminate Vorticism's attitudes toward Aestheticism—and thus the necessity for geometry within Vorticism.

Again, examining Vorticism's complex relationship to Aestheticism can valuably complicate dominant assumptions about a Vorticist movement whose susceptibility to caricatured representation often precludes more subtle understandings of it. Moreover, refining awareness of Vorticism's dialogue with its Aestheticist predecessors can facilitate a more accurate perception of the campaign against effeminacy—which, far from confined to Vorticism, clearly forms a major effort threading through modernist work of this period. It can help us gain better purchase on the projects informing the images that have become emblematic of Vorticism: angular geometric shapes. Finally, understanding Vorticism more richly can yield greater insight into the modern crisis in masculinity to which the modernist campaign against effeminacy serves as a defensive response.[32]

VORTICIST GEOMETRICS

In 1914, on Ormond Street in London, Wyndham Lewis and a group of fellow artists established their Vorticist headquarters at the "Rebel Art Centre." Given Vorticism's status as merely one more movement in an avant-garde cultural field teeming with such movements in Britain and on the Continent, the rebels were aware that they would have to do their utmost to gain public attention. Amid the yellow walls, gold curtains, bright red doors, and blue rugs of the Centre, the work these artists displayed was strikingly abstract and geometric. Kate Lechmere, the venture's financial backer, even decorated the window boxes of their building with geometric designs to signify the group's characteristic refusal to imitate organic forms.[33] Such geometric shapes would soon become the group's hallmark.

In the two issues of *Blast* that appeared in 1914 and 1915, Lewis developed the bellicose editorial posture that anticipated his later persona of "The Enemy," which, a decade later, would become a mainstay of his political and cultural criticism. Lewis's speaker of *Blast*'s manifestoes broached issues of artistic purity and responsibility, distinguishing Vorticism, defiantly English, from such contemporary Continental movements as Impressionism, Picasso's Cubism, Marinetti's Futurism, and Kandinsky's Expressionism. The speaker placed particular emphasis on defining Vorticism's relationship to what was constructed in the manifestoes as "Nature" and "Life," two terms usually employed interchangeably in *Blast* to denote the same category of organic everyday existence. If the Vorticist artist—aloof, detached, committed to aggressive arrangement of the world's material and to discernment of its patterns—had to deal with "Nature," he should conquer it and use it. As Lewis noted in one of his epigrammatic statements, suggesting the attitude of swaggering machismo often associated with the Vorticists, the artist should make Nature his "Brothel" (*B1* 148). The true Vorticist should let life "know its place in a Vorticist universe" (*B1* 148), relegating it to the position of subordinated mistress or prostitute. Rather than imitate the appearances of Nature, which would be tantamount to relinquishing the Vorticist's proper dominant, detached position and surrendering weakly to the world's charms, the Vorticist should instead emphasize in his art those qualities which are "peculiar to men"—"the stranger stuff" that "men must get out of themselves" (*B1* 129).

In the context of Vorticism's explicit denunciations of "Nature" and "Life," the geometric designs so closely associated with the group would seem to signify a rejection of Nature and its organic forms. And in part, the geometric images did signal the deliberate effort to remove Vorticist art from the "supple, soft and vital elements, which distinguish animals and men" (*B2* 43)—not what the manifestoes call "the stranger stuff" of men, but rather the soft underbellies that allied humans with the natural realm. For the Vorticists, then, the geometric suggested that which was hard and unyielding, in contrast to that which was "supple, soft and vital"; and by implication, according to the way the manifestoes defined the "Natural," that which was not part of Nature: geometry indicated the realm of the man-made, the artificial rather than the organic.

The significance assigned to geometry within Vorticism, however, was in fact not quite as stable as this suggests. At other textual moments, even as geometric figures still suggested hardness, they were coded as not estranged from nature, but instead as representative of nature's underlying skeleton. As Lewis notes in another early characterization of his group's geometric work, it emphasized the "geometric bases and structure of life" ("Cubist Room" 9). At times, then, Vorticist geometric hardness might be read not as effecting a turn away from nature, but rather as revealing the fundamentals—or "essence"—of the natural world (*B2* 45).[34] One of Lewis's early attempts to explain the commonalities that united the artists of the Vorticist program indicates this sliding significance of geometry in the nascent Vorticist imagination:

> All revolutionary painting to-day has in common the rigid reflections of steel and stone in the spirit of the artist; that desire for stability as though a machine were being built to fly or kill with; an alienation from the traditional photographer's trade and realisation of the value of colour and form as such independently of what recognisable form it covers or encloses. People are invited, in short, to change entirely their idea of the painter's mission, and penetrate ... with him into a transposed universe as abstract as, though different from, the musicians [*sic*].
>
> ("CUBIST ROOM" 9)

These comments, from Lewis's introduction in a catalogue for "The Camden Town Group and Others" exhibition in Brighton, actually predate the christening of the Vorticist movement; but given that Lewis refers in this essay to the work of the artists who would soon become the Vorticists, and as he associates the work of his "group" with the "geometric," they pertain to what will become Vorticism's distinctive geometric idiom.

Here, Lewis links geometrics with a host of qualities whose range and difference attest to the slipperiness of what will become the significance of Vorticist geometry. Geometry is said, first, to suggest "rigidity," a "desire for stability" reminiscent of T. E. Hulme's descriptions of the geometric. Insofar as the geometric suggests "an alienation from the traditional photographer's trade and realisation of the value of colour and form as such independently of what recognisable form it covers or encloses," geometry also recalls "pure form" and Bell's "significant form"—the nonrepresentational form attractive to the avant-garde of the time. But at the same time, other signals in this passage suggest that geometry is also signifying mimetically: through its shapes, reflecting the "geometric bases and structure of life," the forms of "machinery" and "steel and stone" of the modern urban environment. On the one hand, then, geometry is assigned significance on the basis of its ability to turn away from the forms of the world, to signify independently of them; on the other, on the basis of its ability to allude to them. Moreover, Vorticism is similarly associated with both "penetration" and "abstraction." Although Lewis uses these terms in tandem, suggesting that the artist reaches a domain of pure abstraction *by way of* a form of penetration, the semantic valences of the two terms conflict in a way that indicates Vorticism's bent for holding opposite tendencies in conjunction: Lewis at once codes geometry as signaling the effort to "penetrate" to the depths of life—to reach its invisible underlying essence, to reach a world of abstractions by moving profoundly *into* it—and the effort to "abstract" from life, which connotes moving *away* from it, up and out beyond its particulars.[35]

Thus overdetermined, the geometric figure floats as a signifier through Vorticism, shifting and changing, defined variously at different moments as emblematic of the movement's rejection of representational form and its turn toward abstraction ("an alienation from the traditional photographer's trade"); as representative of the invisible skeleton of the visible world ("geometric bases or structures of life"); and as reflective of the surfaces of the urban environment ("rigid reflections of steel and stone"). Amid this proliferation of slightly different, though not always altogether contradictory, connotations, what remains consistent is that the Vorticist geometric shape assumes its significance by virtue of its ability to suggest dynamically forceful precision, frequently through qualities of hardness and severity and specifically through its capacity to suggest something skeletal and often metallic. The sculptor Gaudier-

Brzeska, one of the chief Vorticists, referred to the "sharpness and rigidity" of his work (*G-B* 32); Pound appreciated Vorticism's "hard light, clear edges" (Wees, *Vorticism and the English Avant-Garde* 154). This is the common denominator: the inconsistency, then, appears in what the Vorticists enlist severity, hardness, and rigidity to *suggest*. And what fostered this inconsistency, I would offer, was that Vorticism, ultimately, was not all that concerned with what such "rigidity," "sharpness," and "hardness" could connote, whether pure form, essences, buildings, machines, or skeletons. Vorticism concerned itself instead chiefly with the way such forceful severity, precision, hardness, and rigidity in their own right, whether natural or no, whatever else they mapped on to, could combat effeminacy on symbolic terrain.

Obscured by this smoke screen of seemingly different significances for geometry, then, is the consistent role played by the geometric figure in Vorticism's aggressively defensive response to the perceived effeminacy of its Aestheticist predecessors. It is this role that unites, in a coalition of sorts, the group of apparently disparate meanings associated with Vorticist geometry. And it is this effort that also demands that Vorticist precision be coupled with dynamic, aggressive energy, even to be coded so as to imply such energy (as Lewis puts it, the geometrics are handled "as though a machine were being built to fly or kill with").

Beyond this, however, Vorticism's instability of signification with respect to Nature, even as it participates in the vacillation that suggests Vorticism's main focus on effeminacy, also reveals the complexity of Vorticism's relationship to Nature, which I will later address in further detail. This attitude toward Nature, in turn, is intertwined with Vorticism's complicated and equivocal response to the very "supple" and "soft" effeminacy it ostensibly seeks to expunge.

BLAST'S RHETORICAL CAMPAIGN AGAINST EFFEMINACY

The now familiar Vorticist rhetoric against effeminacy appeared in Vorticist writings as early as the group's inception. Again, the Vorticists formed their coterie out of a quarrel with their contemporary, the painter and critic Roger Fry, member of the Bloomsbury group and organizer of the legendary Post-Impressionist art exhibit that had scandalized London in 1910. In 1913 Lewis, Hamilton, Etchells, and Wadsworth together signed an open letter expressing discontent with the Omega Workshops, the Bloomsbury-based atelier launched and directed by Fry, with which they had been affiliated.

Formed out of ideals like those of William Morris's nineteenth-century Arts and Crafts movement—which advocated the creation of handcrafted artifacts to counter the deleterious effects of machine-made objects on everyday life—the Omega Workshops were devoted to updating these Morrisian ideals and bringing to people's home environments the innovations of early twentieth-century Post-Impressionist art. Omega artists designed and constructed products for interior décor such as rugs, wallpaper, chairs, curtains, lampshades, pottery, cushions, and boxes—usually executed in vibrant colors and bold geometric patterns—intended to introduce the "spirit of fun" and "free play" into "furniture and fabrics" (Wees, *Vorticism and the English Avant-Garde* 60–61).[36]

Along with Fry, the Omega Workshops included a circle of Bloomsbury-affiliated artists such as Duncan Grant and Vanessa Bell (listed as the Workshops' codirectors) as well as David Bomberg, Mark Gertler, Nina Hamnet, Gladys Hynes, and Winifred Gill. At first, also contributing regularly were the artists who would become the Vorticists: Lewis, Etchells, Wadsworth, and Hamilton. In October 1913, however, Lewis and his comrades charged that Roger Fry and Omega had done them an injustice: Fry had appropriated a commission that was rightfully Lewis's.[37]

In the publicly circulated letter in which they announced their grievances and officially declared their break with Omega, Lewis's group discredited the Workshops in terms that forecast their imminent Vorticist campaign against effeminacy. Unlike the iconoclastic Vorticists, said Lewis's band, the retrograde Omega Workshops still had an "Idol," which was "Prettiness"; and despite its apparently up-to-date emphasis on early twentieth-century Post-Impressionist values, Omega was still deplorably "mid-Victorian," with a Pre-Raphaelite "languish of the neck" and skin of "greenery-yallery," the green-yellow color associated with the décor of London's Grosvenor Gallery and the Aesthetes who had styled themselves after its aesthetic examples (*Letters of Wyndham Lewis* 49).[38] Lewis's faction dismissed the Omega members as Aesthetes—a "family party of strayed and Dissenting Aesthetes"—who had departed somewhat from their *fin-de-siècle* predecessors but remained Aesthetes nonetheless: "[They] were compelled to call in as much modern talent as they could find, to do the rough and masculine work without which they knew their efforts would not rise above the level of a pleasant tea-party" (49).

This of course implies that it was the proto-Vorticists who possessed "modern talent" and "masculinity" in abundance and who had been "called in" to the rescue. According to this view, though the Vorticists themselves were characterized as "rough and masculine," the Omega group was unfortunately feminine, associated with the "prettiness" and "tea parties" usually connected with the woman's sphere. Moreover, the implication was that to be properly "modern," one should be "rough" and "masculine." In *Blast 2*, Lewis would refer wryly to the Omega Workshops as "Mr. Fry's curtain and pincushion factory in Fitzroy Square" (41).[39]

Of course, the Vorticists did not split from the Omega group solely because they regarded them as insufficiently "rough and masculine." Explaining the schism, the Vorticists cited wrongs done them by Fry. Furthermore, what becomes apparent from the circumstances is that the Vorticists used the occasion of Fry's discourtesy as an opportunity for a break that, strategically, they were seeking to make in any case. In a field of cultural production saturated with developing and competing movements, the Vorticists sought to establish themselves as a legitimate movement in their own right; accordingly, they had to advertise their artistic differences from the Omega group in order to justify their independence not only on personal, but also aesthetic, grounds. There were sufficient similarities between Vorticists and the Omega members that the Vorticists had to accentuate, even invent, the features that distinguished them from the Workshops. The Post-Impressionist aesthetic commitments of Omega—reflected in its characteristic abstract geometric patterns done in vivid crimsons, yellows, purples, and oranges—accorded closely with those of the Vorticists in several respects. Moreover, the aesthetic theories of Fry and such compatriots as fellow Bloomsbury member Clive Bell—especially their arguments about "significant form"—had in fact strongly influenced the Vorticist style.[40] As Lewis put it in 1914, like the Omega artists, the Vorticists believed that the "colour and form" had "value" independent of the "recognisable form it covers or encloses" ("Cubist Room" 9).

In their opening manifesto in *Blast*, however, the Vorticists elided their debt to Bell and Omega. In part, they did so out of spite toward Fry and Bloomsbury, but they did so also out of a need to define themselves in a milieu that required groups to distinguish themselves markedly from one another. As Lewis would note in a memoir of the period, "If you were a 'movement'" in those days, "you were expected to shout" (*WLOA* 58). The "rougher" and more "masculine" attitude of the Vorticists—and their attendant challenge to "Prettiness"—was emphasized, as was their quarrel with Fry, to gain interest and establish identity. As Lyon remarks, by the time the Vorticists published *Blast*, they were culminating "four years of incremental self-differentiation from other flanks of the English avant-garde" ("Militant Discourse" 105).

Bloomsbury was by no means the Vorticists' only target in its strategic process of "self-differentiation." Again, the Vorticists were similarly, if more mildly, critical of many other contemporary movements: Picasso's Cubism, Kandinsky's Expressionism, and Marinetti's Italian Futurism. In *Blast 2*'s "Review of Contemporary Art," Lewis in fact made explicit the Vorticists' commitment to separating themselves from others, even when they bore them no ill will. His reviews of movements similar to Vorticism, he noted, might "appear disparaging." But, he explained,

> this inspection was undertaken . . . to show the ways in which we DIFFER, and the tendencies we would CORRECT. . . . In the several details suggested above . . . Vorticism is opposed to the various groups of continental painting. I will recapitulate these points, and amplify them. In so doing I can best tabulate and explain the aims of Vorticism to-day.
>
> (B2 41)

To best meet its responsibility as a movement committed to progress in the arts, this implies, Vorticism had to divide itself from, and improve upon, both precursors and contemporaries.

Resolved to distinguish themselves from their contemporaries, as they did in their opening salvo against Omega, the Vorticists persistently used the language of effeminacy to separate themselves from other movements. Often, the manifestoes of *Blast* invoke effeminacy directly, damning "England" for the way it breeds the "effeminate lout within" (B1 11). They also frequently target effeminacy's semiotic sibling, "femininity," cursing "snobbery," for instance, as the "disease of femininity" (15) and condemning those who bow to the "feminine contours" of "wild Mother Nature" (19). Effeminacy is also indirectly denounced through adjectives and images culturally associated with "effeminacy": "Mr. Fry's curtain and pincushion factory," for instance, is accused of producing "abject, anemic, and amateurish" art (B2 41). Cubism, for all its admirable "great plastic qualities" (42), capitulates to "languor," "sentimentalism," and "WEAKNESS" (41). The Futurists, likewise, although laudable for their "vivacity and high-spirits" (41), succumb to "Romance" and fail to "sufficiently dominate the contents of their pictures" (42). Kandinsky, finally, is deemed "wandering and slack," "passive and medium-like" (40).

Of the terms associated with the twinned categories of effeminacy and femininity, the terms "sentimentality" and "romanticism" are especially assailed. As the magazine's opening declaration of mission announces, "We stand for the Reality of the Present—not for the sentimental Future" (B1 7). This opening section ends with the assertion that "The 'Poor'... are only picturesque and amusing for the sentimentalist or the romantic" (8). Among the undesirable aspects of France blasted a few pages later is "SENTIMENTAL GALLIC GUSH" (13). Cursing the Victorian era, *Blast* damns its "SENTIMENTAL HYGIENICS" (18). The implication throughout the two issues of *Blast* is that Vorticism must remain aloof from the qualities it associates with a condition of effeminacy, instead maintaining an attitude of "bareness" and "hardness" (41); and holding to the camp opposed to that of "effeminacy" in the Manichean universe that *Blast* constructs.

One further member of this family of signifiers that delineates the realm that the Vorticist rejects is the "BRITANNIC AESTHETE" (15), a figure that *Blast* twice condemns within the opening five pages of its first issue. The Vorticists' invocation of "the Aesthete" here in *Blast* resonates with their use of the figure in their letter to the Omega artists, whom they dismiss as "strayed and Dissenting Aesthetes." As I have suggested, the figure of the Aesthete, in fact, holds a privileged position within this collection of signifiers: it is presented within the world of *Blast* as epitomizing, and therefore as a shorthand way of conveying, all the qualities that Vorticism strives to avoid. As Vorticism took shape as a movement, the Aestheticism of the *fin de siècle* was widely regarded as an artistic mode whose influence was waning and from whose standards newer artists had to distance themselves if they were to make their mark. Accordingly, it is under the sign of the Aesthete that the constellation of characteristics overtly renounced within *Blast* are joined.

Given *Blast*'s reliance on the figure of the Aesthete to perform its work of purgation, it is no surprise that a name that often appears within the journal's pages is "Oscar Wilde." In the opening salvo of *Blast 1*, Lewis asserts that "Wilde gushed twenty years ago about the beauty of machinery" (8). Although *Blast* itself explicitly praises the "restless machines" of England's industrial ports and at other points celebrates machinery's "grandeur and efficiency" (*B2* 43), the journal nonetheless faults Wilde for his alleged attitudes toward machines: his "gush" about them is denounced as deplorably "romantic" and "sentimental." Wilde is thereby quickly aligned with the Futurists, whom Lewis vilifies as "a sensational and sentimental mixture of the *aesthete* of 1890 and the realist of 1870" (*B1* 8; my italics). Later in *Blast 1*, Lewis notes cruelly that "about 1900," England emerged from "Lupanars and Satanics"—presumably, for him, the foul eroticism associated with Baudelaire, Swinburne, and their ilk—once its bourgeoisie had "thoughtfully put Wilde in prison" (133).

Within the pages of *Blast*, "Wilde" only partially refers to the actual man: the name accrues special significance within the magazine as a symbol for the qualities of which Vorticism seeks to cleanse itself. Lewis's use of Wilde within *Blast* echoes the way he invokes Wilde in a letter of 1914, in which he notes that Wilde was "struck down by the bourgeoisie."[41] Given Lewis's avant-garde cultural position, Wilde's having been rejected by the "bourgeoisie" implies his alignment with Wilde, but in the letter, Lewis vigorously dissociates himself from Wilde's downfall, disavowing the connection between him and Wilde that the painter Walter Sickert, he claims, has sought to draw. The resonance between the language of the letter and that of *Blast* suggests that, in 1914, Wilde was uppermost in Lewis's mind as a cultural signifier for that which he and the Vorticists wanted to "strike down." That he foregrounds Wilde's opposition to the bourgeoisie, however, underscores the parallel between the Vorticists' cultural position and that of the figure from which he wants to distance them.

Blast's preoccupation with the figure of Wilde illuminates the way that Vorticism, as constructed by Lewis, engaged in an ongoing, and perpetually fraught, relationship with Wilde and all that, in Lewis's mind, he came to symbolize—a compulsive relationship of identification and opposition fundamental to Vorticism. The treatment of Wilde in *Blast*, then, provides an index of Vorticism's attitude toward Aestheticism more generally: Wilde comes to stand synecdochically for the qualities of Aestheticism with which Vorticism devotes itself to contending. Vorticism's phobic reaction to Aestheticism was spurred by what Wilde had come to represent in the London milieu of 1914—specifically, how Wilde's image by that time had conditioned understandings of the notion of effeminacy.

ANTI-COLLABORATIONS

In the following discussion, I will focus chiefly on Lewis's reactions to Wildean Aestheticism, as, though the Vorticist effort was created by not only Lewis, but also Pound, Gaudier-Brzeska, and other artists associated with the movement, it was primarily Lewis's responses to Aestheticism that guided the movement's campaign against effeminacy.

The dynamic, frictional, and generative relationship between Vorticism and Wildean Aestheticism is well captured, I would offer, by the notion of "anti-collaboration." I borrow the term from Scott Klein, who in turn draws it from Joyce's *Finnegans Wake* (Klein, *Joyce and Lewis* 19): both the relationships Lewis developed with his contemporaries and the relationships he established between characters and elements in his work can be described as "anti-collaborations"—

which I use to mean antagonistic, and fertile, relationships of simultaneous identification and opposition. In Klein's view, the signals in *Blast* indicate that the Vorticist participates in such a relationship, "defined not only through his opposition to but also through his similarity to that which he presents as his opposite" (62). And that which is "presented" in the pages of *Blast* as the Vorticist's "opposite" is the Wildean dandy.

By the turn of the century, the Wilde trials and their attendant wave of sensational publicity had established "Wilde" as a central element in the public lexicon (see Sinfield, *The Wilde Century*, and Cohen, *Talk on the Wilde Side*). Newspaper reports surrounding the trials crystallized what would become the dominant twentieth-century image of the "queer" male figure whose "effeminacy" implied a propensity for same-sex sexual relations. Before 1894, when Wilde was accused by the Marquess of Queensberry, the father of Wilde's lover, Lord Alfred Douglas, of "Posing" as a "Somdomite" [*sic*], the English public had been aware of sodomy-as-anal-sex and had associated the figure of the dandy with both effeminacy and licentiousness. But as Sinfield emphasizes, they had not yet consistently merged the two discourses of sodomy and effeminacy, as they would later, into the image of the dandy as sodomite (*Wilde Century* 27). After the Wilde trials brought the figure of the dandy and the issue of sodomy compellingly together before the public eye, the public increasingly began to read dandyism as implying an inclination for sodomitical acts: the "effeminate" dandy became the public image correlating with the newly formed understanding of the "male homosexual."

As Sinfield and Michel Foucault note, the publicity surrounding the Wilde trials cooperated with sexological studies of the period to construct a public understanding of a new kind of being: no longer, as before, a rakish dandy whose predilections for sodomy formed part of a more general tendency toward "degenerate" behavior, but rather an individual whose "homosexuality" necessarily pervaded his being and formed an essential part of his identity.[42] Thus, although before the Wilde trials, there had been available several models of behavior understood as potentially correlating with a propensity for male-male desire, including Edward Carpenter's male comradeship patterned on the example of Whitman, as a consequence of the trials, the Wildean image of the dandy predominated: the effeminate Aesthete dandy was increasingly assumed to be a male homosexual, and conversely, male homosexuality was assumed to play itself out in the persona of the effeminate Aesthete dandy. That Wilde came to be thought of as epitomizing the figure of the male homosexual was evidenced in the discourse of the time: E. M. Forster suggested this in *Maurice*, written between 1913 and 1914 (completed in July 1914, the same month that *Blast* appeared), whose homosexual male protagonist refers to himself, stammeringly, as "an unspeakable of the Oscar Wilde sort" (145).

Thus by the time of Lewis and the Vorticists, Wilde was an established signifier within the cultural vocabulary, an enormously powerful ghost with whom artists, especially, had to reckon. Appropriately, the Vorticist manifestoes bless Sir Edward Carson (*B1* 28), leader of the Ulster Orangemen, who also served as lawyer for the defense in Wilde's first trial, his libel suit against the Marquess of Queensberry. Like Carson, Vorticism stood in opposition to "Wilde" insofar as Wilde signified a host of cultural practices: Wilde was the criminal, the dandy, the Aesthete, and the sodomite, fusing all these figures and instantiating them in one body, such that in the public mind, each came to imply the others. Wilde's cultural reputation, then, engendered great anxiety among the Vorticists about their relationship to Wilde and all he stood for: the sexual panic about effeminacy that fueled both their geometric forms and the kindred geometric gestures of their art.[43]

In 1919, in his pamphlet *The Caliph's Design (Architects: Where Is Your Vortex?)*, Lewis was still using Wilde to figure the constellation of qualities he considered not only inimical to true artistry but also weak and generally repugnant. (In 1939, Lewis would call this pamphlet "another *Blast*" that "continued the criticism of *Blast No. 1* and *Blast No. 2*" [*WLOA* 129].) In a typical move, here Lewis divided poor artists from true ones on the basis of activity or passivity: "An artist can Interpret," Lewis asserts, "or he can Create" (*WLOA* 175). These two attitudes, Lewis notes, which he deliberately capitalizes for emphasis, correspond "to the roles of the sexes" that result from the "great arbitrary sexual divisions of the race": those who "Create" act more the way men traditionally do in society, and those who merely "Interpret" act as women do (175). Lewis excoriates those who remain passive—like the observer who sits "ecstatic," "gazing at a lily, at a portion of the wall-paper":

> He purrs for some time (he is, Mr Clive Bell will tell you, in a state of sensitive agitation of an indescribable nature) . . . . About everything he sees he will gush, in a timorous lisp . . . . When with anybody, he will titter or blink or faintly giggle when his attention is drawn to . . . a queerly seductive object . . . . I have been portraying to the best of my ability the heir to the aesthete of the Wilde period. (175–176)

In this summation—which gradually accumulates details toward its conclusion—Lewis clearly again uses the "aesthete of the Wilde period" to exemplify the qualities he disdains and rejects. In this caricature, he concatenates three elements—passivity of stance; a figure from Bloomsbury, Clive Bell; and "effeminate" mannerisms such as the lisp, the titter, the giggle and the "gush" (a word which he repeats in this passage for emphasis)—to imply his (pejorative) image of male homosexual practice. He closes the passage above with a smirk and an innuendo, complete with italics to stress his implication: "he is a very good example of how to *receive* rather than *give*" (176). Later in this essay, he makes more explicit the connection he draws between this artistic posture and male-male sexual behavior. Of the swooning "connoisseur," Lewis notes,

> Unsatisfied sex may account for much: you wonder if it is really a picture, after all, and not a woman or something else that is wanted, for the purposes of such a luxurious thrill . . . . These bawdy connoisseurs should really be kept out of the galleries. I can see a fine Renoir, some day, being mutilated: or an Augustus John being raped! (178)

Ostensibly, Lewis accuses these devotees of bringing sex into art where it does not belong (in Lewis's novel *Tarr*, Frederick Tarr has much to say about such vitiation of art), of wanting to "rape" a painting. But he also suggests, and implicitly stigmatizes, their preference for male-male sex. After all, these artists may not want a woman, but instead "something else"; the implication is that they may want to "rape" not Augustus John's painting, but rather John himself.

Throughout this section of *The Caliph's Design*, Lewis reinforces this suggestion by his compulsive repetition of variations of the word "queer," which he often italicizes, as though pressing us to recognize the double entendre (the italics throughout this piece, in fact, nudge readers to recognize what remains unstated but is nonetheless *obvious*).[44] The connoisseur "titters" before "a queerly seductive object." If "you" do tend to swoon in front of delicious paintings, "the odder the thing, the *queerer* that you should find yourself fainting and ecstatic about it" (*WLOA* 177). And Lewis stresses what Roger Fry has said of Walter Sickert's paintings: "Sickert was *already getting hold of stuffed birds and wax flowers just for his own queer game of tones and colours*'"(emphases in the original); Lewis then needs to repeat, on the next page, that Sickert's "game," as Fry terms it, is "queer" (*WLOA* 178–179). Far from working with any evidence that these men actually have a preference for male-male sex, Lewis simply uses this concept as a convenient way of casting opprobrium upon them—and suggests that if their attitude toward art is as it is, they necessarily also evince what he constructs as the deplorable tendency toward male-male sex. Clearly, Lewis wants us to believe that these poseurs he disdains want not a woman, but instead "something else"; and it is the "queer" realm of "something else," linked with these artistic practices, with which Lewis himself is obviously preoccupied.[45] And as both the intensity of this preoccupation and the evidence within *Blast* suggests, the realm of the male "invert" inspires in Lewis both fear and attraction.[46]

Important to note here is that Lewis's homophobic rhetoric against effeminacy was not only responding to the cultural discourse of his time that had coded the man perceived as effeminate as the male "homosexual." It was also guided by contemporary discourse that read such "effeminacy" and its attendant homosexuality as symptoms of a more widespread societal disease: what *fin-de-siècle* social critic Max Nordau termed the "degeneration" of society. According to Nordau, this "degeneration" manifested itself not only in figures like Oscar Wilde—pictured, in Nordau's account, with his sunflower and his "queer costumes" (*Degeneration* 317)—and in the Decadents and Aesthetes of whom Wilde came to be known as chief British representative, but also more generally in the "morbid" art, literature, and philosophy of the period (among others, Nordau targeted Wagner, Tolstoy, Ibsen, Zola, Whitman, Verlaine, and Nietzsche) and in the feverish, "hysterical," and neurasthenic mood of *fin-de-siècle* culture.[47]

As Lisa Tickner suggests, especially threatened during this period by the various forces associated with "degeneration" was the culture's standard of masculinity.[48] This crisis in masculinity, in fact, which Tickner reads as reaching its zenith between 1905 and 1915, provides a crucial context for understanding Vorticism's phobic reactions to effeminacy and its concomitant efforts to imagine a condition uncorrupted by such effeminacy. Events of the late nineteenth and early twentieth centuries—ranging from the rise of suffragism to the eugenicists' rhetoric about the unnatural "masculinization" of modern women and the "effeminization" of modern men—had destabilized conceptions of modern masculinity.[49] In the midst of challenges to traditional gender roles, questions arose about what a modern masculinity should entail, and fears abounded about the possibility of masculinity's degradation or destruction. As Elaine Showalter notes, although commentators have generally presented the *fin de siècle* as a period generating a battle *between* the sexes, it should also be regarded as a period of battles *within* the sexes: and men, especially, faced intense internal crises about what being a man should entail (*Sexual Anarchy* 9). Forces thought to threaten masculinity—associated with conceptual categories such as sodomy, homosexuality, and effeminacy, many of which were at this point linked with Aesthete figures such as Wilde—were usually construed as facets of a common phenomenon.[50]

In response, many artists of the time, particularly because they were associated with professions that tended to be regarded as "feminized," begin to infuse their public poses and rhetoric with an exaggerated "self-conscious virility" (Tickner, "Men's Work?" 9). Such compensatory responses, apparently intended to shore up both individual and more general cultural reserves of masculinity, which were perceived as subject to depletion, served to protect the artists against, and to disavow their vulnerability to, an erosion of masculinity seen as increasingly widespread. Both *Blast*'s geometric gestures and its attacks on Wilde, then, formed part of a defensive, compensatory project of this historical moment.

This leads me to the work of Andrea Freud Loewenstein, who offers detailed psychoanalytic commentary on the paranoiac psychological drives contributing both to Lewis's construction of Vorticism and his frequent attacks on the figure of the male homosexual. As Loewenstein notes, Lewis clearly wanted to develop a picture of the ideal Vorticist who was as impervious to threats of the "feminine" and the "effeminate" as he himself wanted to be—and never felt he safely was (*Loathsome Jews and Engulfing Women* 119–148).[51] Even more than Loewenstein does, however, I would underscore that in the way Lewis played out his structure of paranoia, he was guided by concerns specific to his historical moment. The shape of Lewis's phobias, in other words, reflected contemporary cultural preoccupations: about masculinity under siege from forms of effeminacy; about Oscar Wilde and what he stood for; and about the question, vital for artists of Lewis's milieu, of how to reckon seriously with the legacy of Aestheticism. Lewis's psychological pattern was inflected by and manifested through the salient issues of what Anne Quéma terms his "sociocultural matrix" (*Agon of Modernism* 87).[52]

Contrary to what we might assume, however, Lewis resisted calling the results of this Vorticist project "masculine," and in fact explicitly problematized the Vorticist relationship to masculinity. The following sections, which address in greater detail the nexus between Vorticism and Wildean Aestheticism, will explore the surprising distance Lewis strove to develop between the conventionally "masculine" and the successfully Vorticist.

VORTICISM AND WILDEAN AESTHETICISM

In *Blast 2*, the speaker Lewis constructed for his polemics assailed Oscar Wilde even more directly and extensively than he had in *Blast 1*. In the prose commentary of "The Art of the Great Race," Lewis enlists his adversarial manifestic persona to enact a match with Wilde, resolving to critique the "Aesthetic blarney" about Nature's tendency to "plagiarize" art for which Wilde was a prime spokesman:[53] Lewis's speaker will "take up" Wilde's "old aesthetic quip" that "Life imitates Art" and set about the "light holiday task" of "blasting it indolently away" (*B2* 70). Lewis here deliberately presses on a characteristic Wildean adverb—"indolently"—removing the connotation of desirable dandyish languor Wilde has attached to it and using the term instead to belittle Wilde's claims. Note too that in Lewis's remarks, whose tone meets Wilde's famous airiness with his own, Wilde's Aestheticist position is slighted as "old"—by implication, outdated and in need of supersession—and the effort needed to "blast" Wilde's "quip" characterized as merely "light holiday" work; Wilde's force is suggested to be so trifling as to require little labor.

Moreover, the proximity of the quintessentially Vorticist verb "blast" to the Wildean adverb "indolently" in the resolution indicates that, as Lewis pursues this quarrel with the Aestheticist claim that "Life imitates Art," he will also be engaged in another task: appropriating Wildean "indolence" and transforming it into a specifically Vorticist indolence—supplanting, in other words, the Wildean with the Vorticist. The nearness of Lewis's images to typically Wildean gestures here (the conquest of Wilde's "quip" that Lewis forecasts is imagined as taking place as a dandy would perform it, "indolently," engaging only in "light work") suggests this character of Lewis's endeavor: to both invoke and revise, to invoke *in order to* disparage, permute, and thus replace, Wildean assumptions and style.

Lewis contests Wilde's claim that "Life imitates Art" by countering that, on the contrary, when artists bring to prominence a "type"—of beauty or something else—those individuals who exemplify that type begin to assert themselves more forcefully and to receive notice. "On the promotion of their type to a position of certain consideration in art circles, and gradually in wider spheres of life itself, they all emerge from their holes, and walk proudly for a decade . . . in the public eye" (*B2* 71). Later in the piece, Lewis further damns Wildean *fin-de-siècle* culture by noting with hyperbolic, even phobic, relief, that the "debile [sic] and sinister race of diabolic dandies and erotically bloated diablesses and their attendant abortions, of Yellow Book fame, that tyrannized over the London mind for several years, has withdrawn from the capital" (71). Yet despite the consistently derogatory tone Lewis adopts in *Blast* toward Wilde and all he stands for, similarities between Lewis's and Wilde's aesthetic philosophies abound. Vorticism's campaign against Wilde would not be so phobically virulent if Vorticism did not bear so many affinities, generally underacknowledged, to Wildean Aestheticism. Accordingly, throughout *Blast*, even as its overt statements about Wilde express a desire to expel the Wildean, many of its textual gestures draw upon Wildean Aesthetic doctrine. Admittedly, some of *Blast*'s evocations of the Wildean are strategic, as above, deliberately directed so as to summon the target deemed in need of "blasting." At other moments, however, Vorticist maneuvers themselves proceed from assumptions associated with Wildean Aestheticism.

Many of Lewis's central ideas, in fact, clearly derive from Wildean Aestheticism. The basic terms of Vorticism, for instance—Life, Nature, Mind, Art—are distinctively Wildean, as are Lewis's overt insistence on the radical disjunction between Nature and Art and his demand that the artist reject Nature to devote himself to Art. In his study of Vorticism, Materer recognizes Lewis's "reanimation of the nature versus art debate, which had cooled down since the days of Oscar Wilde" (*Vortex* 108). Materer notes further that a passage in *Blast 1*, in which the "hairdresser" is "blessed" for "attack[ing] Mother Nature," "trim[ming] aimless and retrograde growths/into CLEAN ARCHED SHAPES and/ANGULAR PLOTS" (25) recalls *fin-de-siècle* thought, specifically, Max Beerbohm's claims in "A Defence of Cosmetics" from the first volume of *The Yellow Book*.[54]

The point Materer raises here about the likeness between the Wildean and the Vorticist merits even more elaboration than he devotes to it. Many of Lewis's phrases echo Wilde's almost exactly. Wilde's Vivian from "The Decay of Lying," often read as a mouthpiece for the "doctrines" of Wilde's "new aesthetics," for instance, maintains that "Art is our spirited protest, our gallant attempt to teach Nature her proper place" (Wilde, *Complete Works* 970). Lewis of the Vorticist manifestoes, likewise, exhorts artists to let "Life know its place in a Vorticist universe!" (*B1* 148). Vivian claims that "Nature is so indifferent, so unappreciative" (970), and Lewis of the manifestoes declares, "For those men who look to Nature for support, she does not care" (*B1* 130). Wilde's Vivian laments that "the popular cry of our time is 'Let us return to Life and Nature; they will recreate Art for us'" (977). Lewis of the manifestoes likewise dismisses this "popular cry": "An idea which haunts ... many people is that 'Nature' is synonymous with freshness, richness, constant renewal" (*B1* 129). Both Wilde and Lewis vehemently reject worship of Nature and the commonplaces about Nature's abun-

"Bless the Hairdresser," page from manifestoes of Blast 1

dant resources for creativity and art: Vivian scoffs that Nature is always "behind the age" (977); and Lewis of the manifestoes pronounces Nature a "sterile . . . Tyrant," no more "fresh" and "welling up with invention" than "life is to the average man of forty" with his customary "groove," "disillusion," and "little round of habitual distractions" (129). Vivian's assertion that "nothing is more evident than that Nature hates Mind" (971) — often taken as one of Wilde's principal dicta — echoes Vorticism's similar fundamental opposition between Nature and the human mind.

In a 1925 commentary upon the ideas suggested by the action of his play that appears in *Blast*, *Enemy of the Stars*, Lewis insists even more directly that the "human mind" plays a "traditional role" as "the enemy of life" ("Physics of the Not Self" 195). Here, too, Lewis recalls Wilde's terms: Vivian has called life the "enemy" that "lays waste" the "house" of art (*Complete Works* 977). Finally, much as Wilde subverts the bourgeois habit of validating art on the basis of utility, insisting in the preface to *The Picture of Dorian Gray* that "all art is quite useless" (17), Lewis in *Blast 2* maintains, "[T]he artist is NOT a useful figure . . . In fact the moment he becomes USEFUL . . . he ceases to be an artist" (*B2* 40). The phrasing here — beginning with a condition, then proceeding to the consequence that something does *not* belong to the realm of art — echoes Wilde's from "The Decay of Lying": "As long as a thing is useful or necessary to us, or affects us in any way, either for pain or for pleasure, or appeals strongly to our sympathies, or is a vital part of the environment in which we live, it is outside the proper sphere of Art" (*Complete Works* 976).

If the terms of Lewis's artistic manifestoes are set by Wilde, so too are the terms of his style: his epigrams, for instance, though employing the humor of the bludgeon rather than rapier wit, often recall in structure Wilde's *Phrases and Philosophies for the Use of the Young*. Lewis also consistently resembles Wilde in his endorsement of the use of personae—not only in his work (in this regard, he also recalls Browning, Yeats, and Pound, all known for skillful assumption of literary masks) but also in his own poses as an artist.[55] As biographical accounts attest, Lewis was renowned for his theatrical postures, clearly continuing Wilde's famous celebration of dandiacal artifice, style, and deliberate self-dramatization.[56] According to Materer, early in his career Lewis not only encouraged the Wildean adoption of personae but himself for a time appeared in public as "the Wildean aesthete."[57] And in the *Little Review* in July 1917, fittingly through a persona, Lewis enjoins readers to costume themselves deliberately and variously: "Cherish and develop, side by side, your six most constant indications of different personalities . . . A variety of clothes, hats especially, are of help in this wider dramatisation of yourself. *Never* fall into the vulgarity of being or assuming yourself to be one ego" ("Code of a Herdsman" 4). This declaration is clearly a tongue-in-cheek rendition of and response to (and however parodic, not altogether a refusal of) the Wildean doctrine advanced through the persona of Dorian Gray:

> Is insincerity such a terrible thing? I think not. It is merely a method by which we can multiply our personalities.
>
> Such, at any rate, was Dorian Gray's opinion. He used to wonder at the shallow psychology of those who conceive the Ego in man as a thing simple, permanent, reliable, and of one essence. To him, man was a being with myriad lives and myriad sensations, a complex multiform creature.
>
> (WILDE, *COMPLETE WORKS* 112)

Both Materer and Morrisson have offered incisive commentary on these clear linkages between Wildean and Vorticist thought. Both, however, move quickly from an acknowledgment of the unmistakable indebtedness of Lewis to Wilde to remarks about Vorticism's overt rejection of Wildean Aestheticism—without explaining the relationship between these two phenomena. Materer merely shifts from asserting, for instance, that "the play Lewis published in the 1914 *Blast*, *Enemy of the Stars*, might almost illustrate Wilde's dictum 'Nature hates Mind,'" to stating that "Lewis, however, explicitly rejects Wilde and 'THE BRITANNIC AESTHETE'" (*Vortex* 108). Morrisson, meanwhile, effects the transition by maintaining that "despite these affinities [between Lewis's Vorticist thought and Aestheticist thought], Lewis often positions himself against a vision of a contemporary feminized bloodless aesthete" (*Public Face of Modernism* 124). Morrisson simply lets the ostensible aporia stand; Materer accounts for it by maintaining that, if Lewis was pleased with some aspects of Wilde's thought, he was dismayed with others. For example, he notes that "despite Wilde's attacks on conventional art," of which Lewis approved, Wilde nevertheless failed to "escape the mimetic conception of art that Lewis was attempting to subvert" (*Vortex* 108–109).

I would argue, however, that Lewis's striking combination of fierce denunciation of and indebtedness to Wilde warrants more extensive discussion than a brief statement cast in "despite this, nonetheless this" terms can accommodate. Of course, such insistent gestures of dissociation in view of clear inheritance and continuation point to a Bloomian anxiety of influence. But beyond the desire to disavow a debt to a precursor that clearly both exists and drives the disavowal, what deserves attention also are the specifics of the vexed relationship here between Vorticism and Wildean Aestheticism. Given the historical moment out of which Lewis writes, this desire is shaped and directed by the focus on Wilde and the Aestheticism of the time, as well as the related widespread public discourse of the period about what Judith Butler has called "gender trouble." To explain this more fully, the next section will address the climate in which the Vorticist relationship to Wildean thought was formed.

A "STILL
ACTIVE POWER":
WILDE'S
INFLUENCE ON
THE VORTICISTS

Admittedly, the Aestheticist ideals and behaviors to which Lewis was responding did not belong exclusively to Wilde. During Lewis's formative years as an artist, however, Wilde was one of the best-known models for artists; and as an artist in London at the turn of the century, Lewis was certainly well positioned to receive influence from Wilde and his circle, as were his fellow Vorticists. Lewis arrived in London in 1898, three years after the Wilde trials that Lewis himself acknowledged had "electrified" England ("Skeleton in the Cupboard" 335). The year before, Wilde had been released from prison, and, estranged from former friends, was now living in France in exile under an assumed name. While a student at the Slade School of Art in London in 1898–1901, Lewis befriended William Rothenstein, who remained, albeit uneasily, among Wilde's small number of associates during his final years (Ellmann, *Oscar Wilde* 541) and who knew about Wilde's last days of poverty, frequent inebriation, embarrassing public displays, and maudlin pleas for attention and friendship (515–550).[58] While in Paris in the early years of the twentieth century, Lewis developed a close friendship with someone else who knew about Wilde's final period: Augustus John, the bohemian painter who had access to tales of Wilde through friends such as Robert Ross and Reginald Turner, both of whom were at Wilde's bedside at his death.[59] In his memoirs, John even suggested a further link between Lewis and Wilde: that Lord Alfred Douglas at one point had come to sit for Lewis (*Finishing Touches* 106).

When Wilde died in 1900, his reputation had been deeply compromised by the scandal of his three trials, his conviction for what British law then called "gross indecency with another male person," and his two years of hard labor at Reading Gaol. He was cast in the cultural imagination as the protagonist of a cautionary tale: an epitome of the brilliant, leonine, rebellious artist unhappily felled by pride and the overindulgence of depraved desire.

By 1914, as Lewis and his fellow Vorticists designed their *Blast* campaign, talk of Wilde had taken a new turn. A series of events from 1912 to 1914 attests to the continuing power of the Wilde legend—in fact, to a resurgence of interest in it after the lull of the decade following Wilde's death.[60] In 1913 Holbrook Jackson published *The Eighteen Nineties*, a widely read retrospective account of the 1890s that featured not only Wilde but also many other figures such as Aubrey Beardsley, Max Beerbohm, and George Bernard Shaw. Jackson attempted a sympathetic portrait that would recuperate the period as one not only of "decadence" and "degeneration" but more often, Jackson maintained, of "regeneration" (19). In 1912 Arthur Ransome tried to redeem Wilde by depicting him as "artist and critic rather than as criminal" (*Wilde: A Critical Study* 13). In 1914, the year of *Blast*, Lord Alfred Douglas published his own account of the relationship with Wilde: *Oscar Wilde and Myself* (Jackson, *Eighteen Nineties* 11; this reference is to a 1927 edition of Jackson's book). Thus by the time that *Blast* appeared in July 1914, Wilde had once again been brought before the public eye, acting as a powerful ghost against which artists of the time had to define—and defend—themselves. As Ransome observed in 1912,

> so far were Wilde's name and influence from ending with his personal disaster that they are daily gathering weight. Whether his writings are perfectly successful or not, they altered in some degree the course of literature in his time, and are still an active power when the wind has long blown away the dust of newspaper criticism with which they were received . . . . [Wilde's] indirect influence is incalculable, for his attitude in writing gave literature new standards of valuation, and men are writing under their influence who would indignantly deny that their work was in any way dictated by Wilde.
>
> (*WILDE: A CRITICAL STUDY* 20–21)

Although Lewis and the Vorticists would indeed "indignantly deny" that their work was in any way "dictated by Wilde," they were clearly among those profoundly influenced by what Ransome termed Wilde's "still . . . active power" and his "new standards of valuation."

The Vorticists were working in a climate, then, pervaded by vivid memories of the scandal of Wilde's trial, which kept alive the stigma associated with him and his associates, its force attested to by efforts such as Ransome's to defend Wilde's reputation. If the Vorticists were to acknowledge any link to Wildean principles and practices, in their view, they had to do so with caution. The character of the Vorticists' uneasy alliance with Wilde is captured in a response Lewis made in 1914 to painter Walter Sickert's assessment of his art. The "us" Lewis uses here seems to be that of the royal "we," but the pronoun also suggests his Vorticist allies.

> Arrived in our neighbourhood, he [Sickert] gathers a little crowd, mixes us a little with it, and would then Koepenick [i.e., guide

Monument by Jacob Epstein, Tomb of Oscar Wilde, Père Lachaise Cemetery, Paris (photograph by Maggie Kilgour)

> like a Prussian officer] us all, shepherd-like, towards that prison where Oscar Wilde lay for two years, struck down by the bourgeoisie. We have been amused at his antics; but at this point we withdraw.
>
> (*LETTERS OF WYNDHAM LEWIS* 58)

Lewis is defending his art against Sickert's charges that it is excessively preoccupied with sexual organs—by subtly implying that with his accusation, Sickert seeks to align him with Oscar Wilde, but Lewis will have none of it. It is Sickert, Lewis suggests, not he, who bears the taint of "the Yellow Plague-spot" of *The Yellow Book* and *fin-de-siècle* bohemian life, with its attendant profligacy (58). But the way Lewis portrays himself here, I would offer, suggests the character of Vorticism's conflicted relationship to Aestheticism: as his description implies, Vorticism drew near Wildean Aestheticism, engaged briefly with it, and then "withdrew," fastidiously accepting only certain carefully chosen elements of it and rejecting others.

In 1912, more than a decade after Wilde's death and three years after Wilde's remains had been moved from Bagneux to Père Lachaise in Paris,[61] it was fitting that Wilde's grave should be commemorated by a large funerary sculpture carved by Jacob Epstein, an artist associated with Vorticism whose work had appeared in *Blast 1*.[62] Because Epstein's monument was initially considered indecent, provoking many months of controversy in Paris, it was not fully uncovered until 1914, the year of *Blast*'s publication. Epstein's tomb emblematizes, with a literalism almost humorous, the Vorticist relationship to Wildean Aestheticism: the ways in which the Vorticist project "translated" the body of Wilde—in some ways rejecting and reentombing it, in other ways paying tribute to it and even resurrecting it.

The controversy surrounding the tomb, in fact, points to the dangers the Vorticists feared from association with Wilde. In his memoir, Epstein remains tantalizingly elliptical about why officials in Paris insisted that a tarpaulin be thrown over his winged sphinx. He hints, however, at what might have been so objectionable by saying that Wilde's friend and literary executor Robert Ross affixed a plaque to the monument as a kind of "fig leaf" (*Let There Be Sculpture* 46). Presumably, then, what had offended spectators was Epstein's representation of male genitalia. Ross corroborates this theory, noting in a letter that the decision of the French authorities regarding the statue may lie "in the lap of the gods," which "is precisely the part of the statue to which exception is taken" (48). The display of male genitalia, of course, without a "fig leaf" might in itself have been considered shocking, but no doubt what made it even more disconcerting here was that the genitalia were associated with Wilde: genitalia that, in the aftermath of the trials, were seen as depraved and diseased, as a catalyst for scandal, and thus as a disturbing metonym for the act of sodomy. Moreover, given the association of Wilde's activities with the semiotic realm of "effeminacy," and the belief that effeminacy threatened masculinity, there was also likely an underlying belief that Wilde's genitalia were not rightfully male at all—that their apparent maleness told a perverse lie.

The geometric gestures of Vorticism, then, formed a major part of an effort to counteract the threat of emasculation-by-effeminacy that the specter of Wilde, as understood by Lewis and his compatriots, brought dangerously close. I will turn now to how this effort played out within the pages of *Blast*.

AGGRESSIVE
SEMIOTIC
GESTURES

To purge Vorticism of Wildean effeminacy, the geometric gestures of *Blast*, through a series of strategic framings, came to be coded as suggesting precision and dynamism, even aggression. The rhetoric of the Vorticists, together with their visual art, were thus directed to forge a semiotic link between geometry and three semantic regions used to counter the domain of effeminacy: accuracy, hardness, and forceful action.

Within *Blast*, "geometrics" elicit assessments such as that of Jeffrey Meyers—who, in capturing the style of Vorticist art, uses adjectives such as "hard, angular, geometric" and "dynamic" (*The Enemy* 63), such that the "geometric" is associated with the "hard" and "dynamic." The geometric shapes, with their clean lines, imply precision; their angularity implies hardness; and it is the diagonals of Vorticism's images that often make these geometrics read further as "violent and explosive."[63] As Dasenbrock remarks, the fierce dynamism of Vorticist shapes issues from the "sense of motion produced by diagonal lines" (*Literary Vorticism* 41). The Vorticists worked according to the assumption voiced by Futurist architect Antonio Sant'Elia: that "oblique and elliptic lines are dynamic, and by their very nature possess an emotive power a thousand times stronger than perpendiculars and horizontals" (Apollonio, *Futurist Manifestos* 171). As Pound remarks of the drawings from Lewis's *Timon of Athens* series (one of which is included in *Blast 1*), which involve such careening diagonals, they sug-

Wyndham Lewis, Timon of Athens, from Blast 1 (McGill University Library)

gest "fury"—specifically, the "fury of intelligence baffled and shut in by circumjacent stupidity" (G-B 93).

In *Blast 1*, Lewis's *Plan of War*, *Timon of Athens* and *Slow Attack*, positioned on successive pages, hurtle across their spaces with an explosion of diagonal lines. Two pages later, *Portrait of an Englishwoman* presents a tilting array of precariously balanced beam-like rectangles seemingly on the verge of collapse. The cover of *Blast 2* displays a similar welter of long lines crashing in all directions: from the scattering of triangles and diagonals emerge two figures that suggest soldiers loading rifles. The work of other Vorticist painters within *Blast* closely resembles Lewis's, offering yet more aggressive geometry: in *Blast 2*, Jessica Dismorr's *Engine* and *Design* (27, 29) feature rigid, tilting, jagged shapes; William Roberts's *Combat* displays another tower of thin diagonals ready to fall (55); Helen Saunders's *Atlantic City* resembles a pane of glass shattering into shards (57); and even Dorothy Shakespear's small drawing displays a collection of fierce tiny spikes (47). The angles, lines, and spears of the Vorticist paintings, together with titles such as *Plan of War* (as well as by the proximity of actual war in Europe at that moment) suggest battle, soldiers, discipline, hardness, and aggressive motion. Even when more static, the lines of the paintings within *Blast* imply taut attitudes of poise and discipline that implicitly oppose Wildean "indolence" and the characteristically languorous posture of the Wildean Aesthete.

Lewis further suggests this association he wants to create specifically between geometry and aggression, and his celebration of both of these, in an essay about the Futurists. Once again deploring the sentimental "AUTOMOBILISM" (*B1* 8) of Futurism, he distinguishes the painter Giacomo Balla from the rest of the Futurists ("Balla is not a 'Futurist' in the Automobilist sense") and encourages Marinetti and the others to learn from his example: "Cannot Marinetti . . . be induced to throw over this sentimental rubbish about Automobiles and Aeroplanes, and follow his friend Balla into a purer region of art?" (*B1* 144) Balla's "purer region of art" Lewis characterizes admiringly as "violent and geometric" (144). The proximity of the two words—"violent" and "geometric"—both reflects and contributes to the semiotic linkage binding these two qualities throughout *Blast*.

Although the geometric figures of *Blast*, thus coded, bear most of the burden of conveying Vorticism's aggression, other related textual signals—other "geometric gestures"—perform similar work. The magazine's bold typography, reminiscent of the enormous black letters across the cover of *Blast 1*, recalls geometric figures with its sans serif forms. The rhetoric of the manifestoes, coursing with belligerent statements, similarly communicates aggression: "CURSE/WITH EXPLETIVE OF WHIRLWIND/THE BRITANNIC AESTHETE/CREAM OF THE SNOBBISH EARTH/ROSE OF SHARON OF GOD-PRIG/OF SIMIAN VANITY" (*B1* 15). Chiming in also with the journal's mood are the turbulent events of Rebecca West's story "Indissoluble Matrimony" and the equally violent occurrences of Lewis's play, *Enemy of the Stars*.[64] Within the force field of *Blast*'s manifestoes, then, the climate of aggression and severity created by all of these elements is enlisted in the service of the project of combating effeminacy.

LEWIS'S AMBIVALENT RELATIONSHIP TO THE MASCULINE

In their belligerent letter to the Omega Workshops, the Vorticists initially characterized themselves as capable of "rough and masculine work" that members of Bloomsbury could not achieve. It has been commonplace to tag the Vorticists as exhibiting a "he-man approach"; Cork, for example, speaks of "Lewis and his self-styled exemplars of virility" (*Vorticism and Its Allies* 11, 8). For all their aggression and severity, however, the geometrics of Vorticism are only problematically deemed masculine. Fredric Jameson notes that although during this period, Lewis's "sexual ideology," as displayed in the thematics of his early novel *Tarr*, is "openly misogynist"—and accordingly, vigorously antieffeminate—it is not, as one might accordingly expect, therefore "phallocentric." For all the condemnation of the female principle in Lewis's work, Jameson maintains, "there is no correlative celebration of the male principle" (*Fables of Aggression* 97). And indeed, much as Lewis satirizes all things linked to the "female principle," he castigates with equal venom characteristics linked to the overtly manly man, from the "crude manhood" of Hanp in *Enemy of the Stars* to the violent aggression of Kreisler in *Tarr* to, years later, the "natural man" antics of Jack in *The Revenge for Love* (1937).[65] Lewis further suggests his rejection of phallocentrism when in 1914 he responds to Walter Sickert, who reads Lewis's painting "Creation" as unduly concerned with "sexual organs":

> Mr. Sickert's description of my painting "Creation" [is] a deliberate misstatement and invention. I have always found pornography extremely boring and regarded it as the hallmark of the second-rate. As for Phallic aesthetics, I have no quarrel with them, only I don't happen to participate myself, that is all: though much preferring the naked and clean thing to the boudoir suggestiveness and Yellow Book Gallicisms.
>
> (*LETTERS OF WYNDHAM LEWIS* 59)

The pattern of response here conforms to Jameson's characterization: on the one hand, Lewis rejects "boudoir suggestiveness and Yellow Book Gallicisms" (again, which he believes, Sickert himself represents) and, by association, the scandal of *The Yellow Book*, Aestheticism, the *fin de siècle*, Beardsley, sexual licentiousness (often coded as French), effeminacy, sodomy, sexual disease, Wilde, and homosexuality. Yet lest we think that he therefore privileges masculinity, Lewis also disavows a "celebration of the male principle" with an overt denial of his "participation" in "Phallic aesthetics."

Interesting, however, is that in the article to which Lewis responds, Sickert never actually uses the word "Phallic": he says only that in this artistic climate of abstraction, "non-representation is forgotten when it comes to the sexual organs" (Sickert, "On Swiftness" 655). He also invokes the term "pudenda" and ascribes to Lewis, along with Gaudier-Brzeska and Epstein, the "Pornometric gospel" (655). But it is in fact Lewis who introduces the term "Phallic," suggesting that such "Phallic aesthetics" may be more dominant in his imagination than he will admit. To "boudoir suggestiveness," Lewis prefers the "naked and clean thing," an ambiguous phrase, ironically itself quite coy, that suggests "clean" heterosexual sex (as opposed to the "queer" sex Lewis would consider smutty), or perhaps even a "clean" rather than diseased penis. However, by joining his preference for the "naked and clean thing" to the notion of "Phallic aesthetics" with the conjunction "though," Lewis implies that although he may not directly "participate" in such "aesthetics," he nonetheless feels some sympathy for them.

Despite his implied hospitality to "Phallic aesthetics," however, Lewis refuses complete allegiance to them. And this is because, in his Vorticist vision, in order to resist effeminacy, he must purge his stance even of any qualities conventionally associated with the "masculine" that might contribute to "effeminate" weakness. To do proper battle with effeminacy, that is, he must avoid even the foibles of conventional masculinity, which for him involve weakness: what he will call in *Enemy of the Stars* the "ragged spirt [sic] of crude manhood, masculine with blunt wilfulness [sic] and hideous stupidity of the fecund horde of men" (*B1* 65). Reminiscing about Vorticism years later, Lewis would note that the outlook of Vorticism was

> not entirely a "tough guy" attitude.... There were no schoolboy heroics, of the emotional Hemingway order about it. It was just the sternness and severity of mind that is appropriate to the man who does the

> stuff (in contrast to the amateur who stands rapt in front of it once it is done and stuck up to be looked at); especially when that stuff is a harsh, reverberative, and indeed rather terrible material .... [The attitude] was, yes, *professional*. (Lewis's italics)
>
> (WLOA 342)

"Professional" Vorticism here, with its "sternness and severity of mind," recalls the "bareness and hardness" that the rhetoric of *Blast* pits against what it characterizes as "gush" (B1 41); the "durable" and "imposing," "tense and angular" forces that *Blast* invokes to challenge that which is "supple, soft and vital" (B2 43).

Despite Lewis's disclaimers, however, these qualities would likely have been read by audiences of the time as manly. Given, that is, Lewis's outright rejection of "femininity" and "effeminacy"; given his readers' interpretive habits, especially their binary tendency to consider anything not feminine necessarily masculine; and given Lewis's own endorsement of the use of dichotomies—especially his explicit recognition of the power of the "Male-and-Female" duality (B2 91)—the characteristics Lewis advances within Vorticism to reject that which is weak and effeminate would probably have been interpreted as masculine. Indeed Gaudier-Brzeska, reviewing the work of the Rebel Art Centre in 1914, celebrated Vorticism's "manliness" (G-B 34).[66]

Lewis himself, however, to whatever degree we trust his disavowals of "Phallic aesthetics," claimed to be carving out for Vorticism a place of "severity" that was neither overtly "Phallic" nor feminine, neither "tough guy" nor "gushy" in attitude. Lewis evidently did not believe that men, even conventionally masculine men, necessarily possessed the qualities he sought for the Vorticist. If one successfully achieved "sternness and severity of mind," one was most likely male; but to be male, even in some way masculine, was not necessarily to evince the requisite severity. To celebrate and attain conventional manliness was not perforce to reach Lewis's ideal—which might be thought of as masculinity in, as Alan Sinfield notes, the "terms ... set by Aristotle," who opposed "continence" and "incontinence," "endurance" and "softness" (*Wilde Century* 26). To evacuate Vorticism of weakness, Lewis had to reject even those aspects of conventional masculinity of his time that he considered dangerously "emotional" and, hence, effeminate.

Arguably, then, Lewis was elevating some characteristics traditionally associated with masculinity: mastery, continence, and self-command. But he was wary enough of nineteenth-century and early twentieth-century versions of masculinity—and their possible contamination by effeminacy—that, to preserve his realm of pure severity and professionalism, he wanted to keep even the category of ordinary masculinity at bay.[67] He wished to ensure that, if the universe of *Blast* celebrated "violent" geometrics, the violence was "harsh" and "terrible"—not just the attempted "heroics" of Hemingwayesque "emotional" "tough guys."

VORTICISM'S COVERT ATTRACTION TO THE EROTICIZED MALE DYAD

Vorticism's forcible rewriting of Wilde, designed to evacuate any lingering association with effeminacy, makes it at once Aestheticism's inheritor, betrayer, and transformer; it both emulates it and strains to "correct" and purify it. To use Kristeva's terminology, the relationship between Lewis and Wilde, and accordingly between Vorticism and Aestheticism, is one of abjection: the expulsion of something that one is—that comes out of oneself—but with which one wants to disavow all connection. Within the psychic maneuver of abjection, Kristeva maintains, "there looms ... one of those violent, dark revolts of being, directed against a threat that seems to emanate from an exorbitant outside or inside"—that *seems* to emanate from outside, that is, but in fact emerges from within (*Powers of Horror* 1). The abject "lies there" (in this case, Wilde lies there) "quite close, but it cannot be assimilated.... Unflaggingly, like an inescapable boomerang, a vortex of summons and repulsion places the one haunted by it" (in this case, Lewis) "literally beside himself" (1). One of the major forces conditioning Vorticism's "vortex," I would maintain, is this alternation of "summons and repulsion," of attraction and anxiety, with respect to Wilde and all, by the *avant-guerre* years, he has come to represent. "[F]rom its place of banishment, the abject does not cease challenging its master," Kristeva notes (2): Wilde and what he stands for will constantly "challenge" and threaten the stable identity of Lewis and the Vorticists, as they direct toward Wildean Aestheticism the admixture of disgust and desire that not only shapes the direction of their project, but in fact, I would argue, initially engenders it. Vorticism is founded upon, formed out of, an abjection of Wildean Aestheticism.

Again, the way in which, despite his uneasiness, Lewis is drawn to Wilde stems in part from the inescapability of Wilde's example in Lewis's formative artistic environment and, furthermore, from the nearness of Wilde's Aesthetic doctrines to his own. But I would argue further that Lewis is also pulled into the Wildean orbit by his attraction to the eroticized male-male relations associated with Wilde, those that he takes such pains to condemn. In *The Caliph's Design* Lewis may denounce those artists who want to "rape" an Augustus John, but elsewhere his texts inscribe desires for interactions between men that are both eroticized and violent.

Officially, of course, Lewis's Vorticism rejects not only effeminacy but also, specifically, sodomy and the male homoerotic practices with which, at this historical moment, the category of sodomy is associated. In "Code of a Herdsman," Lewis's persona announces that "sodomy should be avoided, as far as possible. It tends to add to the abominable confusion already existing" (6). Although "sodomy" does not, strictly speaking, refer exclusively to male-male sexual intercourse, during the period following the Wilde trials (which were sparked by Queensberry's accusation that Wilde had "posed" as a sodomite), it did suggest this. Thus, according to the opponents of "degeneration," any gesture read as such a Wildean "pose" merited denunciation by virtue of its association with male-male anal intercourse.

It is no accident that Lewis's "Herdsman" places this comment about sodomy immediately after another directive: "As to women: wherever you can, substitute the society of men. Treat them kindly, for they suffer from the herd" (6). The two commands join, then, under the sign of the battle against the "feminine": in this view, one can elude the feminine by avoiding the company of women and by abstaining from sodomy, which is linked with the feminine insofar as it is considered indicative of and conducive to weakness and insofar as men with a propensity for sodomy, it is assumed, resemble women.

The connection between the two injunctions, however, goes beyond this. Women and sodomy are also linked because it is precisely the Herdsman's—and Lewis's and Vorticism's—recommendation of eschewing the society of women that necessitates the injunction against sodomy. Shunning women, in other words, brings its dangers: one must try to keep company exclusively with men, but only in certain permitted ways; one must guard against the temptation of sodomy and its assumed probable entailments. The continuation of the desired Vorticist male homosocial sphere, then, depends on keeping at a remove the threat of outright male homosexuality.[68]

On the one hand, it is the very intensity of Lewis's defensive gestures against effeminacy that suggests a suppressed, latent desire for the very male-male erotic bonds he so insistently disparages in Vorticist rhetoric. Also attesting to this hidden desire, however, are the many figural displays, even endorsements, of erotic bonds between men in Lewis's Vorticist work. Certainly, as Jameson has noted, Lewis's texts display "an obsessive phobia against homosexuals" (*Fables of Aggression* 4) — and Lewis most often focuses on male homosexuals — but, significantly, his protests are accompanied by frequent seductive textual dramatizations of intimate male dyads.

To address these further, and to deepen the understanding more generally of Vorticism's complex and formative "vortex" of "summons and repulsion" with respect to elements Lewis associates with Wildean Aestheticism, I turn to another piece in *Blast*: Lewis's play *Enemy of the Stars*. This text will clarify what I have outlined thus far and elucidate a few further points about Lewis's deeply anxious, ongoing engagement with Wildean Aestheticism. As I have noted, the complex of Vorticist attitudes in response to Aestheticism involves, on the one hand, Lewis's clear agreement with some of the doctrines of Aestheticism and, on the other, his underlying attraction for the male-male homoeroticism and passivity with which Aestheticism, at this historical juncture, has come to be associated.

Lewis's simultaneous effort to stave off Aestheticism, meanwhile, also arises from two impulses. First, it stems from a deep-seated fear of the "unmanning" that Aestheticism might entail. But as I will explain, Lewis's ambivalent desire to keep Aestheticism at bay arguably also arises from a quarrel with the Aestheticist attitude toward Nature, an attitude that Vorticism at times even appears to endorse — a quarrel that is bound up in the dormant desire for passivity that his Vorticism expresses.

Enemy of the Stars, in fact, provides a much more accurate portrait of Vorticism's defining postures than do the pronouncements of the manifestoes of *Blast*. This still comparatively little-read text of Lewis's repays attention because it registers so powerfully the conflicted relationships that serve as coordinates for the positioning of Vorticism: Lewis's relationships to Aestheticist thought, to the realm of effeminacy, and to the prospect of eroticized intimacy between men. Intended by Lewis as an explication of Vorticist doctrine, placed in the midst of Vorticist manifestoes, and thus inviting the reader to interpret it as related to their pronouncements, *Enemy of the Stars* exhibits seldom-noticed aspects of Vorticist thought that both draw it near to the "effeminacy" that Vorticism ostensibly rejects and, at the same time, unexpectedly separate its attitude toward Nature from that of Wildean Aestheticism.

Furthermore, these two unexpected efforts of Lewis's Vorticism, with respect to Nature and effeminacy, are allied: Lewis expresses the desired Vorticist relationship to Nature by way of postures explicitly coded as "feminized," postures that are accompanied by strikingly brutal, eroticized encounters between men. This attests to the way that Vorticism's underlying attitude with regard to Nature is not only expressed, but also fueled, by passive, masochistic, male-homoerotic desire—which constitutes a significant strain of latent desire within Vorticism.

ENEMY OF THE STARS: FAILURE?

In 1914, Richard Aldington called *Enemy of the Stars*—"play or story or poem or whatever it is"—the most "portentous" and "surprising piece of work" in all of *Blast*: "It stirs one up," he wrote, "like a red-hot poker" (Aldington, "Blast" 272). Lewis was probably quite pleased by such a response (although he might have winced at its phallic connotations): after all, in the manifestoes, he had advertised Vorticism's "red-hot swiftness" (B1 149).

In *Rude Assignment*, Lewis claimed that he had intended the play to epitomize Vorticist principles, to supply a literary equivalent of the abstractions of his Vorticist paintings. "My literary contemporaries," he wrote, "I looked upon as too bookish and not keeping pace with the visual [Vorticist] revolution. A kind of play, 'The Enemy of the Stars' . . . was my attempt to show them the way" (129).[69] Although it has received much less serious critical notice than much of Lewis's other work,[70] the play merits attention as a successful showpiece of Vorticism, a parable that effectively exhibits the principles announced in *Blast* and that does so as much through its plot, characters, and themes as by way of its remarkable linguistic strategies.

The difficulty of its writing, however, along with the problematic nature of its genre, has prompted even Dasenbrock, one of a handful of critics who recognize the play's importance, to declare it "almost unreadable" (*Literary Vorticism* 127). Readers generally feel confusion akin to the kind Aldington expressed even as he paid tribute to *Enemy*: "Of course, I don't 'understand' it, in the sense that I cannot tell you exactly what the characters looked like, what they dressed in, or quite what they did" ("Blast" 272). Consequently, most commentators have turned away from the play's plot, character, and themes to focus instead on the historical milieu of the Vorticist movement in which the text participates.[71] As Scott Klein notes, if critics do address *Enemy*'s textual details, they usually comment only on the play's stylistic "audacity" and explosive textual surface, veering away from sustained critical exploration.[72] Most, as Toby Foshay points out, neglect the work's thematic significance.[73] And ultimately, most critics accept at face value Lewis's own appraisal of the play as a failed exercise in Vorticist prose.[74]

This latter-day commentary notwithstanding, the play clearly occupied a central place in Lewis's own thinking about his *oeuvre*. A copy of *Blast* at Cornell University displays a wealth of Lewis's marginalia on the play, attesting to the attention he devoted to it. Although these scribblings are undated, an apparently contemporaneous reference to "Fascism" elsewhere in this copy suggests that they were made in the late 1920s or early 1930s when Lewis was revising the play toward a new version published in 1932. At that juncture, he expanded *Enemy* and rendered more comprehensible what he considered its principal ideas. In fact, the play continued to be so important to Lewis that, as a few undated sheets in the Cornell archive suggest, at one point, probably in the early 1930s, he even attempted to transcribe it for the screen.[75]

The play's linguistic strategies, however, unquestionably challenge readers.[76] A note to the 1932 *Enemy of the Stars* indicates that even in 1914 Lewis had arrived at the *Blast* version of the play only after much consideration and selection: "This version of *Enemy of the Stars* differs in detail from that to be found in *Blast No. 1*. There were several versions—the author has restored passages removed from, or not used in, the *Blast* version" (*Enemy of the Stars* 1932, 61). Given the didacticism and comparative clarity of the 1932 version, Lewis thus quite probably initially conceived of the play as a much more straightforward explication of the ideas and values of Vorticism than the text that ultimately appeared in *Blast 1*. The relative lucidity of the 1932 version, if we read it along with the 1914 version, highlights the unconventionality of the *Blast* version: what Aldington termed its "telegraphic" syntax; its cryptic, often verbless, isolated phrases; and its grotesque images, presented in a turbulent whirl. Creating the play's distinctive mysteriousness is the obscurity of connections among elements within phrases, among phrases, and among images and events. Elements are paratactically juxtaposed and concatenated, but we are rarely sure by what principle.

Moreover, *Enemy*'s generic signals are undoubtedly mixed: the *Blast* version occupies with conspicuous unease its place as what the title page announces as "THE PLAY" (57), its large capital letters seeming to enact a defensive assertion against anticipated skepticism about its legitimacy as a dramatic text—or perhaps designed to compensate for, and thereby point up, the ambiguity of its generic identity.[77] Many of its techniques seem so clearly most appropriate for the silent reader that it has been called a "closet drama" and compared with such similarly "unperformable" plays as Byron's *Manfred*.[78] That the preponderance of narration in the text is never assigned to a distinct character; that the play is presented in the form of a story rather than a script; and that many of its phrases remain largely unintelligible—all certainly mean that it would have to be significantly modified for performance on the stage. It reads like a play straining to become something else, inviting a category shift to realize itself more effectively—an invitation to which Lewis himself was perhaps responding when he attempted to translate it for the screen.

Yet beyond the play's unexpected linguistic maneuvers and its generic indeterminacy—both unquestionably central to its effect—I (like Foshay) would offer that we also need to attend to "what the characters looked like, what they dressed in," and, most important, "what they did." We need to focus on the play's characters, plot, and themes not only because these have hitherto been so comparatively little considered in the critical literature, but also because they can illuminate Lewis's Vorticist relationship to Nature and its concomitant attitude toward male-male intimacy. I contest the widespread consensus that the play is a "failure" and that it charts a failure, reading it instead as a piece that reveals, through its action and themes as well as through the difficulty of its language, currents of desire fundamental to Lewis's Vorticism that would otherwise remain unseen.

ENEMY OF THE STARS AND THE "EFFEMINIZED" VORTICIST

For this analysis, I use the 1914 *Enemy of the Stars* published in *Blast*. Critics such as Flory and Beatty have interpreted the 1932 text as simply an elucidation of the 1914 version, accepting at face value Lewis's claim that, a few details notwithstanding, the two are "substantially the same" (*Enemy of the Stars* 1932, 61). Accordingly, when puzzled by obscurities in the first version, these critics often use the more lucid and conventional 1932 text to gloss it. Foshay notes, for instance, that given Flory's assessment that Lewis's "changes" in the 1932 "do not correct the earlier version so much as amplify it," he will use the 1932 version for his analysis (*Politics of Intellect* 22–23; Foshay quotes from Flory, "Enemy of the Stars" 92). In this study, although I do occasionally draw on quotations from the 1932 version, I chiefly build my argument upon the 1914 version—because it is this text that appeared alongside the manifestoes in the Vorticist milieu. Since this is the version that emerged from the *avant-guerre* moment, it is most suitable for studying the drives fuelling Lewis's Vorticist strategies at their inception. I also prefer the 1914 text because it succeeds in the terms in which the 1932 text fails. In rendering the language of the 1914 version less elliptical, smoother, and more accessible, Lewis removed from the 1932 text the perversity and obscurity indispensable to its Vorticist project.

As *Enemy of the Stars* opens, the figure of Arghol, dubbed in the introductory material as the "condemned protagonist" of the play (*B1* 61), emerges, only immediately to be "neglected" by "two fellow actors." One of them, a mysterious "supernumerary" character, suitably silent, rushes in and then vanishes for the rest of the play, leaving his function inscrutable. Lewis thus introduces a red herring that, with its willful violation of the principles of dramatic unity, sets the tone for the play. This text will mischievously ignore our requests for conventional sense and an Aristotelian indispensability of all parts: we will be left guessing which textual elements are superfluous and which necessary.

The other character, Hanp, Arghol's comrade and disciple, is welded to him like a Beckettian companion. Their universe swells and contracts with fierce energy, alternately pictured in bloody red and electric white. Arghol, perversely aloof from life, withstands violent blows from his surroundings with a martyr's intoxication, fully aware of his plight—as it is presented to us—as a scapegoat of "Humanity" (61). Even when Hanp tries to dissuade Arghol from what we understand to be his usual victim's posture, Arghol continues to offer himself up to the pain, suggesting that he enjoys it as part of his destiny. P. K. Page's lines come to mind here: his "suffering" becomes his "[b]est friend, bestower of feeling / status-giver."[79]

But whereas Arghol seems passively to surrender to this fate, he is active about something else: he spends a good bit of the text attempting to purge from himself the revolting everyday "Self" that he so despises: "I have smashed it against me," he says of the "Self," "but it still writhes, turbulent mess" (*B1* 71). Cleansing himself of this "Self" involves denying his name to former friends, casting off his possessions in a fury of attempted "hygiene," and castigating Hanp, his "mate" and disciple—as much a man of the body as Arghol is a man of the mind—whose interaction with Arghol, Arghol believes, brings this undesirable "Self" into being.

Ultimately, Arghol and Hanp whirl into a frenzy of violence, their combat seemingly part of Arghol's effort at "hygiene." In the aftermath of the battle, when Arghol realizes that his efforts at exorcism have failed, he falls into a deep sleep. Now apparently revolted by his master, Hanp seizes the opportunity to stab and murder him, inadvertently releasing Arghol from self-loathing. Spent and despairing, now seemingly bereft of something essential, Hanp ends the play by leaping from a bridge to kill himself.

Again, in critical treatments of the play, the narrative is seldom summarized in this way because readers find its trajectory so difficult to follow. Beyond the obscurity of the play's linkages, causal or otherwise, among textual elements, presenting further obstacles to interpretation is the way in which its opening pages are interrupted by a series of Lewis's abstract paintings—*Plan of War, Timon of Athens, Slow Attack, Portrait of an Englishwoman,* and *The Enemy of the Stars*— along with a photo of one of Lewis's decorations done for the house of the Countess of Drogheda. The placement of these visuals suggests that they are, if not illustrations, at least companion pieces to the verbal text, visual correlatives of its linguistic gestures, and necessary as part of the set-up for the play.

As we begin the play, we are alerted that we are in "SOME BLEAK CIRCUS" (*B1* 55), a world very much in accord with the atmosphere of Vorticism evoked by the manifestoes of *Blast*, which is both supremely artificial and intensely severe. Removed from a specific time and place, we are thus invited to read the action of the text as a parable. A brief paragraph before the "action opens," which by virtue of its position functions as a dumbshow, tells us that our "condemned protagonist" is a "gladiator who has come to fight a ghost, Humanity" and that he will ultimately be executed and sacrificed to the "UNIVERSE" (*B1* 61). The questions the text prompts us to pose, then, are why Arghol is condemned; whether the way he ultimately dies, as predicted, constitutes a victory or defeat; and finally, what argument this suggests about Vorticist aesthetics and the mission of the Vorticist artist.

Arghol is often considered an exemplar of "Lewis's Vorticist Übermensch" (Beatty, "Experimental Play" 44)—the superlatively egotistical Vorticist artist, aloof, self-sustaining, a committed adversary to what *Blast*'s manifestoes have constructed as "Nature." But a close examination of Arghol, I would argue, troubles this characterization—and yields insight into the little-noticed stances of Vorticism with respect to effeminacy and Nature toward which I have gestured. Arghol does seem to be at odds with Nature, in that, as displayed by the assaults he withstands from the universe, his qualities and actions provoke Nature. Remarkable about Arghol's attitude, however, is that he seems to relish Nature's abuse. When we first encounter him, he lies on the ground, battered by Nature's violence:

> His eyes woke first, shaken by rough moonbeams. A white, crude volume of brutal light blazed over him. . . .
>
> The ice field of the sky swept and crashed silently. Blowing wild organism into the hard splendid clouds, some will cast it's [*sic*] glare, as well, over him. . . .

> The stars shone madly in the archaic blank wilderness of the universe, machines of prey.
>
> Mastodons, placid in electric atmosphere, white rivers of power....
>
> Throats iron eternities, drinking heavy radiance, limbs towers of blatant light, the stars poised, immensely distant, with their metal sides, pantheistic machines.
>
> (B1 64)

The world of the stars—signaled subsequently in the play by the qualities suggested here, such as immensity, distance, archaic blankness, electricity, roughness, brutality—is presented as powerful and "splendid." In comparison to the magnificent stars ("over him" in that they are both above him and superior to him), Arghol pales: his blood runs "weakly" (64).

It is appropriate that Lewis intersperses geometric images among the pages of the play—for here he creates an atmosphere akin to that which he has conjured elsewhere in *Blast* by way of geometric gestures. The placement of the paintings before the action begins is not our only signal that geometry should be connected with *Enemy*'s domain of the stars. Given the semiotic realm of austere precision and ferocity Lewis has coded geometric shapes as indicating, the electric dimension of this universe in *Enemy*, connoting similar qualities, serves as a clear atmospheric analogue to these earlier "geometrics." The manifestoes of *Blast* have celebrated "bareness and hardness" (B1 41), "force and action" (B2 44). Images used to capture the desirable Vorticist climate in *Blast* have included "snow," "ice," "BLIZZARDS" (B1 12), and "the steppes and rigours of the Russian winter" (B1 33). The realm of the stars in *Enemy of the Stars*, meanwhile, is described in similarly icy terms: we hear of the "ice field of the sky" (B1 64), with a "white, crude volume of brutal light" or "blatant light" (B1 64); and Hanp is associated with an "icy steppe" (B1 65). Further, the manifestoes have celebrated "snow," "ice," and "blizzards" according to the same value system that prizes "violent and geometric" shapes (B1 144). We are thus led to associate ice and geometry; and because we have been invited to link stars and ice in *Enemy of the Stars*, by a transitive property of interpretation, we thus connect the realm of the stars in *Blast* with the cold ferocity of Vorticist geometry.

The linkages Lewis gradually develops among signifiers in the play suggest how we are to read Arghol's treatment by the stars. By the time we encounter Arghol's subjection to the stars' attack, we have already witnessed his being assailed by an unknown boot (*B1* 63). The stars lash him in much the same way as does this boot, which is identified a few scenes later as belonging to his uncle, who beats him regularly. When Hanp demands incredulously why Arghol suffers his uncle's abuse, Arghol answers by making explicit the connection between the stars and his uncle's attacks: "Here I get . . . the will of the universe manifested with directness and persistence" (*B1* 66): he accepts his uncle's kicks because they resemble those of the universe, which is linked to the stars ("The stars shone madly in the archaic blank wilderness of the universe, machines of prey" [*B1* 64]). Arghol has received similar, and presumably similarly desirable, evidence of the "will of the universe" from Hanp himself, who initially "stirs" him "roughly" with his "foot" (*B1* 65). Later, the text suggests that Arghol accepts these blows as punishment for his offenses against the universe—for some kind of "remote sin" (*B1* 68).[80]

Given the way we have been encouraged to value and regard the stars by this point, these "punishments" are presented as both justified and desirably emblematic of admirable strength. Receiving them as such, Arghol seems to enjoy them. When attacked by Hanp, for instance, he luxuriates in the pain. And as he does so, the text positions him as reacting "like a woman" (*B1* 65): he "stretches elegantly," and, this new assault having put him into a "childish lethargy," he kisses Hanp on the cheek (65). In the 1932 version, which we are led to believe restores some material excised by the 1914 text, we hear that Arghol responds with ardor to the boot's "brutal caress" (9): the language here evokes a sadomasochistic dynamic. Furthermore, after we witness Arghol's "kiss," a cryptic paragraph in the 1914 intrudes: "Harsh bayadere = shepherdess of Pamir, with her Chinese beauty: living on from month to month in utmost tent with wastrel, lean as mandrake root" (65). Another ambiguous verbless phrase follows, attached to no specific referent: "Excelling in beauty, marked out for Hindu fate of sovereign prostitution, but clear of the world, with furious vow not to return" (65). Given that the surrounding text refers to Arghol, and given what we already know about Arghol's resolved attempt to stay "clear of the world," these images probably refer to him, especially given that he later says directly to Hanp, "I shall always be a prostitute" (73). Presumably, Arghol is thus placed in the position of a "prostitute" who reacts "like a woman" to natural forces magnificently stronger than he and all the figures that metonymically recall them. Other descriptors place him as a feminized prostitute, or as the 1932 version reads, "bed-cramped mistress" (9), given to "the female gesture to facilitate aggression" (7). At the outset of the 1914 version, for instance, we hear that Arghol possesses a "type of feminine beauty," one significantly called "'manish'" [*sic*] (*B1* 59)—which places him in the realm of feminized maleness, or effeminacy.

Since he enjoys rough treatment at the hands of Nature, then, Arghol here is not only placed in a passive posture but is clearly also marked by the text as effeminate. His languor, in fact, recalls the male Aesthete so demonized in the manifestoes of *Blast*. If, as Beatty suggests, Arghol is the "Vorticist Übermensch" ("Experimental Play" 44), what are we to make of this? Admittedly, at first, we see in Arghol many of the qualities we expect from a Vorticist: as the universe attempts to "SHAKE" him, for example, he remains immovable, "CENTRAL AS STONE" (*B1* 61). As we learn more about his relationship to the surrounding universe, however, we find postures of femininity—and, given that this is conspicuously a no-woman's-land, effeminacy, that brand of femininity found (unrightfully and "unnaturally," according to the ideology attendant upon the term) in males. We also find masochistic relish as well as signs of male-male eroticism, in this case appearing in the form of male-male fellatio. When Arghol first meets Hanp, we hear that "the deep female strain" (presumably, Arghol's)

> succumbed to this ragged spirt [sic] of crude manhood, masculine with blunt wilfulness [sic] and hideous stupidity of the fecund horde of men, phalic [sic] wand-like cataract incessantly poured into God. This pip of icy spray struck him on the mouth. He tasted it with new pleasure, before spitting it out: acrid. (65)

The "pip" of "spray," though "icy," is identified clearly as a "phalic [sic] wand-like cataract." If Arghol is a "mistress" or "prostitute" (to use Lewis's terms), as this and other signals of the text suggest, he is so within a male-male dyad: as the text declares, he inhabits a "rough Eden of one soul," "mated" not to "EVE" but rather to "another man" (*B1* 62).

The manifestoes of *Blast*, however, have enjoined the Vorticist to make Nature his "brothel," not to be a "prostitute" himself. Arghol would thus seem to be the Vorticist Übermensch manqué, the effeminized Aesthete constructed and vilified by Vorticism—a negative exemplar, a mistake that the text has to "correct." I would argue, however, that this is not ultimately the case: Arghol's passive, masochistic stance toward the stars and all that attacks him figures a crucial aspect of the Vorticist's deferential relationship to Nature. And in turn, this relationship to Nature points to Vorticism's concomitant ulterior investment in male homoerotic masochistic enjoyment.

Of course, as noted above, although we normally link Arghol to stances of passivity—he is "too superb" to "lift a finger" against his attackers (*B1* 67)—he does later lash out violently against Hanp, who represents "the world" and its "family objections" to him (73), as well as against the "loathsome deformity called Self" (71) of which he wants to cleanse himself. Arghol turns to violence, then, in what might seem a rejection of his former passivity, perhaps suggesting that the text does want to expel such passivity from its system. From the outset of the play we know that Arghol wants to "leave violently slow monotonous life" and "take header into the boiling starry cold" (67). This seems fitting, not only because the stars are valorized in this text, but also because, as Kenner remarks, Lewis is said to have taken Arghol's name from that of a double star, Algol (*Wyndham Lewis* 23). It is when Arghol and Hanp engage in battle with each other that Arghol seems closest to achieving this paradoxical "boiling starry cold," to reaching Nature's "cadaverous beaming force" and its "white rivers of power" (*B1* 64). As the two characters grapple, their hut achieves a star-like transcendence, becoming "inebriated with electric milky human passion" (75)—milky white like the stars of the Milky Way, and, in this homoerotically charged atmosphere here, also white like semen. At this point, the text tells us, "Once more the stars had come down" (74).

The violence associated with Arghol is then perpetuated through two more gestures: driven by much the same disgust toward Arghol that Arghol has felt toward him, Hanp kills his master, helping Arghol to achieve the "suicide's knife" (*B1* 71) he has called for earlier in the text as a way of excising the "ailment" of "Self." As Hanp kills Arghol, the text tells us that "something distant, terrible, and eccentric, bathing in [Arghol's] milky snore, had been struck and banished from matter" (84). By this point in the text, given the "distant hardness" of the stars, that which is "distant" and "terrible" has been established as good. Because of this, and because Arghol has long struggled toward self-purification, we tend to read his death as a desirable liberation. As Arghol's "milky" snore reminds us, it is "electric milky human passion"—in this context, coded as male homoerotic desire—that allows the human to attain such terrible "distance" and "electricity." As Hanp kills himself, we are apt to read his action likewise as an achievement of the desirable ferocity of the stars, the answer to the text's demand for purifying violence.

Indeed, then, the realm of the stars has been reached in part through Arghol's shift from his passive mode of the opening to later gestures of active violence. But Arghol's aggressive behavior when he attacks Hanp is actually more continuous than discontinuous with his previous effeminate languor. In both the early section of the play during which Arghol kisses Hanp and revels in the "brutal caresses" of his boot, and in the later sections in which Arghol himself is actively violent, he is driven by a desire for a condition of "brutal light" (*B1* 64), whether he reaches it by way of subjection to the violence of others or via his own aggression: the only difference is that, ultimately, he takes action to catalyze movement toward the fuller achievement of that "brutal light." His latter gestures, in other words, move toward the same goal as his earlier ones; they simply involve a change in approach. Moreover, Arghol's aggression provokes the "stars" to "come down," and when the stars "come down," both Arghol and Hanp are relegated to a position of passivity with respect to Nature, one that ushers them toward their final release.

When brought together with the Vorticist's persistent need to deny any likeness to the languid "aesthete," these phantasms of *Enemy of the Stars* indicate within Lewis's Vorticism a strong—though ostensibly denied—strand of masochistic, male homoerotic desire that accompanies its aggression.[81] And this ulterior masochistic desire, I would offer, is in turn bound up in an ulterior Vorticist attitude toward Nature.

When the Vorticist as constructed by Lewis displays violence, he does so in order to emulate the ferocity of Nature; when he receives violence, he enjoys it as a manifestation of the admirable ferocity of Nature. Arghol's passive enjoyment of the "boot's brutal caress" and his violent attack of Hanp thus are two sides of the same sadomasochistic coin. The impulses revealed by these phantasmic dynamics, I would offer, show the Vorticist to be at once, to use the parlance of *Blast*, "master" and "mistress": on the one hand, "master" with regard to the material of the natural world that he must conquer, refusing mere aesthetic imitation and representation of Nature; and on the other, subservient "mistress," in a posture both passive and eroticized, with regard to Nature's splendid violence. One could say further that the aggressive refusals to imitate Nature's forms are in fact a tribute to Nature in another respect: an effort to do what Nature itself does. The Vorticist acts as "master" in some realms, then, out of the same values that actuate his desire, in other contexts as "mistress" toward the natural universe's splendid severity.

And ironically, although the passive postures pictured here certainly move the Vorticist closer to the poses that Vorticism would, albeit problematically, associate with male-male—and hence Wildean—erotic desire, the doctrinal implications of these poses in fact distance Vorticism from Wildean Aestheticism. The eroticized violence figured in *Enemy of the Stars* points to the Vorticist construction of Nature (one alternative to the common understandings of it Lewis denounces in *Blast*) as stark and pure, uncorrupted by sentimental anthropomorphizations. It indicates the Vorticist admiration of this construction of Nature and the Vorticist desire to, as the manifestoes have it, "do" what this version of Nature "does" (*B2* 46): to emulate the violence of Nature. And in all of this, the Vorticist differs markedly from the Wildean Aesthete, who remains nonchalantly unconcerned with Nature, as indifferent to Nature as Nature is to the artist.

Whereas at first, then, the Vorticist seems akin to the Wildean in a disdainful rejection of Nature, and unlike the Wildean in a disdainful rejection of effeminacy, *Enemy of the Stars* reveals a phantasmic dynamic associated with Lewis's Vorticism that effects a reversal of that view, an inversion of it, as it were, in a chiasmic move. These Vorticist phantasms could be read as showing Lewis's effort, not necessarily deliberate or conscious, to indicate not a refusal of Nature but rather reverence for it and, moreover, to replace the stereotypical male-male erotic linked with Aestheticism—in his mind, associated with languor, weakness, and passivity—with a set of eroticized male-male relations that are rougher and more violent.[82] Understood more fully, then, Lewis's Vorticism does not altogether reject the erotic bonds between men suggested by Wildean Aestheticism, but rather preserves such erotic bonds and rewrites them.[83]

Although such bonds are both eroticized and between men, even somewhat reminiscent of male gay-macho sadomasochistic interaction, as Lee Edelman suggests, it is problematic to identify them as "homosexual" because they so clearly participate in the demonization of the feminine central to homophobia and misogyny ("Redeeming the Phallus" 41–42).[84] But whatever we decide to call them, these sadomasochistic bonds between men here resonate with Lewis's efforts elsewhere to replace what he considers weak masculinity with what he sees as a purer condition, one that will accept no effeminacy, either from the femininity of women or from the "schoolboy heroics" of Hemingway or from "Phallic aesthetics."[85]

Lewis's phantasms offer these male homoerotics, then, not only to erase effectively another undesirable version of male homoerotics, but also to use sadomasochistic bonds between men to figure an ideal state of purity. However, though Vorticism supplants conventional relations of "effeminate" inverts with this sadomasochistic vision, for the Vorticist the threat of effeminacy conventionally associated with such bonds between men always hovers perilously near. The phantasms here indicate the proximity between, on the one hand, the feminized masochistic position with regard to violence, Nature's and otherwise, that, in Lewis's vision, produces desirable Vorticist discipline and, on the other hand, the "effeminate" Aesthete's realm. It is the first "feminization" Lewis wants to promote, one that perpetuates purification by violence; accordingly, he must always be on guard against the other kind, the Wildean kind, that leads not to discipline but instead to effeminacy. The closeness of the two realms tempts the Lewisian Vorticist to move from his realm of surrender to Nature's violence into another kind of surrender that would not achieve the requisite ferocity. And thus the Vorticist must constantly police himself for signs of that other passivity that leads to the wrong kind of male-male interaction and thence to effeminacy. Moreover, given Vorticism's injunctions against women, the Vorticist must stave off that passivity without relying on the heterosexual interactions often used to banish effeminacy. Instead, he must keep them away by carefully maintaining properly Vorticist relations between men.

The atmosphere of control and aggression fostered within Vorticism, then, expressed by geometric gestures, is designed to keep at a remove the threat of effeminacy that lurks around the edges of Vorticism, especially close to its attitude of subservience to the wild violence it associates with its ideal construction of Nature (again distinct from "Wild Mother Nature" [B1 19]). Ultimately, the insistent Vorticist rejection of Wilde by way of geometric gestures makes evident the Vorticist boundary, the line that indicates the proximity between (and the corollary insistent separation between) Vorticist male-male eroticized sadomasochism and the caricatured construction of Wildean effeminate male homosexuality. The insistence on maintaining that line is clearly homophobic insofar as it involves a construction of the effeminate male, here assumed to be homosexual, and a judgment of that figure as necessarily weak, degenerate, and objectionable. But significantly, the Vorticist vision does not rule out the possibility of eroticized bonds between men: in fact, it is these very bonds that conduce to the achievement of Vorticist ideals: electricity, ferocity, white rivers of power.

Strikingly, Arghol's—and implicitly, the Vorticist's—position as "master-mistress" resembles one articulated by the Italian Futurists, from whom the Vorticists were always at such pains to separate themselves (both despite and because of their abundant common ground with them). Marinetti, for example, describes flying in an airplane in terms remarkably like those dramatized in *Enemy of the Stars*:

> When I flew for the first time with the aviator Bielovucic, I felt my chest open up like a great hole through which, smooth, fresh, and torrential, all the blue of the sky plunged exquisitely. Instead of the slow watered-down sensuality of walks under the sun and amidst flowers, one ought to

> prefer the ferocious and blood-tingling massage of the raging wind.
>
> (QUOTED IN SCHNAPP, "PROPELLER TALK" 166)

In the midst of flying, an activity the Futurists code as hypermasculine, the Futurist poet thus experiences what Jeffrey Schnapp calls an "effemination whose overall effect is virilizing" ("Propeller Talk" 166). As the plane penetrates the sky, the poet flying is penetrated by the sky and by the "raging wind" whose "ferocity" recalls the grandeur of Lewis's stars, of Nature as Lewis constructs it.

As suggested both by the manifestoes of *Blast* and by *Enemy of the Stars*, the Vorticist likewise achieves what is constructed as an ideal virility through an experience of effeminization with respect to the "cadaverous beaming force" (*B1* 64) of his ideal conception of Nature. But only effeminization with relation to something as cold, fierce, and powerful as Vorticist Nature is acceptable; only the kind of effeminization that can function as a rite of passage and foster virility is permissible; hence the need to abject the image of the languorous Wildean dandy.[85]

The Vorticist campaign against effeminacy, then, arises from the Vorticist project, along with the establishment of its aesthetic doctrines, to develop an attitude of "professionalism" and "severity" that reads as a kind of masculinity, though Lewis, given the associations the category has accrued in his climate, is reluctant to use the term. Again, Lewis's ideal is neither entirely "crude manhood" nor male effeminacy (as it was constructed, and construed, through publicity about Wilde), but rather something of them both. At stake in the Vorticist abjection of Wildean Aestheticism, in other words, is a desire for the founding of an aesthetic and philosophical doctrine that also serves as a model of conduct. In the name of a purer condition and code of behavior—one far enough removed from the conventional masculinity of his moment that Lewis preferred later to call it not masculine but rather "professional"—Vorticism implicitly advocates a rite of passage to a specifically Vorticist manhood that brings the initiate dangerously close to the relinquishment of masculinity. It is a ritual redeemed only insofar as it allows ultimately for the achievement of an ideal of invulnerability.

This chapter has endeavored to trace the genesis of Vorticism's geometric gestures: how geometric figures come to be coded within the project of Vorticism's formation so as to serve an early twentieth-century project of combating effeminacy. As forged chiefly through Lewis's desires and anxieties, which were in turn conditioned by his cultural milieu, Vorticism's relationship to the category of effeminacy—which the Vorticists understood through the example of Aestheticism—is clearly fraught, ambivalent, and complex. As the dynamics of *Enemy of the Stars* illuminate, it involves not only a rejection of Aestheticist effeminacy, but also a covert attraction to male-male eroticism involving a passivity that, rendered shameful in a homophobic context, must be denied. This need for disavowal, which gives rise to the defensive abjection of the figure of the effeminate Aesthete within Vorticism, also drives the coding of Vorticist geometrics. Within a Vorticist context, the geometrics come to stand for the "sternness and severity" (*WLOA* 342), the "mastered, vivid vitality" (*B2* 38) that will counteract effeminacy and serve the project of disavowal.

Over ensuing decades, in the work of other modernists, the values that Vorticism celebrates out of its battle with effeminacy came to be played out in different arenas in a variety of ways. The commitment to "sternness and severity" certainly evidences itself not only in an allegiance to geometric form, but also, by extension, in a preference for taut postures and streamlined material bodies, as well as in an objection to forms of passivity. As later chapters will discuss, it is these different modalities of the Vorticist quarrel with effeminacy—how that quarrel works itself out in attitudes toward line, material bodies, and passivity of attitude—that will inform the later modernist work of Pound, H.D., and Yeats. Harnessed within Vorticism to expunge the spectre of the Wildean Aesthete, Vorticist geometric gestures will be employed in the later work of Pound, H.D., and Yeats, to counter other forms of lethargy, slackness, languor, inefficiency—and to promote other kinds of precision, discipline, vigilance, aggression, and force. These other moderns will redirect the geometric idiom toward different problems, those that belong to the years between the wars. But likewise seeking a combination of rigor and active force, they will use geometry, a Vorticist geometric idiom, to imagine their way toward the mastery and improvement of insupportable conditions.

> *Seeming already a legend, the history of those years leaps out at our eyes synchronically and thrusts us into a vortex.*
>
> ADA NEGRI, on the Mostra della Rivoluzione Fascista, the exhibition in Rome celebrating the first decade of the Italian Fascist regime (1932)

> *letters stripped of ornamental serifs, sober, geometrical, and bold.*
>
> JEFFREY SCHNAPP, "Epic Demonstrations," describing the letters displayed in the 1932 Fascist exhibition

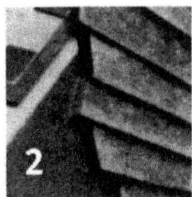

A Vorticist Renaissance?
Ezra Pound, the Geometric "Clean Line," and Facist Italy

Between 1925 and 1930, as he warmed to the project of *The Cantos*, Ezra Pound brought out three deluxe editions of installments of his "Poem of Some Length": *A Draft of XVI. Cantos* appeared through William Bird's Three Mountains Press in Paris in 1925, *A Draft of the Cantos 17–27* through John Rodker in London 1928, and *A Draft of XXX Cantos* was published through Nancy Cunard's Hours Press in Paris in 1930. By deliberately featuring the word "draft" in each title, Pound underscored the still provisional nature of his endeavor, signaling that he was only at the beginning of a major project, exploring and testing ideas. That he was ready to publish these installments in ornate deluxe editions, however, arresting their impermanence in artifacts whose conspicuous solidity implied durability, indicates that he saw no inappropriateness in presenting his initial trial segments of the *Cantos* in rich settings. This method of publication suggests that these "drafts," though still in process, were certainly nonetheless worth display and consideration: Pound's choice here implies a celebratory validation of the molten status of the work in progress.

Initial from "The Fourth Canto," Pound, A Draft of XVI. Cantos (1925) (Beinecke Rare Book and Manuscript Library)

THE FOURTH CANTO

PALACE in smoky light,
Troy but a heap of smouldering boundary stones,
ANAXIFORMINGES! Aurunculeia!
Hear me. Cadmus of Golden Prows!
The silver mirrors catch the bright stones and flare,
Dawn, to our waking, drifts in the green cool light;
Dew-haze blurs, in the grass, pale ankles moving.
Beat, beat, whirr, thud, in the soft turf
                under the apple trees,
Choros nympharum, goat-foot, with the pale foot alternate;
Crescent of blue-shot waters, green-gold in the shallows,
A black cock crows in the sea-foam;

And by the curved, carved foot of the couch,
       claw-foot and lion head, an old man seated,
Speaking in the low drone . . . :
              Ityn!   Itys
Et ter flebiliter, Ityn, Ityn!
And she went toward the window and cast her down,
    "All the while, the while, swallows crying:
Ityn!
    "It is Cabestan's heart in the dish."
    "It is Cabestan's heart in the dish?"
    "No other taste shall change this."
And she went toward the window,
                    the slim white stone bar
Making a double arch;
Firm even fingers held to the firm pale stone;
Swung for a moment,
                and the wind out of Rhodez
Caught in the full of her sleeve.
          . . . the swallows crying :

Initial from "Canto I," Pound, A Draft of XXX Cantos (1930) (Beinecke Rare Book and Manuscript Library)

I

AND then went down to the ship,
Set keel to breakers, forth on the godly sea, and
We set up mast and sail on that swart ship,
Bore sheep aboard her, and our bodies also
Heavy with weeping, and winds from sternward
Bore us out onward with bellying canvas,
Circe's this craft, the trim-coifed goddess.
Then sat we amidships, wind jamming the tiller,
Thus with stretched sail, we went over sea till day's end.
Sun to his slumber, shadows o'er all the ocean,

T HUS THE book of the mandates:
Feb. 1422
WE desire that you our factors give to Zohanne of Rimini
our servant, six lire marchesini,
for the three prizes he has won racing our barbarisci,
at the rate we have agreed on. The races he has won
are the Modena, the San Petronio at Bologna
and the last race at San Zorzo.
     (signed) Parisina Marchesa

. . . pay them for binding
un libro franxese che si chiama Tristano . . .

Carissimi nostri
    Zohanne da Rimini
has won the palio at Milan with our horse and writes that
he is now on the hotel, and wants money,

Initial from "The Twenty Fourth Canto," Pound, A Draft of the Cantos 17–27 (1928) (Beinecke Rare Book and Manuscript Library)

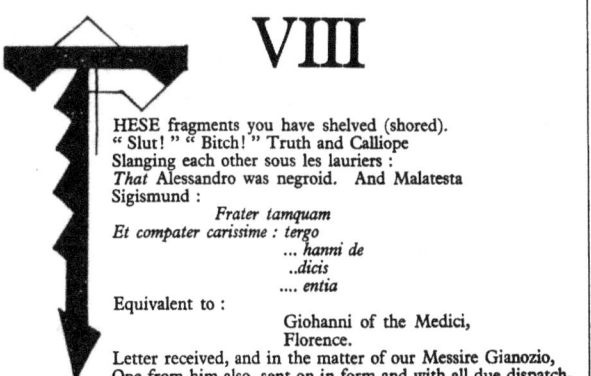

T HESE fragments you have shelved (shored).
" Slut! " " Bitch! " Truth and Calliope
Slanging each other sous les lauriers :
That Alessandro was negroid. And Malatesta
Sigismund :
    Frater tamquam
 Et compater carissime : tergo
     ... hanni de
     ..dicis
     .... entia
Equivalent to :
    Giohanni of the Medici,
    Florence.
Letter received, and in the matter of our Messire Gianozio,
One from him also, sent on in form and with all due dispatch,

Initial from "Canto VIII," Pound, A Draft of XXX Cantos (1930) (Beinecke Rare Book and Manuscript Library)

In the 1920s, Pound was displaying a proclivity, both aesthetically and economically motivated, for deluxe editions—what he would later call "De looks bookz" (*Pound/Zukofsky* 18). Like its predecessors, the Hours Press edition of 1930 features fine printing, lavish materials, and ornate initials at the beginning of each Canto. But the 1930 edition, although it indicates Pound's continuing interest in deluxe editions, also signals a new direction in his thought. Unlike the 1925 and 1928 deluxe editions, whose framing designs display graceful arabesques and richly storied visual vignettes, the 1930, smaller and sparer in appearance than its precursors, exhibits stark geometric designs that Jerome McGann calls "clearly vorticist" (*Textual Condition* 131). Drawn by Pound's wife, Dorothy Shakespear, the streamlined, generally angular shapes of the initials to each Canto, reminiscent of Art Deco work of the 1920s and 1930s, indeed also recall Vorticist images of the *avant-guerre* years.[1] Pound's endorsement of such geometric Vorticist visuals in 1930, far from trivial, indicated one of his most important projects of this moment: his intense effort, nearly twenty years after the publication of *Blast*, to revive Vorticism in the context of Fascist Italy.[2] And deeply involved in this effort was Pound's commitment, solidified through his work with Vorticism, to the geometric "clean line": in fact, his justifications for his introduction of Vorticism into Fascist Italy, as well as for his support for Mussolini's regime, entailed his belief that the material forms of Fascist Italy display clean lines akin to those of geometric Vorticist shapes.

In the early 1920s, Pound had mined the archives in several major Italian cities for artifacts that would enhance his understanding of the Italian Renaissance, particularly the exploits of condottiere Sigismondo Malatesta, on whose formidable personality and adventures he focuses Cantos 8–11: his Cantos were reflecting his preoccupation with the values, projects, and rivalries of fifteenth-century Italian states. By the early 1930s, Pound was seeking to kindle another kind of Renaissance in Italy: the rebirth of the Vorticist project. In 1932, shortly after the publication of the first edition of *A Draft of xxx Cantos*, Pound commissioned the translation of his 1914 article "Vorticism" into Italian, a gesture that epitomized his larger attempt at this point to translate Vorticist ideals and projects into the terms of the new Italy.[3] Tellingly, when Pound's wife, Dorothy, produced a watercolor, "Hommages—To Vorticism," in the late 1930s, featuring allusions to the work of Gaudier-Brzeska, Lewis, Pound, and Eliot, she included an image representing a castle in Rapallo, the resort town on the Italian Riviera where she and Pound had resided since the mid-1920s, as though attesting to a perceived connection between the Vorticist moment and her life with her husband in Italy; Pound commented of the painting that it was the "best" she had done.[4]

During the 1930s, Pound's commitment to the resurrection of Vorticism began to inform in crucial ways his increasing advocacy of Mussolini's regime. This is not to say that Pound's Vorticist loyalties initially inspired his interest in Mussolini, nor even that they provided the leading factor in his support of Italian Fascism. Rainey offers insightful commentary about the conditions that first sparked Pound's interest in Mussolini in the early 1920s, and Redman provides an extensive and nuanced account of how Pound's increasing devotion to Mussolini in the 1930s was shaped by both economic concerns and hero worship.[5] What I would add to the record here is that during the period in the early 1930s that saw a marked intensification of Pound's interest in Italian fascism, Pound's investment in Vorticist assumptions and values notably colored his arguments for the Fascist regime.[6]

In part, Pound devoted himself to reviving Vorticism in the early 1930s because he had long wanted to carry on the projects of his Vorticist heyday, to realize Vorticist goals in a way not possible in 1914. He was especially interested in actualizing, at last, what he construed as Vorticism's potential for effecting political change—a potential that had remained unrealized during the years before the Great War. In 1914, despite the Vorticists' grand ambitions to transform society, Vorticism had accomplished little in the way of actual social and political revolution.[7] During the early 1930s, Pound wanted to involve Vorticism in an overtly political project such that it could finally contribute to real-world societal reform.

By this time, of course, Vorticism was a thing of the past: a decade had elapsed since Vorticism had last been in any way visibly part of the London avant-garde scene.[8] Pound's markedly increased focus on politics and economics in the early 1930s provided the major impetus for the resuscitation of his interest in Vorticism at this point, and, more specifically, spurred his desire to enlist Vorticist values and aesthetic commitments in the service of overtly political projects. By 1931, in response to a climate of political uncertainty and economic crisis, Pound was shifting away from his earlier principal focus on the arts and devoting himself chiefly to economic and political commentary: given what the age demanded, he increasingly concentrated on what he called "econ/ and politics" (quoted in Kadlec, *Mosaic Modernism* 58).[9] As the phrase suggests, for Pound during these years, economic and political issues were necessarily intimately interwoven; and in his view the best way to political improvement lay through amelioration of economic conditions. In the early 1930s, his commitment to underconsumptionist economic thought—which sought to redress the lack of consumer purchasing power—came to the fore.[10]

As early as 1911, Pound's interest in underconsumptionism had been awakened through his work with A. R. Orage's journal the *New Age*; his exchanges with Dora Marsden, editor of the *Egoist*; and his exposure to the writings of Proudhonian underconsumptionist Arthur Kitson.[11] Subsequently introduced by Orage to Major C. H. Douglas in 1918, Pound became persuaded of the ideas of Social Credit, the school of underconsumptionist economic thought that Douglas had founded and that Orage strongly supported. It was not until the first years of the 1930s, however, as Pound was taking cognizance of the consequences of the Great Depression and as renewed contact with his Social Crediter friend Orage revived his interest in economics, that economic convictions began seriously to dominate his work.[12] In 1933, Pound meditated on this change of course: "What drives, or what can drive a man interested almost exclusively in the arts, into social theory or into a study of the ... economic aspects of the present?" ("Murder by Capital," *SP* 228).

For Pound, as for many other writers and artists of the 1930s in Europe and North America, the urgent economic and political troubles of the world merited the full attention of every intelligent observer; the artist, no longer able to afford detachment from such concerns, would have to keep strictly aesthetic considerations in abeyance until such concerns were addressed. Pound might be trespassing into areas about which he was not entirely qualified to speak, but the transgression seemed to him a matter of responsibility: as he would put it in 1936, "A man who is too stubborn or silly to learn economics IN OUR time has NO moral value whatsod/never."[13]

Pound chastised fellow modernist poets such as Marianne Moore for remaining cloistered within a "glass case," for avoiding pressing public issues like the "idiotic continuance of poverty disease etc.," and, above all, for failing to "wake up to ECON as a factor."[14] As expressed by the lines of alliance that developed among the moderns at this time, Pound's separation from his modernist comrades on this point became increasingly apparent: while Pound accused Moore of ivory-tower retreat in the 1930s, she was admiring Wallace Stevens's ability to remain devoted to what he called "pure poetry," aloof on principle from the political and economic fray of the time. T. S. Eliot, meanwhile, was a staunch advocate during this period of Moore's approach to poetry, writing the influential laudatory introduction to her 1935 *Selected Poems*. And William Carlos Williams was expressing the same dismay many of Pound's correspondents felt at this time both at the extreme degree to which economics had overtaken all other concerns in Pound's mind—and at the belligerence of his epistolary tone as he exhorted his associates to learn "ECON." As Williams wrote acerbically to Pound in 1935, "If you can't tell the difference between yourself and a trained economist, if you don't know your function as a poet, incidentally dealing with a messy situation re. money, then go sell your papers on some other corner" (*Pound/Williams* 171).

This is not to say that Pound's modernist cohorts were not also concerned with public issues of their day and the question of how poets should respond to them: on the contrary, the work of Moore, Stevens, and Eliot from the 1930s evidences their parallel struggles to find, to use Stevens's famous phrase, what would "suffice" for their times.[15] Williams shared Pound's allegiance to Social Credit; even Eliot showed an interest in it.[16] Neither was Pound alone in charging poets like Moore and Stevens with an aesthete's isolation and indifference: during the 1930s, Stevens was withstanding attacks from leftist critics such as Stanley Burnshaw, and Moore was charged with callousness to the social and political troubles of the day by such reviewers as Eugene Davidson. Put on their mettle, both poets responded with anxious and thoughtful reassessments of their commitment to poetry.[17]

But Pound's was a far more thoroughgoing and zealous foray into public engagement than those of his comrades, and both the quantity and the intensity of his wrathful invective from this period, as well as his seeming inability to recognize what others regarded as the proper limits of his role as poet, struck them as offensive and extreme.[18] Of course, even Pound suggested he wasn't entirely pleased with this state of affairs: positioning himself as a reluctant Cincinnatus, he initially framed his interest in economics as a temporary expedient measure while conditions demanded his attention—and while, in his jaundiced view, none of the experts seemed to be managing the problems effectively. As he wrote to the economist Odon Por in 1936, "[D]o you expect ME to be still an economist by 1937? It ought to be DONE by then. . . . I xxxspekk to be ritin muzik and poesy by 1937. . . . [E]con/ shd/ by then be handed over to . . . [a] trained staff of accountants."[19] But, as Surette points out, Pound "did not finish with economics in 1937—or ever" (*Pound in Purgatory* 46).

During the 1930s, Pound dedicated himself to "econ/ and politics" by publishing *The ABC of Economics* (1933), articles on Social Credit, poems on economics, the pamphlet *Social Credit: An Impact* (1935), and his notorious treatise, *Jefferson and/or Mussolini* (1935), which praised Mussolini by addressing what Pound read as the likeness between il Duce's variety of genius and that of Thomas Jefferson. His Cantos of these years—the "middle cantos," 31–73—displayed his new sense of mission: they were written, as he noted to Archibald MacLeish, "pro bono pubco."[20] By carrying Vorticism into an environment in which he believed a new political and economic system was coalescing, Pound hoped to endow Vorticism with a practical political dimension that, in such fraught times, he believed any responsible aesthetic movement should have. To quote Robert Spoo and Omar Pound, during these years Pound felt "tormented by the desire to be useful" (Pound, *Letters in Captivity* 9).

Pound dedicated himself to reviving Vorticism not only out of this desire to contribute usefully, which was bound up in his new devotion to economics and politics, and not only out of his longstanding ambition to continue the work the Vorticists had begun. In addition, I would offer, Pound was also guided by a belief that he saw signs in his Italian environment of the affinity between the projects and values of Vorticism and those of Fascist Italy: signals that a Vorticist revival was already under way and that conditions were propitious for its continuation. For evidence of this, he relied largely on the visual forms and lines of the surrounding culture, features that he increasingly came to interpret in the 1930s as indices of a civilization's character and health.

For Pound, geometrically simple shapes and lines had long represented the collection of Vorticist qualities he admired: precision, energy, action, streamlined and efficient motion. By the early 1930s, Pound's Vorticist allegiance to the geometric shape and its eloquence had developed into a belief that the "quality of line" (*LEP* 188) in material artifacts could express the essential values and principles of the culture to which they belonged, and into a concomitant belief that the geometric "clean line" suggested cultural vigor.[21] As a result, he interpreted the clean lines he witnessed around him in Mussolini's Italy as indicating both the Vorticist tendencies of the Fascist regime—because, for Pound, Vorticism suggested intelligence and power—and its success as well. Pound displayed his Vorticist inheritance here not only in his desire to perpetuate Vorticism, but also in the way he argued for the compatibility between Vorticism and Italian Fascism (as I will explain, his tendency to interpret material forms for significance was a distinctly Vorticist maneuver), as well as in his persistent celebration of Italy's geometrically streamlined forms.

Pound's interest in Italy's visual forms evinced itself especially clearly in his response to one of the great Italian cultural events of the time: the Mostra della Rivoluzione Fascista (MRF), which Pound, permuting the Italian word *decennale*, tended to call the Esposizione del Decennio. In 1932, just a few months before he was granted an interview with Benito Mussolini, Pound traveled to Rome to attend this exhibit, which commemorated the first ten years of the Italian Fascist regime. Pound had lived in Italy since 1924, so the *mostra* reviewed nearly all the years he had been witnessing Italy's development under Mussolini. A multimedia extravaganza, the show presented more than five thousand spectators a day with room after colossal room of posters, photographs, newspaper clippings, pamphlets, and other artifacts, arranged according to modernist principles of collage and photomontage—all meant to converge in an inspiring narrative of the fascist government's glorious rise, accomplishments to date, and ambitions for the future.[22] Pound's enthusiastic reactions to the exhibit, I would offer, suggest his desire to be able to read the values of Italian culture from its visual forms, to see the forms and values he associated with Vorticism—which he read as evidence that the moment was ripe for a continuation of Vorticism on Italian soil—and thus to find assurance that his credentials as a former Vorticist would afford him legitimacy as a participant in the construction of Mussolini's new regime.

By exploring the relationship between Pound's desire to regenerate Vorticism and his arguments in favor of Mussolini's Italy, this chapter addresses the ongoing riddle for modernist scholars of the connection between Pound's aesthetic and political commitments—and, by extension, between modernist aesthetics and authoritarian politics.[23] Here, rather than treat the question of how awareness of Pound's links to fascism should affect how we read his poetry,[24] I examine the nature of those links to fascism—and how Pound's aesthetic allegiances, even at a moment when he was subordinating them to work with economics and politics, affected his turn to Fascist Italy.

At this point, Pound's Vorticist loyalties began to exert a significant influence upon his growing devotion to Mussolini and the Italian Fascist regime. Given the conventional wisdom about Vorticism and Italian Fascism, we might assume that Pound's former affiliation with Vorticism would have contributed to his attraction to Fascism because Vorticism's well-known association with aggression would render him receptive to the violence associated with Mussolini's regime. After all, Vorticism was in many respects closely related to Futurism, which—in part because of its glorification of violence and in part because the founder of Futurism, F. T. Marinetti, was later sympathetic to Italian Fascism—has long been read as a kind of aesthetic correlative, even precursor, of Italian Fascism. What connected Vorticism and Italian Fascism more importantly for Pound, however, was the way that Pound's hunger for the geometrically "clean line" and all it suggested to him—a hunger that emerged from his celebration of Vorticism and his desire for Vorticist projects to continue—disposed him favorably toward Mussolini's projects.

In the early 1930s, as his sympathy for the streamlined forms of the new Italy deepened, Pound displayed a concurrent shift in attitude toward the format of his books: generally, he turned from more overtly ornate editions, the deluxe editions so prominently featured in his work of the 1920s, to markedly plainer ones. Although apparently unrelated to his growing support for the new Italy, this change in publishing practice in fact bears witness to the same increasing concern with cleanness and simplicity of line—especially line as displayed in the material artifact—that so markedly conditioned his responses to Fascist Italy.

HISTORICIZING POUND'S RELATIONSHIP TO FASCISM: THE ROLE OF THE BOOK

Through an examination of how Pound's Vorticist commitments influenced his growing sympathy for Mussolini's regime, I will consider Pound's relationship to Mussolini's Italian Fascism (what Pound believed Mussolini's Fascism to be, in any case) at a particular historical moment.[25] Such historicizing work can promote enhanced understanding of what drew Pound to Italian Fascism—as well as of what, more generally, may have made Fascism appeal to others, modernist artists and otherwise, during this period between the wars when one of the chief political challenges at hand was finding a viable alternative to liberal capitalist democracy, widely believed to be bankrupt.[26] Many critics have grouped Pound's sympathy for Fascism with the authoritarian leanings of various other modernist writers, including Yeats, Lewis, and Eliot.[27] Although we undoubtedly need to recognize the affinities among the attitudes these artists developed toward totalitarian governments—even among the ways their artistic principles related to their political allegiances—we must also attend carefully to the specificity of each, recognizing distinctions as well as similarities. Examination of individual cases at individual moments—in this case, Pound's attraction to Italian Fascism at one cultural juncture—can help us to avoid glib generalizations and received ideas about the relationship between Fascism and modernist art.

Here, one dimension of Pound's modernist artistic convictions, his Vorticism, did indeed play a significant role in the development of his sympathy for a Fascist regime. But this is not to say that modernist aesthetic principles necessarily lead to fascist commitments, nor even that all of Pound's aesthetic principles did so. Precise understanding of which did and exactly why they did, I would offer, can help us not only understand and describe more finely the relationship between modernist poetics and the political allegiances of modernist writers, but also prevent such movement toward fascism again. As Rainey notes, fascism "thrived" and compelled "intelligent contemporaries" during this period because it could assume "homely form in homely contexts"; "only through the protracted description of those sites," where fascism's premises became part of the fabric of daily living, Rainey suggests, "can we hope to understand its operations" (*Pound and Culture* 3). Following Rainey's lead, I regard it as crucial to examine the "homely" environments, physical and intellectual, in which fascism took hold, in order to understand why it "thrived" and how it operated. Like Surette, I believe that we have a responsibility to make "the imaginative effort" necessary to understand what fascism, which attracted so many, "looked like from the other side of WWII and the Holocaust" (*Pound in Purgatory* 18).[28] Careful attention to Pound's case can enrich our understanding of the cultural and intellectual climate that guided not only Pound, but also many others, toward Mussolini—so that we can be better equipped to avert such a path in future.

Crucial to such a historicization of Pound's views of Italian Fascism, I would offer, is examination of the specific books in which Pound's texts of the period were embodied, ranging from his deluxe editions of the late 1920s to his significantly simpler editions of the 1930s. Recently, scholars such as Jerome McGann, Lawrence Rainey, and George Bornstein have encouraged such attention to the significance of the format of books—their physical features, constituting their "bibliographical code"—as well as writers' choices concerning editions of their work.[29] As Cary Nelson argues in *Repression and Recovery*, study of the specific editions in which a writer's texts are physically instantiated can yield valuable insight into the ideological commitments and cultural projects in which the texts participated. Often, these commitments and projects, powerfully registered in the visual features of an edition—illustrations, design, typeface—are erased and forgotten when the texts are later issued in new editions or assembled in collections and anthologies.[30] In Pound's case, the many authoritative New Directions editions of *The Cantos* and his other work have made it easy to overlook the physical characteristics of the books of the 1920s and 1930s that tellingly document his philosophical and ideological allegiances of the time.

If such an examination of Pound's books fosters valuable historicization, such a study is also particularly well suited to Pound because of his own persistent preoccupation with the shapes and lines of material artifacts—of which books, for him, were prime examples.[31] Moreover, such a focus on books as material artifacts is especially appropriate to an exploration of Pound's sympathies for Italian Fascism because of the centrality of his concern with the physical artifact to his arguments about Mussolini. The book as material object thus provides an especially advantageous index to the philosophies that inform Pound's developing devotion to Mussolini's project in the late 1920s and 1930s.[32]

"VORTICISM HAS NOT YET HAD ITS FUNERAL": POUND'S CAMPAIGNS FOR VORTICISM IN ITALY

As Pound strove to resuscitate Vorticism in Fascist Italy in the 1930s, he was acting out of a desire he had harbored, and displayed, for many years. From 1914 onward, he had served as Vorticism's committed propagandist,[33] dedicating himself to continuing the movement long after its apparent demise in 1915, which had been brought about by the advent of the war, the attendant stoppage of *Blast*, and the movement's loss of momentum. In 1916, Pound published a memoir about the sculptor Henri Gaudier-Brzeska—who had died at the front— which devoted many of its pages to general commemorative commentary on Vorticism's first days. That same year, Pound wrote to John Quinn of a plan to "do a Lewis book to match the Brzeska. Or perhaps a 'Vorticists' [book] (being nine-tenths Lewis, and reprinting my paper on Wadsworth, with a few notes on the others)" (*LEP* 74). In 1916, he was also writing on Quinn's behalf to Vorticist painters such as Helen Saunders about Quinn's desire to buy their paintings for his Vorticist collection. At this point, two years after *Blast 1*, Pound was already defensively resistant to claims that Vorticism had come to an end; Quinn's lavish outlay of £375, he wrote defiantly to Saunders, "ought to contradict the premature reports of the death of 'le mouvement.'"[34]

This strain of commentary continued: in 1917, Pound was noting with satisfaction of a show of Alvin Coburn's Vorticist photographs that "it will serve to upset the muckers who are already crowing about the death of vorticism."[35] During the war, Pound contacted Lewis about the possibility of bringing out another issue of *Blast*, an idea Lewis was still entertaining as late as 1920.[36] In 1919, in an unsigned piece in the *Little Review*, Pound again protested the reports of "many half-caste reporters" that Vorticism was dead. "Gaudier-Brzeska's life work" may have been "stopped by a german bullet," he declared, but "Vorticism has not yet had its funeral."[37]

By 1924 Pound was waxing nostalgic to Wyndham Lewis about their Vorticist period: "I have just, ten years an [sic] a bit after its appearance, and in this far distant locus, taken out a copy of the great MAGENTA cover'd opusculus. We were hefty guys in them days; an [sic] . . . we seem to have survived without a great mass of successors." The question was now, "Can we kick up any more or any new devilment??" (*Pound/Lewis* 138–139). By this point, wavering between "any more" or "any new" devilment, Pound showed himself, albeit reluctantly, moving toward acceptance of the fact that Vorticism had died and accordingly needed not continuation, but resurrection.

By the 1930s, having fully conceded the point,[38] he began a campaign to renew Vorticism. In 1930, he was lamenting that so few recognized the greatness of the Vorticists, especially their exemplary enactment of the principle that success in the visual arts resided not in accuracy of representation but instead in the quality of their "form": "combined curves and straights, etc., masses, combinations of same" (*P&P* 5:217). In England, Pound claimed, this laudable ability had "reached its known maximum in the period 1911 to 1914 as shown in the work of Wyndham Lewis, Gaudier, and in a few works of Epstein" (217): here he deliberately featured, and celebrated, the work belonging to the Vorticist group.[39] In 1931, again bringing the work of Vorticism before his readership, Pound complained that Italy had never held "a decent exhibit of Wyndham Lewis."[40] He also heralded Vorticism's merits in *ABC of Reading* (1934), in which he observed that his test advanced there for determining the quality of artwork, whether it could be "made more efficient in some other medium," was "simply an extension of the 1914 Vorticist manifesto" (76). And in *Guide to Kulchur*, he noted that he based his idea of culture in part on his remembrance of the work he and Wyndham Lewis had produced for *Blast* (95).

As Pound's 1924 comments to Lewis indicate, however, he not only wished for people to remember Vorticism and recognize its value in the past, but also wanted Vorticist "successors" in the present. By the 1930s, Pound thought such heirs might be found in the new Italy. If what he perceived as Italian Fascism's already Vorticist tendencies could be further augmented, and if Italians could be persuaded of the value of Vorticism, Italian Fascism itself might come to serve as Vorticism's active, politically and economically engaged "successor."

By the early 1930s, Pound was striving in various ways to participate in the Italian government. In 1932, he agreed to collaborate with film director F. Ferruccio Cerio on a documentary chronicling the achievements of Mussolini's regime.[41] After submitting a copy of the documentary script to Mussolini's office in December 1932 as part of a petition for an interview with Mussolini, he was permitted to meet with il Duce in January 1933 (Carpenter, *Serious Character* 490). Pound planned to spend the meeting relaying ideas and counsel to the Italian leader. Although by all accounts the encounter was brief, perfunctory, and superficial, it nonetheless confirmed Pound's awe of Mussolini.[42]

To bring together his wish to contribute to the Fascist regime with his desire to create Vorticist heirs, Pound began promoting Vorticism in subtle ways as the official aesthetic of Italy—and, accordingly, presenting himself as uniquely qualified to educate Italians about Vorticism. Between February and May 1933, when his Italian translation of "Vorticism" (1914) was appearing in Rapallo's newspaper *Il Mare*, he included with it a note suggesting that conditions in Italy had helped him clarify his understanding of Vorticism.[43] Further, in his other contributions to periodicals Pound campaigned for Vorticism—and strove to present himself as an expert Vorticist—by cultivating a publicly staged relationship with F. T. Marinetti. Once the notorious Futurist of avant-garde circles in Milan, Paris, and London before the First World War, by the 1930s Marinetti was both an established artistic luminary in the new Italy and an enthusiastic supporter of Mussolini.

Although the Vorticists of 1914, as they strove to establish their identity, had always publicly disavowed similarities between themselves and the Futurists, connections between the two groups had abounded.[44] The propinquity between the groups—generated in part by the fact that Marinetti and his fellow Futurists had been lecturing and exhibiting frequently in London in 1910–1914 just before the Vorticists developed their movement[45]—had derived both from their publicly dramatized antagonisms and their private alliances. The press had linked the two movements (often nearly conflating them); their constant, deliberate public skirmishes with each other had joined them in the public eye; many of the members of the two groups had been friends; and despite claims to the contrary, the two groups had shared many artistic goals and entrepreneurial strategies.[46] The Vorticists indeed seem to have been inspired toward the rhetorical bombast of *Blast* by the Futurist example.

This richness of shared history between the Vorticists and the Futurists, I would argue, facilitated the revival of relations in the 1930s between Pound and Marinetti. The immediate catalyst for their reunion during this decade was their joint support of Mussolini: as Robert Casillo notes, Pound's 1932 visit to Marinetti enhanced his reverence for il Duce ("Fascists of the Final Hour" 100). During this period, a personal relationship between the two men was clearly in evidence: in 1932 they were corresponding; Pound traveled to see Marinetti in Rome; and a card from Marinetti to Pound from that year indicates Marinetti's intention to return the visit.[47] Their friendship grew so strong during the 1930s, in fact, that in 1944, just after Marinetti's death, Pound wrote Cantos 72 and 73 in part to commemorate him—and featured him among his pantheon of great men.[48]

Although Pound seems to have felt genuine regard for Marinetti, we still need to consider the strategic dimension to his cultivation of this friendship, i.e., how Pound may well have advertised his truce with Marinetti to gain legitimacy in

Italy by his association with the widely known leader of the Futurists. By the early 1930s, Marinetti was leading a campaign in Italy, in many ways analogous to Pound's, to make Futurism the official aesthetic of the new Italian regime. Although, as Marla Stone notes, Marinetti's Futurism was not the only movement seeking the position of primary Fascist aesthetic—several movements were vying for that title (*Politics of Production* 262)—Marinetti's profile at this moment was unquestionably high. Even Mussolini had publicly recognized Marinetti as a poetic innovator, a passionately committed comrade in arms, and an old friend.[49] Thus, to whatever degree Pound admired Marinetti, he quite probably also wanted to capitalize on Marinetti's cultural authority, wanted to advertise his connection with him to gain credibility for himself in Italy.

In an article of April 1931, Pound declared that although he had resisted Futurism in 1914, every day that he remained in Italy, he moved closer to Marinetti's position.[50] Further, in a 1932 interview in *La Stampa*, Pound recanted much of his earlier public hostility toward Futurism and acknowledged the debt that all European literature owed to Marinetti, stressing especially Futurism's influence on the modernist movement.[51] Pound's statement was widely circulated and quoted in many pieces advertising Futurism as the key movement—in fact, the "pride"—of the new Italy (*P&P* 5:334).[52] In his column of November 26, 1932, in *Il Mare*, Pound again saluted Marinetti's activism and his ability to combine it with his art. By 1933, in *Jefferson and/or Mussolini* Pound was writing in an appreciative tone:

> Any smart schoolboy can make fun of some detail or other in Marinetti's campaigns, but the same clever sneer-sprouter would find it much more difficult to match the mass record of Marinetti's life, even if you limit it to his campaigning for public education in aesthetics and omit the political gestures, which any good writer might envy. You must judge the whole man by the mass of the man's results. (107)

With this, Pound implicitly apologized for and rescinded his own "schoolboy" antics of the Vorticist era.[53]

In a 1932 column for *Il Mare*, Pound then used the public gestures of admiration he had made thus far to proceed to the next step in his campaign. Drawing upon this history of connection between Futurism and Vorticism, Pound argued for the suitability of Vorticism for Italian Fascism.[54] He opened the article with excerpts from a piece by Marinetti describing how artists who designed the MRF had drawn from Futurist work. Marinetti had lauded the mostra's magnificent metallic, polychrome, warlike mien, claiming that everything in it was "directly or indirectly influenced by Italian Futurism."[55] Given the obvious appropriateness of the Futurist style for the regime, Marinetti had demanded, among other things, "the presence of an authentic Futurist" in all governmental commissions."[56] This demand, Pound commented, seemed too "modest," given that, as he believed, it was impossible to create a truly contemporary public monument or exposition without informing the work with one of the vital contemporary Italian aesthetic styles, of which he positioned Futurism as prime exemplar. In this comment, Pound's appreciation for Futurism is clear.

But here, at a crucial juncture, after praising Futurism, Pound explicitly broached its similarity to Vorticism. The best works of Futurists like Boccioni and Sant'Elia, he observed, also satisfied "Vorticist criteria." Here he described Vorticism as a more rigorous version of Futurism, originally born out of a desire to criticize and refine Futurism. Pound's implication here is that Vorticism and Futurism were actually two variations on the same essential movement, of which Vorticism was the purer and more disciplined. Because Vorticism had improved upon the fundamentals of Futurism, it thus could be even more appropriate than Futurism for Italy. Pound's strategy, then, appears to have been first to praise Futurism; then to stress the affinities of Vorticism and Futurism in order to gain the approval of Futurism's Italian supporters; and then, having swayed them this far, to persuade them of Vorticism's superiority. If Italy accepted his proposal, he was well positioned take his place as an expert who could educate Italians about Vorticism.

THE MOSTRA CONVINCES POUND

Vorticism's historical connections with Futurism and Marinetti, however, contributed only one among several funds for Pound's argument that contemporary Italy would benefit from an infusion of Vorticism. Again, further solidifying his own convictions about the rightness of Vorticism for Italy were the visual forms of Italian culture—especially the forms displayed by the MRF, which Pound sometimes referred to as the Esposizione del Decennio.

Pound's admiration for the mostra (whose first full day open to the public,

October 30, 1932, fell on his birthday, a coincidence he would not have overlooked) manifests itself in the references to it he wove through his texts of the next several years. Canto 46, for example, registers the event: Pound's drawling poetic narrator, amid frequently repeated assertions that he has been "on the case," pursuing the "hoggers of the harvest" who perpetrate usury, interjects: "Didja see the Decennio? / ? / Decennio exposition, reconstructed office of Il Popolo" (*c* 231). The speaker then compares the office of "Il Popolo" (*Il Popolo d' Italia*, the newspaper founded by Mussolini in 1914, a reconstructed version of whose office was included as part of the MRF) to one which he describes ("ours waz like that"). Because the speaker says little more, the valence of this passing remark is difficult to determine. The comment, however, falls directly after Canto 45, the Canto notorious for excoriating usury, as well as just after the opening of Canto 46, which suggests that "the tale" of the Cantos teaches a "lesson" about how to pass out of the "hell" of usury (*c* 231). Thus the reference to the "Decennio," with its animated tone, suggests that the Fascist regime may offer a remedy to contemporary manifestations of what Canto 46—and the *Cantos* more generally—present as the perennial crime of usury.

In 1933, just after visiting the mostra, Pound was certainly responding positively to the exhibit. In *Il Mare*, he remarked that the majority of his fellow citizens in Italy did not sufficiently understand the importance of what the MRF was marking. Even given his familiarity with contemporary developments in Italy, he said, the exhibit had nonetheless brought him a new awareness of the Fascist regime's power and achievements.[57] As he noted in *Jefferson and/or Mussolini* (which he was writing in 1933), "Some details [of the Fascist regime] I never heard of at all until I saw the Esposizione del Decennio" (51).

The MRF had emerged from four years of planning by officials hired by Mussolini to create an exhibit that would define and express a coherent, if hybrid, Italian Fascist cultural identity. Responding to several years of debate about what that identity entailed and should entail, the exhibit sought to crystallize, legitimate, and publish Italian Fascism's cultural character. To this end, it aimed to persuade spectators with an ideological narrative about the regime's history, achievements, and future goals—and out of this to unify and to inspire the Italian people. Jeffrey Schnapp characterizes the image the exhibit tried to present of Italy as fundamentally oxymoronic: held in the Palazzo delle Esposizioni, whose Beaux Arts façade was modernized for the event, the show attempted to present Fascism as at once traditional and modern, as both a continuation of Italy's glorious imperial past and a cataclysmic break from it ("Epic Demonstrations," 3–4, 26). The tone of the exhibit, much like that of Vorticism, involved both "hot," chaotic, turbulent dimensions and "cool," streamlined, sober, for-

Cover of exhibition catalogue for the Mostra della Rivoluzione Fascista *(1932)*

Image from MRF exhibition catalogue

Image from MRF exhibition catalogue

Image from MRF exhibition catalogue

malistic ones (28). Stone suggests that this hybridity emerged from the Italian government's effort to reach a diverse audience, as well as to include artists from a variety of schools from all over Italy: ranging from the cool Rationalists to the tumultuous Futurists to the conservative Novecento group (*Politics of Production* 251, 293).

Intensely publicized through cinema, radio, advertisements on trains and buses, posters, postcards, and catalogues, the exhibit attracted more than 1.2 million visitors during the first seven months of its two-year run, more than 3.8 million visitors in all (Stone, "Staging Fascism" 233). Many reached Rome on Mussolini's famously efficient railway system with tickets discounted specially for the occasion; others made pilgrimages to Rome by bicycle or on foot.[58] Originally scheduled to close in April 1933, the mostra was so popular that it was held over until October 1934, then exhibited again in revised versions in both 1937 and 1942.[59]

In the first fifteen rooms that depicted the genesis of the regime, 1914–1922, as Pound noted, "The first impression ... is confusion," a welter of diverse objects tumbled together, their usual ontological differences erased as they were all thrust forward as part of a common project to embody Fascist culture and identity.[60] In a contemporary essay, Ada Negri wrote of the exhibit:

> Grandeurs and horrors figured or realized with a representational audacity I never dreamed of: the gigantic statue ... bears witness alongside the printed and written document. ... [P]aintings, caricatures, photographs, are peers with the historical dates and names recalling the heroic battles. Seeming already a legend, the history of those years leaps out at our eyes synchronically and thrusts us into a vortex. There is no defending oneself against its violent assault.[61]

As visitors progressed through the exhibition, this "violent assault" ultimately gave way to the four final central chambers—the Hall of Honor, the Gallery of the Fasci, the Mussolini Room, and the Chapel of the Martyrs—whose comparative coolness and stateliness celebrated Mussolini and the legend of the regime. The spectator thus moved from a sequence of rooms depicting a historical narrative of turbulence and struggle to rooms whose quiet, dim, impressive stasis evoked a mythic atmosphere—and suggested an ideal at last arrived at through strenuous effort (Stone, "Staging Fascism" 226; Schnapp, "Epic Demonstrations" 28–31). Visiting the exhibit, Pound would have been primed to recognize how the exhibit's visually tumultuous section resembled, as Ada Negri said, a "vortex" and, more specifically, how this structure's combination of tumult and stillness resonated with *Blast*'s description of a Vortex, which whirled furiously around a still center.[62]

Furthermore, Pound is likely to have noticed that the exhibit marked the first formative period of Fascism's history as having taken place between 1914 and 1922, precisely the bookend years that Pound associated with the inauguration of Vorticism and the development of modernism out of the Vorticist crucible.[63] *Blast* had first appeared in 1914, and 1922, of course, had been hailed as the annus mirabilis of modernism, when Joyce's *Ulysses* saw publication in book form and Pound and Eliot brought out Eliot's *The Waste Land*. Thus as Italian Fascism's initial period of growth had culminated in the March on Rome in 1922, analogously, Vorticism's first "blast" had likewise come to fruition in the publication of two texts in 1922 that exemplified the watershed achievements of which the new modernist writers were capable: Pound had dubbed *The Waste Land* "the justification" of the modernist movement (*LEP* 180).[64] These chronologically parallel trajectories quite probably further suggested to Pound the compatibility of Vorticism with Fascism and thus the possibility of enlisting Fascism to carry on where Vorticism had left off.

There were still other ways in which the MRF likely convinced Pound of both Fascism's Vorticist tendencies and its success (which, in his view, amounted to much the same thing). First, that Mussolini's regime staged its triumphal narrative in an exposition hall—that il Duce and his organizers devoted such effort to creating and publicizing an aesthetic exhibit to express its identity—implied not only Mussolini's valorization of artistic endeavor as integral to the new Italy but, furthermore, the resemblance between Fascism itself and a movement in the arts. Pound showed his liking for this analogy when he described Mussolini as an artist, or "artifex."[65] The idea of Fascism as an artistic movement would clearly have appealed to Pound: if Italian Fascism itself was like an artistic movement, it could therefore be interpreted by aesthetic hermeneutical methods and judged according to aesthetic standards, in which case an artist such as Pound would possess the credentials—especially, in his view, as a Vorticist—to participate in its political projects. During an era, then, in which he increasingly valued overtly political projects as more crucial and legitimate than chiefly artistic ones, Pound could rightfully extend his artistic abilities toward the evaluation and development of a political regime. Because Pound believed he had found a situation in which a political regime was in many respects allying the spheres of art and politics, rather than have to leave the arts behind in order to participate in politics, he could participate in politics *by way of* his contributions to the arts.[66]

Second, no doubt impressive for Pound was the way that the MRF achieved its narratives, both historical and mythic, through objects, images, shapes, and lines. The exhibit featured room after room of photographs, drawings, maps, signs, newspapers, and statistics, together with objects like badges, medals, and pins.[67] Culled from myriad contributions sent in from all over Italy, the elements of the exhibit were chosen on the basis of their ability to create a pictorial language through which to articulate the history, ambitions, and myth of the fascist regime (Stone, *Politics of Production* 249). As commentator Margherita Sarfatti remarked in 1933, "The show makes the Revolution plain, palpable, and intelligible"[68] — and it was the exhibit's intelligibility through palpability, through tangible objects, that so appealed to Pound. In general, the exhibition's effort to make the spirit of Fascism manifest in easily readable familiar objects answered Pound's own desire for, and attendant belief in, the legible artifact and the eloquent form. On the opening day of the mostra, as officials greeted Mussolini in the Salon of Honor, the secretary of the Fascist Party chose not to make a speech, because, he said, the exhibit "speaks eloquently for itself."[69] Ada Negri likewise commented of the impact of the exhibit on visitors: "No one speaks. It is the Exhibition that speaks" (quoted in Schnapp, "Epic Demonstrations" 23).

During this period of the early 1930s, Pound became increasingly invested in the idea that the objects of a civilization could "speak" for themselves — and be read for ideological significance. His work with the Vorticists had persuaded him of the eloquence of shape and form, but it was his engagement in the early 1930s with the work of German anthropologist Leo Frobenius, whom he had met in 1930, that solidified his belief that the physical artifact could express the values — as Frobenius put it, the *paideuma* or "spiritual essence" — of the culture to which it belonged.[70] "Frobenius has outstripped other archeologists and explorers," Pound noted, "because he does not believe things exist without cause" — and "because he considered that the *forms* of pottery, etc., had causes" (J/M 83). Or, as Pound put it in "Murder by Capital," "Frobenius is a bitter pill" because of his belief that "bad art indicates something more than just bad art" (SP 227). According to Frobenius's perspective, Pound noted, "an age SHOWS in its forms, in its material forms" (J/M 83).

Pound's prose during the early 1930s repeatedly displays this conviction that the artifacts of a culture spoke volumes: "Anyone who has seen the furniture at Schönbrunn ought to understand the flop of the Austrian Empire" (J/M 83).

In 1934 Pound celebrated what he construed as the antidote to the disaster of the Schönbrunn: "The white-gleaming intelligence in Gaudier's [-Brzeska's] studio ... in comparison with the podgy and bulbous expensiveness of Schönbrun [sic], the tawdry, gummy adhesive costliness of the trappings of the bourgeois drawing rooms of the period, had a meaning"—for Pound, clearly "meaning" the cultural superiority of the former over the latter (P&P 6:191).[71] When a culture was healthy, Pound noted in *Guide to Kulchur*, one would find "civilization"—an approbatory term for Pound—"in the seals"; it would be "carried down and out into details" (159).

Admittedly, Frobenius's assumption warranted Pound's interpreting any components of a culture, not just its material forms, for information about its health and foundational ideas. As he said, styling himself after Frobenius with his foundational assumption about the interconnectedness of all elements of a culture, "one thing you shd. not do is to suppose that when something is wrong with the arts, it is wrong with the arts ONLY. When a given hormone defects, it will defect throughout the whole system" (GK 60).[72] But swayed by both Frobenius's archeological bent for material cultural exhibits,[73] as well as the Vorticist emphasis on visual form, Pound gravitated chiefly toward the visual features of the art and artifacts of a culture—its paintings, seals, coins, pottery, and furniture—for news about its health, especially about the degree to which it was pervaded by usury, the cultural malaise with which, in the 1930s, Pound was increasingly preoccupied. Thus Pound was surely delighted to find the MRF advancing its argument through objects tantamount to the furniture, seals, and pottery of the Fascist regime.

Finally, Pound valued not only the legibility of these forms of Italian fascist culture, but also specifically what, given their appearance, they signified: the characteristically clean lines of the MRF recalled both Vorticist forms and the strength that, for him, Vorticism had implied. Moreover, during the 1930s, as Pound became increasingly consumed with work on economics, clean lines more and more began to connote for him a culture's economic health, i.e., its freedom from usury. His speaker in Canto 45 declares: "with usura the line grows thick / with usura is no clear demarcation" (C 229).[74] In a letter to Carlo Izzo of 1938, Pound glossed this line, "with usura the line grows thick": "[It] means the *line* in painting and design.... I can tell the bank-rate and component of tolerance for usury in any epoch by the quality of *line* in painting. Baroque, etc., era of usury becoming tolerated" (LEP 303). Because, as Pound believed, in a usurious culture, "the line grows thick" and a culture dominated by "gombeen men" (i.e., usurers) and "stealers of harvest by money" will run "concurrent with a fattening in all art forms" (GK 109), he conversely favored the clean, thin, geometric line—not only in painting, but in "all art forms": architecture, sculpture, and stone work. Further, as it had for the Vorticists, the clean line connoted for Pound not only unobstructed economic circulation but, more generally, "swiftness or easy power of motion" (*Translations* 23) and, more specifically at this point, "freedom from traffic blocks" (SP 225). The very cleanness of the clean geometric line suggested to him that it had been traced in the absence of impediment—and that it indicated the kind of rapid, vigorous efficiency that he sought.

Accordingly, Pound was impressed by the hard-edged forms of the MRF's visual rhetoric: massive, colossal, and stark. Though not geometric per se, the sans serif letters and shapes of the MRF were as block-like and clean-edged as geometric figures. They were formidably large; when three-dimensional, they appeared in the contemporary materials, such as concrete and steel, favored by the Vorticists (as Wyndham Lewis had said in 1914, "All revolutionary painting today has in common the rigid reflections of steel and stone" ["Cubist Room" 9]). Schnapp comments of the appearance of the mostra:

> Approaching the Mostra from either end of Via Nazionale the visitor would first have been struck by the Palazzo delle Esposizioni's new streamlined Moderne black, red, and silver façade . . . . With its four twenty-five-meter tall tin-plate fasces and its twin six-meter X's, this fiercely contemporary "face" would have been almost as recognizable as that of *il Duce*.
>
> ("EPIC DEMONSTRATIONS" 25–26)

Margherita Sarfatti expressed appreciation for the entrance's "clean vertical lines of ascension and action, of domination, audacity and empire."[75] As Craig Dworkin points out, in the context of the early 1930s such hard-edged, sans serif forms had clearly come to signify modernity, concord with the emphases and values of the machine age, and a gesture toward the future.[76] Just after encountering this initial image, a visitor would proceed up the stairs of the entrance to face the inscription "MOSTRA DELLA RIVOLUZIONE FASCISTA" set above the lintel in 1.6-meter tall three-dimensional Roman letters—"letters stripped of ornamental serifs, sober, geometrical, and bold" (Schnapp, "Epic Demonstrations" 27). Clearly, here, Pound would have discovered the values he desired.[77]

READING CULTURE: "DEALING WITH THE HETEROCLITE MASS OF UNDIGESTED INFORMATION"

Pound's investment in the legibility of form reveals his quest not only for efficiency of action, but also for efficient interpretation of the character of a culture. As he sought credentials as a participant in the Italian revolution, Pound strove for the authority to diagnose, at a glance, the ills of his surroundings. At this point, Pound began to develop his own method of reading culture. In part, he gravitated toward this method because it was the most effective—it went "straight to the centre" (J/M 66)—but also guiding his preference for the approach he took, I would offer, was an underlying concern that, in a world increasingly dense with information and facts—what Marshall McLuhan would later call the "information overload"—he did not possess the wherewithal usually considered necessary for such explication. Seeking to extend his influence into overtly political arenas, Pound seemed to be responding to what he regarded as the sometime inadequacy of his intellectual resources for such a task by constructing an epistemological system that allowed him to infer a culture's character from a few telling objects. He created a method of reading, in other words, that allowed him legitimately to use his powers of aesthetic appraisal, already proven, toward judgments about realms in which he had no official credentials.

Ever since unveiling his "New Method in Scholarship" in 1911, Pound had believed in such an epistemological approach, which allowed one to ascertain the big picture from a few carefully chosen parts. According to this method, based on the principle of synecdoche, one could arrive at a sufficient understanding of a culture through the perusal of a few "luminous details," which told one all one needed to know.[78] His hermeneutical methods of the 1930s, although in many ways similar to this earlier approach, also differed from it in several significant respects. First, given the urgent circumstances of the 1930s, his desire for diagnosing the culture around him had intensified: surrounded by what he regarded as a corrupt Western civilization on the verge of collapse and in need of corrective commentary, Pound more than ever desired the credibility to be able to make large and authoritative claims about a culture.

Furthermore, in the 1930s he shifted from an emphasis on "luminous details" in general—which could be found anywhere, in a culture's ideas, language, or physical expressions—to those specifically manifested in a culture's "material forms." Before the 1930s he had certainly attended to architecture and artifacts, but now, guided by Frobenius and quite possibly by the example of the MRF, he directed his attention much more markedly toward them. His emphasis on the visual features of "material forms" quite probably emerged also from his desire for rapid judgment: reading a culture's most readily accessible surface forms could expedite the process of interpretation. In *Guide to Kulchur*, he displayed this desire to read a culture quickly from its forms by projecting this ability onto one of his idols, Thomas Jefferson. "Jefferson never saw a roadside bill-board," he wrote, but "if he had he wd. have loathed the underlying diseases" (255). Here, Pound presumably meant that the very phenomenon of the billboard, bound up in capitalist processes, suggested economic and cultural "diseases," but we can also use this comment to capture the way that, more generally, Pound construed the objects of a culture as signs, or "billboards," of cultural trends: like Jefferson, the astute Poundian interpreter would be able to read the objects of a culture as easily as one read a billboard for what they signalled about "underlying diseases."

The way Pound characterized the overall project of *Guide to Kulchur*, in fact, indicated a desire for a method of interpreting culture that would, on the one hand, enable swift reading and, on the other, would not require conventional erudition. *Guide* was designed, Pound suggested, to help his readers to form opinions about issues with which they were not thoroughly familiar. He described his own frustration at trying to sort through "masses" of "undigested information" to arrive at a position:

> About thirty years ago ... [in the British Museum], I lifted my eyes to the tiers of volumes .... Calculating the eye-strain and the number of pages per day that a man could read, with deduction for say at least 5% of one man's time for reflection, I decided against it. There must be some other way for a human being to make use of that vast cultural heritage. (53–54)

Accordingly, *Guide to Kulchur* counseled readers how best to "make use of that vast cultural heritage," and aimed to "provide the average reader with a few tools for dealing with the heteroclite mass of undigested information hurled at him daily and monthly and set to entangle his feet in volumes of reference" (23). In response to the need for some "other way for a human being to make use of" information, Pound offered an epistemological approach that allowed one not only to avoid the laborious compilation of facts and figures but also to dismiss such painstaking compilation as futile:

> [I]t does not matter a two-penny damn whether you load up your memory with the chronological sequence of what has happened, or the names of protagonists, or authors of books, or generals and leading political spouters, so long as you understand the process now going on, or the processes biological, social, economic now going on. (51)

Although Pound might be said to have been making a virtue out of necessity here, he presented his method as using necessity to discover a hermeneutical procedure whose virtue lay in its efficiency.

A GENEALOGY OF POUND'S HERMENEUTIC OF THE LINE

Before proceeding with the narrative of the intensification of Pound's relationship to Fascist Italy, I will take a moment to consider the genesis, in Pound's earlier thought, of this method of reading that came to the fore in the 1930s. This hermeneutic undoubtedly resolved itself into an especially concentrated form in response to the pressures and needs of the 1930s, and the work of Frobenius certainly provided an alembic within which Pound distilled it to a new potency, but its chief claims and assumptions had already been present in Pound's work for several decades. Of the strains of thought generating his practices of the 1930s, some were specifically Vorticist; others, though not directly Vorticist, involved values and assumptions that clearly resonated with those of Vorticism.

I. ARCHITECTURE AND "SIMPLE LINES"

Pound's method of reading material objects was conditioned, most obviously, by a longstanding concern with the line in architecture, and, specifically, a celebration of buildings with clean lines. As Richard Sieburth notes, over the course of his career Pound often showed a "puritanical suspicion of ornament" along with "a functionalist asceticism that we have come to recognize as characteristic of the international style of high modernism" ("In Pound We Trust" 148–149). Pound's reasons for such "suspicion," however, shifted over time. In a 1918 article, for instance, he denounced nineteenth-century British architecture because of its "mendacity": "Complications and convolutions in these machine-made 'ornaments' are lies," he wrote, "because the ornamented surface is an implication that it has cost more trouble than the plain" ("Art Notes" 320). At this point, then, Pound criticized these ornaments for their "dishonesty" about the money and effort devoted to creating them. Whereas ornament implied that the building had required much "care," "affection," and labor, these fussy surfaces had in fact emerged from a mere "desire to get through a mean job with the least possible expenditure of thought, taste, time, money, or the better habits of craftsmanship." Instead, Pound favors simplicity rather than this deceitful ornament: "One sighs for the stone window-frames of Verona. Simplex munditiis, how fine the simple notching and grooving of the stone" (320).[79]

By 1928, Pound would similarly celebrate clean lines in his essay "The City," in which he outlined his vision of the ideal metropolis of the future. Pound's images and exhortations here recall the work of Le Corbusier, who similarly insisted upon clean lines and order in such studies as *Vers une Architecture* and *Urbanisme*. More than calling for ornament honestly made, Pound here went so far as to demand, like architect Alfred Loos (to whom he paid tribute on the architect's sixtieth birthday in 1930),[80] the eradication of ornament: Pound advocated the abolition of all "pastry-cook gothic" and any buildings that recalled "the horror of Florence" in its "wilfully [sic] ornate sections" (*SP* 225). He recommended "simple lines, all made for utility" (225). He wanted streets that would "follow the stream line or speed line," that had "a sweep rather like the curves in a rail-road siding" (224). This "sweep," then, recalls the clean lines celebrated in his 1918 article, but here he valorized uninterrupted, fluid lines not for their honesty but instead for their association with swift, unimpeded motion: as Pound put it, he wanted in every way possible to achieve "freedom from traffic blocks" (225). In 1928, then, he prized the simple line not so much because it signalled careful, ethical, genuine workmanship, but rather because it both suggested and facilitated various forms of traffic flow.

The conceptual linkage Pound made between speed and clean lines appeared in his work as far back as 1910, when he suggested that a line "marks the passage of a force": "[A]ll our ideas of beauty of line," he observed, "are in some way connected with our ideas of swiftness or easy power of motion, and we consider ugly those lines which connote unwieldy slowness in moving" (*Translations* 23). The linkage made within Vorticism between geometric clean lines and dynamic action had then reinforced this "connection" of Pound's, such that Vorticism became for Pound the locus classicus for geometric clean lines, their concomitant implicit dynamism, and both their aesthetic success and capacity to indicate other forms of success. Pound's 1928 use of this linkage, then, constituted a transposition of an argument from his earlier work that he had not hitherto applied to architectural ornament per se.

II. THE GEOMETRIC IMAGINATION

In addition to his work on line in architecture, also informing Pound's commitment to the clean line during the 1930s was his longstanding allegiance to geometric figures, expressions, and analogies, as well as the assumptions, related to this allegiance, that emerged from his work with the writings of Ernest Fenollosa.

Although one might assume that Pound's loyalty to geometric figures emerged from his involvement with Vorticism, his frequent use of the geometric trope actually predated his Vorticist period by several years. As early as 1910 and 1912, as he was establishing himself as a critical essayist, Pound often drew upon the language of geometry to fashion for himself an analytical and descriptive vocabulary. In *The Spirit of Romance* (1910), for instance, he likened the work of poetry to that of geometric formulae, calling poetry "a sort of inspired mathematics, which gives us equations, not for abstract figures, triangles, spheres, and the like, but equations for the human emotions" (14). By 1912, in "The Wisdom of Poetry," Pound had refined the analogy between the domains of geometry and poetry: "What the analytical geometer does for space and form, the poet does for the states of consciousness" (*SP* 362). He then went on to describe the poet's task as the construction of kinds of equations—akin to $(a\text{-}r)^2 + (b\text{-}r)^2 = (c\text{-}r)^2$, which "imply the circle and its mode of birth"—no particular circle, but the "circle absolute . . . unbounded, loosed from the accidents of time and place" (362). The poet's work, as Pound then saw it, was to express such "absolutes" abstracted from particulars.

As Ian Bell notes, the terms of analytical geometry introduced in Pound's earliest work would "provide the fulcrum for Pound's vorticist tracts within the next two years" (*Critic as Scientist* 36). By 1914, geometry seemed doubly appropriate for Pound's purposes: not only could it express, in efficient shorthand, the detached artistic stance that fostered understanding of the absolute, but it also befitted the geometric shapes and forms that the Vorticists, with whom he was now allied, were producing. It was as though, with their famous geometric shapes, Lewis and the other Vorticists had answered Pound's call for a geometric artistic project by enacting such a mission with actual geometric shapes.

The Vorticists, however, conceived of and used the geometric shape in a way slightly different from the way that Pound initially had. Pound at first used the idea of geometry to stand symbolically for an attitude of artistic mastery, an ability to express "states of consciousness" through verse. Through his work with the Vorticists, however, particularly with the sculptor Gaudier-Brzeska, Pound began to move away from enlisting the geometric shape, insofar as it represented abstraction from particulars, to capture the activity of artistic creation — and to move toward, instead, using its quality of line (as opposed to its ability to suggest abstraction) to express dynamic motion and emotional states. He became gradually more interested in how geometric shapes could figure, as Lewis put it when describing Vorticism, "a mental-emotive impulse" that "is let loose upon a lot of blocks and lines . . . and encouraged to push them round and to arrange them at will."[81] Pound's thought became increasingly dominated by the belief that shape itself, as Hugh Kenner phrases it, "manifests psychic intent," that "all shape" is "eloquent" (*Pound Era* 258).[82]

Simultaneously contributing to Pound's developing interest in the eloquence of shapes was his work with the notebooks of the American sinologist Ernest Fenollosa, which he received in 1913, five years after Fenollosa's death, and on which he would focus for the next several years. In his essay "The Chinese Written Character as a Medium for Poetry," Fenollosa had praised the Chinese ideogram, as he construed it, for its ability to provide a "vivid shorthand picture of the operations of nature" — "of actions or processes" (*Chinese Written Character* 8–9). As Pound revisited this essay again and again during the 1910s,[83] this idea of the "shorthand picture" diagramming processes further influenced him to construe shapes as expressive of both emotions and movement: they could diagram trajectories. Fenollosa's statement, in other words, bolstered Pound's contention from 1910 that a "line" marked "the passage of a force."

Vorticist geometrics, which often suggested turbulent movement, would likewise have steered Pound to construe lines as expressive of trajectories of motion. Evidence suggests, in fact, that Pound even began to liken Fenollosa's ideograms to Vorticist geometric shapes. In 1914, as he was working concurrently with both Fenollosa's notebooks and Vorticist projects, Pound reviewed Wyndham Lewis's sequence of designs for *Timon of Athens*. Here he credited Lewis with having expressed through his shapes the "youth-spirit, or what you will, that moves in the men ... between their twenty-fifth and thirty-fifth years"; Lewis, he says, had made Timon "a type emotion and delivered it in lines and masses and planes" (*P&P* 1:251).[84]

Notice the emphasis here on "delivery" of emotion in "lines and masses and planes," an indication of how Pound was reading shapes at this point as capable of conveying emotion. Significantly, Pound chose to print alongside his review two small designs from Lewis that strikingly resembled Fenollosa's ideograms. Given the similarity of Lewis's images to Fenollosa's, given that the ideogram according to Fenollosa provided a "vivid shorthand picture" of "operations," and given that Pound was working with both Vorticism and Fenollosa simultaneously, Pound was quite probably assigning to Lewis's shapes the ideogrammic ability to diagram processes, to convey not only "spirit" and "emotion" but also action. Pound's engagement with Fenollosa, in other words, likely affected how he was understanding Vorticist forms, or, to put it another way, this engagement reinforced in him the Vorticist approach of reading lines as connoting force. Shapes, whether ideogrammic or Vorticist, increasingly served for Pound to suggest actions, processes, lines of force.[85]

By 1914, given the various associations with geometry Pound had accumulated by this juncture, his logic probably ran somewhat like this: if an artist used geometric shapes, he was most likely achieving an artistic stance properly aloof from the material world's particulars; he likely subscribed to standards like those of the Vorticists, whose work by then Pound thought epitomized artistic intelligence; and he was quite probably capturing, through his art, rushing motion, process, and energy. Further influenced by T. E. Hulme's lecture "Modern Art," which Pound heard at the Quest Society in 1914 and which emphasized the geometric "character" of emergent innovative art of the times, Pound came more and more to construe geometric figures as signals of artistic success.

Given all these factors—Pound's own use of geometric metaphors, his work with Fenollosa, Hulme's influence, and his involvement with the Vorticists—Pound ever more favored the geometric shape and all that recalled it: the simple unadorned line, the bold and block-like shape, the contour looking as though incised in stone. And judging by the frequency with which Pound mentions Lewis and Gaudier-Brzeska in his later work, of these factors, it was the alliance with the Vorticists in 1914–1915 that exerted the most lasting impact on Pound. Vorticism solidified his preference for the geometric idiom, served as the project in which his various arguments for the geometric could be invested and within which they could be consolidated, and fixed the notion of the "geometric" in Pound's imagination, through a host of vivid visual examples, as emblematic of the values, aesthetic and otherwise, to which he subscribed — the values of Vorticism. Again, Vorticist geometry became for Pound paradigmatic of geometric clean lines that implied dynamism and therefore success.

By the 1930s, then, the allegiance to the geometric evidenced in Pound's commentary on Italy was Vorticist not only insofar as it was enlisted in the service of reawakening Vorticism, and not only because the geometric cast of the shapes he witnessed in his Italian environment reminded him of those from *Blast* and Vorticist paintings, but also because Vorticism had played a pivotal role in its making — and had come, in his mind, to epitomize the qualities that he was celebrating.

"THE PURE LINES OF THE ROMANESQUE ARE DUG OUT"

For Pound, the admirable clean lines of 1930s Italy were manifest not only in the MRF, but elsewhere as well: in every sense, as far as Pound was concerned, Mussolini had drained the swamps.[86] The "Italian awakening," he noted in 1933, "began showing itself" when "from one end of the boot to the other, the blobby and clumsy stucco [was] pried loose from the columns; the pure lines of the romanesque [were] dug out" (J/M 84–85). Pound admired the "beginning of a critical sense" demonstrated in "the four tiles and the dozen or so bits of insuperable pottery, pale blue on pale brownish ground, in the ante-room of the Palazzo Venezia," where Pound had waited before his meeting with Mussolini in 1933 (85). Mussolini had been able to carve out "pure lines" from the "cluttered rubbish and cluttered splendour of the dozen or more strata of human effort" in the midst of which he had found himself on his arrival; he had managed to clear Italy of "the romanesque cluttered over with barocco" (66). ("Cluttered" clearly became for Pound a term redolent of everything he wished to avoid and overcome.) For Pound, the "pure lines of the romanesque" were an immediate sign not only of freedom from the blockage of usury, but also, through the way they suggested the inscription of a trajectory of motion, evidence of Mussolini's immense "*directio voluntatis.*" This was Pound's term, borrowed from Dante and medieval scholarship, for the "direction of the will," the will moving into action: as he characterized it elsewhere when praising Mussolini, the "capacity to pick out the element of immediate and major importance in any tangle" and "to go straight to the centre" (66).

THE BOOK AS LEGIBLE ARTIFACT

During the 1920s and 1930s, the convictions informing both Pound's effort to resurrect Vorticism and his hermeneutics of culture began to play out not only in his attitude toward architecture and toward artifacts such as pottery and sculpture, but also in his decisions about the appearance of books. By 1933 he was explicitly acknowledging that he regarded books as "MATERIAL OBJECTS," which meant for him that their visual features, like those of all material artifacts, formed a crucial part of their significance (P&P 6:106).

Pound first began to transfer his attitudes about other material artifacts to books most noticeably in 1922–1923, as he undertook research for the Malatesta Cantos.[87] In July 1922, just after the trip to Italy during which he combed through archival materials about the "Tempio" built by Sigismondo Malatesta in Rimini, which impressed him deeply, Pound wrote a letter to Felix Schelling that employed a lexicon reflective of his study of Malatesta's Tempio and its art: he describes his own poetic work in a combination of painterly and architectural terms. "The first 11 cantos are preparation of the palette. I *have* to get down all the colours or elements I want for the poem . . . I hope, heaven help me, to bring them into some sort of design and architecture later" (*LEP* 180).[88] Both "architecture" and "design" suggest Pound's desire for more formal structure in his poetry. He expressed the same wish to Eliot when noting his frustration at never "getting an outline": he wanted to discipline his work into a form he felt it lacked.[89] Pound's preoccupation at this juncture with architectural and painterly metaphors, with "outline," attests further to how much shape and line had come to dominate his vocabulary and imagination.

At this point, he likewise began to strive for "architecture," "design," and "outline" in the formats of his books. In 1924, for instance, he was arranging with William Bird to bring out a deluxe edition of *A Draft of XVI. Cantos*. As

Vincent Sherry suggests, Pound's "formalist values," brought to a head as he combed through archives to find artifacts related to Malatesta's Tempio, were "strikingly visible" through the features of this deluxe edition: "the inscriptional head-lettering mimics the architectural motifs of the Tempio" (*Radical Modernism* 147). Given Pound's impulse to liken the project of the *Cantos* to the Tempio Malatestiano that impressed him so mightily, his effort to make the physical features of the 1925 deluxe book recall those of the Tempio is not surprising.[90] In a letter to Lewis of a few years later discussing the lettering and format of an edition, Pound suggested the commonality between impulses that might be realized in architecture and painting and those that could be manifested in the format of books: "As one can't get architecture or even mural stuff DONE one retreats to printed page" (*Pound/Lewis* 168–169).

In the 1920s, Pound's concern with the physical book played out in his attraction to ornate, assertively physical deluxe editions. He brought out his *Cantos* in William Bird's 1925 edition of *A Draft of XVI. Cantos* and John Rodker's 1928 edition of *A Draft of the Cantos 17–27* (*A Draft of XVI. Cantos* appeared in an edition of 90 copies; *A Draft of the Cantos 17–27* in 101). These elegant productions featured lavish work: elaborate illuminated lettering, illustrations, and printing in black and red, reminiscent of that of William Morris's luxurious books. Both the 1925 and the 1928 editions were bound in covers of richly colored vellum, stamped in gold, and printed on paper of high quality, ranging from Roma to Whatman to Imperial Japan. Although Pound had cogent entrepreneurial reasons for producing these deluxe editions—through them, he knew, he could reach an audience of wealthy collectors—he also had aesthetic reasons for publishing in such a form: in 1923, for example, he wrote exuberantly to Kate Buss of the upcoming *A Draft of XVI. Cantos*, which he declared of "UNRIVALLED magnificence": "It is to be one of the real bits of printing; modern book to be jacked up to somewhere near level of mediaeval mss." (*LEP* 187).

With the advent of the 1930s, however, Pound turned toward simpler formats, and accordingly, his attention to the line of the book began to show itself in a different way. When arranging for the several deluxe editions in the 1920s, Pound had informed his decisions about format with the Vorticist principle of eloquent form: at this point, his desire for a beautiful object of conspicuous solidity, reminiscent of a physical building like the splendid Tempio, had led him to favor ornate editions, the style of whose visual features differed markedly from that of streamlined Vorticist geometrics. In the 1930s, however, as Pound became increasingly impelled by hopes for a Vorticist revival, he turned to shapes more directly similar to unadorned Vorticist forms.

THE SHIFT TOWARD PLAINNESS

During this shift of the 1930s, Pound continued the preference for the clean line that had pervaded his thinking in the 1920s; in the later decade, he simply changed the ways in which he manifested that preference.

In 1923, Pound had hired little-known artist Henry Strater to illustrate Bird's edition. Subsequently, Pound assessed the success of Strater's work on the basis of its line, clearly showing his preference for simple lines. As the edition neared completion, Pound commented irritably to Bird, "*Point* was to restrict Strater to *design*. Instead of staying in the design, he has wandered all over the page." He continued:

> [T]he only course now open is to cut away superfluous rubbish. *Ci inclus*: the tail of "P" and the scene across the top of the page. And other such delenda in other caps. Such operations as can be performed by simple scission and omission.... As to the quality of line in the "P," it is equal to any 1890, Walter Crane hammered brass.
>
> (*LEP* 188)

Even here, early in the 1920s, then, Pound not only stressed his concern with the "the quality of line," but also specified his desire to "cut away" all "superfluous rubbish" (he uses similar language in *Jefferson and/or Mussolini* to praise il Duce, who dispenses with "clutter" and "tangle") by processes of deletion, "scission," and "omission." His comments here clearly indicate both his impulse toward streamlining and an equation between the streamlined and the properly modern: because of the curlicue on its tail, to Pound, Strater's "P" looked dated.

After 1930, as Pound's interest in Mussolini and the potential resurrection of Vorticism intensified, he began to modify his notion of streamlining, to redefine what he regarded as "superfluous rubbish" that needed to be "cut away." More and more, in fact, Pound came to regard the whole idea of the deluxe edition as "superfluous." Accordingly, by the early 1930s Pound was no longer publishing his *Cantos* in deluxe editions but instead almost exclusively in plain trade editions through commercial firms such as Faber and Faber or Farrar and Rinehart.[91] Pound's other work, though not always published through such large commercial firms, was likewise generally issued during this period in simple, inexpensive editions.

In part, Pound began to favor simpler lines in his books because of a desire to mimic both the lines of Vorticism and the streamlined designs associated with Mussolini's regime. Admiring Mussolini's having "dug out" the "romanesque" from the ornate "barocco," impressed by the MRF, and powerfully swayed by Vorticist memories, Pound increasingly preferred the simple line in its own right. The plain line implied a quickly traversed trajectory, the "swiftness" he ascribed to Mussolini and all those who successfully evinced the *directio voluntatis*.

At this point, however, Pound was also guided toward simpler lines by a concern with another, more actual "swiftness" that plain editions could enable: swiftness of circulation among readers. Because of the economic depression that had struck North America and Europe during this period, deluxe editions had become a much less viable way of circulating his work and the work of the other moderns. For several years, the deluxe edition had allowed moderns like Pound to obviate the imperative of most commercial publishers that a book be marketable to a wide audience before being accepted for publication. During the 1920s, small presses like William Bird's Three Mountains Press, Nancy Cunard's Hours Press, and John Rodker's Ovid Press, issuing deluxe editions and making their money from libraries, bookshops, and collectors, had, with their deluxe editions, facilitated the circulation of work Pound considered worthwhile. A limited and ornate edition, first, enabled writers to make good money without having to appeal to a broad public: in 1922, for instance, Pound emphasized to William Carlos Williams that publishing in fine limited editions

> is a means of getting in 100 dollars extra before one goes to publisher.
> Yeats' sisters' press in Ireland has brought him a good deal in this way. I got nearly as much from my little book with them as from the big Macmillan edtn. of *Noh*.
>
> (*LEP* 183)

Later, during the Depression years of the 1930s, more and more small private presses were being forced to shut down. Moreover, because large firms such as Random House were increasingly recognizing a "great craze for fine press books—beautifully made limited editions" (Cerf, *At Random* 63) and issuing deluxe editions, the significance of the deluxe in the publishing world was changing: even when small firms were able to continue producing deluxe editions, these books no longer either possessed the same cultural meaning nor performed the same cultural work they had hitherto, when they had often been associated with the avant-garde. Pound registered his awareness of this change in the significance of the deluxe in a letter to Caresse Crosby, head of the Black Sun Press:

> The de luxe book was (has been) useful in breaking the strangle hold that the s. o. b. [i.e., large publishing firms] had on ALL publication. But the minute the luxe was made into a trust (Random Louse etc.) and forced into trade channels it ceased pretty much to be useful.
>
> (CONOVER, "CROSBY CONTINENTAL" 110)

Because a mainstream publisher like Random House, for instance, was affiliated with so many private presses and wielded the power to advertise and make successful those deluxe editions in which it had an interest, the deluxe began to lose its formerly subversive significance and counterhegemonic power.[92] Moreover, through the intervention of firms like Random House, deluxe editions were increasingly used to publish the work not only of the moderns but also of established authors or contemporary authors whose work Pound considered negligible. This, of course, enraged Pound, as it removed the deluxe edition from the cultural space it had occupied when it had frequently been associated with modernist innovative work and had helped the moderns make money through purchases by collectors. Painfully evident to Pound was the waning of the deluxe's capacity to facilitate the circulation of his own work and that of writers whose work he wanted to promote.[93]

But Pound had still another reason for his turn away from the deluxe, one which probably would have engendered his turn from ornate editions even had their significance within the publishing world not changed. At the time, his opinions were in transition regarding what books he wanted to see circulated and how he wanted them to be circulated. Responding to the urgent political climate of the day, more and more driven to "cut away" the "superfluous rubbish" of ignorance about economics, Pound concomitantly wanted to "cut away" superfluities in the production process, to simplify both the process of book production and the books themselves. Because he increasingly wanted to educate as large and diverse a public as possible about economics and politics, he wanted his texts to be inexpensive and widely available.[94] Books with a simple format could better achieve this purpose because they required less effort and money to make, could get out to the public faster, and, since they were less expensive, could achieve broader, swifter circulation.

By 1935, Pound's negotiations with London publisher Stanley Nott, a Social Crediter sympathetic to Pound's economic convictions who brought out some of Pound's directly economic writing during the 1930s, clearly showed both his desire to educate the public in economics and his attendant desire to publish in inexpensive, plain formats. "I believe," he wrote to Nott, "all propaganda etc/ shd/ be ... brought out in paper covers."[95] Nott agreed, issuing much of the work on economics that came out through his firm in pamphlet form. When Nott later quoted costs for other books by Pound he hoped to publish, Pound noted that he was "alarmed" at the prices and said that, to avoid such exorbitant costs, he had "been looking into pamphlets for years." Pound conceded that Nott could make a more expensive edition if he thought it advisable, but still expressed his disapproval of ornate books.[96] These and other letters to Nott in the 1930s indicate that, given the times and his subject matter, Pound clearly no longer had either much patience or use for the deluxe. Animated by a complex cluster of reasons—economic, aesthetic, and philosophical—he had come to prefer in his books the geometrically simple, uninterrupted line.

By the early 1930s, swayed by the underconsumptionist economic thought of the Social Credit movement, which espoused the circulation of money—as Maurice Colbourne's analogy put it, like blood through veins—as a means to economic health, Pound was increasingly worried about clogs and blocks in the economic system. According to Social Crediters, these clogs, produced by the hoarding of individuals or the shenanigans of banks, impeded the rightful distribution of purchasing power, leading, in the famous Social Crediter phrase, to "poverty in the midst of plenty." In the realm of publishing, Pound sought a goal analogous to that he advocated in economics: swift, uninterrupted circulation and distribution. And this publishing objective, in turn, became part of his campaign against usury. As he noted in *Guide to Kulchur*—in what seems an echo of Canto 45's famous litany—"Usury endows no printing press. Usurers do not desire *circulation* of knowledge" (62; my italics). Much as he believed that money must circulate freely to produce a healthy economic system, Pound believed that knowledge must circulate; and usury had to be combated because it prevented the circulation of both money and knowledge. As in his Vorticist days, Pound's thought during this era boiled with images of rushing activity, insistence on the "necessity of motion" (*SP* 254).[97]

In other words, Pound began to value streamlining in the physical format of books not only because of its resemblance to geometric Vorticist forms per se, but also because it could foster two other kinds of streamlining: the streamlining of the circulation of his writing, which would augment his influence; and the streamlining of economic and governmental processes, which he hoped his writing would facilitate. And in Pound's imagination, given the capacity for dynamic action he had long associated with Vorticism, these other forms of streamlining came to be as closely related to Vorticist values as geometric figures themselves.

SIMPLICITY AND INFLUENCE IN THE 1950S

Inscribed in Pound's simple, plain formats of the 1930s and afterward, then, were impulses akin to those that drove his effort to revive Vorticism. Although the designs of the *Draft of xxx Cantos* (1930) may be the ones that look "clearly Vorticist," more generally, Pound's bent for visual streamlining during the 1920s and 1930s registers the motives governing his effort to resurrect Vorticism, which was in turn bound up in his passion for the new Italy.

Twenty years later, across the chasm of experiences during the Second World War, as Pound was confined to St. Elizabeths Hospital,[98] his overtly political outlet for transmitting his convictions about Vorticist streamlining had disappeared; he could no longer foster the revival of Vorticism through an external system. Even at this late date, however, he continued to enact values he had associated with both Vorticism and Italian Fascism, through his ongoing dedication to plain and inexpensive editions. Having lost the regime that he believed might have translated his dreams into real political and economic reform, he now more than ever "retreat[ed]" to the "printed page" to achieve both the visual simplicity and the capacity for influence that he desired.[99] Before this, his turn to the printed page had accompanied his engagement with exterior political and economic systems; now, it substituted for such engagement, compensated for its loss.

During his years at St. Elizabeths, although he did sanction the publication of a few limited or deluxe editions of his own work and of thinkers he admired, he primarily occupied himself with assembling inexpensive paperback educational anthologies.[100] Dominating his correspondences of the period are references to the "Square $ Series" of John Kasper and David Horton: slim dollar pamphlets of the work of such members of Pound's pantheon as Confucius, naturalist

Louis Agassiz, economist and historian of money Alexander del Mar, statesman Thomas Hart Benton, and jurist William Blackstone.[101] In Pound's commitment to the Square Dollar Series, we see his effort toward simplicity (simplicity that he prized because of the values, aesthetic and otherwise, that it connoted, as well as because it evidenced conditions that would in turn enable influence) transformed by the dramatically changed conditions of the 1950s. At this point, attaining simplicity and influence had come to mean inexpensive formats and a focus on the educational "basics"; it had come to mean asking his friend Louis Dudek about the cost of a Varitype machine in the hope that he could "multiply copies of a text" without having to depend on the "godDDDam printer or artizan" (*Dk* 39). Pound urgently wanted to communicate with a minimum of impediment what he considered to be texts essential to an education.

KASPER'S BOOKSHOP

At this point also, having perforce "retreated" behind the walls of St. Elizabeths, Pound began to engage with the world vicariously through an assorted host of disciples who came to visit him in D.C. (his circle of acolytes became known as the "Ezuversity"), seeking wisdom from the man many had come to regard as a guru and maligned visionary. John Kasper, of the Square Dollar Series, was one such disciple. Blatantly anti-Semitic, racist, and increasingly pro-Nazi, Kasper did significant further injury to Pound's reputation when reports of his segregationist activities in the American South, together with news of Pound's close ties with him, made the headlines of the *New York Herald Tribune* in 1957 (Carpenter, *Serious Character* 828).[102]

In Greenwich Village in 1953, Kasper had opened a bookshop called Make It New, which reflected his vision of the gospel according to his master, Pound. It is tempting to juxtapose the images of the MRF and the window of Make it New in a conceptual ideogram to consider the relation between them. Through the windows of Kasper's bookshop, it is as though we see the MRF through cracked, soiled glass that, on the one hand, distorts the view but, on the other, also reveals truths not immediately apparent in the mostra itself. In 1932, Pound was attracted to a display of il Duce's achievements; twenty years later, John Kasper sought a similar crystallization, in the display of visual images and material artifacts, of the ideas and career of *il Maestro* (as his St. Elizabeths disciples sometimes called him), Pound.

Kasper set up his window display to exhibit Pound's poetry, translations of

Confucius, and economic commentary; he especially featured the ideogram from Pound's *Make It New*. Much as Mussolini's officials had sought to portray the successful history of their regime and its hero in a shorthand of assembled objects and documents, so Kasper strove to capture the epic narrative of Pound's development. That during these years Pound was able to associate with Kasper—organizer and executive secretary of the "Seaboard White Citizens Council" in Alabama and member of the KKK—to correspond with him, and to transact business with him, without sending him away, of course bespeaks, if not a complete endorsement of Kasper's views, at the very least a deeply disturbing tolerance of violent prejudice, with which, as we address Pound's association with Italian Fascism, we must also reckon. What made such tolerance possible? I would suggest that one of its conditions of possibility was the urgent desire of Pound's featured throughout this chapter: "to be useful"—a desire that was quixotic and often deeply misguided, often obsessive, and often thwarted to the point that it inspired Pound's rage and further torment.

This chapter has focused on Pound's commitment to the geometrically clean line. The notion of the line, of course, almost invariably evokes the concept of the boundary, and boundaries, in turn, almost inevitably come to mind in connection with Pound. I am thinking particularly of the boundary often said to separate the domains of art and politics, or the boundary often thought to divide between the "inside" and "outside" of any text. Events of the 1930s, the late modernist decade during which writers had to consider deeply their role within a Western culture in upheaval, both made these boundaries apparent and fueled the desire to cross them—to cross from the domain inside literary texts to the realm outside them, to cross from art to politics. This was the essence of Pound's desire. In view of all the crossings that took place, Pound's and otherwise, we need to continue to consider what happens when images and ideas from within the literary text emerge onto the street outside and affect people in the world. We need to examine cases in which that boundary is dissolved, when the windows separating inside from outside are broken, such that outside and inside intermingle and the world of the literary text is no longer safely in the realm of the hypothetical where nothing happens (as Auden mysteriously suggested) and nothing is made to happen, where textual actions are immune from consequence. We need to consider when that crossing becomes transgression, to consider what happens when a text or a writer, through influence, contributes to the injury and even the destruction of lives.

As the 1930s unfolded, Pound, like many other writers of the time—such as Auden, Orwell, Woolf—demanded that the windows be broken (as Blaise Cendrars once put it, "*Les fenêtres de ma poésie sont grand' ouvertes sur les bou-*

levards" ["The windows of my poetry are wide open to the boulevards"]),[103] that his ideas begin to have real effects, to do work in the external world. And as he strove for more real influence, as he advanced from rather than retreated to the printed page, he also affiliated himself with more real harm. During the 1950s, Pound received a letter from Marshall McLuhan about the *Cantos* that asked if they were a "reconstruction of a crime": presumably he was thinking about the perennial crime of usury against which Pound waged an ongoing battle. Addressing Pound's career now, we necessarily summon the crime of treason with which he came to be associated and the fervent alliance with Fascist Italy from which issued the actions for which he was arrested in 1945. Pound was never actually convicted of treason per se — deemed mentally unfit to stand trial, he was instead sent to the relative sanctuary of St. Elizabeths — but his links to anti-Semitism and Fascism remain nonetheless an indelible part of his record of struggle.

The question remains, of course, of what exactly Pound's crimes consisted in. I am unwilling to believe that they resided in his decision to venture beyond the boundaries of the sphere of art, in a *trahison des clercs*. Many artists have done the like, and have done so rightfully and responsibly, assuming their roles as public intellectuals. Pound's decision to involve himself in "econ/ and politics" did not lead inevitably to the world of John Kasper. I am even willing to say that it was not even his interest in Italian Fascism that was, in itself, his gravest error: during a period when many urgently sought an alternative to liberal capitalist democracy and remained skeptical of communism and socialism, the option of fascism was not out of the question. As compatriots of Pound's such as Yeats and Eliot likewise expressed admiration for Mussolini and fascism in the 1930s, "fascism" simply hadn't the connotations it does, in hindsight, today. Ultimately, of course, Pound not only considered Mussolini's Fascism a possibility, but actively supported it; however, as Redman and other have noted, he did so in the absence of adequate understanding of what it entailed, such that his approbation remained conspicuously insubstantial, even vacuous.

Where one of Pound's chief errors lay, I would offer, was in that very lack of understanding, which in turn arose from his excess of wishful thinking and epistemological desire coupled with a paucity of information, a paucity maintained in part because of a willful reluctance to seek and absorb information that thwarted his desires, among them the passionate desire to be of use. The system of cultural hermeneutics Pound developed, which assumed the ability to read cultural health from the "quality of line" in material objects, attested to his hunger to obviate the time-consuming process of observation, inquiry, and the evaluation of facts necessary for a responsible assessment of the condition of a culture. His urgent need for answers, as well as for a revival of the Vorticist values he cherished, bred a craving for epistemological shortcuts: this fueled his signature habit of hasty generalization as well as his even more pernicious habit of looking for something and someone to blame, which in turn funded his anti-Semitism, bound up in his denunciations of usury.

In his interpretation of culture, then, Pound was reading from a poverty of data and a plenty of wishful fictions. Driven by both his desire to believe that he knew definitively what was happening and his yearning for the realization of his own longstanding wishes, he increasingly insulated himself into an irresponsible naivete about the way actual conditions in Italy deviated from his assumptions about what he thought was occurring. Ironically, the writer who famously exhorted artists in 1913 to "[g]o in fear of abstractions" was ultimately felled by his own abstractions, unable to accept into his abstract, wishful picture of Italy's success the particulars, the "rain of factual atoms" he had long claimed would engender the richest knowledge. One of Pound's severest betrayals, I would offer, was of his own antiabstractionist epistemological wisdom: a treason born of the mixture of his impatience for authoritative knowledge and his rage, ever greater as he was increasingly thwarted, to realize his ideals.

> The house was her spirit .... It was parallel and modern and ran level with lines of mountain, it was squares to be bisected and parallelograms and rhomboids. In the sparse and geometric contour of the house, there was all wisdom. She wanted to walk along the corridors, just that; she wanted to walk from one end of the flat roof to the other far end. She would be so embodied in long parallelograms and in square and cube and rectangle. She wanted those things.
>
> H.D., Nights

"Embodied ... in Square and Cube and Rectangle":
H.D. and the Vorticist Body

Near the end of H.D.'s novella *Nights* (1935), protagonist Natalia Saunderson meditates on the geometric forms of her sister-in-law's house.[1] With lyric intensity—developed through H.D.'s characteristic prose techniques of parataxis, syntactic parallelism, and insistent repetition—Natalia not only admires the building, finding "all wisdom" in its "geometric contour," but clearly also identifies with it ("the house was her spirit"). Although the first sentence of the passage implies that she already feels coincident with the building, the sentences that follow suggest instead that she has not yet quite reached the point to which she aspires, that she is impelled by a desire to unite more completely with the house: the diction here suggests that the house presents her with an ideal body toward which she strives. The shift from a present condition ("The house was her spirit") to one potentially to be realized in the future ("She would be so embodied") correlates with, and is accounted for by, a shift of attention in this passage from "spirit" to "body." Although the house may already be Natalia's

Kenwin, villa in Switzerland, residence of H.D. (Beinecke Rare Book and Manuscript Library)

"spirit"—presumably because she feels such affinity for it—now she wants it to become her *body* ("she would be so embodied"): only then will her desire be entirely fulfilled.

This passage emerges from a novella that focuses not only on Natalia's body, but also on her experiences of sexual transport that make her keenly aware of her body. Natalia repeatedly achieves ecstatic states through erotic arousal that afford her access to a "holy" realm of visionary consciousness: like a mystic, she travels what she calls "the high-road to deity" (52). Before this passage, *Nights* has consistently attended to Natalia's shifting condition of embodiment, signaling moments when she feels "incarnate" (80) and moments when she is instead "disembodied" (43) or gets "out of" her body (64, 66). By the time of this passage, her desire to be "embodied" in "square and cube and rectangle" indicates yet another instance of her longing to escape from her everyday corporeal identity—ironically, by way of the erotic stimulation of her body—into an alternative state of ideal embodiment figured by geometry. Natalia's persistent geometric fantasies mark her continual effort to transmute her ordinary bodily state into a transcendent one, and thereby to surpass several different boundaries—the boundaries of her body, conventional sexual practice, conventional womanhood, even conventional humanity—en route to visionary consciousness.

This chapter examines how H.D. enlists geometric language in *Nights* to construct this desired state of embodiment, arrived at through erotic stimulation, that fosters visionary states of consciousness.[2] It also interrogates the implications of the geometric fantasies that H.D. stages by way of Natalia Saunderson. I frame my discussion of H.D.'s use of geometry in *Nights* with a treatment of her uses of geometry elsewhere in her oeuvre, considering both how geometry accrues its various significances within her lexicon and how these significances inform the geometric body of *Nights*.

H.D.'s treatment of the geometric body in *Nights* can illuminate the character of her relationship to Vorticist thought, in part because of the widely accepted semiotic association between geometry and Vorticism during the modernist decades, as well as because H.D. herself suggested that she tended to link Vorticism with geometric forms. But, furthermore, in *Nights* H.D. also codes geometry to indicate a cluster of aesthetic qualities celebrated with notable intensity within Vorticist rhetoric—hardness, tautness, severity, and intense energy—and by way of a geometric vocabulary, she attributes these qualities to the ideal body that Natalia imagines.

In the inaugural issue of *Blast*, Pound publicly associated H.D. with Vorticism by featuring her poem "Oread"—he quoted the poem without supplying the title—as his sole exemplar of Vorticist poetic technique (*B1* 154). Despite this, and despite her close association with Pound and acquaintance with other Vorticists and their work, H.D. never explicitly acknowledged what she thought of Vorticism (Guest, *Herself Defined* 65).[3] Given H.D.'s comments in an unpublished review of Yeats's *Responsibilities* written during the First World War, however, many critical accounts have emphasized H.D.'s stated antipathy to, if not the Vorticist movement per se, at least the values and practices she associated with Vorticism.

Gary Burnett notes that in this review of *Responsibilities*, H.D. used geometric images ("cubes and angles," "the black magic of triangles and broken arcs" [H.D., "Responsibilities" 53]) to represent the aesthetic programs of Vorticism and Futurism, which she condemned for cooperating with forces that brought about the bleakness of mechanized modernity and the violence of war. For H.D. in the 1910s, Futurism and Vorticism possess an aesthetic, as Burnett puts it, "which most reflects and is most determined by the militarism and industrialism of the early twentieth century" (*Between Image and Epic* 11), and since Vorticism is "more visible" to H.D. than Futurism at this point, it is chiefly toward Vorticism that she directs her critique. As Burnett notes, in a "dangerous pun" in her review, H.D. likens the geometric "planes" of a "Vorticist canvas" to the

"EMBODIED . . . IN
SQUARE AND CUBE
AND RECTANGLE"

"aeroplanes" of war ("Poetics out of War" 57–58). When describing H.D.'s attitudes toward Vorticism, critics tend to cite this review of H.D.'s, along with Burnett's reading of it.[4]

But ascertaining whether or not Pound considered H.D. a Vorticist, how much H.D. interacted with those who styled themselves Vorticists, or how H.D. herself felt about Vorticism still fails to address how much her work actually demonstrates values associated with Vorticism. Here I consider how her work's implicit endorsements, especially as they address the body, resonate with those that are conspicuously articulated within the manifestoes of Vorticism, such that the geometrics of her work, surprisingly, often function much as do the "planes and angles" of Vorticism.

In this chapter, although at times I may seem to define "Vorticist" according to the degree of resemblance a set of textual maneuvers bears to those in the work of Ezra Pound and Wyndham Lewis, what I mean to show instead is that, like H.D., Pound and Lewis both engaged in the construction of ideal bodies in their work—and, like her, imagined a body composed of features "blessed" in the *Blast* manifestoes. By way of their fantasies of ideal bodies, all three artists notably display a subscription to Vorticist ideals. Like Lewis and Pound, H.D. could be said to stage a desire—albeit an equivocal one—for an attenuated, rarefied Vorticist body.

Through her use of geometry in *Nights* and other similarly valenced texts, H.D. signals her attraction to an ideal body cast in geometric terms—indicating, accordingly, a desire for a transformation of the ordinary body that fosters a liberation from everyday corporeality, and thus a receptivity to visionary consciousness. More precisely, H.D.'s version of the geometric body registers a desire for refinement away from the heavy, fleshly qualities traditionally associated with the female childbearing body; and, as I will explain, suggests a heterodox erotic distant from, even predicated upon a refusal of, maternal nurture. This rejection of the fleshly, conventionally womanly body and the traditional notion of the maternal in favor of an eroticized rarefaction of the body that will conduce to visionary consciousness manifests itself not only in *Nights* but also, though less overtly, in several other of H.D.'s texts as well—such as her autobiographical romans à clef HERmione and *Bid Me to Live*. The kind of ascesis implicitly recommended by the geometric body (the process of purification that gives rise to this body receptive to visionary consciousness) is valued not only by H.D. but also by Pound, Lewis, and Vorticism more generally. The geometric body—as displayed in the texts of H.D., Lewis, and Pound—is a Vorticist visionary body.

Moreover, the geometric body H.D. presents in *Nights* has the potential to complicate valuably several dominant critical constructions of H.D.: it can trouble the assumptions and investments that have informed such constructions and that, more generally, have sustained efforts of the past three decades to introduce a greater range of women writers into the modernist canon. Specifically, H.D.'s geometric body necessitates a reconsideration of the accounts of H.D. prevalent in recent critical work that emphasize her supposed endorsement of the maternal childbearing body and her development of what Susan Stanford Friedman terms a "modernist gynopoetic" (*Penelope's Web* 11).[5] As the geometric body indicates, this "gynopoetic," as usually defined within H.D. studies, fails to accommodate the moments of clear ambivalence in H.D.'s texts toward the childbearing body.[6]

The geometric images of *Nights* also suggest the inadequacy of the assumption, also widespread in critical discussion, that H.D.'s use of geometric images necessarily marks her refusals of Vorticism. H.D.'s geometric vocabulary does generally register the qualities of starkness, tension, and energy associated with Vorticism, but it does not always signal a rejection of these. In *Nights*, the way geometric forms are enlisted clearly signals a celebration, albeit a qualified one, of the kind of severity and precisely controlled intense energy endorsed by Vorticism. If H.D. sometimes opposes the values she associates with Vorticism—hardness, mechanization, violence—she does not do so unequivocally. Ultimately, H.D.'s geometric vocabulary, especially as it becomes involved in her constructions of an ideal body, signals neither predominantly condemnation nor celebration, but rather something of both, inscribing a complex ambivalence toward Vorticist principles and all that she associates with them.

As H.D. wrote *Nights*—completing the main text in 1931 and the Prologue in 1934—she was in the midst of confronting both personal and public crises. On the one hand, her psychoanalytic work with Mary Chadwick (1931), Hans Sachs (1931–1932), and Freud (1933–1934) was prompting her to revisit, and to seek to gain command of, many of her traumatic experiences of the years neighboring the First World War. As Rachel Blau DuPlessis summarizes,

> A series of formative tragedies between 1915 and 1919 (as central to H.D. as the terrible chain of family deaths of 1895–1906 were for Woolf) had marked H.D. ... In 1915, there was a stillborn baby .... Her brother Gilbert was killed in action (1918), and her father, precipitously dead in response to that loss (1919). Metaphorically, she lost a husband, for Richard Aldington

"EMBODIED ... IN
SQUARE AND CUBE
AND RECTANGLE"

> and she were permanently estranged .... She lost two male friends, D. H. Lawrence, a "twin brother" with whom she had strong bonds in 1916–1918, and Cecil Gray, the father of Perdita [her baby daughter]. And she almost lost that baby and herself as well, for she was near death-stricken with the influenza (and/or pneumonia) in 1919, just before her daughter's birth in March.
>
> (H.D.: THE CAREER 72)

H.D.'s psychoanalytic work, at its most intense as she was writing *Nights*, brought her into especially direct contact with painful memories of that period. Exacerbating a sense of vulnerability at this point was her growing awareness that a political storm was brewing in Europe and danger imminent. As she would put it in *Tribute to Freud*, between the wars she and her compatriots experienced a "period of waiting" in which they knew that tensions were escalating and the "flood" coming, but remained uncertain about what direction to take in response (57). "We were drifting," she notes (13). Accordingly, the geometric body in *Nights* reads as a response to both the actual political jeopardy she felt building around her community and the personal dangers resurfacing as she engaged in psychoanalytic work—as she tried, once again, to understand the significance of her own chain of misfortunes. The geometric body in *Nights*, I would offer, comes to figure a fantasy of invulnerability; to stand for conditions conducive to a visionary state of consciousness that will, in turn, transcend forms of personal and political confusion and enable removal from threat. The rhetoric of H.D.'s geometric body is directed especially toward the concept of childbearing, constructing a bodily state that surpasses the act of having anyone's child. In H.D.'s lexicon, childbearing represents a kind of vulnerability peculiar to women, an exposed position that H.D.'s Natalia seeks to evade.

Most immediately, then, it is in response to conditions of the 1930s that H.D. enlists a Vorticist geometric vocabulary. But the fantasy of the geometric body, in *Nights* and elsewhere, bears significance beyond that which it carries in the context of her project of replying to political and personal threat. The end of this chapter will address how, apart from the function it serves in H.D.'s own narrative of self-protection and attempted transcendence, the geometric body offers possibilities for feminist emancipation.

"THIS
DIFFICULT PIECE
OF WRITING":
THE CRITICAL
NEGLECT OF
NIGHTS

The very availability of *Nights* in published form today attests to the radical changes H.D.'s reputation has undergone since her death in 1961. The past thirty years have witnessed a committed effort to recuperate H.D. from a marginalized position within the modernist canon, establish her crucial place within modernism, and enrich awareness of the range of her work. Thanks to the pioneering scholarship of such critics as Susan Stanford Friedman, Alicia Ostriker, Albert Gelpi, and Rachel Blau DuPlessis, H.D. is now recognized not only for her early Imagist poetry but also for her epic poems of the 1940s and 1950s, her prose fiction, and her memoirs. Growing recognition of her importance has spurred new editions of her work, much of it hitherto unpublished, and much of it her prose.[7] The cluster of new publications of the last twenty years includes *Nights*, reissued by New Directions in 1986, which until then had remained largely unknown after its first publication in 1935. Especially given the wealth of new material from H.D. now available, the moment is ripe for reflection about what the last few decades of critical labor on H.D.'s work has yielded (Spoo, "H.D. Prosed" 202). Now that H.D. criticism of the 1980s and 1990s has rightly liberated H.D. from the confines of her identity as an Imagist, we need to question the boundaries established by the very critical interventions that have revised and enhanced interpretation of her work. Although unquestionably H.D.'s canonization over the past two decades is both a major achievement and a just one, it has sometimes been accomplished at the expense of a robust understanding of her work.

Despite the wealth of critical attention devoted to H.D. over the last few decades, notably little has focused on *Nights*.[8] *Nights* may have been overlooked partly because it was only reissued recently—in 1986—but this cannot be the sole reason for its comparative neglect. Several of H.D.'s works published, or reissued, more recently—such as *Asphodel* (1992) and *Paint It Today* (1992)—have drawn much more notice than *Nights*. In the few scholarly accounts that do address the group of novels to which *Nights* belongs, commentary on it has often been cursory, suggesting a reluctance born of discomfort. DuPlessis, for example, begins a chapter that promises to survey H.D.'s prose of the 1920s and 1930s, then largely evades the group of works that includes *Nights*, confining her remarks to brief notes on their connection to cinema. She underscores that

"EMBODIED . . . IN
SQUARE AND CUBE
AND RECTANGLE"

H.D.'s other prose of the period is "more important" than the group to which *Nights* belongs (*H.D.: The Career* 60).⁹

Nights, this "difficult piece of writing" (*Nights* 28), has been passed by, I would argue, because it displays dimensions of H.D.'s work and thought not easily assimilable to many currently salient critical narratives about H.D.'s oeuvre, dimensions that can productively resist assumptions founding many claims about H.D.'s success as a feminist artist. The geometric body in *Nights* implies a valorization of qualities and desires usually assumed to be those that H.D., as a feminist artist, rejects. I read H.D. as both a feminist and a successful artist; what *Nights* and its notion of the geometric body invite us to reconsider are the terms on which H.D. has been constructed as such—terms which, in turn, have often led to critical neglect of crucial aspects of her work.

Critical recuperation of H.D.'s work has often fostered an emphasis on her distinctively female voice, a "gynopoetic," "anchored in the maternal" (Friedman, *Penelope's Web* 11), that "directly writes the female body, female desire" (9). More recently, related claims have characterized her work as displaying an *écriture féminine* and a Kristevan semiotic force.¹⁰ It is largely thanks to such readings that emphasize the "feminine" in H.D.'s writing that, over the past twenty years, the importance and subversive power of H.D.'s work have been established. A text like *Nights*, however, prompts reevaluation of such readings—of both the reasons for them and their ramifications.

In Friedman's view, the gynopoetic is most evident in H.D. prose, begun in the 1920s out of an effort to escape the limits constraining her in the 1910s, when she primarily wrote verse and worked under the tutelage of male mentors such as Pound and Lawrence. H.D. developed her gynopoetic by writing "female desire": as Friedman notes, "Some fifty years before Hélène Cixous and Luce Irigaray called for an *écriture féminine*, H.D. forged a prose discourse that wrote the female body" (*Penelope's Web* 11). For Friedman, H.D.'s prose, unlike her early verse, displays a "language of excess, of plenitude," of "feminine fluidity" (6). Moreover, H.D.'s writing is "anchored in the maternal" (11): in Friedman's account, the "female body" usually suggests the maternal body. Finally, in creating her gynopoetic, H.D. is said to have developed a modernistic practice considerably different from the work of her male modernist contemporaries.

As Susan Edmunds notes, such arguments are characteristic of the strong wave of Anglo-American feminist criticism that brought H.D.'s work to prominence in the 1970s and 1980s (*Out of Line* 3). Even in an era of poststructuralist feminist work—which, in building upon earlier feminist work, has challenged many of its assumptions (questioning, for instance, the possibility of achieving an "authentic female voice")—Friedman's argument that H.D.'s prose illustrates a gynopoetic that "writes the female body" remains influential.[11] The notion of H.D.'s gynopoetics, however, can easily accommodate neither the geometric body nor the relationship to Vorticist ideals it suggests. Nor does it consider sufficiently the affinity between H.D.'s work and that of her male compatriots. Whereas at times during her career H.D. clearly did seek to distinguish herself from, even challenge, her male contemporaries, what her geometric body illuminates is that long after Imagism and her novitiate of the 1910s, H.D. was at times producing claims and subscribing to values clearly akin to those of Pound and Lewis.[12] As Michael Kaufmann laments, the widespread "perceived need" in criticism to "define the work of female modernists as strictly countering that of male modernists ... sometimes obscures women writers' contributions to modernism—if their contribution happens to be what some consider a masculinist version of modernism" ("Gendering Modernism" 59).[13] Here, because of the values that inform it, the geometric body indeed might be regarded, albeit problematically, as belonging to a "masculinist" project. At the close of this chapter, I will turn again to the issue of how H.D.'s geometric body might trouble received ideas, ensconced in criticism, about how to read H.D.'s relationship to her male contemporaries.

VORTICIST GEO-METRICIZATIONS OF THE BODY

H.D.'s use of a vocabulary of "square and cube and rectangle" in 1935 to imagine a transfigured human body reinscribes a practice common to artists associated with Vorticism twenty years before—and, specifically, participates in the dichotomy between the "abstract" and the "organic" prevalent in discourse of the 1910s. In his 1914 lecture "Modern Art and Its Philosophy," critic T. E. Hulme noted among contemporary artists of the time the widespread tendency to depict the body geometrically. In this address, Hulme emphasized the work of Wyndham Lewis and sculptor Jacob Epstein, both closely associated with Vorticism, as his chief examples of this phenomenon. Although Hulme turned away from his association with the Vorticists as they launched *Blast*, before this he had been intimately connected with the artists of the Vorticist circle: during the *avant-guerre* years he had been a chief exponent of their views, grounding many of his claims about modern art in their work (see Introduction).[14]

In his lecture, as he addresses modern art—the most progressive of which is, for him, strongly geometric, proto-Vorticist art—Hulme uses as his point of departure the opposition between the realms of the "abstract" and the "organ-

"EMBODIED ... IN SQUARE AND CUBE AND RECTANGLE"

ic." These are the categories, central to Worringer's *Abstraction and Empathy* (1908), into which, for Hulme, geometry and the human body fall, respectively. Hulme wonders why artists so evidently committed to geometric shapes bother to include the body at all.[15] "Why make use of the human body in this art," he asks (*Speculations* 105), if it is so clearly inimical to what he calls the "geometrical character" (81) of their modern work? Why include the body—and make it "look like a machine?" (105–106):

> Take for example one of Mr. Wyndham Lewis's pictures. It is obvious that the artist's only interest in the human body was in a few abstract mechanical relations perceived in it.... The interest in living flesh as such... is entirely absent. (106)

Hulme notes that rather than show an "interest" in "living flesh as such," artists who produce "geometrical art" want to "translate" flesh—i.e., what is "changing and limited," frail and mortal—into something "unlimited and necessary" (106), to transmute the "organic" into something "hard and durable" (107). Modern artists such as Lewis focus on the body, he suggests, because the desire for abstraction is best fulfilled when a nonabstract object (one that is "organic"), such as the human body, is subjected to the process of abstraction:

> [T]he desire for abstraction ... cannot be satisfied with the reproduction of merely inorganic forms. A perfect cube looks stable in comparison to the flux of appearance, but one might be pardoned if one felt no particular interest in the eternity of a cube; but if you can put man in some geometrical shape which lifts him out of the transience of the organic, then the matter is different. (106–107)

Although Hulme does not explain exactly why the "matter" is "different," presumably transmuting the organic human body into geometric shapes can better satisfy the "desire for abstraction" because it involves displaying the deliverance of something clearly "organic" from its inherent "transience." As the philosopher José Ortega y Gasset (who, like Hulme, had studied in Germany as the ideas of Worringer were circulating) would describe such a representation of the process of transformation in "The Dehumanization of Art":

> The question is not to paint something altogether different from a man, a house, a mountain, but to paint a man who resembles a man as little as possible; a house that preserves of a house exactly what is needed to reveal the metamorphosis; a cone miraculously emerging—as the snake from his slough—from what used to be a mountain. (22–23)

Some of the best demonstrations of such a satisfying "metamorphosis," Hulme suggests, are provided by sculptor Jacob Epstein's geometricizations of the process of birth:

> The tendency to abstraction, the desire to turn the organic into something hard and durable, is here at work, not on something simple .... Abstraction [here] is much greater ... because generation, which is the very essence of all qualities which we have here called organic, has been turned into something as hard and durable as a geometrical figure itself.
>
> (*SPECULATIONS* 107)

The greater the degree of "the organic" present in the thing to be transformed, then, the more change evident in the process displayed and the more satisfying the "metamorphosis."[16]

Hulme's hypothesis about the goal of the process of abstraction represented by geometric figures—that it aims to transform the organic into that which is "hard and durable"—is both problematic and valuably insightful. On the one hand, as suggested by the work of Lewis, Pound, and H.D., geometricization is not always employed as part of an effort toward durability or eternity. But Hulme highlights important questions here: Why include the body at all in a geometric project? Why geometricize the body? What is at stake?

Hulme observes of Lewis's work that "the interest in living flesh as such ... is

"EMBODIED ... IN
SQUARE AND CUBE
AND RECTANGLE"

entirely absent"; in *Blast*, Wyndham Lewis's editorial voice supports this view by declaring that in this Vorticist era "THE ACTUAL HUMAN BODY BECOMES OF LESS IMPORTANCE EVERY DAY" (*B1* 141). Yet given the heavy irony pervading *Blast*, we cannot take such pronouncements at face value. Moreover, as Hulme himself demonstrates, the attention devoted to the "ACTUAL HUMAN BODY" in Lewis's and other Vorticist work reveals, on the contrary, that the body possesses great importance for Vorticism. Vorticism in fact displays a preoccupation with the body: a need to exhibit the body and act upon it, to transform it toward states of being represented either by geometric figures per se or by qualities linked to geometry through metonymic chains of signifiers.

Hulme also implies that it is a dislike of the body that prompts the Vorticist effort to make the body "look like a machine." I would offer, however, that the desire on the part of Vorticist artists such as Lewis to transform the body does not entail the disgust for the body's vulnerability or transience that Hulme's statements, as well many critical commentaries about the moderns more generally, tend to imply.[17] Coexisting with the desire to reform the body geometrically is not only a fascination with it, but also an admiration for its wild potency.[18] If, in their desire to geometricize the body, these writers display an Aristotelian desire to impose a *schema* upon the untamed *hule*, a geometric form upon body-as-matter, they do not accordingly disparage the bodily matter as mere potential awaiting actuation; rather, they regard the body as an indispensable element of the process toward revelation.[19] They treat the body as what Caroline Walker Bynum, discussing medieval attitudes toward the body, calls a "locus of redemption" ("Why All the Fuss" 15), inscribing the terms of that redemption in the language of geometry. Bynum might well be referring to the moderns when she notes of the medieval period that the "extravagant attention to flesh" suggests not so much a "flight from" as a "submersion in" the material of the body (14–15).

What Pound, Lewis, and H.D. share in their treatments of the body is not only a bent for the geometricization of the body, but also a specific desire expressed through that geometricization: to play out on the site of the body a constellation of values endorsed by Vorticist thought. All three writers imagine and celebrate a body that encodes a desire to transform the body, discipline and refine it away from heavy corporeality into something ethereal, rare, and strange that can foster transcendent awareness. The geometric body in all three indicates an investment in a kind of "ascesis" that Eileen Gregory identifies as one of H.D.'s leading ideas, drawn from Walter Pater's Dorian Hellenism: this Paterian ascesis is achieved by disciplining the corporeal body into a purer, etherealized condition "susceptible to visionary epiphany" (*H.D. and Hellenism* 86).

Using terms like those of *Blast*, Lewis, Pound, and H.D. posit an ideal body that is "tense" (*B2* 43), "hard," "exquisite" ("The Meaning of the Wild Body" 58), dynamic, and rarefied into currents of energy. They register a desire to transform the ordinary body by subjecting it to a "sternness" and "severity" (as Lewis puts it) associated with Vorticism (*WLOA* 342). And for all three, such transformative subjection involves the erotic arousal of the body. Where Lewis, Pound, and H.D. part ways somewhat is in the slightly different, although clearly related, strategies they recommend for attaining the requisite discipline. For Pound, it is accomplished through restraint and moderate, controlled eroticism; for Lewis, through physical, often eroticized, violence, and for H.D., through highly intense, often violent erotic experience. Furthermore, although all three use a geometric vocabulary to represent the body transfigured by discipline, each assigns to the geometric idiom a slightly different semiotic valence.

The desire expressed in Lewis's, Pound's, and H.D.'s work to transmute the ordinary physical body into a rarer, more etherealized form notably resembles the process associated with the mystical "subtle body" theorized by Neoplatonic and Gnostic thinkers and associated with astrology and alchemy. Many of the moderns would have had access to the concept through the descriptions of Theosophist G. R. S. Mead, who invoked the idea both in his articles of the 1910s and in *The Doctrine of the Subtle Body in Western Tradition* (1919). According to Mead, the "subtle body" is a "corporeal" but "invisible" and "ethereal" body, attached to the ordinary physical body (the "hylic" body) at one point near the head. The task of the mystic initiate undergoing a process of *palingenesis*, or mystical rebirth, as Tryphonopoulos glosses it, is to achieve a progression that leads from "hylic" to the "subtle" body (*Celestial Tradition* 172–173).

Pound was certainly influenced by Mead's account of Alexandrian "psychophysiology," and H.D. likely absorbed some of Mead's thought through both Pound and her own reading, but it is doubtful that Lewis had any contact with either Mead or the "subtle body." Nonetheless, all three writers are guided by an ideal of a "radiant" and "luminescent" body (Tryphonopoulos, *Celestial Tradition* 172). Moreover, in the way they imagine both the ideal body and the discipline required to achieve it, all three evince values that resonate with those of Vorticism. In imagining the ideal body as geometric and possessing those qualities of dynamism and stark precision valorized by Vorticism, as well as in suggesting that the "etherealized" bodily state is arrived at through pressure and severe discipline, all three writers move the concept of a "subtle body" in a Vorticist direction.[20]

H.D.'s project differs most significantly from Pound's and Lewis's in that her effort to refine the body away from "gross" corporeality registers an unease specifically with the heavy childbearing body. Lewis and Pound likewise turn

"EMBODIED . . . IN
SQUARE AND CUBE
AND RECTANGLE"

away from the contours of the female body as it is traditionally imagined, largely by excluding the female body from their visions, but, in contrast, H.D. encompasses the female body within her picture, summoning it as a specter toward which she directs a focused and insistent ambivalence.

POUND'S AND LEWIS'S VORTICIST BODIES

En route to a discussion of H.D.'s geometric bodies, I will turn to Pound's and Lewis's ideals of the pure geometric body to establish coordinates for positioning H.D.'s similar ideals. In "Cavalcanti" (1934), Pound explicitly invokes the term "geometry" in connection with the notion of embodiment as he praises the medieval Tuscan poets for their sane and balanced attitudes toward the body.[21] In Pound's view, the wisdom of medieval Italians such as Cavalcanti, poetic and otherwise, derives from their rejection of "idiotic asceticism and a belief that the body is evil" (150) and, more specifically, from their ability to achieve mystical visionary states through controlled sensual and sexual activity.[22] Pound prizes such control because it involves neither indulgence nor celibate asceticism, but rather, as he put it in "Psychology and Troubadours," "refinement of, and lordship over, the senses" (*Spirit of Romance* 90). Pound's advocacy of moderation, delay, and restraint in one's relationship to the body amounts to the endorsement of a form of discipline—often a discipline arrived at through careful sexual engagement and subtle management of sensual experience—that keeps the individual to the via media between repudiation of the flesh and surrender to it.

In "Cavalcanti," Pound goes on to link this ability to inhabit the body properly to *geometry*. This he does by associating the medieval poets' healthy relationship to the body with two other capabilities: the capacity to discern forms in the material world and the ability to produce a "clean line." Emerging from the medieval philosopher's sanity about the body and the material world, Pound suggests, was his ability to perceive in his surroundings a "world of forms": every plant, every air current, would prompt in him an awareness of forms ("Cavalcanti" 155). Pound laments that we no longer possess such an ability. "We appear," he notes elegiacally, "to have lost the radiant world where one thought cuts through another with a clean edge, a world of moving energies . . . magnetisms that take form, that are seen, that border on the visible" (154). Perhaps, he suggests, the "algebra" of the modern world "has queered our geometry" (155).[23]

In this text, Pound uses "geometry" to stand for two abilities simultaneously: the ability to relate to the physical world with a salutary stance midway between detachment and engagement, and another ability arising from this one: of ascertaining form. Inhabiting one's body so that one neither renounces physical sensation nor completely capitulates to it renders one sensitive to the "world of forms"—forms seen at their purest, when they possess a geometric simplicity, when their shapes possess a "clean edge." When one enters this subtle bodily state that fosters the capacity for vision (for Pound, a state of mystical awareness), "The senses . . . seem to project for a few yards beyond the body," making the body a "perfect instrument of the increasing intelligence." The "nerve-set" of the body is "open" to "tune in" to the "ambience" of one's surroundings (152). Transformed into a conductor, the body in this state is no longer merely physical, but also "animate," active, and radiant. In such a condition, the body's own "shape" simply "occurs" because the body is easily able to manifest currents of force traveling through it (152).

Pound thus associates this ideal bodily state with geometry because it transforms the individual's body into a condition in which its own form becomes evident and in which the individual's sensitivity to the forms of other bodies increases. In part, Pound uses the notion of geometry to express this because for him the geometric figure, as he has come to understand it through his work with Vorticism, emblematizes the ability to understand and represent form—the "form sense" (GK 134). One further reason for Pound's assertion that the medieval Italian poets possessed a geometry that latter-day readers no longer have is that, for Pound, their bodily sanity correlated with the ability to produce a "clean line," the capacity to represent forms at their purest. How individuals inhabit their bodies, in other words, governs not only their perspective on the world and their ability to recognize forms, but also their capacity to depict the forms that they perceive. And for Pound, such a facility results in the production of forms that are graceful and elegant. Conversely, the ascetic belief that the "body is evil" is always, he says, "accompanied by bad or niggled sculpture"—by the production of shapes that are "bulging and bumping and indulging in bulbous excrescence" (150–151).[24]

In his edition of Pound's *Literary Essays*, T. S. Eliot dates "Cavalcanti" as "1910–1931," suggesting that the ideas in this essay are ones that Pound has been working with since publishing *The Spirit of Romance* in 1910; indeed, for years, Pound's thought has been traveling, and evolving, along such clean lines. For an indication of how Pound was conceiving of the relationship between geometry and the body just after the Vorticist heyday, for example, we can look to his 1918 review of Vorticist sculptor Gaudier-Brzeska's "Red Stone Dancer"

"EMBODIED . . . IN
SQUARE AND CUBE
AND RECTANGLE"

(1913). Here, too, Pound links geometry with the idea of "pure form." Meditating on the significance of Gaudier-Brzeska's having marked the body of his sculpture geometrically, Pound remarks that the sculpture "is almost a thesis of [Gaudier-Brzeska's] ideas upon the use of pure form":

> We have the triangle and circle asserted, *labled* [sic] almost, upon the face and right breast. Into these so-called "abstractions" life flows, the circle moves and elongates into the oval, it increases and takes volume in the sphere or hemisphere of the breast. The triangle moves toward organism it [sic] becomes a spherical triangle (the central life-form common to both Brzeska and Lewis) . . . . The "abstract" or mathematical bareness of the triangle and circle are fully incarnate, made flesh, full of vitality and of energy.
>
> (G-B 137–138; POUND'S ITALICS)

Framing this comment with expressions of his admiration for Gaudier-Brzeska's work, Pound thus celebrates the sculptor's ability to achieve a balance between geometry and "flesh" (here again is the opposition between the geometrically abstract and the organic); in so doing, he implies both what geometry can accomplish and what it potentially sacrifices. Pound suggests that geometry registers the artist's capacity to abstract from raw material its central forms—in Pound's view an ability requisite to artistic success. Ideally, however, this activity of abstraction will be combined with the ability to invest the sculpture with sufficient vitality and fleshliness to save it from "mathematical bareness" (138) or, as Pound puts it in "Cavalcanti," the "devastated terms of abstraction" (151).[25] As in "Cavalcanti," here Pound prefers that recognition and representation of form be tempered by attention to the "flesh" and "vitality" that extreme geometric abstraction may endanger. In the 1918 essay, then, geometry stands for the ability to recognize forms, which brings with it the risk of "mathematical bareness"; whereas later, in "Cavalcanti," the referent for "geometry" per se has shifted slightly, signifying Pound's desired balance between appreciation of abstract form and appreciation of flesh.

As earlier work attests, the abilities for which Pound praises both Gaudier-Brzeska and the medieval poets he admires are those he associates with Vorticism more generally. In 1915, Pound initially celebrated Vorticism for having awakened him to "new and swift perceptions of forms" and "new ways of seeing" form: Vorticism gave him new "ways of seeing the shape of the sky as it juts down between the houses. The tangle of telegraph wires is conceivable not merely as a repetition of lines; one sees the shapes defined by the different branches of the wire" ("Affirmations II" 278). In the early 1930s, Pound continued to invoke Lewis, Gaudier-Brzeska, and Epstein—for him, all integral members of the Vorticist project—as exemplars of artists who exhibit the eminently desirable "form-sense" (*GK* 134). "[F]ew plastic artists have been strong enough to depend on form alone, dispensing with the stimulus or support of a literary content," such that their work stands or falls on the basis of the effectiveness of its formal composition (*P&P* 5:217). "In England," Pound says, "the courage" to rely on form only "reached its known maximum in the period 1911 to 1914 as shown in the work of Wyndham Lewis, Gaudier, and in a few works of Epstein" (217). If, in Pound's view, the "form-sense" is not exclusively Vorticist, Vorticism nonetheless remains its locus classicus.

For Pound, then, the concept of geometry signifies a balanced, healthy, disciplined attitude toward both one's body and the physical world, an attitude that enables one to discern and portray the forms of the physical world underlying its surface appearances. And this attitude, successfully maintained by the medieval troubadours, has been quintessentially manifested in the twentieth century by the Vorticists.

Early in his career, in a piece for the *New Age*, "Our Wild Body" (1910), Wyndham Lewis issues a call for a healthy acceptance of the body, one similar to Pound's in several significant respects. Lewis does not suggest that such acceptance can lead to the "conception of the body as perfect instrument of the increasing intelligence" ("Cavalcanti" 152), but like Pound he deplores what he perceives as a "vast Anglo-Saxon conspiracy against the body": the way that the British, out of somatophobia, subject their bodies to intense discipline, attempting to "drown," "daunt," and "tame" them. As a model of a "first step" ("Our Wild Body" 10) the English might take to correct this state of affairs, Lewis recommends the open and candid French attitude toward the body. He urges recognition of the body as, far from eroding dignity, in fact fostering dignity if regarded and treated in a healthy manner. He advocates moving away from the bodily contact afforded by the carefully regulated games of English sport and toward more instinctual engagement between bodies. If two men do not agree, rather than skirmish according to the artificial "Queensberry rules" designed to palliate and contain bodily force, they should instead surrender to the sheer desire to fight in all its wildness (9).

"EMBODIED . . . IN SQUARE AND CUBE AND RECTANGLE"

This endorsement of open, instinctive fighting reappears in several of Lewis's fictional texts of this early period; he will convey it implicitly through staged fights between male characters in texts such as *Enemy of the Stars* (see Chapter 1) and his novel *Tarr*. Although in "Our Wild Body" Lewis predicates his advocacy of fighting on a rejection of what he calls "discipline" of the body—discipline, as he construes it here, that emerges from unhealthy skittishness and prevents true connection with the body—his narration of these fights in his fiction in fact indicates a desire to discipline the body in ways other than the ways the English usually do. Lewis's textual fights, although they in many ways play out the desires expressed in "Our Wild Body," in fact come to exhibit much more furious violence than the gentle picture of "roll[ing] around a bit" (9) and "occasional good honest fighting" (10) suggested in the 1910 essay. This violence, which so exceeds the congenial descriptions of 1910, suggests that as Lewis's thought about the body and its wild potency evolved, he desired the fighting body not only to be open to its instincts, but even ultimately to be purified by forms of physical impact, even punishment.

Furthermore, as his fictional scenes imply, for Lewis, combat between men involves a markedly erotic component. In this way, the program Lewis suggests through his fiction for expression of what he calls the "wild body" (in contrast to that which he outlines in "Our Wild Body") coincides with Pound's notion of purification of the body by way of forms of erotic engagement. But unlike Pound, who focuses exclusively on male-female erotic interaction, Lewis pictures men with men, and unlike Pound's, Lewis's erotic scenes generally involve overt violence.

As Lewis developed a more fully articulated set of views about the body during the 1910s and 1920s, he rejected the possibility advanced in "Our Wild Body" that people can achieve harmony with their bodies by removing the barriers of "sham and conventional" perspectives that they have "interpos[ed]" between themselves and their bodies (9). Instead, he posits as fundamental to human existence an inexorable divide between the consciousness of an individual and his body; Lewis in fact suggests that this necessary "detachment" from our bodies constitutes the wellspring of comedy.[26] Remaining consistent during this shift in his thinking about the body, however, was Lewis's admiration for the body's wild potency, as evidenced in the lavish textual attention he devotes to it in his fiction. It is this veneration for the body's power, I would argue, that engenders the desire for violent discipline of the body inscribed in his texts. As displayed in fictions such as *Enemy of the Stars* and *Tarr*, Lewis's desired severity toward the body pushes the notion of discipline from Pound's realm of self-control into the territory of physical violence. Lewis imagines the achievement of a purified body—one capable of extraordinarily heightened perceptiveness—in a context of violent combat rather than, as Pound does, in a climate of moderation, subtlety, and restraint.

Unlike Pound, Lewis does not explicitly link the term "geometry" to his desired state for the body. Lewis's early Vorticist visual art often portrays the body by way of geometric figures, yet Lewis does not directly code his geometrics as inscribing a desire for eroticized violence upon the body. However, the scenes in which he presents male bodies subjected to eroticized violence are so often conspicuously framed by visually geometricized bodies—as in the pages of *Blast*—that the contiguity implies an association between such violence and geometry, and thus between geometry and the process whereby the body is purified by the experience of physical aggression.

Further, as Chapter 1 addresses in detail, *Blast* has coded geometric forms as signaling aggressive "vivid and violent" forces (*B1* 7). Lewis makes most evident the association between violence and his geometrics through his remarks in *Blast 1* about the Futurist painter Giacomo Balla. Although, as usual, decrying Futurism, Lewis distinguishes Balla from the other Futurists and suggests that the others should follow his example: "Cannot Marinetti . . . be induced to throw over this sentimental rubbish about Automobiles and Aeroplanes, and follow his friend Balla into a purer region of art?" (*B1* 144). Lewis characterizes Balla as not a "'Futurist' in the Automobilist sense" but instead as a "rather violent and geometric sort of Expressionist." Lewis does not directly say here that Balla is "violent" *because* he employs geometrics—correlation is not causation—but he nonetheless implies a linkage here between the "violent" and the "geometric": the purity of Balla's abstraction (his commitment to abstraction is signaled by the word "geometric") is presumably connected to a violence of attitude that enables him to escape unwelcome "Automobilist" sentimentality (144). The linkage is in fact not only between violence and geometry, but also among violence, geometry, and purity, as Lewis often links geometry with purity. Geometric abstraction here ushers one into a "purer region of art"; accordingly, the further implication here is that violence can foster purity.[27]

Given such linkages between violence and geometry, when we encounter scenes of eroticized violence in the context of Lewis's Vorticist work, we are likely concomitantly to imagine geometric images. Specifically, as the infliction of bodily aggression comes to be linked in Lewis's texts both with the process of purifying the body itself and with a more general purification of one's condition of being, his geometric idiom, itself also associated with purity, comes to suggest emancipation and progress toward health—ironically, health achieved through the impact of eroticized aggression. In *Enemy of the Stars*, for example, which is conspicuously placed in *Blast* among paintings that geometricize the body, Lewis presents bodily violence as enabling such desirable purification.

Arghol and Hanp, doubles linked in a subtly eroticized dyad of identification and opposition, consummate their anger toward each other in a frenzied battle. Textual signals preceding their conflict have invited us to appreciate the mad violence of the stars in the text, such that when combat between Arghol and Hanp involves a similar violence, we are apt likewise to admire it:

> The sky, two clouds, their two furious shadows, fought.
>
> The bleak misty hospital of the horizon grew pale with fluid of anger.
>
> The trees were wiped out in a blow.
>
> The hut became a new boat inebriated with electric milky human passion . . .
>
> First they hit each other . . .
>
> Soul perched like aviator in basin of skull, more alert . . . than on any other occasion. Mask stoic with energy: thought cleaned off slick—pure and clean with action.
>
> Bodies grown brain, black octopi.
>
> Flushes on silk epiderm and fierce card-play of fists . . .
>
> Arms of grey windmills, grinding anger on stone of the new heart . . .
>
> The attacker rushed in drunk with blows.
>
> (B1 75)

Clearly, this scene displays near-erotic intoxication (Arghol and Hanp are "inebriated with . . . passion," "drunk with blows") and purification by violence ("grinding anger" and "fierce card-play of fists" correlate with a "new heart"; "Thought" is "cleaned off slick" in this battle to become "pure and clean with action," possessing the purity of a "stoic"). Especially significant here is that the furious battle rarefies Arghol's and Hanp's bodies into "brain" so that the bodiless "soul" perches in a condition of abnormally heightened mental awareness ("more alert . . . than on any other occasion") (*B1* 75). Given the scene's strategic placement at a point at which we desire respite from the tension accumulated between Arghol and Hanp, we are likely to welcome the violence, relieved that the storm has finally broken. Both the scene's diction and its location suggest the desirability of what it enacts: a ritual purification and bodily transformation achieved by way of eroticized bodily violence.

In Lewis's roughly contemporaneous novel *Tarr*, the duel between the characters of Kreisler and Soltyk displays a similarly eroticized battle. Kreisler, ostensibly fighting Soltyk to avenge an insult born of their common desire for Anastasya Vasek, instead seems more governed by an inscrutable desire to engage in violence with another man. Lewis's comments from "Our Wild Body" seem apropos here: "A man driven . . . to strike another, often . . . at the contact of his victim's nose or chin . . . realises the futility of the pretext that had led to the struggle" (9)—that is, realizes the inadequacy of the putative reason for the fight as well as the existence of an ulterior motive: an instinctive desire for physical contact with another.

At this point in the novel, it is already apparent that Kreisler is suicidal and that his erotic passions, notably cruel, generally lead to self-sabotage. His sadistic erotic drive is evident as he stands before Soltyk.[28] Ready to duel Soltyk, having hitherto hated him viciously, Kreisler feels for his rival a sudden access of "love":

> A cruel and fierce sensation of mixed origin rose hotly round his heart. He *loved* that man! But because he loved him he wished to plunge a sword into him, to plunge it in and out and up and down! Why had pistols been chosen? (270)

As the scene develops, Kreisler becomes increasingly ardent, further displaying how his erotic and violent drives intertwine. After what the text describes as "heavy coquetting" (271), he says, "If Herr Soltyk will give me a kiss, I will forego the duel!" (272). Then "Kreisler thrust his mouth forward amorously, his body in the attitude of the eighteenth century gallant, as though Soltyk had been a woman" (272). Of course Kreisler's gesture can be regarded as male bravado designed to humiliate the enemy through irony and effeminization, but it also clearly suggests Kreisler's sadistic homoerotic desire for Soltyk, especially in conjunction with his wish to "plunge a sword into him."

Following Kreisler's overtures, in a scene reminiscent of the battle from *Enemy of the Stars*, Soltyk is galvanized into action:

> His hands were electrified. Will was at last dashed all over him, an arctic douche. The hands flew at Kreisler's throat. His nails made six holes in the flesh and cut into the tendons beneath. Kreisler was hurled about. His hands grabbed a mass of hair .... Then they gripped along the coat sleeves, connecting him with the engine he had just overcharged with fuel. (272–273)

Once again, as in *Enemy of the Stars*, readers are likely on some level to welcome this violent encounter because it discharges the inexplicable anger that Kreisler has harbored and that has impelled him to increasingly drastic action: as he has smoldered, we have waited for relief. The text encourages us to feel release at this juncture through not only its action but also through its diction: we hear that "Will was *at last* dashed all over him," the phrase "at last" suggesting that this is what Kreisler, Soltyk, and we have been waiting for: no matter that it is Soltyk, and not Kreisler, who is jolted into high-intensity action. Moreover, the violence here is certainly associated with purification: the force of "will" pours over Soltyk like an "arctic douche."

Again, however, neither in this novel nor in *Enemy of the Stars* does Lewis ever make explicit the connection between such purgative bodily violence and geometric images; we must infer it from paintings of the immediate context, as in *Blast*, and from what we know of Lewis's work of the period. It is H.D. who will more directly inscribe such violence by way of geometric forms.

Pound's and Lewis's fantasies of the body—conducive not only to efficient action, but also to "alertness" and "intelligence"—can help to locate H.D.'s. Like Pound and Lewis, H.D. imagines and celebrates a body purified, rarefied, and therefore ready to act as an instrument for extraordinary perception and vision. I call this tendency to construct such a body Vorticist because it so clearly plays out Vorticist ideals on the site of the body—Vorticist ideals, that is, of the achievement of purity through the experience of forms of discipline, severity, and intense, active force. In her textual constructions of such a Vorticist visionary body, H.D. oscillates between an advocacy of the "sane" body more like Pound's and an ambivalent desire for a body that more closely resembles Lewis's, a body subjected to eroticized violence.

H.D.'S GEOMETRY

I. "RESPONSIBILITIES"

A rich understanding of the significance of the geometric body in H.D.'s work requires not only awareness of how her contemporaries are using geometric form but also how she employs it elsewhere in her oeuvre. Critical commentary on the meaning H.D. ascribes to geometry often relies on her review of Yeats's *Responsibilities*—thought to have been written about 1916 and unpublished during her lifetime—in which she uses geometric figures to articulate a refusal of the aggression, mechanism, and violence of her generation. Praising Yeats for his "worship of beauty," she aligns herself with the 1890s from which he emerges, regretting that the present generation, "inasmuch as its cubes and angles seem a sort of incantation, a symbol for the forces that brought on this world calamity [the First World War], seems hardly worthy to compare with the nineties in its helpless stand against the evils of ugliness." Artists of the 1890s were superior to her contemporaries, she suggests, because they refused to "fall down before some Juggernaut of planes and angles." Now, with the unfortunate complicity of her generation, "The black magic of triangles and broken arcs has conquered and we who are helpless before this force of destruction can only hope for some more powerful magic . . . to set it right" (53). By twice acknowledging the "helplessness" of her worshippers of beauty in the face of this onslaught of aggression, H.D., as she laments the forces that she reads as having ushered in the Great War, also recognizes their power.

H.D.'s cascade of geometric images here forcefully implies that of the artists of her generation that she addresses, it is specifically the Futurists and Vorticists—both working in a conspicuously geometric idiom and associated with aggression—who, with their "praise" of "guns" and their "love" of the "beauty" of machines, have prepared the way for war. As Burnett rightly notes, for H.D., the "planes" of the "Vorticist canvas"

> echo and support the "aeroplanes" of the war; together, they comprise the "Juggernaut" before which her generation has fallen . . . . [T]he angular abstractions of the Futurists and Vorticists provide her with an aesthetic she can identify as equivalent to the war.
>
> (*BETWEEN IMAGE AND EPIC* 56)

"EMBODIED . . . IN
SQUARE AND CUBE
AND RECTANGLE"

As Burnett points out, the allusions to a geometric idiom and to violence indicate both Futurism and Vorticism, yet given the milieu in which H.D. lived during this period and her personal connections to Pound and Lewis, it was Vorticist art and rhetoric to which she was closest. As a result, whereas her critique of the geometrically abstract aesthetic that both reflects and cooperates with, even perpetuates, the forces that lead to war, encompasses both Vorticist and Futurist aesthetics and their attendant values, it is Vorticism that is especially on display here. In this essay, the geometric idiom, understood through the lens of Vorticism, is indeed portrayed as connoting machinery, violence, and complicity with the group of forces that H.D. here terms the "enemy"—those forces that lead to war—and accordingly vilifies.

We should resist the temptation, however, to read H.D.'s statements in her review of *Responsibilities* as representative of the significance she assigns geometry everywhere or as indicative of her more general relationship to the values associated with Vorticism. In "Responsibilities," H.D. does indeed equate geometry with Vorticism, Vorticism with violence, and rejects all three. By the 1930s, however, in *Nights*, she treats both geometry and violence quite differently. Although she continues to link geometry to the severity and force associated with Vorticism, at times even with violence, in *Nights*, she uses geometry to express a desire, albeit equivocal, for the very values she rejects in "Responsibilities."

II. NOTES ON THOUGHT AND VISION

Further contributing to prevalent assumptions about H.D.'s rejection of Vorticist values is *Notes on Thought and Vision*, H.D.'s essay-*cum*-manifesto from about 1919, a meditation on visionary consciousness developed in a gnomic, Blakean idiom. Unpublished in her lifetime, first published in 1982, it is now often invoked as epitomizing the commitments that funded her creation of a gynopoetic in the 1920s and 1930s. Hollenberg, DuPlessis, and Friedman all construe *Notes* as an early text vital to understanding H.D.'s oeuvre because it articulates many of the feminist ideals that will later become pivotal to her work. It has become customary to position *Notes* as a locus classicus for the modernist gynopoetic assumed crucial to H.D.'s writing: as Kathleen Crown observes, feminist critical work has often "focused on the *Notes* as a modernist poetics that writes the female and maternal body" ("Visible Body" 218).

Moreover, critics such as Burnett and Friedman have read *Notes* as continuing the rejection of geometric values H.D. articulates in "Responsibilities." It is fitting, in fact, that "Responsibilities" and drafts of *Notes* are bound in the same manuscript volume, given the sympathy usually assumed between their attendant value systems.[29] As Friedman characterizes the relationship between the two texts, "The muted gender inflection of H.D.'s modernism" in "Responsibilities" and other reviews is "developed into a full-blown ... gynopoetic in *Notes*" (*Penelope's Web* 9). Many textual signals of *Notes* indeed invite readers to interpret it as a confirmation of H.D.'s rejection of geometry and the violence geometry connotes for her, as well as an affirmation of maternal images that can be read as opposing and erasing both. But although some aspects of *Notes* do indeed contribute to this kind of affirmation, other aspects do otherwise; furthermore, what H.D. suggests in *Notes* does not always coincide with what she suggests elsewhere.

Overtly, H.D.'s manifesto focuses on how to achieve a balanced, healthy body that can foster the achievement of visionary consciousness. The essay's speaker opens with a statement of the interdependence of "body," "mind," and the part of the being capable of visionary knowledge (the "overmind")—and posits an elite of those who can develop all three in concert with one another. "Aim of men and women of highest development," the speaker maintains, is "equilibrium, balance, growth of the three at once" (*Notes* 17). In her opening pages, the speaker makes clear that the body can most readily attain vision when erotically aroused. "All reasoning, normal, sane and balanced men and women need and seek at certain times of their lives, certain definite physical relationships," the speaker contends (17), then explains how erotic experience can promote visionary awareness. Like candidates for initiation into the ancient Greek Eleusinian mysteries, H.D.'s seekers of "over-mind consciousness" must have "healthy bod[ies]" (27) and sufficiently "sensitive, fastidious" attitudes toward sex to capitulate neither to "crude animal enjoyment" nor to "hypocritical aloofness" (29). Sounding much like Pound, H.D. advances a notion of superior consciousness attained through careful, healthy, controlled sensuality and sexuality.

Yet many critics distinguish *Notes* from Pound's work by reading it as articulating not a paean to the body, but rather a tribute particularly to the female body, and even more specifically, to the childbearing body. Indeed the speaker of *Notes* avers that "it was before the birth" of her child that a visionary state first came upon her (20). To capture the experience of visionary moments, H.D.'s speaker uses amniotic images: "jelly-fish," for instance, or a "cap, like water, transparent, fluid yet with definite body" (18–19). As DuPlessis suggests, the speaker in *Notes* celebrates "the advantages of female physicality, of female Otherness" in the quest for "vision" (*H.D.: The Career* 40–41): she offers the possibility of "vision of the womb" (*Notes* 20), an intensified ability to achieve visionary consciousness through the experience of childbearing.

In this context, Friedman's term "gynopoetic" clearly suits many of the rhetorical declarations of *Notes*. Friedman's definition of the term suggests that a text is most "gynocentric" when it celebrates women's bodies and qualities distinctive to those bodies qua childbearing bodies, such as fluidity and viscosity, and when it rejects, conversely, qualities such as those associated with the Vorticists: hardness, geometricity, angularity. Defining "gynopoetic" this way, however, implies several related assumptions about the significance of a geometric idiom: that it belongs in a realm both "masculine" and opposed to the fertility of childbearing and that it is inimical to the creation of a gynopoetic.

Kathleen Crown and Bonnie Kime Scott suggest that such a dichotomy was indeed in currency among H.D.'s contemporaries: amniotic images may well have been read in H.D.'s context as countervailing the significance of Vorticist geometry as developed by Lewis and his cohorts. As Crown notes, for instance, H.D.'s choice during this period to champion the "jelly-fish" and its qualities, given a prevalent public discourse of the time that enlisted the jellyfish as symbol, implicitly suggested her rejection of the value systems demonstrated by Lewis, who uses jellyfish imagery in textual moments that disparage women and the "feminine."[30] In light of the discourse of the time, H.D.'s embrace of the jellyfish image does read as a rebuttal to Lewis's denigration of it — and, accordingly, as both a validation of women and the "feminine" and a repudiation of the geometric language with which Lewis, by 1919, was closely associated.

Although these are unquestionably persuasive readings of *Notes*, the assertions in H.D.'s visionary meditation do not always accord with what other texts in H.D.'s oeuvre suggest. To extrapolate from the statements of this manifesto the notion of a gynopoetic that guides H.D.'s work more generally is mistakenly to assume that her claims here are representative of her views more broadly.[31] The statements of the speaker in *Notes* certainly don't capture, for instance, the values that she implies in *Nights* by way of the geometric body. Even certain moments in *Notes* itself, in fact, diverge in the values they imply from the values H.D. demonstrates throughout much of the text. The more overt aspects of *Notes*, in other words, accented by critics who read the text as offering a gynopoetic, coexist with other dimensions of it that make its valorization of amniotic qualities and women's childbearing bodies more ambiguous than it at first appears.[32]

In his introduction to *Notes on Thought and Vision*, Albert Gelpi observes that in the *Notes* H.D. shows herself "[u]nencumbered by the misogynist phallicism of Pound and Lawrence" (*Notes* 13). In fact, however, the essay conspicuously displays qualities and gestures often associated with what has been termed "misogynist phallicism": *Notes* exhibits much more advocacy of the hard and chiseled images usually linked to "phallicism," and supposedly inimical to the project of celebrating the female body, than the critical picture of *Notes* as an exemplary articulation of H.D.'s gynopoetic will allow.

To avoid both an inaccurate reading of *Notes* as synecdoche for H.D.'s views more generally and a misreading of *Notes* as suggesting an uncomplicated gynopoetic, we need to read the declarations of *Notes* together with those of *Nights*. Containing signals in many ways much like those of *Notes* about the erotic body's capacity for fostering visionary states of consciousness, *Nights* not only reveals a later, different chapter in H.D.'s textual considerations of the erotic visionary body, but also casts into relief some of the little-noticed dimensions of *Notes*. In *Nights*, H.D. reexamines the notion of the conditions necessary for the cultivation of the visionary body, presenting a much starker, and arguably bleaker, picture than she offers in 1919. When read in conjunction with *Notes*, however, *Nights* not only brings out possible motives for and consequences of vision-through-the-body that *Notes* does not consider explicitly, but also highlights aspects of *Notes* that have gone largely unconsidered in the effort to claim the text as a consummate gynopoetic manifesto. *Notes* indeed at moments enshrines the "healthy body," especially the woman's body as a childbearing body, and suggests that this childbearing body affords privileged access to vision. Reading the manifesto in light of *Nights*, however, brings into view the ambivalence toward the childbearing body that *Notes* evinces as well.

NIGHTS

Nights features the story of Natalia Saunderson, whose absent husband, Neil, has gone abroad to engage in amorous dalliances with a group of young male comrades. The action of the narrative consists mainly of Natalia's erotic encounters with David, her young and stable English lover whose sexual prowess assuages her loneliness. As the novella opens, we learn from the narrator of the Prologue, John Helforth, of Natalia's suicide. The narrative that ensues—Natalia's—is thus positioned so as to account for her choice to kill herself, though it ultimately provides only a partially satisfying, ambiguous explanation. Natalia's moments of ecstasy with David are often presented in terms reminiscent of those used to describe visionary experience in *Notes on Thought and Vision*. At one point, after sexual arousal, Natalia describes her feeling by calling herself "holy" and "purified":

> "EMBODIED . . . IN
> SQUARE AND CUBE
> AND RECTANGLE"

> If she were a Christ, she would use, distribute this power; she would think only holy thought; she would be purified like a clod of earth, drawn up into the radiant texture of some fragrant lily. Weren't they all, in their way, experimentalists in this very-vibrant power, this holy radium? (51–52)

Natalia characterizes her transport here in a language of the sacred that recalls the terms H.D.'s speaker uses in *Notes* to imagine the candidates for initiation into the Eleusinian mysteries: although the candidates in *Notes* are clearly mystical seekers, and Natalia's imagined "they" are instead characterized more scientifically as "experimentalists," both strive toward a holy realm.[33] In her discussion of *Nights*, Chisholm underscores the mystical nature of Natalia's "experiments": "*Nights* focuses its psychic research on the perverse eroticism of one woman's mystical ecstasy . . . In content, *Nights* reads like the confessions of ecstatic mystics of the late Middle Ages" (*H.D.'s Freudian Poetics* 82, 83). Further, Chisholm observes, "Natalia describes what Luce Irigaray identifies as a mystic's, or *mystérique*'s, masochistic *jouissance*" (85). Like Pound, H.D. demonstrates a "mediumistic sexuality," a sexuality with an "ability to stimulate visions" (Oderman, *Pound and the Erotic* xi).

Natalia's accounts echo the visionary experiences presented in *Notes* in several other ways as well. In *Notes* the oracular voice pronounces, "The body of a man is a means of approach . . . to ecstasy" (46). In *Nights*, Natalia positions "the body of a man" similarly when she realizes that David and Neil were "bridges, they led her to her dream, they were the rainbow arch" (87). The speaker of *Notes* contends that "[M]y line of approach [i.e., to "over-world consciousness"], my sign-posts, are not your sign-posts" (24). Natalia likewise asserts that "Each must find his own high-road to deity" (*Nights* 52). In *Notes*, the voice speaks of receiving quasi-electrical impulses from beautiful objects: "If we had the right sort of brains, we would receive a definite message from that figure, like dots and lines ticked off by one receiving station, received and translated into definite thought by another telegraphic centre" (26). Natalia, too, describes her communication with David in terms of signals and transmission: "She could not explain that it was a thing between them, the wire he was, the wire she was, the positive and the negative . . . nor discuss it in electrons" (*Nights* 86).

Finally, *Notes* maintains that "the body . . . like . . . coal, fulfills its highest function when it is being consumed" (47), suggesting through delicate textual linkages that such "burning" can occur through sexual interaction. In *Nights*, burning, sexual arousal, and vision are likewise associated. We hear from John Helforth, the figure who narrates the Prologue, that Natalia had said of her manuscript (her comment, he says, "slightly savouring of Saint Paul"): "'but better burn'" (4). Literally, of course, Natalia wants to burn her manuscript. But by recalling for us Paul's injunction from I Corinthians 7:9—"It is better to marry than to burn"—Helforth reveals Natalia's permutation of the Pauline pronouncement. For Natalia, it is better to burn, sexually, in order to attain a visionary state: she advocates achieving spiritual ecstasy not through the repudiation of desire but rather through surrender to it.

Thus both *Notes* and *Nights* demonstrate a visionary eroticism, staging similar processes of achieving visionary consciousness by way of the sexually aroused body. In *Nights*, scenes of erotic transport apparently evoke an erotic atmosphere much different from the one conjured by the "healthy bodies," "jelly-fish," and "vision of the womb" of *Notes*. As I will discuss later in the chapter, however, the atmospheres of the two texts are not so unalike as they might at first seem.

To understand the implications of geometry's being enlisted in *Nights* to describe states of erotic arousal, as well as the implications of Natalia's wanting to be "embodied" in "square and cube and rectangle," what needs to be considered is the way the signifier of geometry gradually accrues associations and significances throughout *Nights*—and, accordingly, how it functions in the text. H.D.'s character John Helforth (a friend of Natalia's sister-in-law Renne whom Renne asks to write the "Prologue" to Natalia's "Nights") initially uses geometric terms to signal Natalia's ongoing quest for truth and a severe beauty of maximum intensity. Natalia's effort to "have the peak or nothing" (7), he recounts, she pursued through both "fervid" writing and "erotic experiments" (4). He describes Natalia's suicide by drowning in geometric terms: Natalia's skates inscribed on the ice two "very straight lines . . . The two lines ran straight out, two parallel lines—they met in a dark gash of the luminous ice-surface" (45).

This geometric image recurs insistently throughout his Prologue: "She drove two straight lines to infinity and she got her answer" (6). By calling her death an "answer," Helforth subtly implies that Natalia's suicide, rather than derailing her effort, in fact culminated her search for intense beauty. Although displaying ambivalence throughout the Prologue about everything Natalia did and was, here he expresses admiration for the way she completed her quest, got her "answer" (6), as he and others like Renne cannot: "Only Natalia had the courage to cut two straight lines, on a flat surface of an Alpine lake, running to infinity" (10). The geometric image of the parallel lines thus comes to be semantically linked not only to Natalia's death, but also to her whole active effort toward attaining the most intense states of consciousness—linked to the "erotic experiments" and feverish writing through which she strives to fulfill her desires.

As the text unfolds, geometry comes to be associated with a cluster of other signifiers that also come to express the realm of extremity for which Natalia yearns. Working much like an Imagist poem that elaborates an emotion through a collection of related images, the text accumulates a vocabulary for the articulation of Natalia's desires. The severe beauty for which she reaches provides the common referent of this constellation of different, though in several ways qualitatively similar, signifiers: geometry, abstraction, ice, the ice-like colors of blue and silver, and forms of energy such as "radium," "white lightning," "electricity," and starlight. We begin to forge connections among these elements, since they are all employed by Helforth, along with the initial geometric image of the parallel lines leading to infinity, to describe Natalia. Of her writing, Helforth says, "Every line seemed to bleed . . . [i]ce and fire" (21); "She seemed to work . . . in radium or electricity" (22); "She wanted the realism of white lightning" (26). The semantic burden initially borne by geometry thus soon comes to be distributed among these other signifiers; they come to serve a function similar to that of the geometric figures. They come to be so interlinked, in fact, that each begins to evoke the other. Natalia has said that her writing resembles music (4): we might say here that the text builds the vocabulary for describing Natalia's desires such that the sounding of one image, one note, can summon a whole chord.

Other qualities then come to be linked with geometry by way of association with Natalia's husband, Neil. As Natalia's narrative opens, we discover that the extreme beauty for which she longs, which the text has taught us to align with geometry, is the "inhuman" beauty she connects specifically with Neil: "Neil magnified and de-humanized and his sort of beauty sterilized all other beauty" (39). Through Helforth's descriptions, we have come to attach such beauty to notions of geometry and ice, and to the "radium" of Natalia's writing. Now, since the kind of beauty Neil stands for is akin to the beauty first described, we relate all these images, previously introduced to describe Natalia's desire, to Neil. Further, we then join them with a string of other images that Natalia goes on to use to describe Neil and that bear qualitative affinities to the collection of images she uses initially, insofar as they participate in a similar range of colors (silver, ice-white, electric gold, blue) and similarly connote austerity, intensity, and icy cold. "Neil was the platinum note of nature, lightning, frost on bracken, the pattern of molecules, moving in radiations, through glass, under a lens" (39).[34] Neil possesses "ice-insistence" (77). At first, Natalia suggests that she means to obliterate her memory of Neil's "platinum blue" with her new lover David, who is utterly different: "hardy," "smug" (37), and "Saxon, Empire-making, British"

(36). David, she notes, "would be antidote, cure, heal-all" (35). Natalia decides that the love between her and Neil is "too intensely cerebral" (40) and "prays" that the memory of "Neil's lightning" won't disturb the new world she has with David, in which she feels herself "David's" Natalia rather than Neil's (39).

Yet her longing for Neil continues, marked in the text by images associated with him, persistently repeated and often geometric. After an encounter with David, we find Natalia reverting to memories of Neil by desirously imagining the act of drawing images of geometry into herself: "Her eyes are wide open to parallelogram of shadow and light, in bars" on the ceiling (42). This "openness" to geometric figures is confirmed as being connected to reminiscences of Neil when we hear directly after this observation that she wants to fall out the open window of the bedroom, "forward into platinum" (43). "Neil," she has said just a few pages earlier, "was the platinum note of nature" (39).

Later in the text, as geometric images and the signifiers related to them are increasingly associated with Natalia's moments of erotic transport, we can interpret them to mean that Natalia has found a way of attaining a state of being through erotic arousal that recalls Neil without relying on Neil himself to bring her to such a state. This accounts for the similarity of the images associated with Natalia herself to those linked with Neil. In part, these qualities belong to her because she desires them. But more than this, like one of Freud's melancholic subjects from *The Ego and the Id*, Natalia has dissociated from Neil the qualities she has hitherto depended on him to provide and has introjected them into herself, such that she can now evoke them by autoerotic stimulation. David she requires only as a catalyst: after he arouses her, she needs to be alone in order to enter her desired realm of beauty:

> [A]s the radium gathered electric current under her left knee, she knew her high-powered deity was waiting.... [S]he would hold muscles tense, herself only a sexless wire that was one wire for the fulfilment [*sic*]. She was sexless, being one chord, drawn out, waiting for the high-powered rush of the electric fervour.... She wanted the electric power to run on through her, then out, unimpeded by her mind. (51)

In this scene, Natalia's sexual ecstasy is described not in geometric, but electric terms. But again, as the text has developed, geometric images have come to be strongly linked to images of electric current. As a result, such scenes as these can illuminate the significance of Natalia's later wish to be "embodied" in "square and cube and rectangle": it expresses a desire for the same realm of taut, tense, "high-powered" fervor as that which is described here through electrical metaphors. This connection between the geometric and the electric in the novella's lexis is verified by the way in which, immediately before her meditation on Renne's geometric house (90), Natalia recapitulates this earlier scene—in which she has excited herself after David's departure—this time using not electric, but rather geometric, images to describe her ecstasy, implying their interchangeability. "[Y]ou see you excite me," she says to David, "and, after you left, I excited myself more":

> But she didn't want to explain it. She must get away, must lie alone, must let lines and patterns and the two interlocked triangles of light and shadow ... draw her out. She wanted to watch triangles of light and shadow, on her ceiling. She wanted to lie, parallel with a ceiling and she wanted to be a parallel, running to infinity and never touching that twin other-line. She wanted David there. But she must be free. (89–90)

Geometry thus here serves to capture the state of erotic transport she achieves through (though not with) David. Most obviously, its "parallel lines" symbolize the relationship she wants to maintain with David, in which they travel along together but never converge. Because of the way it has been coded and linked to other signifiers in the text, however, geometry also suggests that her ideal state of ecstasy possesses qualities associated with Neil: his inhuman beauty evoked by platinum, lightning, electricity, silver, and Brazilian blue. This linkage between Neil and geometry is presented most directly when, late in the book, the only thing capable of turning Natalia's attention away from the memory of Neil just after he abandons her—the only thing keeping her from falling off the roof to her death—turns out to be the "geometric square" of Pegasus (98). Presumably, the square of Pegasus possesses qualities sufficiently like Neil's that it assuages her need for him.

Most importantly, however, geometry and these other signifiers suggest that Natalia's ideal bodily state involves a rarefaction of the body. In part, geometry suggests a kind of attenuation toward dematerialization because it is linked to

Neil—and Neil, in turn, is associated with bodilessness. Whereas David has a "hardy body" (37), Natalia wonders if Neil has a body at all (38), suggesting the likelihood that, in Natalia's terms, he hasn't: he is most real to her as a dematerialized force. Given her desire to move toward Neil and his atmosphere, Natalia's sexual transport thus involves a drive toward bodilessness, the transmutation of solid molecules into intense running currents of energy. She tells David of her ecstasy after she "excited" herself "more": "'[I]t was almost sexless. It was almost automatic contraction. It was white and lavender. It was radium. I wanted to get out of my body.' He said, 'you did get out of your body'" (63–64). Here again is an effort reminiscent of the mystical project, as described by Mead, to overcome the gross and ordinary "hylic" body by transport into the ethereal "subtle" body.

Geometry also comes to imply the rarefaction of the body in *Nights* through the semantic connection that develops between the geometric and the electric body. Geometry and electricity are associated in the text not only because Natalia describes the same experiences in both geometric and electric terms, as though they can substitute for each other, but also because the text represents Natalia's body as responding to electric charges of desire by attenuating into a taut wire as thin as a geometric line: electrified, her body becomes a geometric mesh of wires conducting surges of power. Her "high-powered deity" will "sting" her, and she will be "one wire for the fulfilment [sic]... one chord, drawn out, waiting the high-powered rush of the electric fervour" (51). Transfused with "electric current," geometric, her body achieves the state of bodilessness often invoked, and often celebrated, in the text.

The geometric body, then, composed of wire-like lines, "drawn out," stretched taut, is the body rarefied through erotic stimulation into a state that transports one out of one's ordinary body. When Natalia expresses her desire to be "embodied" in "long parallelograms and in square and cube and rectangle," she evokes such rarefaction of the body.

We soon find that the geometric body is achieved not only through erotic transport but also, increasingly, through erotic violence of a kind much like that staged in the texts of Wyndham Lewis. The tautness of the geometric body comes to be one associated with—because it is achieved through—strain, pressure, and pain. In other words, here the linkage between geometry and violence introduced in H.D.'s review of *Responsibilities* reappears—but this time eroticized and ambivalently celebrated rather than condemned.

Accordingly, Natalia achieves the severe beauty she associates with Neil through sadomasochistic intercourse that moves her toward self-annihilation. As Alicia Ostriker notes, Natalia uses David "to get herself into a visionary state—for which the near-suffocation of his kisses is essential" (in Friedman, *Penelope's Web* 400). As the novella opens, we assume that Natalia wants from her relationship with David a chance to destroy memories of Neil. Although stung by Neil's "unfaithfulness," by way of David's sexual force she will survive: "I am blotted out," she says, "but not dead" (34). In subsequent encounters with David, however, her desire for self-obliteration becomes more and more urgent, and she seems increasingly less committed to eradicating the memory of Neil. Instead, she seems to want to return to Neil, to reach the severity she associates with him, by way of her own death. Gradually, we discover the degree to which sex with David seems to bring her close to the death she desires. When David bears down upon her, she often almost stops breathing:

> His mouth, closed over her mouth. He breathed into her . . . strangling, she cried, "you must let me breathe." She forgot to breathe, shook shoulders, gasped, "make me come back, I must breathe." (49)

When David leaves her, she comments of their encounter: "She saw no force for it but death, and as the aura of radiant life sped through her, she saw that she was not so much healed as shocked back, re-vivified, for fresh suffering. Would she die sometime in some such shock-aura of pure light?" (53). Later, she remarks, "She would lie in his arms, die, be so blotted into darkness" (65). Still later, feeling her personality extinguished, she takes her image of electrification to its extreme: "She felt herself go cold, static; electrocuted, dead corpse. She felt death creep in" (73). And when he kisses her deeply: "She would get out, under that kiss. It was possible that it would kill her . . . She believed that David's kiss was death because there was only blackness as she dropped under it and it spread (when she stopped breathing) a black canopy over her head" (79).

Natalia's masochistic desire is more explicitly signaled as David "jokes" at one point, "I won't offer you violence" (71); and then later, still more clearly, just after he inadvertently holds her too tightly: "she was caught in the arms, they would break her . . . If he tightened now, by one fraction of a millimetre, the bones would crack" (99). She says aloud to him, "Sadist"—but then remarks to herself, signaling the pleasure she takes in this: "he did not know that the crunching of her bones was the highest ecstasy" (100). Natalia's ecstasy, then, whether pleasurable because it allows her to "blot out" the part of her that is still joined to Neil, or perhaps to return to Neil through her own death, clearly arises from violence.

This world of ecstasy achieved through violent assault on the body seems, at first glance, the antithesis of the world of *Notes on Thought and Vision*: the novella appears to reflect in a ghoulishly distorting mirror the early manifesto's advocacy of the "healthy body"—which is often figured in *Notes* by the childbearing, life-giving body—as a means to vision. Instead of achieving visionary states through this hale body, Natalia instead achieves "holy radium" (52) through the mutilation of her body, the "crunching of her bones" (100). Rather than dwell on the giving of new life through childbirth, her accounts of erotic transport in *Nights* instead focus on a desire for death. In fact, as placed in relief by the prevalence of images associated with childbearing in *Notes*, Natalia's drive toward the attenuation of the body, and her attendant compulsion toward ecstasy attained through violence, seems at least partly fueled by disgust at the notion of childbearing and at the heavy female body associated with pregnancy. When Hulme comments in "Modern Art" on Jacob Epstein's geometricization of the process of childbirth, he posits a fundamental difference between the quintessentially organic nature of childbirth and the abstraction of geometry. Premised on a similar opposition, *Nights* uses geometry to enact an aversion from childbearing and its entailments.

Natalia's turn away from childbearing is suggested most explicitly when we find that her realm of "holy radium" contrasts with what she considers the "tiresome things" of life: "Was her fervour, after all, an illicit escape, an inhuman intolerance of the casual, tiresome things of this life?" (53). Feeling a pang of guilt, Natalia wonders immediately after this if she should atone for her transgression by participating in one of the activities she considers "tiresome": "Should she have Neil's children?" (53). Her sister-in-law Renne has rejected the possibility of Natalia and Neil's having a child: Renne suggests that it would ruin the special bond they have by replacing it with one involving more traditional female and male roles: "If you have his child then *you* are woman, *he* is man, that's smashed" (46). By classifying "childbearing" among the "tiresome" things of life, Natalia seems to agree with Renne that childbearing would "smash" the sustaining heterodoxy and ambiguity of her relationship with Neil.

From another image in the text, we gather that Natalia feels revulsion not only toward the prospect of childbearing and its concomitant traditional heterosexual dyad, but also toward the heavy female body that metonymically represents both those possibilities. In a vision much like that which H.D. herself experienced while vacationing with Bryher, and that she textualizes in *Tribute to Freud* (albeit seen here through a darker glass), Natalia imagines the figure of a woman:

> Her heart leaps out towards the woman who will not turn round and the curve of her spine tells that story, tells how Natalia herself had lain last night, her emotion spreading electric aura, so that she lay in the white sheet-lightning of her aura. An aura must be fastened like a butterfly, like angel wings to a naked, scraped spine. (56)

There follows a pair of cryptic sentences:

> Flesh must be scraped off, we must eat what will make us live. The woman became pre-Ionic, gross, with large breasts, she looked out, over another stretch of water. (56)

In the context of *Nights*, we react to the "gross" woman with "large breasts" as a jarring note, suddenly aware of how devoid of such images the text has been and how undesirable, amid Natalia's desires for ice and radium and lightning, it seems. This fleshy woman, with maternal breasts, is the figure from which the text seems to drive away, seeking instead vision ("aura") born not of naked flesh, but rather of "naked, scraped spine." Positioned as they are in this context, the images imply that it is the "naked, scraped spine," from which flesh has been "scraped off," that enables the generation of the desirable "white sheet-lightning" of the "aura" (56)—what Natalia calls elsewhere a "shock-aura of pure light" (53). Accordingly, Natalia's project, the project of *Nights*, is—through electric, erotic, geometric bodies—to "scrape off" the flesh and get down to spines and bare bones.[35]

Nights, then, might easily be read as the opposite of *Notes*, insofar as it challenges, even refuses, the values associated with childbirth and the fleshly female body. The relationship between the two texts might be read as one of complementarity: *Notes* might be construed as showing one dimension of H.D.'s attitude toward the female body, a celebratory affirmation of the female body's childbearing potential and the consequences of that potential; *Nights* might be read as displaying, obversely, the fear of entrapment by the female body and the conventional cultural script implied thereby. Together, the texts could be regarded as suggesting H.D.'s profound ambivalence toward the maternal role. And although H.D. does indeed exhibit such ambivalence, what this claim (and most critical constructions of *Notes*) overlooks is that, like *Nights*, *Notes* also evinces, albeit in a much subtler fashion, a discomfort with the childbearing body. And it signals this unease, I would argue, partly by way of its own geometric images, which coexist alongside its conspicuously amniotic images.

In *Notes*, for instance, H.D.'s speaker describes in geometric terms the cues that inspire her to vision: "Certain words and lines of Attic choruses, any scrap of da Vinci's drawings, the Delphic charioteer, have a definite, hypnotic effect on me. They are straight, clear entrances, to me, to over-world consciousness" (24). A few paragraphs later, she continues, "The Delphic charioteer has, I have said, an almost hypnotic effect on me: the bend of his arm, the knife cut of his chin . . . the fall of his drapery, in geometrical precision; and the angles of the ingatherings of the drapery at the waist" (24–26). H.D. sounds much like Pound here in both prizing the geometrically precise line and using it as a means of access: in H.D.'s case, not to knowledge of a culture's health (which Pound believes the nature of the line indicates), but rather to a higher plane of consciousness. H.D.'s speaker might be said to possess the "form sense" with which Pound credits the medieval Tuscan troubadours in "Cavalcanti"—the sensitivity to form that correlates with sanity of the body. Slightly later, the speaker pursues further the notion of geometrically precise lines that act as "entrances" to "over-world consciousness": a "[m]an's body" may be used as a "means of approach" (46) to visionary awareness because "[t]he lines of the human body . . . are like the body of the Delphic charioteer" (47).

These moments, in which the prophetic speaker invests geometrically precise images with desire, and suggests that the body can transmit such geometrically precise images, give the lie to the assumption, prevalent in commentary that reads H.D.'s rejection of geometry in her review of *Responsibilities* as coextensive with the celebration of the "vision of the womb" in *Notes*, that a text that valorizes the womb-vision necessarily also devalues geometric figures and lines. The layout of *Notes*, with its sparsely printed pages, filled with white space around its often brief and epigrammatic statements, together with the spareness of its prose, further suggests approval of geometrically clean lines. Rather than elevating the fluid at the expense of the geometric, the text instead oscillates between celebratory imagination of the body as composed of viscous, amniotic fluids and valorization of the body as chiseled in precise lines like those associated with the "Delphic charioteer," with the "knife cut of his chin," and "the fall of his drapery, in geometrical precision."

Slightly later in *Notes*, the realm of the jellyfish that H.D.'s speaker initially invokes in fact gives way to a realm of geometric precision and concentration. After having introduced her amniotic jellyfish images, H.D. subsequently begins to alternate and even to displace these with the more compact image of a seed: "These jelly-fish, I think, are the 'seeds cast into the ground'" (50). H.D. then introduces another image to capture the speaker's spiritual condition, one even more concentrated: a pearl.

In commentary whose syntax recalls the sentences of Gertrude Stein, H.D.'s speaker remarks, "Probably we pass through all forms of life and that is very interesting. But so far I have passed through these two, I am in my spiritual body a jelly-fish and a pearl" (50). At this point, she presents these two images of spiritual consciousness as equally valid, even interchangeable. In subsequent descriptions, her syntax, involving a paratactic sequence, suggests a relationship of substitutability among the jellyfish, the seed, and the pearl: "[O]nce a man becomes conscious of this jelly-fish above his head, this pearl within his skull, this seed cast into the ground, his chief concern automatically becomes his body" (50). And in the following section she says explicitly: "I saw that the state of mind I had before symbolised as a jelly-fish was *just as well* symbolised differently" (51; my italics), i.e., as something "concentrated," "small" and radiating a "very soft light" like the light of a "pearl" (51). But despite the equation this statement suggests, by this point the text has actually begun to tend toward favoring the pearl: "[T]oday," the speaker writes, "I saw . . . that the jelly-fish . . . had become concentrated" (51). One state has shifted into another, and the pearl is presented to us with a lovely description that makes our attention rest upon it: "it was small and giving out a very soft light" (51). The paragraph closes with an allusion to the Christian "pearl of great price," likely to direct our allegiances toward the concentrated image.

By the close of the commentary about jellyfish and pearls, the concentrated pearl has superseded the jellyfish as the text's dominant endorsed image. As Crown observes, H.D.'s privileging of the pearl here implicitly values hardness over softness and concentration over viscosity; and, accordingly, undermines the celebration of jellyfish images so striking elsewhere in the manifesto ("Visible Body" 219).

At this point, the body is dismissed as "an elementary, unbeautiful and transitory form of life," redeemed only by the pearl-like "concentrated essence" it can produce (*Notes* 51). This moment recalls one at the outset of *Notes*—one easily forgotten during the praise of the body that ensues over the first few pages—in which the speaker damns a "body without reasonable amount of intellect" as an "empty fibrous bundle of glands as ugly and little to be desired as body of a victim of some form of elephantiasis or fatty-degeneracy" (17). The suggestion here is that the body becomes worthy only as it can become spiritualized into purer form.

Reading *Notes* in light of *Nights*, then, makes evident that even *Notes*, the gist of much critical commentary notwithstanding, dramatizes a conflicted attitude toward jellyfish and fluidity, which is coded in this text as suggesting the maternal realm. Moreover, *Notes* could be said to indicate an uneasiness with the physical body more generally. In *Notes*, even before the section on the pearl, H.D.'s speaker has asserted that the body, like coal, "fulfills its highest function when it is being consumed," "transmuted" through a process of burning into a "different form, concentrated, ethereal, which we refer to in common speech as spirit" (47–48). This passage validates the body by noting that "We cannot have the heat"—i.e., the beneficial energy produced by the burning—"without the lump of coal."

However, this passage also draws attention to the fact that although *Notes* is certainly a text that focuses on the "body" ("Where does the body come in?" the text asks insistently), it conspicuously does *not* focus on fleshly bodies, but rather on bodies represented in such a way that averts attention from their ordinary corporeal condition (through, for instance, fluid images or Dorian chiseled lines), or focuses on bodies in the process of sublimation. In other words, through these images of burning and transmutation, of the amniotic rather than the fleshly, of visions and "jellyfish consciousness" rather than infants—through this effort of ascesis, that is, to etherealize actual physicality into "spirit"— *Notes*, like *Nights* but in a subtler form, in fact demonstrates a discomfort with the body, and especially with the kind of heavy body associated with childbearing. Just before the end of the manifesto, we again hear that "the body" has "its use," but here the diction implies even more emphatically that the body's value inheres in its redeemability as something rarer—that "in time" it "casts off the spirit." The body is good only insofar as it can ultimately produce "concentrated essence," which delivers it from "emotions and fears and pain" (51). Signals here indicate a swerve away from not only the body per se, but also the female childbearing body specifically: because of the alternation at this point between the images of jellyfish and pearl, we are likely to associate "emotions and fears and pain" with the jellyfish-like qualities the text has earlier endorsed and from which, at the last, it moves away. And because these "jellyfish" qualities have been coded as associated with the womb and childbirth earlier in the text, the final turn here—toward an etherealized "subtle body"—becomes tantamount to a turn away from the childbearing body.[36]

"EMBODIED . . . IN
SQUARE AND CUBE
AND RECTANGLE"

*HER*MIONE AND THE TRANSFORMATION OF GEOMETRY

Even if we concede, however, that *Notes* is more like *Nights* than it initially seems, the difference in emphasis and tone between the two texts is still clear. It is equally evident that, although *Nights* may share with "Responsibilities" a linkage between geometry and violence, *Nights* endows geometric language with a significance markedly different from that which it carries in H.D.'s review. To capture this transformation of the significance of geometry between "Responsibilities" and *Nights*, this repetition with a difference, I will look briefly at a similar maneuver that appears within H.D.'s autobiographical roman à clef, *HER*mione.

Over the course of this novel, thought to have been composed about 1927, H.D. enacts a shift in significance much like the one that occurs between "Responsibilities" and *Nights*: a reencoding of the language of geometry to represent something desirable rather than undesirable—something that bears some of the same qualities, in a different guise, originally critiqued through the language of geometry. Whereas in "Responsibilities" and *Nights* geometry signifies forms of violence, in *HER*mione geometry is initially linked with scientific austerity, mathematical rigor, and abstraction. Violence and austerity, however, both fall within a common semantic realm of severity—and thus also within the range of what the value system of Vorticism approves. Furthermore, in *HER*mione mathematical rigor in fact comes to be connected to violence because it proves so psychically traumatic to the eponymous main character.

In *HER*mione, geometric figures are initially coded so as to represent the protagonist Hermione ("Her") Gart's "entire failure to conform to expectations" (4), her inability to meet the standards of scientific and mathematical excellence that her father and brother have set for her. Having failed out of Bryn Mawr, Hermione compulsively repeats images of "conic sections" from the math class that she failed: "Pennsylvania whirled round her in cones of concentric colour .... [C]onic sections was the final test she failed in" (5). Thus as the novel begins, geometry signifies the world of "biological-mathematical definition" (76) in which Hermione's brother and father thrive, from which she has been banished, and which she must "supercede" (76) if she is to free herself from her state of paralysis.

Yet surprisingly, the vocabulary of geometry initially associated with the events of her failure reappears later in the novel to mark some of Hermione's positive experiences. Remembering the pain of failing mathematics, Hermione at first notes that "the least thought of add, subtract made Her feel blurred" (17). Ironically, however, as the text develops this semantic valence of "blurring" as connoting helplessness and oppression, Hermione's ideal state of being, harmed by such blurring, is explicitly figured as geometric. Later, when her fiancé George clumsily makes love to her, Hermione describes her revulsion as a geometric clarity—her own geometric clarity—subjected to threat: "The kisses of George smudged out her clear geometric thought" (73). Hermione thus comes to associate the "geometric" not only with the scientific and mathematical order from which she has been expelled, but also with her own state of desirable mental focus.

When Hermione meets Fayne, the compelling young woman who will later become her lover, geometric terms are again used to signify desirable experiences, in this case moments of epiphany and erotic connection. When Fayne is first introduced, the language used to establish the atmosphere associated with her is strikingly geometric:

> A face drew out of people grouped like teacups and people bisected by long lines of blue curtain hanging from miles above one's head .... The floor was polished and showed diagonals of the blue curtain in space between chairs going down and down. Bits of the floor went down, reflected between table legs; long lines of pure blue .... The wall and the floor were held together by long dramatic lines of curtain falling in straight pleated parallels. (52)

In this scene, geometry is still also associated with Hermione's trauma, which is here figured as a physical blow: "What did one take, as they say, 'up,' after one had been banged on the head and sees triangles and molecules and life going on in triangles and molecules [?]" (51). But even as "triangles" still symbolize shock, we also see here, as with the "clear geometric thought," that Hermione has begun to separate out for herself another, separate rhetoric of geometry, appropriating it to signify her fascination with Fayne. Hermione's most intensely erotic encounter with Fayne is represented in geometric terms:

> Her Gart saw rings and circles, the rings
> and circles that were the eyes of Fayne

"EMBODIED ... IN
SQUARE AND CUBE
AND RECTANGLE"

> Rabb. Rings and circles made concentric curve.... Her and Fayne Rabb were flung into a concentric intimacy, rings on rings that made a geometric circle toward a ceiling. (164)

Moreover, when Hermione is with Fayne, "Parallelograms came almost with a click straight" (128). "You put things, people under... the lenses of the eyes of Fayne Rabb and people, things come right in geometric contour" (147). Through Fayne, Hermione has found a way of achieving, in her own fashion, an activity equivalent to the scientific projects of her father and brother as they gaze through the lenses of telescopes and microscopes (147) and make pictures "click" into place.

Hermione joins with Fayne after having turned away from an increasingly oppressive engagement to George Lowndes. We could thus read Hermione's union with Fayne as a welcome liberation from her arrangement with George, and construe geometry as ultimately suggesting desirable subversion and emancipation. Within the text, however, the degree to which Fayne is a force for good is constantly problematized, given that Hermione's judgment is often constructed as questionable and that several voices in the text repeatedly denigrate Fayne and her relationship to Hermione. George, for instance, pronounces that Hermione and Fayne should be "burnt for witchcraft" (165), and Hermione's and George's mothers call Fayne "*most* unwholesome" (176). The end of the novel, which presents Hermione as emerging from a period of mental illness, does nothing to resolve the ambiguity of whether, through Fayne, Hermione has moved to a space of greater freedom and autonomy or simply reinscribed her oppressed condition in different terms. The last line of the novel indicates that Hermione will see Fayne again, but the significance of the reunion remains opaque. Thus the second significance of geometry, although clearly distinct from the first, is only problematically an improvement upon it: we could interpret even the second version of the geometry as a figure for entrapment.[37]

Yet however we judge Hermione's choices toward the end of the novel, important to notice here is Hermione's maneuver of expropriating for her own purposes the terms of a system that initially failed her and that she feels has oppressed her. Although she wants to escape "biological-mathematical definition" (76), we know that she nonetheless seeks "clear geometric thought" (73). And we also know that she chooses to achieve that clear geometric thought through erotic encounters that transport her to visionary states: as in *Nights*, geometric figures here are linked with erotic intensity. This preservation of one aspect of geometry's original significance within the novel—clarity and precision—coupled with a shift from one set of associations to another, and possibly one valuation to another, echoes the transformation in geometry's significance that occurs between "Responsibilities" and *Nights*.

In "Responsibilities," H.D. offers a clear condemnation of geometry because of what, within the force field of the war years, it has come to signify. In *Nights*, although geometry retains connotations of violence, it also comes to signify the atmosphere of an erotically aroused state, and in the context of the novella, this significance comes to be celebrated rather than entirely refused. The celebration, however, is compromised by ambiguity. In *Hermione*, the erotic relation expressed through geometry, as staged in Hermione's relations with Fayne, has been equivocally presented as possibly liberatory but also as potentially entrapping and pathological. In *Nights*, by surrounding the story of the central character with a complex introductory frame, H.D. renders it equally difficult to assign a definite value to the state of erotic arousal described in geometric terms.

"ONE HAS TO BE TRUE TO ONE'S DAEMON": NARRATIVE FRAMES AND SEDUCTIONS

In *Nights*, H.D. uses the framing devices and multivocality available to her within the genre of the novella to leave ambiguous how much the text endorses Natalia's desires and her drive toward death—endorses, that is, the values marked by geometry. Guided by the mixed feelings John Helforth presents about Natalia in the novella's Prologue, we begin her narrative uncertain about how much credence and sympathy to direct toward her. Helforth admires the way she found her "answer," and he envies her uncompromising ability to go for the "peak" or "nothing" (7). But he also repeatedly undercuts her: "I never took her seriously, and didn't really like her" (15–16). He concedes that Natalia had "a gift, an unquestionable talent"(21). But, he suggests derisively, "Her battery was surcharged. . . . She seemed to work actually in radium or electricity. Is that, I ask you, the medium for a novel?" (22).

"EMBODIED . . . IN SQUARE AND CUBE AND RECTANGLE"

Given Helforth's ambivalence, we are left to our own devices to decide exactly how to evaluate Natalia's "courage." Even Natalia herself expresses dividedness about the desirability and worth of her quest for extremity. As the "crunching of her bones" feels like the "highest ecstasy," she "quiver[s] involuntarily away"; she realizes that "her stupid humanity would save bones from breaking" (100). This resonates with another moment when she has, in the aftermath of a moment of ecstasy, found "her face, salt-wet with tears" (52). Although she wants to enjoy erotic ecstasy "unimpeded by her mind" (51), "[m]ind yet checked the flow of white electricity" (52). Here, too, her "humanness" seems to "check" her search for "white electricity." (The diction here recalls the "white, crude volume of brutal light" featured in Lewis's *Enemy of the Stars*; the "immense bleak electric advertisement of God"; the "white rivers of power" [*B1* 65]—even the "electric milky human passion" of Arghol and Hanp, [*B1* 75], though H.D.'s version of this electric passion is explicitly coded as not human.) But whereas at the first juncture, Natalia has shown impatience at her "stupid humanity," here she is "happy" to find a part of her resisting the inhumanness (52). Natalia's own ambivalence about her inhuman quest for intensity, our own probable tendency sometimes to favor the "humanity" in Natalia, our equally probable tendency to be at least partly seduced by the powerfully lyrical descriptions of Natalia's erotic flights, and our memory of Helforth's mixed assessments—all these make us likely to feel powerfully undecided about how to evaluate Natalia's drive toward death.

Ultimately, however, I would maintain that *Nights* presents as admirable Natalia's yearning for the geometric body, her uncompromising quest for the utmost intensity, for fire and ice, radium and electricity. Friedman suggests instead that *Nights* offers a portrait of a dangerous "erasure of the feminine through suicide" (*Penelope's Web* 270). For Friedman, Natalia's flight toward suicide is much like that of the character of Rhoda in Virginia Woolf's *Waves*, who internalizes misogynistic violence and self-destructs. Accordingly, Friedman reads the sadomasochistic dynamic between David and Natalia as a profoundly disturbing inscription of Freud's death drive; Natalia's "erotically charged wish to overpower and be overpowered in a sadomasochistic economy of desire explains why Natalia is not healed in her affair with David, but brought ever closer to death" (275).

Young notes that critics like DuPlessis and Friedman regard *Nights* and other "autobiographical" texts of this moment in H.D.'s career as "therapeutic exercises preparing H.D. for her later epic mode," as "working through certain themes . . . and aesthetic modes . . . in order to discard them" ("Between Science and Psychology" 325). According to this view, the representation of Natalia's suicide allows H.D. to "work through" a rejection of a hampering possibility and thereby to advance toward an art that is more affirmative and mature. Friedman's reading is certainly plausible: in the 1920s and 1930s, H.D. was indeed writing her way out of torment, revisiting with nearly obsessive repetitiveness the events of 1915–1919 that had scarred her. In view of what H.D. at this point was surfacing and reliving, what she wanted to relinquish, Natalia's death, like a ghoulish echo of the death of Pound's Hugh Selwyn Mauberley or Woolf's Septimus Smith, might well have staged H.D.'s exorcism of a part of herself that both fascinated and terrified her and that, ultimately, she wanted to reject.

And as I have suggested, the geometric body in *Nights* might also be read as a compensatory fantasy of imperviousness, aimed, on the one hand, to counter the extreme vulnerability H.D. remembered feeling during the years around the First World War, particularly the vulnerability of the woman's body that H.D. herself registered acutely, especially when pregnant or when remembering the traumatic circumstances of her pregnancies.

Given its linkage with violence, the geometric body might well also act as a response to H.D.'s fear in the 1930s that the violence she associated with the First World War—the "Juggernaut of planes and angles" that brought with it the "force of destruction" (53) that she remembered in connection with her sequence of personal traumas—would return. From this viewpoint, the geometric body might serve as a sign of self-protective introjection of the violence she dreaded, a preemptive attack of sorts expressed through textualized masochistic encounters: the textual inscription of a psychological maneuver aimed at defensive transformation of the violence, likely impending, into something more welcomed than feared. During this period, H.D. was indeed thinking about how to meet adequately the violence of the war that might be coming, rather than simply to be overwhelmed by it as she had been during the First World War. In this reading, too, the geometric body, given the textual suicide with which it is linked, comes to read as a desperate response to traumatic experience, as a sign of trauma.

But this, I would suggest, does not exhaust the significances of H.D.'s Vorticist geometric body. Moving beyond the project of H.D.'s responses to the personal and public crises of the 1930s, which do seem to act as the immediate spur for her construction of geometric body, I would offer the possibility of reading Natalia's death not only as an inscription of failure or despair, and not only as a defensive search for immunity in the face of danger, but also as the trace of desire for emancipatory transformation. Natalia's death may indeed imply the outcome of unhealthy forces gone too far; it may also, however, at the same time signify otherwise.

"EMBODIED . . . IN
SQUARE AND CUBE
AND RECTANGLE"

Some of Natalia's statements, for instance, suggest the text's endorsement of her desire to be obliterated by David's erotic force: "She believed that David's kiss was death because there was only blackness as she dropped under it . . . The kiss was, in that sense, authentic" (79). Here, Natalia's search for death is marked as a quest for "authenticity," one with which, despite our uneasiness, we may feel some readerly allegiance. Admittedly, much of what H.D. herself suggested guides us toward reading Natalia's "fervour" as "illicit" (53) and a potentially hazardous condition. In response to Robert McAlmon's expression of concern at Natalia's section of *Nights* (he said he was "distressed" by it), H.D. conceded on August 18, 1933,

> But you yourself have been pointing out—and rightly—that my writing had reached a vanishing point of sterility and finesse. Awful—I feel it when I read the stuff . . . . But one has to be true to one's Daemon—or what is one true to?
>
> (QUOTED IN FRIEDMAN, *PENELOPE'S WEB* 30)[38]

In this same letter, H.D. in fact attributes to her own writing of the period the very qualities she associates in *Nights* with Natalia's writing and erotic experiences: her stories of this moment, she says, are "all on that high-vibration to the breaking-point level." As she writes, she says she even feels the influence of Freud, with whom she engaged in psychoanalytic work in 1933–1934, "burn away" in her like "radium" (also quoted in Friedman, *Penelope's Web* 30).

DuPlessis suggests that H.D. began her sessions with Freud prompted in part by the fear she expresses here, when she refers to texts like *Nights*: that her writing had reached a perilously intense and "sterile" point and that perhaps her currents of desire and thought had as well. H.D. in fact created the frame of John Helforth after she wrote Natalia's section of *Nights*, just after completing work with Freud.[39] In light of this, Helforth's assertions might plausibly be read as the voice of reason that H.D. was trying to cultivate in herself as she felt herself, along with Natalia, moving dangerously toward the "vanishing point." H.D. did choose to use "John Helforth" as her pseudonym for *Nights*, implying an alignment between her views and his. And H.D. even said in a letter of 1943 to Norman Holmes Pearson that *Nights* represented for her a rather "lost" and "sad" period (Hollenberg, *Between History and Poetry* 29).

Given all this, we cannot believe H.D. entirely unsympathetic to Helforth's practical ways, as they seem to express her own fears of falling over the edge; accordingly, H.D. herself might well have agreed with some of Friedman's assessments. But given the way *Nights* is constructed, neither can we believe her entirely unsympathetic to Natalia's aspirations. Moreover, as D. H. Lawrence, H.D.'s onetime friend and mentor, once suggested, here we may need to trust not the teller but the tale. Helforth is presented as a double to Natalia, a "half-and-half sort of person" much as she is (5), more like her than he would like to admit. We know that, given Helforth's von Aschenbachian inability to "let go," Natalia demonstrates a form of courage he has never been able fully to achieve. Furthermore, the section of *Nights* on Natalia is so compelling that we are apt to read Helforth as the prosaic voice of common sense whose ways Natalia vaults over and outwits—whose inhibited systematicity sets into relief the inspiredness of Natalia's euphoric, if agonized, path. And Natalia's compelling discoveries, in turn, implicitly satirize Helforth's penchant for "psycho-analytic dissection" and "vivisection" (23); for Natalia, there can be no rightful "vivisect[ion]" of a "miracle" (49).[40] It is also, I would argue, the rhythms of H.D.'s prose in *Nights*—incantatory, hypnotic, graceful, insistent—that prompt our admiration for Natalia's elegance and superb errantry. Like Robin Vote in Djuna Barnes's *Nightwood*, Natalia ultimately eludes attempts to define and describe her, to pin her down.

What the carefully formed frame of *Nights* achieves is the implication that the geometric body that Natalia envisions, insofar as it culminates her inspired efforts toward visionary knowledge and transcendence, marks not only failure (which it does) but also brilliance and uncompromising desire. Ultimately, we may need to disregard even what H.D. herself may have thought about Natalia's wild arc toward apotheosis. We need to take the frame, whose effect on our reading of Natalia is crucial, into account; we need also to consider how the rhythms of H.D.'s prose—what Friedman calls her "hypnotic repetition, a latticework of interlocking motifs" (*Penelope's Web* 91)—invite us to respond to the seductions of Natalia's narrative.

Once having accepted the possibility that the geometric body in *Nights*, which figures the visionary state for which Natalia strives, is held up as an ideal, if ambivalently, we then also need to reckon with the implications of the similarity of this body to Pound's and Lewis's. H.D.'s affinities with Pound and Lewis—in her valorization of the geometric body arrived at by way of erotic stimulation, violent or otherwise, that affords a vantage of transcendent vision—can usefully complicate received ideas, widespread in criticism, about the distance, even antagonism, between H.D.'s work and that of her male contemporaries.[41]

A recent article by Demetres Tryphonopoulos indicates the difference usually assumed between H.D.'s sexual politics and, for instance, those of Pound, whom Tryphonopoulos charges with not only "phallocentrism" but also an "egregious misogyny" that contrasts with H.D.'s "gynocentrism," using this divergence to account for their different relationships to eroticism and occult thought ("Fragments of Faith" 235). By counting on this same set of assumptions, Albert Gelpi is able to observe with conspicuous lightness in his introduction to *Notes on Thought and Vision* that H.D. was "unencumbered by the misogynist phallicism of Pound and Lawrence" (13). Kendra Langeteig also signals with her phrasing the high degree of acceptance the notion of this division has received (such that, I would offer, it has become almost de rigueur to genuflect to it): after noting several ways in which the projects of H.D. and Pound are aligned, she notes, "however, the poetics of H.D. and Pound are diametrically opposed when it comes to the legislation of gender and sexual politics. No surprise here, given Pound's ingrained misogyny and H.D.'s undaunted feminism" ("Visions in the Crystal" 57).

What seems "ingrained" here, I would offer, is the nearly automatic gesture of assigning Pound and H.D., as well as H.D. and male contemporaries such as Lewis, usually placed with Pound along a "masculinist" axis of modernism, different positions along the spectrum of sexual politics, in a blanket move that elides instances in which H.D. may not be as distant from them as is usually thought. What troubles me here is not the claim that H.D. at times differed from her male contemporaries: she quite obviously did, often for principled, and often feminist, reasons, and critics are quite right to point this out. At issue here is the tendency, indicated by the almost glib phrasing of such comments as these, to conclude too quickly, a priori, that a division between H.D. and such "masculinist" male contemporaries as Pound and Lewis and Lawrence exists always and everywhere. This habit fosters the risk that readers will remain blinkered to affinities between H.D.'s work and the work of compatriots like Pound and Lewis, even in the realm of sexual politics, acknowledgement of which is crucial to a rich understanding of both H.D.'s work and that of her peers.

In her thought about the body, H.D. is certainly not so removed from her male contemporaries Pound and Lewis as critics such as Friedman often have suggested. Nor, again, is she so far from the Vorticist values Pound and Lewis articulate as critical literature has often suggested. Moreover, her propinquity to Pound, Lewis, and the Vorticist values they express does not necessarily indicate her capitulation to masculinist and misogynistic values. Instead I would suggest that the Vorticist geometric body enables H.D. to articulate a set of feminist desires.

"BOUNDLESS, FURIOUS PASSION": H.D.'S DISSIDENT EROTIC

Through the Vorticist geometric body, H.D. illustrates an erotic that constitutes an important form of sexual dissidence with feminist implications—one largely illegible through interpretive paradigms that search for what has been called the "maternal" in H.D.'s work. Chisholm has recently identified in H.D.'s poetry such a current of sexual dissidence, which, as Chisholm notes, has little to do with the maternal or the conventionally womanly that is emphasized in much current revisionist feminist criticism on H.D. Chisholm describes H.D.'s erotic as an intoxicating "lyrical intensity" of "sensual excess" ("Pornopoeia" 72). It is "sexual ecstasy" as a "religious and aesthetic experience" that, as Meryl Altman has likewise offered, has little to do with the search for a "mother goddess" ("Prisoner of Biography" 39).[42] Chisholm rightly suggests that H.D.'s eroticism seems to supersede the discursive spaces many readers have assumed it inhabits—to hurtle beyond the "threshold" not only of "romantic love" ("Pornopoeia" 76) but also of maternal nurture, into a "vertiginous intoxication" (73) and "boundless, furious passion" (76).

I would move further to separate what Chisholm mischievously calls the "narco-electro lusts" of *Nights* ("Pornopoeia" 89), expressed by way of the geometric body, from the other currents of eroticism that Chisholm delineates and groups with that of *Nights*. Chisholm's account does pertain to *Nights* in many respects: the erotic force expressed by Natalia, like those Chisholm describes, is indeed linked to the Eleusinian mysteries that fascinated H.D., in that it initiates Natalia into a "holy" region; Natalia does come across as an "ecstatic mystic" (*H.D.'s Freudian Poetics* 83). And like the texts Chisholm explores, *Nights* expresses a wish for violence that will foster achievement of a sublime state that resonates with similar desires expressed in H.D.'s *Sea Garden*. The erotic force of *Nights*, like that which Chisholm describes, is indeed impersonal, beyond gender, individuals, and names. As Natalia says in *Nights*, "Personality was the thing that didn't matter" (72), and "We aren't now, people" (101). When she is with David, Natalia insists that they have no names (40).

But unlike Chisholm, I would offer that H.D.'s transgressive erotic is not articulated primarily in her verse: in fact, it is the incantatory rhythms and pulsings of H.D.'s prose fiction that better express this heterodox, ecstatic erotic force important to her work. Further, the erotic currents H.D. inscribes in her work are not always best captured by the voluptuous language of flowers that Chisholm offers (quoting from H.D.'s "The God") as epitomizing the nature of H.D.'s erotic: "cyclamen-purple / cyclamen-red, colour of the last grapes / colour of the purple of the flowers" (*Collected Poems* 47). This is indeed the color of one kind of passion in H.D.'s work, but it is also the kind of languid, voluptuous, and decadent passion that H.D. associates with Aphrodite and Greek Ionian culture and that, as Eileen Gregory has convincingly argued, engenders H.D.'s unease (*H.D. and Hellenism* 105–106). Moreover, the vivid red and purple here are certainly not the colors of passion in *Nights*, where the desire for the geometric body is clearly expressed through a palette composed of blue, silver, and white.

Gregory argues that, given the influence on H.D. of Walter Pater's valorization of a palette of white and blue reminiscent of the cool colors of marble statuary—which he in turn draws from Dorian Greek art—white and blue come to be linked in H.D.'s imagination with homoerotic desire of the chaste, ascetic, "spiritualized" variety that Pater celebrated, as well as with similarly chaste androgyny and bisexuality (*H.D. and Hellenism* 85–107).[43] But although H.D. does at moments employ this palette for the articulation of ascetic homoerotic or bisexual desire, in her work these colors also signal more generally forms of desire beyond the pale of conventional sexual relations. In *Nights*, in her vision of the geometric body, H.D. does invoke an ecstatic burning of the body toward purification, vision, and ascesis reminiscent of the Paterian "gem-like flame," and like Pater, she rejects a voluptuous Ionian erotic. But she certainly does not consistently prefer the kind of Dorian restraint that Pater favors. In *Nights*, H.D.'s vision of the geometric body shares little with the serene and chaste erotic associated with Pater. Building her imagistic lexicon composed of not only white and blue, but also ice, frost, platinum, radium, and geometry, H.D. expresses an intense erotic current whose cascading force also has little to do with the gender or sex of its stimulus.

In *Nights*, we are invited to focus not on whether this erotic force is directed at man or woman, whether it is heterosexual, homosexual, or bisexual, but instead on the nature of the current itself. In fact, as Natalia demonstrates, the erotic current no longer needs an object for its realization: Natalia's strongest fervor is achieved when she is alone, when David has left her, when she "excites herself." David and Neil, she notes at one juncture, have been only "bridges" to the knowledge of a sexual intoxication that in turn can bring vision (87). The erotic that H.D. presents here through Natalia is autoerotic, irrepressible, transgressive, impersonal, even inhuman, a "note of nature" (39).

It becomes plain why such a heterodox erotic force, inscribed in *Nights* by way of the geometric body, is not readily incorporated into accounts of H.D.'s gynopoetic—or if it is included, why it is usually read as an undesirable possibility rejected as H.D. moves toward more salutary attitudes. This unorthodox erotic force, highlighted in *Nights* but also crucial in much of H.D.'s other work, is not maternal, warm, giving, rich, loving. It is neither voluptuous nor chaste. It is not about compassion or love or friendship; and not necessarily about masculinity. It may indeed have to do with what DuPlessis has termed "thralldom," but perhaps ironically liberatory, transformative thralldom. It certainly has to do with phantasmic violence. As Natalia describes the erotic current:

> There is no localization of their force. It
> creeps into bones, dissolves personality,
> so that they lie, sex undifferentiated yet,
> through some magnetic law, one receives,
> one gives. (102)

Ultimately, Natalia's desires for visionary consciousness through erotic arousal, expressed by the geometric body, may not simply be an inscription of trouble. We should also consider the possibilities H.D. indicates through the Vorticist geometric body as offering avenues toward feminist liberation. We might think of a notion of ascesis not only as articulated by Walter Pater, but also as expressed in the work of scholars like Leo Bersani.[44] And perhaps, too, there is a Harawayian logic here: a supersession of the merely organic (body) through a movement toward, and transformative fusion with, that which evokes the inorganic (geometry).[45]

Valuable scholarship of the past decade has illuminated the way that H.D.'s work powerfully inscribes "difference," especially woman's difference and queer difference. Given this, and given the compelling assertion of the geometric body in *Nights*, we need to recognize in this sexually dissident current, aligned with the erotics of Vorticism, H.D.'s provocative distance from the values of many current feminisms dominant within H.D. scholarship. We need, first, to recognize this distance if we are to achieve a richer and more accurate picture of H.D. The current of desire represented by the geometric body in *Nights* can both sensitize us to and augment our understanding of many other moments in H.D.'s work. For instance, the erotic associated with this geometric body also appears, in a slightly less developed form, in H.D.'s novel *HERmione*:[46] Hermione's desire for Fayne, like Natalia Saunderson's for David, is conveyed through images of blue, white, electricity, and geometry. H.D.'s *Bid Me to Live* offers another scene of desire that the geometric body of *Nights* can illuminate: Julia Ashton's passion for Rico, born out of her agonized relationship to her unfaithful husband and generative of her artistic vision, is described as associated with "blue lightning" and "flame," and likewise transcendent of "firm-fleshed bodies."[47]

More importantly, we need to think about the emancipatory possibilities H.D. might offer here for feminism—to consider again what we will admit into our feminisms. Clearly, elements in *Nights*—sadomasochistic sex, desires for violence, a trajectory toward suicide—will rightly continue to provoke discomfort among many readers. Natalia's fantasy of the geometric body nonetheless also encodes a wish for sexual ecstasy leading toward visionary consciousness that is presented as potentially liberatory and empowering, and the reason it is liberatory and empowering has nothing to do with maternal nurture. Among the many other currents of H.D.'s thought, it should be noted as well. Through the cracks and fissures of Natalia's tortured way toward transcendence, we might see not only brokenness but also glimmers of other means of emancipation from what Renne in *Nights* calls the state of being in which "*you* are woman, *he* is man," a state associated with conventional gender roles under patriarchal norms. And we might see other ways of understanding the erotic forces that can foster such freedom.

H.D.'s emancipatory strategy may indeed issue, in part, from trauma; the geometric body does seem to emerge in H.D.'s imagination partly as a response to the memories of personal crisis that she experiences acutely through her work with Freud and partly as a response to the despair of what she called her "lost" and "sad" period, during which she feared her writing was nearing a "vanishing point" of "sterility." The geometric body seems to suggest a fantasy of imperviousness and detachment that compensates for a fear of fragility and pain. If the qualities of Vorticism are aimed to counter effeminacy, H.D.'s imagination here, celebrating Vorticist qualities through the construction of the geometric body, may analogously counter weakness and vulnerability.

But perhaps H.D.'s Vorticist geometric body emerges also out of the perennial, but still relevant, recognition of the ideological entrapment that the maternal realm can bring women into even now; perhaps it also arises out of desire. In general, we should not overlook the possibility that through her appropriation of Vorticist values here, through her Vorticist geometric body, H.D. presents us with ways that women might heal, grow, and strengthen that bear no relation to childbearing and nurture. And ultimately, what she points us to is that we may need to be even more cautious about the consequences of implying, even if only faintly, that it is on the basis of an association with the maternal sphere that women writers belong in modernist or feminist literary canons.

Considering the affirmative implications of the geometric body is important, first, because of the routes it leaves open for new readings of H.D., readings that feature voices of her richly polyvocal work to which feminist scholarship has yet to attend. But beyond the work of H.D., there is also wider value in exploring H.D.'s heterodox eroticized possibilities toward vision and freedom—not only for women, but also for all, as H.D. might say, who might become "companions / of the flame" (*Collected Poems* 521). Of the "H.D." I have hoped to adumbrate here, one who soars beyond the critical shelters in which we have sometimes enfolded her, I would say, quoting from H.D.'s *Trilogy*:

> she is not shut up in a cave
> like a Sibyl; she is not
>
> imprisoned in leaden bars
> in a coloured window;
>
> she is Psyche, the butterfly;
> out of the cocoon.
>
> (*COLLECTED POEMS* 570)

"EMBODIED . . . IN
SQUARE AND CUBE
AND RECTANGLE"

> [Freud] explained it carefully. He might
> have been giving a lesson in geometry.
>
> H.D., *Tribute to Freud*

> At the moment my head is all frozen hard
> because of a morning of mystic geometry.
>
> W. B. YEATS, letter to Olivia Shakespear,
May 22, 1928

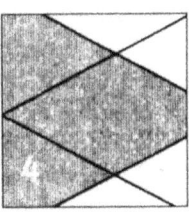

"Mystic Geometry": The Visionary Texts of Yeats and H.D.

Among the moderns, W. B. Yeats and H.D. have become fabled, at times even notorious, for their intense fascination with the occult. As Materer notes, while several of the chief modernists, including Pound and Eliot, have been widely recognized in recent scholarship for their interest in esoteric wisdom, Yeats and H.D. still have the distinction of being the only "practicing occultists" among them (*Modern Alchemy* 87).[1] It is on the nature of their relationships to the occult, and how these relationships came to be inscribed in their narratives about experiences of the occult, that this chapter focuses. Conditioned by both public crises and private anxieties, the attitudes that H.D. and Yeats evolved toward the occult led them to Vorticist conceptions of geometric form.

By 1920, both had been deeply affected by mystical revelations of occult wisdom and were immersed in efforts to explain in writing the knowledge they had gained through their visionary experiences.[2] H.D.'s visions occurred while she was travelling with her companion Bryher through Cornwall, the Scilly Isles, and Greece in 1919–1920. Afterward, plagued by uncertainty about their import, she repeatedly sought to record and gloss them textually—and, through textual expression, to facilitate greater comprehension of their significance—but it took her more than twenty years to gain sufficient command of her memories to narrate them fully. After briefly describing the first of these visionary experiences in her unpublished *Notes on Thought and Vision* (1919), she then scattered oblique references to them through her prose fiction of the 1920s and early 1930s. Ultimately, it was her psychoanalytic sessions with Freud in 1933–1934, begun in part to enlist his help in clarifying the purport of these "psychic or occult experiences" (*TF* 39), that enabled her to consolidate them and bring them to confident exposition. Her fullest and most vivid accounts appear in her memoirs of the 1940s about Freud: "Writing on the Wall" (written 1944) and "Advent" (written 1948), which were later paired by Norman Holmes Pearson in one volume, *Tribute to Freud*. H.D.'s capacity for surefooted narration by the 1940s emerged from her conviction that she had at last been able to make some sense of these once mysterious experiences.

Yeats, meanwhile, was spurred into an especially intense period of writing about the occult when, just after his marriage in 1917, his wife, George, displayed mediumistic powers and began transmitting what Yeats and she took to be messages from spiritual instructors (Harper, *Automatic Script* 1:x), which Yeats referred to as "Communicators" or "Guides" (1:270). Over the next two decades, Yeats labored to do justice to the occult wisdom that collaborative sessions with his wife had revealed. Yeats's most extensive narrative about these sessions occurs in *A Vision*, his occultist text which purports to convey and interpret the claims relayed to him by these otherworldly spiritual instructors about patterns underlying the history of Western civilization, the progress of the individual soul through life and death, and the nature of the creative process.[3] Out of his sessions with George, Yeats produced two editions of *A Vision*, 1925–1926 and 1937, in the second of which he attempted to augment and improve upon the first. After publishing the first version of *A Vision*, Yeats would labor for the rest of his life to perfect his account of what he had received. Bette London comments of his process of revision: "As WBY's letters and journals indicate, *A Vision*, even more so than his other texts (and WBY was a notorious rewriter), was a product of continual reordering and reworking, a repeating and revising of the materials that went into it. It was, in effect, always a re-vision" (*Writing Double* 187). Connie Hood observes likewise that "for Yeats the book was a process which never ceased evolving toward a never-achieved perfection" ("Remaking *A Vision*" 67).

Driven by what they took to be messages from beyond, both Yeats and H.D. strove to understand, transcribe, and translate the information they had received—as well as to chronicle the experiences through which they had received it. And in these efforts at narration, both conspicuously featured a geometric vocabulary. This chapter concentrates on what the geometric figures prominent in their narratives of visionary experience can reveal about their relationship to visionary knowledge. A wealth of scholarship now documents Yeats's and H.D.'s investment in esoteric thought.[4] Building upon this foundation, this chapter explores further the narratives through which they published their visionary contact with forms of knowledge hidden from the everyday world—and the ambivalence, reflected in their narratives as well as in their geometric vocabulary, that they directed toward both visionary epistemology and the secret wisdom it could illuminate.

If, as Surette convincingly argues, we must recognize the centrality of occult thought to the development of modernism, we must also seek to do justice to the specificity of the attitudes of individual modernists toward the occult.[5] In H.D. and Yeats, arguably the modernists who committed themselves most devotedly and publicly to mystical ways of knowing and occult thought, we must accordingly recognize a sometime reluctance to take this realm of knowledge altogether seriously. It is H.D.'s and Yeats's uneasiness with visionary knowledge of the occult that guides the progress of their narratives—and that transposes their accounts into a Vorticist key. The public and personal anxieties that shape Yeats's and H.D.'s attitudes toward vision and the occult impel them to use a Vorticist strategy of response, one that in turn directs their use of a geometric lexicon.

By the time H.D. and Yeats had experienced the visionary encounters they described in these texts, visionary work was hardly new to either. From the 1880s onward, Yeats had been a dedicated participant in the widespread late nineteenth- and early twentieth-century revival of interest in occult knowledge (what G. R. S. Mead called "The Rising Psychic Tide"), steeping himself in Theosophy, mysticism, magical experiments, and attempts to contact the spirit world.[6] His many affiliations with esoteric organizations attest to a committed and ongoing interest: in 1885, he became one of the founding members of the Dublin Hermetic Society, joined the Esoteric Section of London's Theosophical Society in 1888, and entered the Hermetic Order of the Golden Dawn in 1890, the last of which he would remain a member for the rest of his life. He had developed close alliances with such figures as MacGregor Mathers, founder of the Order of the Golden Dawn, and Madame Helena Blavatsky, leader of the Theosophists.[7] By 1892, Yeats was writing to his friend John O'Leary the now famous letter in which he defended his study of the occult in the face of what he took to be O'Leary's dismissive attitude toward it: "[T]he mystical life," he declared, "is the centre of all that I do and all that I think and all that I write" (*LWBY* 211).[8] More than twenty years before beginning *A Vision*, Yeats was publishing much that reflected his occult interests, including an 1893 edition of William Blake's work, coedited with Edwin Ellis, in which Yeats defined and defended Blake's mysticism.[9]

H.D., in contrast, did not undertake intensive exploration of the occult until the 1920s, just after she began writing about her visionary encounters. Through both her upbringing and her contacts, however, she had already long been familiar with visionary consciousness. Both her family and her hometown of Bethlehem, Pennsylvania, were suffused by the ideas of Moravianism, a form of Christianity receptive to the possibility of gaining knowledge by mystical means.[10] Although it would not be until the 1940s that H.D.'s own research would bring her to an understanding the formal historical linkages between Moravians and mysticism, she had nonetheless been introduced to her mystical heritage early in life through hearing both her mother and maternal grandmother speak of the Moravian belief in the "gift" of second sight.[11]

Moreover, in 1905, H.D. developed a relationship with Ezra Pound, who loaned her books in plenty—encouraging her to read, inter alia, work by the Swedish mystical theologian Swedenborg as well as *Séraphita*, a novel by Balzac informed by Swedenborgian mysticism (H.D., *End to Torment* 23). And in 1910 and 1911, H.D. began a romance with Frances Gregg, a woman given to fascination with mysticism and the occult who persuaded H.D. of both the reality of the occult and the possibility of mystical vision and prophecy (Friedman, *Psyche Reborn* 159). Tryphonopoulos even suggests that we should read H.D.'s early Imagist work as informed by occult interests ("Fragments of Faith" 233–234).

It was after her visionary experiences, however, during the 1920s that H.D. began extensive and sustained work with the occult, studying such occult practices as astrology, the Tarot, and numerology. Thereafter, her close engagement with the occult would continue for the rest of her life, reaching special intensity in the 1940s as the conditions of the Second World War prompted her to even more devoted study. During this period, she expanded the scope of her reading on mystical traditions, guided by contemporary explicators of the hermetic tradition such as Robert Ambelain, Denis de Rougemont, and Jean Chaboseau (Friedman, *Psyche Reborn* 157–172). As Friedman points out, she may even have been influenced by Yeats, though Blavatsky's Theosophy clearly did not compel her to the degree it did him (160).[12]

As she strove to narrate adequately her "occult experiences," H.D. was impelled both by a need to make sense of the events of her life and by a desire to respond to the climate of building political tensions of the 1920s and 1930s. She was narrativizing her visionary experiences out of a wish to "piece together" the elements of her visionary knowledge in order to promote healing, both personal and public.[13] Likewise inspired by a combination of private and public motives, Yeats sought to "spend what remained of life explaining and piecing together" what was revealed by the "scattered sentences" produced out of his collaborative sessions with George (AVB 8).

And in these efforts at narration, both, strikingly, frequently employed a geometric vocabulary. In his two versions of *A Vision*, Yeats featured the now famous collection of wheels and interlocking gyres intended to represent the historical cycles and fundamental human types of Western civilization. In H.D.'s "Writing on the Wall," now the first part of *Tribute to Freud*, a significant portion of her narrative is devoted to a description of geometric figures she had witnessed on the wall of a hotel in Corfu while experiencing what she took to be a visionary trance. This geometry, H.D. and Yeats claimed, was given them through visions: H.D. saw geometric figures appear on the wall before her; Yeats received geometric diagrams from the Communicators through the trances and "sleeps" of his wife.[14] But even if transmitted to them from elsewhere, within the context of their narrative projects the geometry soon came to be invested with other significances, significances that stemmed from their own anxieties and desires.

H.D. and Yeats were interested in the occult before these visionary encounters that dominated their imaginations, but after these visionary experiences, their investment in mystical experiences of occult knowledge intensified and changed direction. In part, of course, after this point they were driven by a personal desire to use writing to arrive at a richer understanding of the mysterious wisdom delivered to them. But the trajectory of their work was also inflected by their awareness of the increasingly turbulent political climate around them in the late 1920s and early 1930s — and by the need to find adequate ways of responding to current economic and political questions about poverty, the rise of fascism, the widely bruited bankruptcy of liberal capitalist democracy, and the promise of socialism. Aware that they lacked the conventional credentials usually required to comment authoritatively on the public crises of the day and to offer help, H.D. and Yeats sought to do both through alternative means. Like Pound facing modernity's welter of information and urgent questions in *Guide to Kulchur* (23, 53–54), Yeats and H.D. strove to answer what Pound called the era's "accelerated grimace,"[15] and it was to visionary knowledge that they turned to find suitable replies.

Nonetheless, at the same time both were constantly haunted by doubts about the legitimacy of visionary experience: they feared that the occult knowledge they were receiving through mystical means might be, on the one hand, untrustworthy, and, on the other, undeserved. They were concerned, in other words, about the truthfulness of what they found—and troubled, too, about the potential costs of becoming merely passive recipients of occult wisdom. To borrow and permute Yeats's phrase, this chapter explores the ambivalence that pervaded everything H.D. and Yeats did, thought, and wrote about visionary knowledge.

In *Modernist Alchemy*, Materer addresses in valuable detail an oscillation between skepticism and credulity that he identifies as characteristic of many modernist writers attracted by the occult. Materer attributes the sometime skepticism to typical modernist irony—an unwillingness to place faith too wholeheartedly and naively in any program—and further suggests that some of the moderns may have adopted a strategically deceptive pose of skepticism to protect themselves from those likely to mock their beliefs. He mentions Yeats here, and I agree that, as Stephen Coote puts it, Yeats's "longing for the occult" was always "checked by his skepticism" (*Yeats: A Life* 59).

But whereas Materer excludes H.D. from the group of modernists given to moments of doubt and skepticism about the occult—suggesting that, unlike Yeats, "H.D. did not weave doubts about the validity" of esoteric thought into her work (*Modernist Alchemy* 87)—I would certainly include her. As Friedman suggests, her attitude toward the occult was, like Yeats's, a "blend" of "faith and skepticism," her skeptical detachment manifesting itself in her refusal to join any organization associated with occult study except the Society for Psychical Research, whose scientific investigations of occult phenomena satisfied her (*Psyche Reborn* 200).[16] And as Sword notes, H.D.'s fear of the autonomy, "self-possession," and control she might sacrifice by participating in mystical experiences also bred in her a wariness toward visionary experience. Moreover, although the factors Materer notes may well have played a role in the appearance of doubt in the thinking of both Yeats and H.D.—i.e., irony and defensive posturing—I would suggest that the skepticism that colored H.D.'s and Yeats's views should be recognized as emerging also from the intellectual traditions within which they were raised: specifically, those that their fathers had striven to instill in them.

And as I will show, this ambivalence conditioned—and was thus registered in—how they employed the geometric vocabulary in their narratives. Perhaps encouraged by Yeats's remark in *A Vision* that readers might be "repelled by what must seem an arbitrary, harsh, difficult symbolism" (*AVB* 23), critics have long complained of Yeats's geometric symbols in *A Vision*: as Harold Bloom remarks of the now famous double gyre that Yeats features in the book, it "tends to madden or anyway bore readers of *A Vision* who are looking for passion and insight, and sometimes find themselves staring at an empty geometry" (*Yeats* 217). H.D.'s geometry, meanwhile, because it exerts a much less obvious presence in her visionary meditations than Yeats's geometry does in his, tends to be conflated with her many other metaphors for visionary activity, its specific significance left unrecognized.[17] The geometric lexicons of both Yeats and H.D., however, merit more careful study because they are precisely the place to find, to use Bloom's phrase, "insight" into the anxious passions governing their relationships to, and representations of, visionary consciousness.

Moreover, both the way they use geometry and the values and assumptions prompting their ambivalence about visionary consciousness, I argue, share much with characteristically Vorticist uses of geometry: to enact refusals of weakness (*B2* 41), passivity (40), and "relaxed initiative" (41)—what H.D. and Yeats term the realm of the "amorphous." In *Blast*, Wyndham Lewis had in fact linked the Vorticist renunciation of weakness and passivity with a refusal of the occultism prevalent in his early twentieth-century London milieu: he targeted occultism that required transmission of supernatural wisdom through a medium. Vorticism, of course, favored an active, incisive stance; mediumship, by common definition, a receptive one: what Lewis quarreled with in the work of occultists was the passivity that their epistemological process was assumed to entail.

In the second issue of *Blast*, Lewis devoted a lengthy piece, "A Review of Contemporary Art," to distinguishing Vorticism from the main movements in *avant-guerre* Europe—Picasso's Cubism, Marinetti's Futurism, and Kandinsky's Expressionism. According to Lewis's persona here, Vorticism quarrels with, and seeks to "CORRECT" (41), a major tendency of each group: Cubism concentrates too much on static objects, such that it lacks energy; Futurism is too indiscriminate in its inclusive scientific record of the "hurly-burly and exuberance of actual life"; and Expressionism, finally, is excessively "wandering and slack" (40). It is in his criticism of Kandinsky's Expressionism that Lewis alludes to the interest in the occult that pervades avant-garde circles of this moment. The Expressionists, he notes, are "ethereal, lyrical, and cloud-like—their fluidity that of the Blavatskyish soul" (40). Lewis here repeats the chief argument of *Blast*—that Vorticism supersedes its contemporaries by repudiating all forms of the "relaxed initiative" (41)—in large part to exorcise the effeminacy associated with *fin-de-siècle* Aestheticism.

Here, however, the Vorticist rejection of such a "relaxed" and "inactive" posture of "langour" [sic] (B2 41) is linked specifically to a rejection of contemporary occultism. The Expressionists, Lewis suggests, exhibit tendencies unfortunately reminiscent of Madame Blavatsky and her fellow Theosophists: Kandinsky, though promisingly abstract in his methods, fails because he is so "passive and medium-like" (40). A few pages later, again addressing Kandinsky, Lewis likewise notes that "[t]he Blavatskyish soul is another Spook which needs laying"; haunted by this "Spook," the "Brain" becomes a "mystic house" whose properly "rigid chambers" and "Bach-like will" degenerate in response into a "slovenly and wandering spirit" (B2 43). As the placement of terms in this passage indicates, for Lewis, the "Blavatskyish" and "mystic" are to be equated with the "slovenly and wandering."

Many forces of Lewis's immediate environment guided his use of the "Blavatskyish" occultist as a figure for what he disdained: London in 1914–1915 was still in the flush of the late nineteenth- and early twentieth-century revival of interest in the occult, replete with followers of Blavatsky's Theosophy, members of Mathers's Order of the Golden Dawn, and other participants in esoteric societies. Moreover, Kandinsky was a declared Theosophist. The Vorticists were in fact intrigued by Kandinsky's ideas, as attested by their decision to publish excerpts from his *Über das Geistige in der Kunst* (*On the Spiritual in Art*) (1912) in the first issue of *Blast*. And the irony here is that, like much that Lewis and his Vorticists disavow, "Blavatskyism"—and specifically Theosophy as absorbed by Kandinsky—arguably exerted considerable influence upon Vorticism. Materer makes a persuasive case for the impact of Theosophy's use of geometric forms—as transmitted through figures such Kandinsky, Brancusi, and the Futurists—on the development of the Vorticist geometric lexicon (*Modernist Alchemy* 32–40).

But regardless of what Vorticism owes to Blavatsky's Theosophy, it is Lewis's overt objections to mysticism and esoteric thought that are most relevant here. Lewis's quarrel with the occult, as I will argue, anticipates Yeats's and H.D.'s: like them, he objects to it because of the languor (B2 41) of attitude he believes study of the occult to entail.[18] Yeats and H.D. will be similarly driven by discomfort with the "passive and medium-like"—again, in their terms, the "amorphous"—and will respond to this uneasiness with a similarly geometric vocabulary. The indebtedness of Vorticist geometry to Theosophy and the occult notwithstanding, within Vorticism geometric figures assumed valences different from those they exhibited in a Theosophist context—in fact, shifting significance in reaction to the forces that may well initially have partly inspired them. And whereas H.D. and Yeats were indeed influenced by esoteric uses of geometric figures—I will say more about this—it is the distinctively Vorticist significance of their geometric strategies that I feature here.

This chapter, then, focuses on phases of Yeats's and H.D.'s careers during which the investment of both in the mystical revelation of occult knowledge had reached a particularly heightened state; and during which, nonetheless, both were simultaneously troubled by the prospect of becoming merely "passive and medium-like" recipients of occult wisdom, in part because of the intellectual standards according to which they had been raised. It is telling that H.D. writes to Bryher in 1933, registering a sentiment that resonates with Lewis's: "I am not, as you know, a sloppy theosophist and horoscope-ist" (Friedman, *Analyzing Freud* 331).[19] Here she disavows "sloppiness," though not involvement with the occult altogether. Again, the assumptions fueling H.D.'s and Yeats's anxiety about visionary consciousness, although not solely derived from Vorticist sources, were reinforced through their contact with Vorticism, and resonate closely with Vorticist ideas.

Arriving at occult knowledge through mystical means, of course, need not involve being "passive and medium-like." Yeats in fact differentiated between "mysticism" and "mediumship," reading the latter as entailing an extinction of the intellectual faculties, and even the memory, through the experience of being overtaken by another consciousness, and thus thoroughly passive (an "unconscious condition"), while regarding mysticism as not necessarily involving such passivity.[20] But in *Per Amica Silentia Lunae* (1917), Yeats suggested that the process of arriving at knowledge through visionary means does involve, if not passivity per se, at least a suspension of "will and intellect" (48). H.D., meanwhile, believed that visionary knowledge sometimes involved surrender to a passive condition of receptivity, and at other times, conscious effort and control as well, depending upon how it was experienced and handled.[21] Although Yeats and H.D. shared the belief that it was possible both to obtain knowledge by visionary means and to avoid surrendering to mere "passivity," their common fear of becoming simply passive conditioned their attitudes toward, as well as their textual accounts of, visionary experience. H.D. and Yeats strove to approach their visionary experiences, and represent them, so as to avert the kind of "sloppiness" of approach and passivity of attitude that Vorticism would deplore.

Yeats signals the approach to the occult that he disdains in his 1889 critique of members of the Theosophical Society, delivered during his first period of enthusiasm for visionary work: "[T]hey seem some intellectual, one or two cultured, the rest the usual amorphous material that gather round all new things. All, amorphous and clever alike, have much zeal" (quoted in Foster, *Apprentice*

Mage 102). The conspicuous, repeated use of the word "amorphous" here suggests Yeats's concern with a shapelessness of attitude: a lack of incisive, definite, active intellectual engagement, and a state neither "intellectual" nor "cultured" that Yeats seeks to avoid. In *The Sword Went Out to Sea*, written between "Writing on the Wall" and "Advent," H.D. likewise enlists the word "amorphous" to capture the nature of the work with the occult to which she objects:

> I have found the boundaries so far explored by psychic-research workers, cloudy and amorphous. My chief objection to the recorded findings of the spiritualists is that their messages and voices seem to come from a vague and commonplace no-man's-land . . . . It is almost as if their wordy and amorphous manner of expression were a badge of authenticity.
>
> (QUOTED IN FRIEDMAN, *PSYCHE REBORN* 199–200)

Here, the word "amorphous" is also repeated, used to suggest both a vague understanding of the occult phenomena "explored" as well as a consequent vagueness of "expression," both of which H.D. regrets. That H.D. likens these explorations (by "psychic research workers") to her own, even as she insists on differentiating her approach from theirs, is indicated by the phrase "research worker": in the Hirslanden Notebooks, H.D. will likewise call herself a "research worker" in the psychic realm. The kind of work with the occult that both H.D. and Yeats dislike, I would offer (as signaled by their common use, and shared significant repetition, of the word "amorphous") is characterized both by amorphousness of stance—an attitude lacking definite, active purposefulness and backbone—as well as by amorphousness of discovery and utterance, imprecision of both occult findings and descriptions thereof. What Yeats and H.D. seek instead in their own visionary work is the opposite of "amorphousness" or "shapelessness": that is, definite shape, and in this case, Vorticist geometric shape.

In the pages that follow, I seek to account for Yeats's and H.D.'s anxiety about, and their resultant efforts to resist, vagueness and passivity in their work with the occult. Northrop Frye criticizes what he regards as Yeats's "passive state of mind" while he constructed *A Vision* (*Spiritus Mundi* xii): in this comment, Frye overlooks the dimensions of *A Vision* that show Yeats to be far from passive—that show him, in fact, striving to cultivate what he would elsewhere call "the path of 'deliberate effort'" (*Autobiography* 225). Moreover, the geometric figures pervading H.D.'s and Yeats's accounts, although certainly part of the knowledge they received from an otherworldly realm, are also endowed with significances in their narratives that serve what I would term a Vorticist campaign against the "inactive," the "wandering," the "slack"—and, to use Yeats's and H.D.'s term, the "amorphous." As enlisted in the context of Yeats's and H.D.'s accounts, coded so as to connote rigor and activity, the geometric figures they received through mystical experience take on Vorticist valences.[22]

Not only did their anxieties about passivity and their development of a geometric lexicon accord with those of Vorticism, but their attitudes to visionary consciousness and their strategic use of a geometric vocabulary were also in part directed by encounters with Vorticist assumptions and values. Evidence both from *A Vision* and Yeats's letters suggests that there were many factors summoning Vorticism to mind for Yeats as he wrote *A Vision*—especially the second version of the book, which features the greater number of geometric diagrams. In 1931, Yeats was reading *Savage Messiah*, H. S. Ede's biography of Vorticist Gaudier-Brzeska, admiring Gaudier's "hard and masculine" mind (*LWBY* 782). In 1933, Yeats notes reading the work of yet another figure associated with Vorticism, and specifically a text that refers to the Vorticists: Hulme's "Modern Art," the lecture in which Hulme invokes Lewis and his fellow Vorticists as exemplars of the new and promising "geometrical tendency" in the visual arts (*LWBY* 810).

Clearly exerting the greatest impact on Yeats, however, was Lewis's own work: in the late 1920s, Yeats was reading Lewis's *Time and Western Man* with so much sympathy for its arguments—Lewis, he noted, "is on my side of things philosophically" (*LWBY* 739)—that he recommended the book to several correspondents and even wrote ardently to Lewis, whom he did not know well, to express his appreciation. Tellingly, in the same letter in which Yeats mentions Ede's book and lauds Gaudier, he notes that he dislikes the work of French philosopher Henri Bergson (which in his view, fortunately, Gaudier had resisted) because its worldview "turn[s] the world into fruit-salad (*LWBY* 782)." Yeats's off-the-cuff, playful metaphorical language here suggests his aversion at this juncture to that which is soft, amorphous, and without sufficiently definite geometric shape.

It suggests, moreover, given his reference to Bergson and the reasons for his rejection of his thought, that Yeats has been significantly influenced by *Time and Western Man*, which by this point he had read and praised intensely. In

Time and Western Man, Lewis likewise suggests that the Bergsonian perspective, given its insistence that life is most truly experienced as ongoing flux and "duration," sacrifices (for Lewis, lamentably) the ability to observe form and structure in the elements of our surroundings (148), as well as to analyze experience into its components and apprehend their "clearness of outline" (167).[23] *Time and Western Man*, Yeats confided to Olivia Shakespear in 1928, "fills my imagination": this he maintained during a year when he was laboring intensely on revisions to *A Vision*. Although by this time Lewis had long since shed his Vorticist affiliations, Yeats, as his comments about Lewis attest, quite evidently still identified Lewis with the Vorticist idiom.

Again, Yeats concludes his Introduction to *A Vision* (1937) by comparing his own "stylistic arrangements of experience"—his System as expressed in geometric diagrams—with "the cubes in the drawing of Wyndham Lewis" (25). Here, again, Yeats is clearly evoking Lewis's earlier, Vorticist work, as by the 1930s Lewis is no longer producing such geometric "cubes" in his drawings. Moreover, Yeats dates the Introduction "November 23rd 1928, and later" (25), placing this statement about the date just after the assertion about Lewis's "cubes": this suggests that, even if Yeats revised *A Vision* further during the 1930s, it was in 1928 that this comparison asserted itself most forcibly in his mind, during the years when he was reading Lewis's work most avidly. Yeats thus appears to have completed the Introduction to the 1937 edition of *A Vision* while under the sway of Lewis's ideas. That Yeats juxtaposes mention of the Introduction with a comment about Lewis's *Time and Western Man* in a 1928 letter to Lady Gregory lends this supposition further support.

The link between Vorticism and H.D.'s use of geometric figures in "Writing on the Wall" is less clear. What can be said is that in the early to mid-1930s, as evidenced by her language in *Nights*, H.D. relies heavily upon a geometric vocabulary, which she in turn uses to suggest forms of violence, both psychic and physical (see Chapter 3). This link continues the one that she made years earlier in her review of Yeats's "Responsibilities," when she connects geometric figures—the "black magic of triangles and broken arcs," the "Juggernaut of planes and angles" and "cubes" (53)—to the violence of the Great War. Whenever H.D. links geometric figures with violence, then, she harks back to a bond she first forged when responding to Vorticism—arguably, assigning them a significance that she reads as Vorticist. And she emphasizes such a nexus between geometric forms and violence in her work of the 1930s, during the years when she undertook the work with Freud that in turn gave rise to "Writing on the Wall." Thus I would argue that the use of geometry in her work of the 1930s—as well as in later work, such as "Writing on the Wall" and "Advent," issuing from experiences of the 1930s—bears connection to her memory of Vorticist "planes and angles."

But although both Yeats and (quite probably) H.D. were influenced by Vorticist geometry in their use of geometric figures as part of their accounts of visionary experiences, neither explicitly described their "geometrics" as Vorticist. In fact, they tended to emphasize other significances of geometry, which suggests that neither may have been fully conscious of their ties to Vorticist thought. Like many other writers and artists of the early twentieth century (as epitomized by Pound in his essay "The Wisdom of Poetry"), both H.D. and Yeats interpreted the geometric figures in their narratives as representing transcendent, archetypal patterns that emerge from the details of individual lives and events, and thus, by extension, as suggesting states of heightened awareness in which one could perceive such patterns—could infer from a welter of particulars their attendant conceptual shapes.

The late nineteenth-century surge of interest in hermetic thought in Europe, Britain, and North America, which led to much syncretistic work with esoteric teachings, encouraged both a focus on geometric figures as well as this kind of archetypal interpretation of them. Inspired by a diversity of sources—ranging from the ancient Greeks (Pythagoras, Plotinus, and Empedocles), to the mysterious Hermes Trismegistus (associated with Greece and Egypt), to the Kabbalah, to Hindu mysticism, and to later Western mystics such as Paracelsus, the Rosicrucians, Jakob Boehme, and Emanuel Swedenborg—esoteric study as it was understood in the climate of the late nineteenth and early twentieth centuries frequently drew upon geometric figures to "express" what Timothy Materer calls "the secret patterns of human destiny" (*Modernist Alchemy* 38).[24] And this climate, of course, clearly marked the thought of both H.D. and Yeats.

Yeats's membership in Mathers's Order of the Golden Dawn had led to work with geometric forms as stimulants for vision (*Autobiography* 113–114). Yeats also encountered geometry frequently in his work with the Theosophists: one of his earliest exposures to geometric diagrams representing historical cycles was through the Theosophical text *Esoteric Buddhism* (1883), by Blavatsky disciple A. P. Sinnett, which was given to Yeats in 1884 and is thought to have kindled his initial interest in the occult. Blavatsky's own *The Secret Doctrine* (1888), which also exerted significant influence upon Yeats, offered a discussion of ancient thought on geometric vortices from Greek, Egyptian, Chaldean, and Indian sources (117). And through Theosophy, Yeats often encountered arguments for the existence of geometric "thought forms": vividly colorful geometric shapes, said to be produced out of the impact of mental vibrations on "ether," that were believed to express certain emotions or frames of mind.[25] Especially influential on H.D., meanwhile, was a study by latter-day explicator of hermetic thought Robert Ambelain, *Dans L'Ombre des Cathédrales* (1939), which included a chapter on occult geometric symbolism called "La Géometrie Philosophale."[26] It is therefore no wonder that both H.D. and Yeats were interpreting geometric shapes involved in their visionary experiences as indicating universal patterns discovered through those experiences.

As framed in *A Vision*, Yeats's geometric patterns formed an analytical system that he hoped would enable understanding of both the cycles of Western history and the trajectories of individual lives, even the prediction of the future based upon past events. H.D.'s geometric "picture-writing," meanwhile, she links closely in "Writing on the Wall" with the notion of a "universal language" that belongs to "the whole race," that would allow people to "forgo barriers of time and space" and, through understanding of one another, to "save mankind" (*TF* 71).

But in addition to the public meanings H.D. and Yeats assigned to their geometric figures, which largely accorded with those attributed to them by the occult thinkers whose work they studied, geometry signified something else for them as well. Given the conditions out of which H.D. and Yeats were bringing their visionary experiences to the page—their mixture of personal and public concerns—in the context of their visionary narratives, their geometric figures also came to be freighted with particularly Vorticist significances.

THE GEOMETRIC VOCABULARY

The visionary texts in which H.D. and Yeats featured geometry most saliently were late installments, for each of them, in a long succession of versions. After publishing the 1925 edition of *A Vision*, Yeats labored for another twelve years to produce what he hoped was an improved text.[27] Although both the 1925 and 1937 versions include geometric diagrams, it was in the 1937 version that Yeats displayed them most prominently and commented upon them. H.D., meanwhile, experienced the four visions featured in her discussions with Freud while traveling through Cornwall and Greece in 1919–1920, but it took her more than twenty years to narrate them fully.[28] Even emerging from H.D.'s sessions with Freud were two iterations of the visionary experiences: one in "Advent," an account compiled in 1948 but taken directly from her journal of the sessions with Freud of 1933–1934, and one in "Writing on the Wall," written in 1944 without reference to the journal and published in 1945–1946.[29] (Both texts are now housed in *Tribute to Freud*.) Of all the accounts of her visionary experiences she produced throughout the 1920s and 1930s, it was not until "Writing on the Wall" that H.D. disclosed fully the significant geometric component of her visions.

In these late redactions of their visionary experiences—Yeats's 1937 version of *A Vision* and H.D.'s "Writing on the Wall"—readers are led to believe that geometry was an integral part of H.D.'s and Yeats's original visions: that geometry was the symbolism through which the otherworldly forces initially conveyed their occult information. But the fact that the geometry is more richly exhibited and framed in later narrativizations of their visions suggests that H.D. and Yeats did not include it merely to relay what happened. In these later versions, something else motivated and directed the inclusion of geometry, and that something else, I would offer, was in part the need to respond to the intellectual standards and epistemological modes represented in their imaginations by their fathers.

As these later more markedly geometric visionary texts appeared, H.D.'s and Yeats's increasing investment in geometry also became evident in other ways. During his work on *A Vision*, Yeats clearly showed the central place geometry occupied in his imagination. In 1928, writing to close friend Lady Gregory of his revisions of *A Vision*, he used geometry as a shorthand for the project: "At the moment my head is all frozen hard because of a morning of mystic geometry" (*LWBY* 743). When reflecting on *A Vision* in the Introduction to the 1937 version (which was first published in 1929), Yeats constantly referred to its geometric elements, implying their centrality to their project: "The first version of this book," he wrote, "fills me with shame. I had misinterpreted the geometry" (*AVB* 19). Elsewhere, he likewise stresses geometry, noting that the Instructors' "exposition was based upon a single geometrical conception" (11). And in a typescript of *Dramatis Personae* (1935), further indicating that he had geometry on his mind during the last round of revisions to *A Vision* and associated it with forms of learning, Yeats quotes the famous injunction engraved on the front of the Pythagorean Academy, reiterated by Plato, that none should enter the academy who were "ignorant of Geometry."[30]

H.D., meanwhile, showed her investment in geometry in that although *Tribute to Freud* describes all four of the visionary episodes she had experienced in 1919 and 1920, not just the one that incorporated geometric figures, the one involving geometric figures held a privileged place in her mind.[31] This was indicated by her choosing to name her 1944 collection of memoirs with a phrase she associated throughout the text with the specifically geometric visionary episode: "Writing on the Wall." Moreover, when alluding to the "*hieroglyph[s] of the unconscious*" (H.D.'s italics), the dream images she found increasingly significant during her work with Freud, she used geometric terms to exemplify them, referring to them at one point as "shapes, lines, graphs" (*TF* 93).[32] Freud, she tells us, found her geometric visions especially noteworthy because he thought them a "dangerous symptom" (*TF* 51), so apparently it was also he, and not only she, who emphasized them. It was she, however, who decided to focus textual attention on the figures—and she did this, I would offer, because she needed these geometric figures, along with the discussions with Freud that emerged from their collaborative examination of them, to enable her response to the intellectual standards her father had represented.

DESCRIPTIONS OF THE GEOMETRY

Although geometric diagrams punctuate the text of *A Vision* (1937) only intermittently, they nonetheless exert an insistent presence within the text.[33] The book begins with a wealth of geometric diagrams: in Book I, "The Great Wheel," the first fifteen pages feature geometric figures—interlocking cones, wheels, circles, spirals, triangles—approximately every other page. A few diagrams appear early in Book II, "The Completed Symbol"; then the now famous Yeatsian diagram outlining the cycles of history opens Book V, "Dove or Swan." Geometry actually makes no appearance at all in either of the text's two other books—Book III, "The Soul in Judgment," which details the progress of the soul after death, or Book IV, "The Great Year of the Ancients," which maps onto one another cosmic time-cycles with periods of different duration.[34]

Nonetheless, geometric diagrams dominate a reader's impression of the text. In the case of the 1937 version of *A Vision*, we immediately encounter these dia-

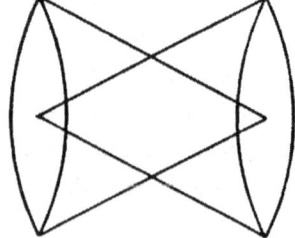
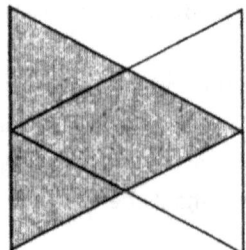

Diagrams from Yeats, A Vision (1937)

THE HISTORICAL CONES

The numbers in brackets refer to phases, and the other numbers to dates A.D. The line cutting the cones a little below 250, 900, 1180 and 1927 shows four historical *Faculties* related to the present moment. May 1925.

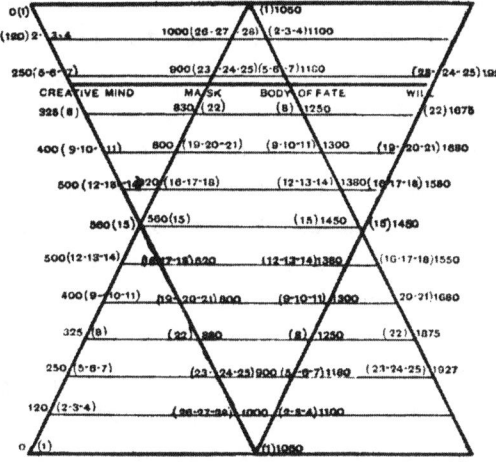

Diagram from Yeats, A Vision (1937): The Historical Cones

grams in abundance, developing our first sharp idea of the book out of this initial impression, and the diagrams conspicuously interrupt the prose such that they imprint themselves on our memories. Furthermore, primed by comments from Yeats in the introduction about his labor to "interpret" the "geometry," we also repeatedly look to the geometry for explanations of the difficult ideas that Yeats elaborates in prose. Concepts illustrated by the diagrams recur throughout *A Vision*, so that when we come upon a term or phenomenon already introduced, we are likely to turn back to the diagrams that originally accompanied it. We are that much more inclined to do so, given that we expect diagrams, by definition, to allay confusion through simplification.

Most of Yeats's diagrams are variations on his now well-known figure of the intersecting gyres, or the pair of interlocking cones (represented as triangles in the diagrams of *A Vision*), the apex of one of which falls at the base of the other. In *A Vision*, these gyres represent the trajectories described by individual souls as they move from life to death back to life, as well as by civilizations as they develop and decline. Yeats notes of the comprehensive explanatory power of the gyres that he need only "set a row of numbers upon [their] sides to possess a classification . . . of every possible movement of thought and life" (AVB 78). The interlocking cones express a relationship among elements that Yeats's Instructors have impressed upon him as a fundamental property of the universe: the life-arc of anything, from a thought to an individual person to a civilization, entails pairs of contrary impulses existing in inverse relation to each other. The

"MYSTIC GEOMETRY"

increase of one of these impulses correlates with, and by implication both depends upon and causes, the other's decline. Yeats often glosses this relationship with a phrase from Heraclitus: "Dying each other's life, living each other's death" (68). These two contrary impulses, or "tinctures," he calls "primary" and "antithetical." "Primary" trends move in the direction of objectivity, toward goals in realms external to the mind and the individual self, such as God, unity, reason, morality, abstraction, and the extinction of individual personality; "antithetical" trends move in the direction of subjectivity, toward the "inner world of desire and imagination" (73), concentrating on emotions, aesthetics, concrete images, and individuality.[35] In Yeats's view, the world's activities are generated out of the constant conflict between these two trends.

Yeats's second major ur-diagram, several versions of which appear in *A Vision*, is "The Great Wheel," an analytical tool that traces and parses the paths taken by the individual soul and, further, that allows for the classification of people. From an individual's location among the twenty-eight "phases" of "The Great Wheel," one can extrapolate that individual's disposition, capabilities, limitations, and ambitions.

In *Tribute to Freud*, geometric images appear in H.D.'s account of the "picture-writing" she saw projected in a hotel bedroom in Corfu while traveling with Bryher in the spring of 1920. Whereas Yeats's geometric images are displayed before us in diagrams that strike our attention just as forcefully as his prose descriptions of how he received them, H.D. offers only lyrical verbal descriptions of the geometry. Involving us in a step-by-step account of how the visions arrived, H.D. often employs present tense, making us feel as though we are moving with her through the gradually unfolding revelation of the series of pictures.

As she gazed intently at the wall, she recounts, there appeared before her first the silhouette of a head, then the outline of a goblet; then, the purely geometric figures began. The first was a "simple design in perspective." Shifting into present tense, she continues, "It is a circle or two circles, the base the larger of the two; it is joined by three lines," a design that finally resolves itself into the "tripod of classic Delphi" (*TF* 45–46). After the appearance of these three initial pictures, further images begin:

> Two dots of light are placed or appear on the space above the rail of the wash-stand, and a line forms, but so very slowly—as if the two rather heavy dots elongated from their own centers, as if they faded in inten-

> sity as two lines emerged, slowly moving toward one another. They will meet, it is evident, and from the pattern (two dots on a blackboard) we will get a single line. (52)

The gradual, sometimes painfully slow, process by which the geometry was revealed to H.D. in 1920 is mimicked here in the pace of her prose. To understand her account, we must concentrate as intensely as she had to do when she first received the images. She continues in the same vein:

> There is one line clearly drawn, but before I have actually recovered from this . . . another two dots appear and I know that another line will form in the same way. So it does, each line is a little shorter than its predecessor, so at last, there it is, this series of foreshortened lines that make a ladder . . . of light. (53)

After this description of the pictures, H.D. goes on to address her intense conversations with Freud about their significance. H.D. thus presents her geometric images by verbally recounting her memory of the process of receiving them, then describing how she worked through this memory with Freud to assign meaning both to what she had seen and to her ability to receive it. Yeats, in contrast, provides not only descriptions of the process of reception and meditations on geometry's significance (not, admittedly, as extensive or elaborate as H.D.'s), but also actual diagrams drawn by his wife (*LWBY* 819).

Clearly, these texts are designed to draw attention to the geometric figures featured within them. More important here than the kind of presence geometry exerts in these texts, of course, are its functions within the projects of *A Vision* and *Tribute to Freud*. In the next sections, I focus less on geometry's obvious functions within these texts and more on its roles within H.D.'s and Yeats's own projects: on the one hand, efforts to contribute adequate responses, by way of narrativizations of occult discoveries, to public crises; on the other, quests to redress the insecurities stemming from conflicts with their fathers. It is the latter that guide the distinctive way H.D. and Yeats frame and use the geometry in their visionary texts.

"THE TREND OF POLITICAL EVENTS": THE IMPACT OF POLITICS ON YEATS'S AND H.D.'S VISIONARY WORK

Presently, I will turn to why both H.D. and Yeats experienced such deep uneasiness about their relationship to the visionary, as well as to how that uneasiness played out at the level of narrative strategy and vocabulary, registering itself in the way geometry came to be coded in their accounts. First, however, I want to address why, between the wars, the investment of both in the occult took on a particular urgency and intensity, as well as why both Yeats and H.D. felt impelled to narrativize their visionary experiences powerfully and effectively. During the years that they were developing the writing that emerged from their visionary experiences—for Yeats, 1917–1937; for H.D., 1919–1944—both were responding to the increasingly uncertain political environment of the time; and their responses, in turn, were shaping their work with esoteric thought. Moreover, as they developed accounts of their visionary experiences, they wanted them to serve as responses to the public crises at hand.

I. YEATS: REACTING TO "THE PRESENT DISORDER"

In the early 1920s, Yeats was painfully aware of the ferment in Ireland that had preceded the creation of the Irish Free State in 1922 and of the brutal violence of the ensuing civil war.[36] As his letters attest, he was also attuned to the intensifying debates in Europe about communism and fascism. Yeats's position as a senator of the Irish Free State, which he took up in 1922, further heightened his awareness of both Irish turmoil and events on the Continent. But although he devoted himself to his role in the new Irish government, took a keen interest in the work, and received much praise for his efforts, Yeats was seldom entirely satisfied with his Senate contributions: when not addressing matters in the sphere of culture and the arts, he often felt out of his element and ill at ease.[37] At this point, I would suggest, the work on *A Vision* appealed to him as a way to participate in the debates of the time in a form that drew more effectively than did senatorial work on his distinctive abilities as artist and student of the occult.

In 1921–1922, he acknowledged his "deep gloom about Ireland" (*LWBY* 675) in its "present disorder" (693). In response to this "disorder," Yeats was aligning himself with a "return to conservative politics" in Ireland, which he read as congruent with the conservative turns occurring "elsewhere in Europe" (693). Specifically, Yeats was displaying an Edmund Burkean conservatism, a desire for Ireland to be governed by an elite of educated, able men aware of, as Yeats quoted Swift as saying, "the universal bent and current of a people"—the traditions, customs, and inheritance of the Irish (*Explorations* 292). Accordingly, he became increasingly invested in efforts to achieve order: as he would note in 1933, summing up the uneasiness with "disorder" that he had expressed in letters throughout the 1920s: "In politics I have but one passion and one thought, rancour against all who, except under the most dire necessity, disturb public order" (Yeats, *Variorum Poems* 543).

In the 1920s, this concern with "disorder" was already becoming connected for Yeats to an interest in fascist systems such as Mussolini's in Italy. More and more disillusioned with democracy, and opposed to communism, Yeats was well placed to become intrigued by Italy's new regime. Just after the March on Rome in October 1922, Yeats was writing to H. J. C. Grierson, "The Ireland that reacts from the present disorder is turning its eyes towards individualist Italy" (*LWBY* 693). Ezra Pound, though ultimately far more notorious than Yeats for his advocacy of Mussolini, was thus not alone in appreciating Italian Fascism both for its desirable order and for Mussolini's "burst of powerful personality" (Ellmann, *Man and Masks* 248). By the mid-1920s, Yeats was expressing approval of Mussolini's Italy more directly. As Michael North points out, Fascist Italy also seemed to Yeats to be designed to respect the "bent and current" of its people, as well as to protect a kind of individualism that was, for Yeats, fortunately distinct from the arid, abstract individualism fostered under liberal democracy—and likewise happily removed from the kind of erasure of individuality promulgated by communism (*Political Aesthetic* 70–73).

In *A Vision* (1937), Yeats announced his reluctance to engage with politics in the book: he did not want to concern himself with "political events," he said, except where obliged (283). But much evidence certainly suggests that as he was writing the first version of *A Vision*, the political scene of the 1920s significantly informed his decisions about the project. Letters of 1922, written during the first committed effort on *A Vision*, reveal that, during this period, he was working intensively on *A Vision* in the mornings and dedicating afternoons to the Senate, alternating activities in a way that would have made it likely that the work with the occult infused his political work and vice versa (*LWBY* 694–695). Ellmann suggests that Yeats indeed wanted to "introduce" the work of *A Vision* "into the political scene" (*Man and Masks* 249). And Cullingford asserts strongly that Yeats saw a "close relationship between esoteric philosophy and practical politics" (*Yeats, Ireland, and Fascism* 166) and that, accordingly, "*A Vision* is central to Yeats's political thought" (121). She maintains that "[a]lthough much of the book appears remote from political concerns, and although Yeats deliberately avoided topical political commentary in the text," *A Vision* turns on an "antithesis" between democracy and aristocracy that reflects how "inspired" it is by political concerns (121).

Signals from the pages of *A Vision* (1937) and the record of its composition suggest that as Yeats wrote the second version of the book, contemporary politics were even more on his mind. In the early 1930s, Yeats's imagination was briefly captured by a form of Irish Fascism manifesting itself through a group known as the "Blueshirts," who told Yeats that they had chosen their symbolic colors, including blue, based on a suggestion of his, though he did not remember having given it (*LWBY* 808). In April 1933, Yeats noted that that he was "trying ... to work out a social theory which can be used against Communism in Ireland—what looks like emerging [sic] is Fascism modified by religion" (808). "Our chosen colour is blue," he wrote, "and blue shirts are marching about all over the country" (812). Hopeful that the Blueshirts might bring some order to Ireland, in 1933 Yeats even agreed to meet with their leader, General Eoin O'Duffy.

Yeats's comments at this juncture point clearly to the important political role he attributed to his occult work: "I was ready," he noted afterward of the meeting, "for I had just re-written for the seventh time the part of *A Vision* that deals with the future" (*LWBY* 812–813). The word "for" here strongly suggests that Yeats regarded himself as preparing for the encounter by way of work on *A Vision*, and thus considered the project of *A Vision* as certainly apropos of, and perhaps even in part guided by, political concerns. As North and Cullingford have documented, Yeats soon afterward became disenchanted with the brute violence of fascism in its Irish, Italian, German, and Spanish varieties: he saw that it would not bring about the rule by educated men that he desired. But accompanying his disillusionment with events in the public political sphere, even fuelled by it, was Yeats's continuing faith in the geometric diagrams of his Spiritual Instructors as capable of offering something valuable to readers of the time—information that might help them to make sense of the "present disorder." Disappointed by developments in the outside world, Yeats, to use Pound's words, "retreat[ed]" to the "printed page" and its geometric diagrams (Materer, *Pound/Lewis* 168–169), but his was a retreat effected in the hope of offering a worthwhile, if heterodox, alternative heuristic to alleviate the confusion of the times.

It is cues on the "printed page," in fact, that suggest convincingly that, as Yeats developed the 1937 version of *A Vision*, politics was guiding his choices as he wrote. One of his opening sections, "The Great Wheel," for instance, is filled with footnotes—not present in the 1925 version—quoting Giovanni Gentile and Benedetto Croce, whose work Yeats was reading in the 1920s and 1930s, in part of out of his interest in Fascist Italy (Cullingford, *Yeats, Ireland, and Fascism* 151), and in part because he saw affinities between their claims and those of Swift and Burke (*Political Aesthetic* 71). The thought of Gentile and Croce, shaped by Giambattista Vico's cyclical view of history, contributed to the theorization of Italian Fascism, though Gentile would ultimately become an apologist for Italian Fascism; Croce, an opponent of it.

Most of the footnotes here simply register Gentile's and Croce's readings of philosophers such as Hegel and Kant. One note, however, observes that Yeats's symbol of "The Great Wheel," which describes the circuits of individual thoughts and lives, as well as the larger cycles of history, resembles "a similar circular movement fundamental in the works of Giovanni Gentile," which, Yeats maintains, is "the half-conscious foundation of the political thought of modern Italy" (*AVB* 81). This offhand remark thus begins, if only lightly, to connect Yeats's "Wheel" not only to Gentile but also to Italian Fascism. Yeats likewise lends a political spin to his footnotes when he observes, "Government must . . . recognize that class war though it may be regulated must never end"; this argument for constant class conflict and hierarchies among levels of society Yeats attributes to Croce and ties to the thought of Heraclitus (82). Then, in a more direct reference to debates of the 1930s, he posits this claim as "the converse of Marxian Socialism" (82). The political valence of Yeats's remarks here is not altogether clear, but that Yeats frames his text with politically charged remarks in the footnotes to *A Vision* implicitly embeds the project of the visionary book in the political debates of the time. Although *A Vision* may not evince an unequivocal political direction of a 1930s "show one's colors" variety, then, it nonetheless clearly engages in dialogue with contemporary claims about "government," "class war," "modern Italy," and "Marxian Socialism."[38]

Moreover, in the 1937 *A Vision*, Yeats chooses to situate prominently as one of his introductory pieces a letter to Ezra Pound, which opens with the commanding lines: "Do not be elected to the Senate of your country. I think myself, after six years, well out of that of mine" (*AVB* 26). The placement of this preface to *A Vision*, and this comment before Yeats's description in the letter of the book's project, suggests that if Yeats is "well out of" his political role as senator in the late 1930s, he may at that point be positioning the work of *A Vision* to participate in political debate and resolve conflict by another means—one more compatible with his temperament than senatorial work. Finally, at the end of *A Vision* (1937), in a section dated 1934–1936, Yeats notes his struggle to apply the symbols with which he has been working to current events: "Day after day," he says, he has been "turning a symbol over in my mind . . . attempting to substitute particulars for an abstraction like that of algebra" (301). Immediately after this, he poses a question arising directly from the political scene of 1936—suggesting, on the one hand, how he links the work on *A Vision* to contemporary political ideas and, on the other, how his work on *A Vision* has been stimulated by them: "How far can I accept socialistic or communistic prophecies?" (301). Again, although Yeats leaves conspicuously ambiguous here the precise nature of the connection between his work with his "symbols" and his meditations on political philosophy, that he includes such remarks at all, especially among the final gestures of the book that serve a perorative purpose, suggests that he sets *A Vision* in conversation with "socialistic or communistic philosophies," and has been trying, if inconclusively, to draw upon the work of *A Vision* to determine what he can, in political terms, "accept." Clearly, *A Vision* was governed in large part by Yeats's felt need to "react" to "the present" political "disorder."

I would offer that the system of thought that *A Vision* presents, along with what Yeats called its "harsh geometry" (*Essays and Introductions* 518), appealed to the desires driving his interest in Mussolini's rise to power: his Burkean conservatism, valorization of order, and desire to respect the individual. Yeats increasingly feared what he read as the Jacobin excesses of the times, and his System suggested a way to restore moderation and balance: with its diagrams, it could trace and respect the importance of the traditions, patterns, and customs of a community developed over an extended period of time, which revolutionary thinkers like the nationalists during the Irish civil war, as Yeats saw it, were inclined to discount and ignore (North, *Political Aesthetic* 65).

In addition, the resources afforded by the System for the analysis and rich description of different types of individuals (as exemplified in the description of the "Twenty-eight Incarnations") could foster a kind of attention to the individual that Yeats felt both liberal capitalist democracy and communism (and, in time, he saw, fascism) had, unfortunately, failed to achieve. If he could not stem the violence he saw building around him, if by 1928 he felt that he was "well out of" his senatorial position and not at his best in the political sphere, he could at least use his philosophical system to make more legible what had happened, politically and historically, as well as what was currently happening, and what was to come. *A Vision* could enable readers to discern patterns governing the development of Western history and to predict the course of upcoming events.

II. H.D.: "AWARE OF THE TREND OF POLITICAL EVENTS"

Likewise, H.D.'s work on visionary consciousness in the 1930s and 1940s was markedly influenced by political pressures of the day. Her letters of the 1930s demonstrate that her interest in the occult was similarly intertwined with, even animated by, her worries about the "constant cycles of war-scares and war-talk" into which she had been "flung." She tended to "see red" when those around her were "foolishly patriotic" and wanted, above all, to "keep out of *War*."[39] During the years between her visions of 1919–1920 and her analysis with Freud, H.D. experienced what she remembered as a "period of waiting" as people in her circles became more and more bewildered by political developments. Some of her contemporaries were suffering from "lethargy" and "stagnation"; others were "aware of the trend of political events" but "were almost too clever, too politically minded, too high-powered intellectually" (*TF* 57). What was clear to H.D. was that a "flood" of some kind was imminent and a response urgently needed. By the early 1930s, H.D. was even more convinced that she and her compatriots were adrift in political confusion, and the desire to allay such uncertainty drove much of her work. As she notes in *Tribute to Freud*,

> There was something that was beating in my brain.... I did not specifically realize just what it was I wanted, but I knew that I, like most of the people I knew, in England, America, and on the Continent of Europe, was drifting. We were drifting. Where? (13)

She remembers walking through Vienna, suddenly being caught in "confetti-like showers from the air" of strips of printed paper with mottoes from Hitler and realizing the imminent danger, especially to Jews like Freud (*TF* 58). She saw swastikas and rifles (*TF* 58–59). She records the desire to make sense of what was happening and her frustration at what she saw as the failure of her contemporaries to respond adequately to conditions at hand.

"MYSTIC GEOMETRY"

As Friedman suggests, disillusioned with the possibility of helping through conventional "political involvement," H.D. saw her "esoteric" work as a crucial means of contributing effectively to the effort of healing (*Psyche Reborn* 178). She combined this esoteric work with psychoanalytic work, since she saw the two as intimately linked, the latter a bridge to occult knowledge. As H.D. noted in *The Sword Went Out to Sea*, "If we think of policies or politics, we are forced to think in vague generalities"; she was therefore "forced," she says, "by a law of compensation, to try to grapple with the forces inside myself, or outside the material world" (41) — psychological or occult forces, which, again, H.D. saw as closely linked, believing that the individual mind often provided access to occult knowledge.[40] In "H.D. by Delia Alton," a set of autobiographical reminiscences, she writes of her sense of mission during the 1930s, using the third person to capture her perspective and efforts of that time:

> We are through with experimenting. We are in the mid-thirties, not the mid-twenties
>
> ....
>
> She has not found it but she goes on assembling her small treasures. This is done feverishly, through a sort of compulsion, you might say. It is necessary to tidy-up, to clear the decks. We are not in the mid-twenties, we are in the mid-thirties. The storm is coming. (211)

H.D. was working out of an acute consciousness, then, that the moment demanded of her something specific to the moment (as she says twice for emphasis, she was *not* "in the mid-twenties," but "the mid-thirties") and that she had in some way to respond adequately to escalating tensions and the imminent "storm." As she came to express in *Trilogy*, her long poem written out of the conditions of the Second World War, as a writer she believed herself distinctively equipped to provide readers with threads binding them to wisdom of the ancient past. Moreover, as someone who had had "psychic or occult experiences" (*TF* 39), she believed that she could offer ancient knowledge that might help to bring about peace in Europe.[41]

Spurring both H.D.'s and Yeats's efforts to narrate their visionary experiences, endowing them with special urgency, then, was their desire to use wisdom gained through visionary experience to assist and heal a troubled contemporary world. Accordingly, the geometric images involved in Yeats's and H.D.'s accounts of their visionary experiences suggested, first, their wish to understand the patterns behind events—to make legible, and thereby to redeem, the seeming chaos of the present. But they also signified something else. Again, the geometry in their work also registers H.D.'s and Yeats's fundamentally conflicted relationship to their visionary projects, as well as to the visionary epistemological mode more generally.

AMBIVALENCE TOWARD VISIONARY EPISTEMOLOGIES

As they felt compelled to contribute to public affairs, both H.D. and Yeats were nettled by increasing self-doubt about their right to speak, the value of their knowledge, and the legitimacy of their epistemological authority. In part, it was the pressure to provide adequate responses to public crises that surfaced their anxieties. Their intellectual modesty, of course, seems ironic. By 1923 Yeats was a venerated public figure, having been appointed a Senator and having won the Nobel Prize; even he acknowledged that he had become a "personage" (*LWBY* 695). Nonetheless, as Daniel Albright remarks, "All his life Yeats considered himself, with some justice, an uneducated man" (*Quantum Poetics* 32). Despite his father's hopes for him, Yeats had not received a university education and remained conflicted about academia. Ellmann comments that "[Yeats's] lack of an orthodox education was to dog him like a guilty conscience throughout his life and to result in an excessive respect for learning" (*Man and Masks* 32). By 1933, H.D., though not recognized as the public intellectual Yeats was, was nevertheless a well-known poet, having moved in advanced artistic and intellectual circles for many years. That Freud would accept her as a "student," rather than simply an analysand, attests to her status. Nonetheless, H.D. regarded herself as inadequately intellectually "endowed."

And this self-doubt, in turn, surfaced latent anxieties that both Yeats and H.D. had long felt about the legitimacy of visionary endeavors more generally—anxieties that stemmed from years before, I would argue, when they had disappointed their fathers through apparent failures of intellect. Thus the way that H.D. and Yeats enlist geometry in their texts reveals the lineaments of an anxiety about visionary consciousness generated in part out of a fear of not being able to respond adequately to the public crises of the day, but also partly by the intellectual standards according to which they had been raised.

"MYSTIC GEOMETRY"

These standards derived from memories of how their own fathers had instructed them, modeled for them methods of intellectual pursuit, and dissuaded them from mystical ways of knowing. Beginning their efforts to narrate their visionary experiences at just about the time of their fathers' deaths (H.D.'s father died in 1919; Yeats's in 1922), both H.D. and Yeats, I would argue, were guided by a need to respond to principles they associated with their fathers.[42] I would offer, in fact, that (in a way appropriate to their work with the occult) they were haunted by the specters of their fathers. Both acknowledged a continuing regret, albeit mixed with many other emotions, at not having lived up to the intellectual expectations their fathers had once set for them.

Yeats's *Autobiography*, H.D.'s memoirs such as *The Gift* and *Tribute to Freud*, and biographical studies of both writers convey how deeply both were impressed by their fathers' examples and by the intellectual and educational standards they represented—and, by the same token, how profoundly inadequate they felt in the face of those standards.[43] H.D. wrote of the character who represents her in her autobiographical novel HERmione, "She was a disappointment to her father" (HERmione 10). In his *Autobiography*, Yeats accumulates before us a picture of a volatile father impatient with his son's reveries and mysticism. And in the cauldron of events of the 1920s and 1930s, H.D.'s and Yeats's discomfort at the memories of their fathers' dissatisfaction reached the boiling point, provoking them into an intense sense of conscience about their work.

H.D.'s and Yeats's ambivalent relationships to visionary consciousness, then, as registered in their use of geometry, were conditioned by a variety of forces—some public, others personal. And these conflicted relationships, in turn, gave rise to a distrust of visionary experience that resonated with the Vorticist skepticism of the occult. Accordingly, the geometric language of their narratives, coded to enact a compensatory response to their uneasiness about vision, assumes a Vorticist set of meanings.

III. YEATS: "ARGUMENTS WITH MY FATHER"

Yeats's father, the painter J. B. Yeats (JBY), was a committed skeptic and rationalist, under the sway of such thinkers as Darwin, Huxley, Tyndall, and J. S. Mill; accordingly, he consistently scorned his son's fascination with the occult.[44] JBY's disdain for his son's increasing ardor for esoteric knowledge during his youth was likely exacerbated by the awareness that by immersing himself in the occult,

WBY was turning away from the intellectual values that JBY had tried to transmit to him. From WBY's childhood onward, JBY had sought to educate his son stringently in literature, science, and philosophy. During WBY's childhood, JBY had been known as intellectually eclectic and dilettantish, but years before, he had matriculated from Trinity College and studied law; he had read widely and masterfully. He was recognized for strong intellectual convictions and high standards. WBY remembers him as an imperious, demanding tutor—and recalls himself as an inattentive and generally lackadaisical student (Yeats, *Autobiography* 14, 71). The elder Yeats watched his son sternly and closely, striving to direct his path and railing when he encountered the inability or the absentminded dreaminess that the younger Yeats often showed. For much of his youth, Yeats remained compelled by his father's intellectual lights, sorry that he didn't measure up to them.

Although JBY was proud both of his son's early interest in science and his later capacity for verse, he was often dismayed by his son's mediocre-to-weak performance in school (Foster, *Apprentice Mage* 25), and later disappointed that WBY opted for London's Metropolitan Art School rather than Trinity, his alma mater. WBY later claimed that his performance in classics and mathematics had been too poor to allow him to pass Trinity's entrance examinations, but he had dared not reveal this to his father (*Autobiography* 48).

In general, as George Yeats noted, WBY remembered his father and other family members "railing about his various inabilities" and especially about his "not going to Trinity" (Foster *Apprentice Mage* 35). His father was supportive of WBY's ambition to be a poet, but he disliked what he took to be the irrationality, and accordingly, the intellectual laxity, of WBY's work with the occult. The young Yeats was keenly aware that everything about his esoteric studies set him at odds with his father, and in later years even recognized that his devotion to the occult was a way of gaining independence from JBY's powerful force field.[45] Averse to his father's atheistic rationalism, he fashioned for himself a kind of religion; unable (and often unwilling) to excel in the areas his father had staked out for him—classics, mathematics, science, art—he ventured through the study of the esoteric into territory that was entirely his own. Aware of his father's valorization of active intellectual effort, he placed a premium on contemplative "passivity" (Coote, *Yeats: A Life* 45); aware of his father's concern that he had become too much like his mother's Pollexfen side of the family, he followed the path of his uncle, George Pollexfen, who had devoted himself to study of the supernatural.

WBY was clearly recognizing the divide opening up between him and his father when he wrote to John O'Leary in 1892, suggesting that O'Leary's disdainful attitude toward WBY's esoteric work had been influenced by JBY:

> The probable explanation... of your somewhat testy postcard is that you were out at Bedford Park and heard my father discoursing about my magical pursuits out of the immense depths of his ignorance as to everything that I am doing and thinking.
>
> (*LWBY* 210–211)

He would later acknowledge that "It was only when I began to study psychical research and mystical philosophy that I broke away from my father's influence" (*Autobiography* 54). But despite the decisive rupture with his father's beliefs this suggests, his early relationship to "psychical research and mystical philosophy" nonetheless remained colored by the elder Yeats's resistance. Chided by a friend for his less than wholehearted acceptance of Theosophy, Yeats felt that he occupied the position of caution, "held there perhaps by my father's scepticism" (55).

J. B. Yeats never hesitated to let his son know of this skepticism: in 1894, he characterized WBY's work with the occult as "hot and credulous" (Materer, *Modernist Alchemy* 25). In April 1918, after seeing the reviews of WBY's devotedly mystical work *Per Amica Silentia Lunae*, JBY wrote to his son, "I am sorry you are returning to mysticism. Mysticism means a relaxed intellect. It [is] of course very different from the sentimentalism of the affections and the senses which is the common sort, but it is sentimentalism all the same, a sentimentalism of the intellect" (Murphy, *Family Secrets* 374).[46]

Despite his father's resistance, however, as he finished *Per Amica Silentia Lunae* and began work on *A Vision*, WBY nonetheless continued to describe his work on the occult to JBY, as though resolved to show him what he was doing. He seemed to be implicitly seeking JBY's approval, and at times even trying to emphasize that their modes of thought, despite JBY's disdain for his mysticism, remained similar. Contrary to what we might expect from a son whose investments in the occult had been so roundly rejected by his father, Yeats at this point still took his father's ideas with intense seriousness. He wrote to JBY with frequency and attentiveness, encouraging his father's endeavors, recounting in detail his own projects, and emphasizing to his father how stimulated he was by the elder Yeats's ideas.[47] Moreover, in his letters he strove to emphasize the likeness between his thought and his father's: "Much of your thought resembles mine in *An Alphabet* [*Per Amica Silentia Lunae*] but mine is part of a religious system more or less logically worked out, a system which will I hope interest you as a form of poetry" (*LWBY* 626–627). Surprisingly, Yeats presses not on differences between father and son—which had been painfully apparent for years—but rather on their affinities, as though invested in convincing JBY that what he was accomplishing with his "religious system" was in fact equivalent to what interested his father.

I will shift now to H.D.'s analogous response to her father, but I will return later in the chapter to the project that drives Yeats's efforts here to persuade JBY of such resemblances. What is clear is that, as he begins the work on *A Vision* in 1917, Yeats is still very much in the habit of directing what he does toward the horizon of his father's ideas and judgments.

H.D.: "A DISAPPOINTMENT TO HER FATHER"

H.D.'s father, meanwhile, Charles Leander Doolittle, a successful professor of astronomy and mathematics, was even more thoroughly associated than J. B. Yeats with rigorous rational thought and scientific method. As H.D. would reminisce in *Tribute to Freud*, her father was a "mathematician, an astronomer, detached and impartial, a scholar or *savant*" (31). Guest notes a "natural linkage" between H.D. and Professor Doolittle and remarks that Bryher, H.D.'s companion, observed that "[n]ot one day went by" when H.D. did not mention "my father, the Astronomer" (*Herself Defined* 14). Recognizing H.D.'s intellect and bent for science and mathematics, her father initially had high hopes for her: recalling that he had at one point noted that "his one girl was worth all his five boys put together," she recognized that this had placed on her a "terrible responsibility" (Augustine, *Gift Complete* 96).

As a child H.D. had revered her father's work, which always remained glamorously mysterious to her: as she wrote in *The Gift*, her memoir from the 1940s, "Papa went out to look at the stars at night. He measured them or measured something, we didn't know quite what" (39). Elsewhere she notes, "What he was, was a pathfinder, an explorer" (96). Retrospecting about her youth in the Hirslanden Notebooks of 1957–1959, she noted that "the Professor of Astronomy and Mathematics ... wanted eventually (he even said so) to make a higher mathematician of me or research worker or scientist like (he even said) Madame Curie" (Notebook II, February 2, 1957, quoted in Friedman, *Psyche Reborn* 200).

This, however, was not to be. In *HERmione*, H.D.'s posthumously published autobiographical roman à clef (thought to have been written about 1927), H.D. registers the circumstances under which she left college at Bryn Mawr, having failed, among other subjects, mathematics.

"MYSTIC GEOMETRY"

> Conic sections would whirl forever round her for she had grappled with the biological definition, transferred to mathematics, found the whole thing untenable. She had found the theorem tenable until she came to conic sections and then Dr. Barton-Furness had failed her, failed her . . . they had all failed her. Science [. . .] failed her . . . and she was good for nothing. (5–6; ellipses not in brackets are H.D.'s)

In its wording, this passage not only registers H.D.'s own sense of failure—its needling repetition evokes the experience of having the subject harped upon—but also suggests the counterreading of the situation that H.D. would later more often launch to resist the sense of defeat: that the world of mathematics and science had "failed" her as much as she had "failed" in its terms.

For years, however, H.D. would nonetheless remain in the grips of a sense of inadequacy. Guest remarks of H.D.'s departure from Bryn Mawr:

> The Doolittle household had rigid scholastic standards. H.D. was the only one of their progeny not to graduate from college. Her status as a prodigal daughter was made clear to her, and she never forgot this lowering of her self-respect.
>
> (HERSELF DEFINED 22)

When, in 1911, H.D. tried to recuperate from her failure by sailing for Europe, Guest suggests that she "saw herself as a prodigal leaving home. H.D. confessed that 'she felt instinctively that she had failed by all the conventional and scholarly standards. She had failed in her college career; she had failed as a social asset with her family'" (27).

The journey to Europe was planned as a vacation from which she would return, yet H.D. ended up remaining abroad to begin a new life. H.D.'s decision to expatriate, then, was informed by her awareness that she had failed by "all the conventional and scholarly standards." She was especially aware of the breach between her and the scientific world associated not only with her father, but also with her grandfather, a botanist and cell biologist, and with her brother, who eventually followed in his father's footsteps as professor of astronomy at the University of Pennsylvania. H.D. had not ultimately been able to meet the "responsibility" visited upon her by her father's "terrible" expectations.

H.D.'s texts often suggest that her interest in mysticism and the occult was intertwined with, and may even have emerged from, this condition of estrangement from the realm of scientific inquiry in which the men of her family had excelled. She came to regard her visionary abilities as enabling her to move beyond, as she would put it in HERmione, the world of "biological-mathematical definition" (76), her shorthand term for the sphere from which she had been expelled. As she noted in the 1933 letter to Bryher quoted in part above,

> I am not, as you know a sloppy theosophist or horoscope-ist, but you know, I do believe in these things and think there is a whole other-science of them.... I suppose that too, is symbolical of my leaving my own home and its surro[u]ndings and the strictly, so-called "scientific."
>
> (MAY 28, 1933; QUOTED IN FRIEDMAN, ANALYZING FREUD 331).

H.D.'s work in mysticism, then, she read as a way of "leaving ... home," claiming a territory of her own, gaining command over a school of thought whose fundamental premises challenged those founding conventional scientific endeavor—and thereby using a "whole other-science" to oppose the realm of science from which she had felt herself barred. Notice that she calls the realm she marks out for herself "science," but, significantly, it is an "other-science," an alternative to conventional science. Moreover, it is "whole"; the word, albeit used casually and colloquially in this context, suggests the robustness and completeness, the legitimacy, with which H.D. wanted to credit this alternative scientific domain. On the original letter she indicates the importance of her statement "I do believe in these things and think there is a whole other-science of them" by typing it in red, while the surrounding passage remains in conventional black ink. Not having been able to succeed in the arena of her father and brother, she would renounce the exclusive rightness of their discipline, its epistemologies, and the knowledge they could gain through it; she would question the value of succeeding on their terms—and, branching off in another direction, seek another form of knowledge, a counterknowledge. Moreover, she wanted to present her occult material in such a way as to register, to herself and others, the equivalency between what she was doing and what her father's scientific standards had asked of her. She may have traveled a route different from theirs, but, she wanted to demonstrate, her skills were as masterly as theirs, even in some ways akin to theirs—and she could offer knowledge as worthwhile as theirs.

By delving into astrology, H.D. was able to gain mastery of a discipline that was enough like her father's astronomy to provide the satisfaction of having reached a site similar to his and having equaled him, as well as of having conquered a discipline that not only differed from his, but whose founding assumptions implicitly challenged those of his. This way, she could at once prove her skills on his terms and demonstrate her resistance to his epistemological convictions. As Friedman notes, "Both Freud and H.D. regarded her fascination for esoteric astronomy as her unconscious attempt to approach her distant, cold, scientific father" (*Psyche Reborn* 166), to accomplish something comparable enough to what he did to gain proximity to him, but to do something different enough from his work to avoid merely echoing him. H.D. suggests this when she notes to Bryher, "I think you will agree that star-fish stuff [i.e., astrology and psychic phenomena] is my real world, and that getting that, I am, in a way, being 'in love' also with my father" (letter to Bryher, May 28, 1933; quoted in Friedman, *Analyzing Freud* 331–332). In this passage, she goes on to link the notion of "father" to a "mystical 'father in heaven,'" but as in the course of the letter she has addressed psychoanalytic transference, her father, her mother, and "home," the word "father" here seems also to point to Charles Doolittle. *By way of* astrology, then, even as she departs from her father's course, she is showing her "love" for, and presumably an affinity with, him.

Elsewhere, she even suggests that more than arriving at territory similar to his, she has succeeded in achieving what he wanted her to achieve, although on her terms rather than his. When, in the Hirslanden Notebooks, she observes that her father "wanted eventually . . . to make a higher mathematician of me or research worker or scientist like (he even said) Madame Curie," she concludes this thought by saying, "He did make a research worker of me but in another dimension" (Notebook II, February 3, 1957; quoted in Friedman, *Psyche Reborn* 200). H.D. had attained the goals her father set out for her, but in her own "dimension," the dimension of mystical rather than empirical epistemology, and occult rather than scientific knowledge. The fact that in the 1950s H.D. employed the phrase "He did make a research worker out of me" suggests further that, however much her work indicated her independence, she was nonetheless ready to credit her father's influence for guiding her down her path.

A VISION AND TRIBUTE TO FREUD

Given what visionary work had come to represent for Yeats and H.D.—a departure from their fathers' ways of knowing and a chance to prove themselves on their own ground, even as they demonstrated the equivalence between their fathers' forms of knowledge-pursuit and theirs—both Yeats and H.D. enlisted their narratives of such visionary work in a project of replying to their fathers.

In *A Vision* (1937), when describing his interactions with the capricious spiritual Instructors, relaying the intense effort he has had to expend to make sense of their transmissions, Yeats introduces his father into the textual picture. At this point, he has just finished describing the struggle with the Communicators, who seem deliberately and mischievously to introduce difficulty into his learning process. They keep "shift[ing] ground," he says, preventing him from grasping their "central idea," as if to ensure that he will remain vigilant in his attention (*AVB* 11). The Communicators forbid him to speak of the System to other people, lest they themselves become confused, unable to differentiate between their own thoughts and those of others (11–12). Furthermore, they enhance the difficulty of the task for Yeats by prohibiting him from reading philosophy, which might help him to follow their communications, until they have finished relaying their information—again, lest they confuse their ideas with his (12). Directly after dwelling on such "difficulties," the Communicators' exacting standards, their capricious ways, and their constant challenges, Yeats observes, "Arguments with my father ... had destroyed my confidence and driven me ... to the direct experience of the Mystics" (12).

This textual juxtaposition—between the description of his strenuous labor with the Instructors and his memory of his father—suggests the link that Yeats made, psychically, between the memory of conflict with his father and his interaction with the Instructors. Moreover, that Yeats mentions his father here suggests that he wished, through his work with the Instructors, to direct this textual display toward his father. As was clear from letters written during the years leading up to his father's death, Yeats wanted to demonstrate his work to JBY. In particular, he wanted to show that he had not, through mysticism, succumbed to a "relaxed intellect," but rather had found through mysticism a way of exerting his intellectual abilities to active and impressive effect. Moreover, in responding faithfully to the demands of the capricious Instructors, he could make gestures akin to those that would have satisfied his father, who, much like the Instructors, was frequently "angry and impatient" (*Autobiography* 14).

"MYSTIC GEOMETRY"

H.D. meanwhile indicates the link between her effort to narrate her visionary experiences and her memories of her father by emphasizing connections between Freud and Charles Doolittle. She repeatedly insists that, as she notes in "H.D. by Delia Alton," "Sigmund Freud is known generally as the Professor; my father was referred to constantly as the Professor; that is an obvious association" (190). In *Tribute to Freud*, the "association" is indeed "obvious": H.D.'s work with Freud (whom she calls "The Professor" throughout the narrative) is presented as having summoned a host of memories about her father. Both Freud's similarities to her father and the psychoanalytic situation facilitated a transference whereby many of the gestures H.D. was directing at Freud—and she had gone to him for his "opinion" about her "psychic or occult experiences" (*TF* 39)—were, on another psychic level, directed at Charles Doolittle.

Accordingly, much as Yeats does in *A Vision*, while narrating her work with Freud H.D. introduces her father into the text, indicating her similar desire to direct toward her father the display of abilities and labor enabled by the project of writing the text. She repeatedly compares Freud to her father. Just after noting having looked at the items on Freud's table, she reminisces about her father's table (*TF* 23–24); she likens the "sacred objects" belonging to Freud to her father's (25); remembering the "shock" from which her father had died, she addresses the similar "shocks" that Freud has sustained (31). Describing Freud's study, she remarks on the several points of affinity with her father's, suggesting how much Freud's "atmosphere" (to use a term employed repeatedly in *Tribute to Freud*) evokes memories of her father's environment:

> There is the old-fashioned porcelain stove at the foot of the couch. My father had a stove of that sort in the outdoor office or study.... There was a couch there, too.... My father's study was lined with books, as this room was. There was a smell of leather, the crackling of wood in the stove, as here.
> (19)

Throughout, H.D. underscores the likeness between her father and Freud, between her relationship to her father and her relationship to Freud: in this narrative laden with commentary about psychoanalytic transference, we see clearly that whatever psychic maneuvers she needs to display to Freud reveal those she needs to demonstrate to the other "Professor."

"TRUTHS WITHOUT FATHER"

Again, however, these replies that Yeats and H.D. felt called upon to direct toward their fathers, replies that involved manifestation of their work with mysticism, involved a great deal of anxiety. And this anxiety comes to be inscribed in their narrative approaches and, specifically, in their use of geometric figures. A metaphor here can help to crystallize how memories of their fathers' intellectual examples spurred H.D.'s and Yeats's radical discomfort with visionary ways of knowing.

Yeats accessed his otherworldly system of knowledge through the automatic writing of his wife. But in the first version of *A Vision*, at George's request, Yeats masked her contribution by fabricating a fantastic story about having received the System from an "Arabian traveller" named Michael Robartes, who, in turn, had discovered it in a book by a medieval theologian named Giraldus. However, also included in *A Vision* (1925) is a poem that indirectly suggests George's role. The poem, "Desert Geometry or the Gift of Harun Al-Raschid," features Kusta ben Luka, a philosopher of whom Robartes learns during his travels, who has received much the same kind of wisdom as has Robartes. Like Yeats, Kusta ben Luka has obtained his information through his young spouse, who has imparted it while in a trance. He describes it this way:

> A live-long hour
> She seemed the learned man and I the child;
> Truths without father came, truths that no book
> Of all the uncounted books that I have read,
> Nor thought out of her mind or mine begot,
> Self-born, high-born, and solitary truths,
> Those terrible implacable straight lines
> Drawn through the wondering vegetative dream.
>
> (*A VISION* [1925] 125)

In context, the "terrible implacable straight lines," reminiscent of the "path of deliberate effort" Yeats invokes in his *Autobiography*,[48] cannot but also remind us of the "harsh geometry" of *A Vision*.

"MYSTIC GEOMETRY"

This fictional scenario, I would offer, captures the nature of the anxiety that both Yeats and H.D. felt about visionary knowledge, in part because of their continuing susceptibility to the influence of paternal expectations. On the one hand, the visionary knowledge they had received, they felt, was wondrous and compelling—"terrible"—seeming to derive from a source more than human, persuasive through both its sternness and its mystery. (One thinks here of Yeats's magnificent golden smithies of Byzantium, who have little patience for the "fury and the mire of human veins.") It also allowed them to separate themselves decisively from their fathers' intellectual realms. But visionary knowledge also brought "[t]ruths without father": truths whose paternity was unsettlingly ambiguous. Perhaps these truths were "high-born," but they were also "self-born," such that their sources could not be verified in human terms: there was always the possibility of their illegitimacy.

For H.D. and Yeats, then, "truths without father" suggest, on one level, visionary truths whose legitimacy could not easily be ascertained because their provenance could not be confirmed. On another level, they were working with truths whose veracity and worth would likely have been called into question by the standards according to which their own fathers had instructed them. Given their commitment to rationalism and empiricism, both J. B. Yeats and Charles Doolittle had imparted epistemological approaches to their children that suggested that unless truths were accessed by rational or scientific means from identifiable sources, ascertainable by reason or verifiable by way of empirical evidence, they were suspect.

Further, according to what their fathers had modeled for them, H.D. and Yeats had to earn these "truths" rightfully by way of their own work. The assumption, growing out of their fathers' examples, was that knowledge gained without active work was inadequate because it involved a merely passive reception of ideas. Visionary knowledge was particularly vulnerable to such a critique: as Yeats's father put it dismissively, "mysticism" involved a "relaxed intellect." H.D., likewise, often felt that during her visionary episodes she simply had to "let go" and surrender all active control over the process of acquiring knowledge. Certainly Yeats felt uneasy about this aspect of mystical experience in part because his father had openly regretted his turn to mysticism for its intellectual laxity. H.D., meanwhile, though not directly admonished by her father on this point, seemed similarly anxious about the prospect of excelling at an epistemology that involved merely passive reception, when she was committed to breaking actively with the intellectual practices of her surroundings. To live up to her father's image for her, she needed to prove herself not a medium, but rather an active "research scientist," much as he had been; the figure she remembered and revered was defined as much by his long days of painstaking work—she remembered him hard at work at all hours in his astronomer's transit house—as by his achievements.

As Sword notes, because H.D. needed to convince herself and others of the validity of her visionary experiences, she worried that taking on the role of a medium for divine inspiration might jeopardize both her control and her expressive autonomy. As Sword argues, H.D. sought, one the one hand, to "legitimize visionary experience" by approaching it scientifically ("Engendering Inspiration" 155), and on the other, to handle visionary experience so as to avoid the "loss of self" she feared visionary experience might entail (122)—to sustain the "self-possession" (135) that certain kinds of visionary experience, which could overcome and "possess" the self from outside, might threaten (126).[49]

BETWEEN HUMILITY AND DEFIANCE: THE CONFLICTED DESIRE FOR VISIONARY AUTHORITY

Thus H.D.'s and Yeats's continued allegiance, on some levels, to scientific and rationalist ways of knowing—those that their fathers had encouraged—left both feeling intellectually inadequate as well as unable to believe that the attainment of visionary knowledge could, in itself, entirely assuage their sense of inadequacy. H.D.'s and Yeats's engagement in visionary projects to compensate for those perceived insufficiencies in some ways worsened their fears—because even as it afforded them forms of authority and independence, it also reminded them of their failure to succeed in conventional intellectual terms. Accordingly, their attitudes toward visionary ways of knowing remained fundamentally conflicted, as revealed in these visionary texts by their oscillation between moments of satisfaction and moments of doubt—between humility and defiance.

"MYSTIC GEOMETRY"

YEATS:
"IGNORANCE"
AND "THE
REVOLT OF THE
SOUL AGAINST
THE INTELLECT"

In the dedication to the 1925 version of *A Vision*, Yeats registers his sense of ineptitude, fearing that his "ignorance of philosophy" (xii) may sabotage his enterprise. In the 1937 version of *A Vision*, he again notes his philosophical naiveté: "I . . . know nothing but the arts and of these little" (*AVB* 279); when he and George began the project, "neither I nor my wife knew . . . that any man had tried to explain history philosophically. I . . . would have said that all written upon the subject was a paragraph in my own *Per Amica Silentia Lunae*, so ignorant a man is a poet and artist" (261). Retrospecting about the 1925 edition, he comments, "The first version of this book . . . fills me with shame. I had misinterpreted the geometry, and in my ignorance of philosophy failed to understand distinctions upon which the coherence of the whole depended" (19). His confessions of ignorance here resonate vividly with his comments in his autobiography—two editions of which were published at approximately the same time as the two versions of *A Vision*[50]—about his lack of scholarly aptitude. In the first two sections of his autobiography, "Reveries Over Childhood and Youth," and "Trembling of the Veil," he notes: "Because I had found it hard to attend to anything less interesting than my thoughts, I was difficult to teach" (*Autobiography* 14) and, later, "I was not an industrious student" (71). Only "terror" he said, could "check" his "wandering mind" (35).

Yet significantly, at one point in the 1937 version of *A Vision*, when Yeats again admits his "ignorance," he situates it in such a way that portrays it not as a drawback, but rather as the result of a resolute choice, even a triumph of sorts. "Apart from two or three of the principal Platonic Dialogues I knew no philosophy. Arguments with my father . . . had destroyed my confidence and driven me from speculation to the direct experience of the Mystics" (*AVB* 12). This remark suggests that Yeats was in some ways proud of his decision to turn from philosophy to a religion of his own making. As Yeats would maintain in a celebrated letter to John O'Leary: "I have always considered myself a voice of what I believe to be a greater renaissance—the revolt of the soul against the intellect" (*LWBY* 211).

A Vision, then, could be construed as the culminating endeavor of Yeats's effort to "revolt" against the "intellect" of his father, as well as against the intellectual methods and practices for which JBY stood. WBY's statements about his own "ignorance," in fact, apart from registering his humility, also show something else: the intensity and frequency with which they are repeated throughout *A Vision* suggests a kind of perverse pleasure Yeats took, on an underlying level, in that very "ignorance." Thus when Yeats acknowledges in *A Vision* that he has not, as his father has, read widely in philosophy, we might read this as other than a lament. Instead, he seems to be accounting for his justifiable turn toward thinkers who model alternative epistemologies more satisfying to him: shortly after admitting that he "knew no philosophy," he notes that "I had once known Blake as thoroughly as his unfinished confused Prophetic Books permitted, and I had read Swedenborg and Boehme" (*AVB* 12). He may have known no traditional philosophy, but he had certainly steeped himself in the thought of complex mystical philosophers.

Although he frequently offers employs the modesty topos, then, we also feel that he prides himself on being part of a "greater renaissance": what he lacks in traditional philosophical learning he makes up for through his contribution to the crucial "revolt of the soul against the intellect." At moments in *A Vision*, Yeats seems to have satisfied his drive for intellectual legitimacy: he opens the Introduction by noting proudly that Augusta Gregory had recently praised him for being "better educated" than he had been ten years before. He then credits the "incredible experience" he has had with visionary work for the transformation (*AVB* 8).

Other moments of *A Vision*, however, suggest that, far from content with his visionary knowledge, Yeats was often still anxiously compelled to work with that knowledge, knead carefully his narrative representations of it, so as to provide himself with a sense of intellectual security. Despite his sometimes staunch remarks, he had not altogether repudiated the standards of the "intellect" for those of the "soul."

When he writes of the Instructors having barred him from reading philosophy, for example, he admits enjoyment at finally being released from his promise so that he can read traditional philosophical sources such as Berkeley (*AVB* 19). In a letter of 1929 to Olivia Shakespear, Yeats maintained that his further reading would strengthen the second version of *A Vision* (*LWBY* 768). Faulted by Frank Sturm for his slipshod scholarship, Yeats actually used Sturm's critical comments to shore up his position: he included in *A Vision* (1937) Sturm's remarks about other respected thinkers—such as Aquinas—who had used geometric diagrams similar to his, in an attempt to shore up his legitimacy by making evident both his placement within a scholarly tradition and the consonance between his work and that of others.[51] Yeats also followed Sturm's example and extended this list of thinkers whose work corroborated and hence validated his findings, locating geometric diagrams akin to his in the work of Empedocles, Swedenborg, and Flaubert.

With these compensatory gestures, then, Yeats showed himself still haunted by the fear that his father might be right: that his mystical knowledge might be merely the worthless product of "a relaxed intellect." Accordingly, he had to strive to assure readers that his occult knowledge was not the product of passive reception alone—and that it possessed value through its accord with the knowledge of other thinkers.

H.D.: "IS IT POSSIBLE THAT I SENSED ANOTHER WORLD?"

Similarly, H.D. oscillates between disdain and envy with regard to traditional ways of knowing; and she likewise inscribes her defensiveness through insistently repeated assertions—not, as in Yeats's case, through repetition of scholarly names, but instead through comments on her own abilities. Meditating on the political climate of the 1930s, she notes that she doubted the cogency of the "high-powered" intellectual theories of some of her associates; they seemed "muddled." She acknowledges, however, that her skepticism stemmed partly from her own sense of inadequacy in the face of their "brilliant" theories (*TF* 57). Elsewhere in *Tribute*, she confesses to similar moments of self-doubt. She explicitly admits, for instance, her jealousy of those with more irreproachable credentials than hers. Of J. J. van der Leeuw, an analysand of Freud's whose hour preceded hers, she notes that he was "richly intellectually and materially endowed. I envied him" (6). Of Marie Bonaparte, the "Princess," who translated much of Freud's work, H.D. remarks similarly that she was "probably not a little envious" of her "intellectual endowments" (42).

At other moments, however, like Yeats, H.D. acknowledged that her visionary capacities could sometimes assuage her envy. Marie Bonaparte, she notes, was "devoted and influential," able to do much for Freud. But directly afterward, H.D. suggests that she may have something to offer that the Princess does not: "[I]s it possible that I sensed another world . . . ? Is it possible that I (leaping over every sort of intellectual impediment and obstacle) not wished only, but *knew*, the Professor would be born again?" (*TF* 39). At times, then, through her power to "know" by way of vision, H.D. felt that her experiences with the occult enabled her to match, even to "leap over," the Princess's "intellectual endowments" (39).

At such moments, H.D. seems hopeful that her visionary capacities, which are not just an inferior ability as measured against "intellectual endowments," in fact allow her to surmount "every sort of intellectual impediment and obstacle" (note that the parenthetical placement of that remark mimics the way that H.D. herself reaches her goal by a side route, an alternative to the main path), and thus to achieve a status equal to that of the Princess. Like Yeats, H.D. is sometimes able to take satisfaction in her position as dark horse and to believe herself ultimately victorious in the race for answers. These other people are respectable, officially endorsed, canonical, whereas she is "uncanonically seated," but she suggests that she is nonetheless strong, perhaps even stronger than they (TF 15). And somewhat unexpectedly, she shores up her position here by suggesting that, in being "uncanonical," she is kindred to Freud, who, though widely regarded as emblematic of authoritative knowledge, is himself "uncanonical enough" (15).

At other points, however, H.D. suggests great insecurity both about her ability to receive visionary knowledge and about the worth and veracity of her visionary findings. As she gazed at the wall in Corfu in 1920, her head throbbing from the effort to focus, unsure of whether she should keep trying, she suggests that she was grateful to her companion Bryher for saying, "Go on." Only when confident of Bryher's support could she continue (TF 48–49). H.D. also betrays uncertainty about her powers by her need to assert them repeatedly. Throughout Tribute she wants, most of all, to assert that her "gift" was "something different" (74). Though initially, she uses "gift" to refer to her search for the right birthday present for Freud, the statement is repeated in the text so as to suggest that it bears a larger significance. The word indicates two paths of H.D.'s desire: she wants, first, to be able to say that she possesses unique visionary "gifts"; in her memoir entitled The Gift, she records that a fortune-teller had once told her mother that that she would have a "gifted" child (22–23). Second, she wants to be able to say that, because of these "gifts," she has the ability to *give* something different from what everyone else has. Through the insistent repetition of her statements, however—she seems to protest too much, trying to convince herself—she reveals herself never quite certain that either of these conditions obtains.

ASSUAGING ANXIETIES THROUGH COLLABORATION

In part, Yeats and H.D. were able to assuage their anxieties about the visionary epistemological mode through a series of collaborations that became central both to the production of their visionary narratives and to the interpretation of the geometry they entailed. Each participated in two distinct kinds of collaborations: one more supportive, and another more contentious and frictional. The first allayed their fears about the legitimacy of their engagement with visionary knowledge and the legitimacy of the visionary findings; the second helped them to avoid adopting too passive a posture with regard to the visionary process. These collaborations reassured them they were achieving truths *with* father: confirmable truths gained in a way that their fathers would have endorsed.

Both writers engaged consistently in such collaborations. From 1917 to 1924, Yeats received the material for *A Vision* from the automatic writing and dreams of his wife. When George entered her mediumistic state, Yeats would repeatedly interrogate her; then he and she would work together to interpret the resulting "automatic script." He therefore collaborated constantly while working on *A Vision*, with both George and the demanding spiritual Instructors. H.D., meanwhile, relied on the support of her companion, Bryher, to complete her visionary experiences; afterward, she was able to recount those experiences fully only through her later collaboration with Freud.[52]

Yeats's collaborations with his wife served at least in part to counter his insecurities about the legitimacy of his mode of vision. In his view, her corroboration of his experiences conferred upon them greater truth value. Through his remarks in *A Vision* (1937), Yeats reveals the thoughts behind this belief: as he commented on how his project resonated with many other similar philosophical-prophetic endeavors over time, he noted his desire to assure himself and his readers that all of this was true, as well as his assumption that repetition constituted a form of proof. In *A Vision*, he implies that if two thinkers — for example, he and Spengler — engaged in analogous projects of finding what Pound called the "repeat in history" and discovered similar patterns, then these patterns were more likely to be true than if only one thinker had produced them. Through his devoted accumulation of examples of philosophers who had undertaken a project like his and produced results akin to his (Vico, Empedocles, Blake, Swedenborg, Pythagoras, Flaubert), Yeats suggests how much he valued the confirmation that stems from repetition, how he desired the "common experience" he invokes near the end of "Dove or Swan."

Yeats's work with his George thus provided him with a similar kind of confirmation through repetition. Given his and George's joint labor to transcribe what he called the spirits' "geometric symbolism," Yeats could feel sure that all this was not merely his own delusion: his wife not only produced information that definitely issued from elsewhere than from himself, but she also sometimes received the same words he did, heard the same supernatural sounds, smelled the same supernatural fragrances. In part, he received the assurance of legitimacy from the way his endeavor echoed the projects of other thinkers, ranging from Swedenborg to Spengler, and the way his information often coincided with theirs. But it was George who provided the day-to-day verification of the truth of these otherworldly messages. It was she, after all, who had initiated the whole project of *A Vision* by announcing to him her gift for automatic writing, and it was she who encouraged him in their daily sessions. She also supplied eerie confirmations of his experiences: "[O]nce," for instance, he writes, "my wife and I heard at the same hour in the afternoon, she at Ballylee and I at Coole, the sound of a little pipe" (*AVB* 16–17). And another time, when Yeats heard a voice saying to him, "You have said what we wanted to have said," George, though she had "heard nothing" and sat across the room from him writing a letter, discovered that she had written the same words in the letter (17).

Yeats not only needed to believe that the "truths" he received were legitimate insofar as they repeated what others had discovered, but also needed to guard against the possibility that such visionary acquisition of knowledge entailed the "relaxed intellect" against which his father had warned. The careful detail with which Yeats recounts his collaborations with the Instructors suggests a high degree of investment in his struggle with them: his frictional collaboration with them assuaged his fears of not taking a sufficiently active intellectual role in the visionary process.

Yeats frequently emphasized all the work the Instructors had made him do. After George had stopped transmitting their messages in her sleep in 1920, he reports that he "began an exhaustive study" of what they had recorded in more than fifty books of notes (*AVB* 17–18). Beyond providing him with an overwhelming amount of information and requiring of him days of toil, the Instructors demanded of him struggle, patience, humility, and agility of mind. The automatic script, a thorough record of which is now available in the three volumes of *Yeats's "Vision" Papers*, attests to Yeats's often frustrating intellectual labor: not only were there actual "Frustrators" who sometimes interfered with the process, trying to mislead him, but even the "Communicators" themselves were difficult, capricious, often—their name notwithstanding—so uncommunicative as to be laconic, and, they said, deliberately out to deceive him (AVB 13). They were frequently impatient:

> I was constantly reproved for vague or confused questions, yet I could do no better, because, though it was plain from the first that their exposition was based upon a single geometrical conception, they kept me from mastering that conception. (11)

The Instructors also betrayed irritation at Yeats's tendency to misunderstand and distort their messages. One Communicator, Yeats claims, had "complained" that he had misused the "geometrical symbolism" supposedly devised to assist him, misinterpreting their thought as "mechanical" (13). Spurred by their demands, Yeats had to exercise "patience" and "curiosity."

As the gestures of *A Vision* show, then, through his effort to transcribe the System, Yeats especially wanted to demonstrate, first, that his project possessed intellectual legitimacy insofar as the existence of its elements was verified by both his wife and other philosophers, and, second, that he had had to expend great intellectual labor and acumen to complete the work for it. This time, as he had not in the past, he could prove to his father that he had achieved the systematicity, prestige, rigor, ambitious scope, and even the company of great thinkers that JBY had always pressed him to attain; further, he had attained all this through the mysticism that JBY deplored.

H.D.: SUPPORT FROM BRYHER AND DEFIANCE OF "THE PROFESSOR"

In parallel fashion, H.D. alleviated her uncertainty about the rightfulness of her receipt of vision and the legitimacy of that vision in part through her collaboration with her companion Bryher. H.D. reports that when she first began receiving her visions in Corfu, she was alarmed at the experience and wondered if she should continue; she was able to persist only when Bryher told her that it was all right to do so (*TF* 48–49). In "Advent," H.D. likewise notes that she could not have had her vision alone: "It was being with Bryher that projected the fantasy" (130). Bryher, then, allowed H.D. to overcome her fear of the strangeness of the visions, her exhaustion at the concentration required, and her doubt that she possessed the credentials to be a visionary. Bryher's role was so crucial that H.D. even suggested that it was she, and not H.D., who was qualified for visionary experience and that what H.D. had seen had in fact been witnessed collaboratively: "perhaps in some sense, we were 'seeing' it together" (49).

H.D. and Bryher actually did see a vision together, and Bryher, playing a role roughly analogous to that of George Yeats, confirmed the substance of the vision: at a moment when H.D. was succumbing to complete fatigue, Bryher "saw what I did not see"—the last image of a sequence, a vision of a man pulling a woman into a sun disk (*TF* 56). Bryher helped H.D. to surmount her fear that she was not entirely capable of receiving the vision, but also confirmed that the vision was more than merely a product of H.D.'s personal, idiosyncratic imagination.

In this scene with Bryher, H.D. also underscores the extraordinary concentration needed to bring these visions into view. She leaves the experience overcome with exhaustion. What still has not been satisfied, however, is the need to invest enough active intellectual effort of her own in the visionary experience to make her believe that she has earned it rightfully. To do this, H.D. displays to us her relationship with Freud.

During their work together, Freud made increasingly clear that H.D. was more a student than an analysand—even a possible successor. When J. J. van der Leeuw, a patient of Freud's whom H.D. construed as a student, someone who could "carry on [Freud's] ideas" (*TF* 6), died suddenly, Freud told H.D. that she had come to replace him (6). H.D. constantly stresses that although she reveres Freud's ideas and courage (71), she also feels a fundamental argument with him in her "bones"—in this case about mystical knowledge and the existence of an afterlife, which the rational Freud apparently rejected.

Through this second collaboration, again in a fashion analogous to Yeats's, H.D. was able to relieve her other anxiety—about not making a sufficiently active intellectual contribution to the process of vision. Her sometimes contentious collaboration with Freud, which she displays narratively, paralleled Yeats's work with the Instructors: it allowed her to show that her visionary work entailed an intellectually assertive posture. In *Tribute*, she does not press as hard as Yeats does in *A Vision* on the actual labor she accomplishes—but like Yeats, she wanted the activity of experiencing vision to be tantamount to an intellectual assertion, a strong accomplishment, and a valuable contribution. She did not want, as she terms it at several moments in *Tribute*, merely to "let go" (*TF*

49, 116). She codes her visionary experiences as entailing intellectual assertiveness both by the way she describes her struggles with Freud as demanding effort, and by the way she describes visionary work as requiring a rare talent of which few others are capable.

She marks her need to exhibit her active challenges to Freud by her repeated assertions that that "the Professor was not always right" (*TF* 18, 98, 101) and by her attendant suggestions that with her visionary abilities, even as she venerates Freud, she can also sometimes defy him: "[H]e was always right in his judgments, but my form of rightness, my intuition, sometimes functioned by the split-second (that makes all the difference in spiritual time-computations) the quicker. I was swifter in some intuitive instances" (98). With relish, she relays her first meeting with Freud, the dynamics of which constituted her initial "wordless challenge" to him and emblematized her ongoing defiance of his authority and some of his ideas. Despite Freud's admonition not to play with his dog, Yofi, because it tended to bite strangers, she bent down and began to engage with it. Freud's warnings notwithstanding, she was easily able to establish a rapport with the dog. H.D. decides to feature her ability to interact with the dog, then, to show that she was better able than Freud to read what a situation demanded, better able to read a "region of cause and effect," a realm of forces, that he could neither discern nor interpret. H.D.'s apparent investment in recounting her defiance of Freud suggests her need to use her visionary capacity (which, even if it required immense effort, still involved a passive posture) toward an active end; in this case a subtle but fierce challenge to Freud's system of thought, much of which she admired but whose inhospitality to the idea of supernatural realms she would not accept. In the presence of the "great man," she did not want entirely to submit to either his directives or the assumptions driving his work. If she could not match him in ratiocination, as she wants to show readers and convince herself, she could outpace him in some "intuitive instances" by employing the abilities involved in her visionary experiences.

GEOMETRIC NARRATIONS

Yeats and H.D. strove to display their visionary work, then, so that both their occult knowledge and the achievement of that knowledge through vision could stand up to the skeptical scrutiny to which their fathers' rationalist and empirical standards would have subjected them. To meet the paternal expectations that remained with them long after their fathers' deaths, they needed to show that their visionary findings could be to some extent corroborated by others, as well as that they had been earned, in part, by their own active, rigorous labor. Accordingly, they coded their visionary writings as defensive responses to their paternal figures. And it is this process of partially defensive coding that the geometry of their visionary texts inscribes.

How they employ geometric vocabulary thus represents their wish to engage with the ghosts of their fathers, at once to satisfy those ghosts and to subvert them. In their visionary texts geometry chiefly registers their desire to demonstrate the kind of active and stringent labor of which their fathers would have approved. Moreover, they coded their geometry to indicate that their work with the mystical and the occult suggested not their inability to master the traditional forms of learning that their fathers represented, but rather their command of a valid alternative to that traditional learning.

Rhetorical maneuvers framing the geometric images signal the intellectual effort of their visionary projects. Yeats registers this in his commentaries on the experience of receiving the geometric figures from his Instructors; in his elaborate fictions that serve as a counterpoint to the geometry; and in his tireless revisions of the text to adequately explain the geometry, which he points to in his narration of the "incredible experience." Like Yeats, by embedding her geometric images in narratives of her personal experiences, H.D. likewise invests them with significance so that they imply her own abilities and her capacity for labor and contribution.

YEATS'S GEOMETRY: OCCASION FOR LABOR AND *SPREZZATURA*

Clearly, the "mystic geometry" of *A Vision*—the "single geometrical conception" (*AVB* 11) that the Communicators relayed to Yeats and that he strove to understand and transcribe—occasioned his struggle with the Instructors. Geometry thus gave rise to and, on the page, signified Yeats's immense labor to comprehend and transmit these visions, intellectual labor he wanted to demonstrate to his father. Furthermore, because he framed the mystic geometry to emphasize its similarity to the geometry employed by a host of famous philosophers and mystics, it also enables and marks his entrance into a world of scholarly repute. Employing geometry allows him to join forces with the many thinkers who have similarly employed geometric diagrams for philosophical explanation—Plato, Empedocles, Swedenborg, Aquinas. The conspicuous appearance of geometric diagrams on his pages indicates his alliance with such predecessors, his participation in the lineage they create, and the equivalence of his work with theirs. In this sense, knowledge of geometry indeed allowed Yeats to enter a kind of "Academy." In defiance of JBY's claim that mysticism made for a "relaxed intellect," Yeats signaled his ability to achieve a reconciliation between mysticism and the effort and intellect that he wished to evince.

But more than this, Yeats mischievously displays the mysticism his father scorned, through geometric terms his father had also disdained: "Euclid," WBY reports JBY as having said, "is too easy. It comes naturally to the literary imagination. The old idea, that it is a good training for the mind, was long ago refuted" (*Autobiography* 35). Through *A Vision*, Yeats implicitly argues back against this statement, suggesting that, to the contrary, a form of geometry, "mystic geometry," had indeed proved "good training" for his "mind."

But even with this, Yeats is not quite finished with his answer to his father. Part of that answer consists, also, of the crazy salad of fictions and fables surrounding the text of *A Vision*, whose fantastical qualities contrast sharply with the largely sedulous and earnest atmosphere of the rest of the book and whose significance in fact derives from its relationship to the geometry. The effect of these fables, in other words, both depends upon and reveals the distinctive significance Yeats assigns to the book's geometry.

At the outset of *A Vision* (1937), Yeats explains that he was originally obliged in 1925 to fabricate these wild narratives about the origin of the text because his wife did not want her role known and because the Instructors had also enjoined him to silence. What resulted in the 1925 version of *A Vision* was the "Introduction" and "The Dance of the Four Royal Persons" by a fictional character named Owen Aherne, who notes that the System was discovered by Michael Robartes, an Arabian traveller who found his way to it through a book published in the sixteenth century, the *Speculum Angelorum et Hominum* (by a mysterious writer named Giraldus) and by a chance discovery of an Arabian tribe named the Judwalis, whose teachings derived from a philosopher named Kusta ben Luka. But in 1937, when Yeats was no longer constrained to silence about the source of his information, he puzzlingly inserted an equally fantastical narrative in the new version (Adams, *Book of Yeats's Vision* 39)—and one that was different, moreover, from the one in 1925, this time called "Stories of Michael Robartes and His Friends." At this juncture, Yeats had already revealed the truth of the book's conditions of production, so why include the narrative at all? Although Yeats himself suggests that he retained the story because some of his poetry is "unintelligible" without it (AVB 19), Adams maintains that this claim is overstated and that Yeats must have had ulterior motives, especially since, inscrutably, the 1937 version of the narrative is even more elaborate and fanciful than the first (Adams, *Book of Yeats's Vision* 39).

In part, the retention of the fictional account of the discovery of the System may suggest Yeats's belief that because the elements of the System arise from the *Anima Mundi* (in Yeatsian terms, a kind of universal unconscious, the treasury for the host of archetypal images shared by all people), they could just as easily be found by anyone, at any time. His juxtaposition of the fictional account of origins with the factual one implicitly interrogates the ontological privilege of the conventionally factual, suggesting that the fiction may be regarded as just as "true" or "real" as the empirical report. And, accordingly, his account also implies that the work of the poet, who fictionalizes, is just as valid as that of the historian.

But to understand this point about the status of fiction, we do not need to know in quite such luxurious detail about the antics of the "friends" of Michael Robartes: Yeats has spun a seeming excess of textual gossamer unnecessary for his purpose. This apparent superfluity, I would offer, functions as Yeats's willful assertion of playfulness, of poetic mischief, against the geometric logic of the "great systems." Yeats has been asked by the Instructors themselves, of course, to "give concrete expression to their abstract thought" (AVB 12), which he does, for instance, in his descriptions of actual individuals whom he uses to body forth the twenty-eight phases of individual personality, and in his specific examples of historical events in "Dove or Swan."

But he also does much more than this. In Book II of *A Vision* he notes that he was "haunted" by "figures" who, "muttering 'The great systems,' held out to me the sun-dried skeletons of birds," which for Yeats implied that he was supposed to turn to "the living bird" (AVB 214). This, I would offer, describes metaphorically the task Yeats assigns himself and completes by way of the fables in the opening pages of *A Vision*. The geometry offered him by the Instructors corresponds to the dry "skeletons"; ironically, to find the "living bird" as they direct, Yeats must necessarily move beyond what the Instructors demand: he must spin the supremely unnecessary fictions that counterpoint their serious geometry—in his terms, that provide the antithetical contrary to the information they relay, which belongs to the primary realm.

That these fictions do, in Yeats's imagination, occupy a status contrary to that of the geometry is made apparent through a sequence of associations. In the Introduction to the 1937 *A Vision*, Yeats initially compares his geometric schemes to the "cubes" in the drawings of Wyndham Lewis and to the "ovoids" of Brancusi. In the 1925 *A Vision*, he has used these two artists, Lewis and Brancusi, to epitomize the contemporary trend toward what he calls "the physical primary" or the "primary tincture": like them, he notes, many artists of the day

> are all absorbed in some technical research to the entire exclusion of the personal dream. It is as though the forms in the stone or in their reverie began to move with an energy which is not that of the human mind. Very often these forms are mechanical.... I think of the work of Mr Wyndham Lewis, his powerful "cacophony of sardine tins," and of those marble eggs, or objects of burnished steel too drawn up or tapered out to be called eggs, of M. Brancussi [*sic*]. (211)

The diction here, with its emphasis on "sardine tins" and "marble eggs," is almost flippant. In *A Vision* (1937), Yeats notes, less precisely but likewise, that he tends to associate contemporary nonrepresentational art with the primary tincture (AVB 258).[53] Geometry, then, seems to signify for Yeats the primary tincture: that which moves toward the direction of objectivity, unity, and the extinction of individual personality, that which lies beyond the limits of the individual self. And presumably, then, Yeats's own participation in the construction of these geometric schemes, by association, forms part of this primary turn toward the "general surrender of the will" (300). But as the last sections of both the 1925 and 1937 versions of *A Vision* indicate, even as Yeats participates in this erasure of individual personality, he also challenges its dominion: even as he foresees

> a time when the majority of men will so accept an historical tradition that they will quarrel, not as to who can impose his personality upon others but as to who can best embody the common aim, when all personality will seem an impurity,
>
> (*A VISION* [1925] 212)

he looks forward to the next cycle, when, in 1927, there will again be a turn again toward the realm of the concrete and the supremacy of individual personality and will.

In one of the final sections of *A Vision* (1937), dated "1934–6," his statements imply less certainty that arrival of the antithetical phase is imminent, but he still alludes to it: "What discords will drive Europe to that artificial unity—only dry or drying sticks can be tied into a bundle—which is the decadence of every civilisation?" (301–302).⁵⁴ Noting the "decadence" of the primary tincture, here Yeats then alludes to the "the *antithetical* multiform influx" (302) that may arrive and that will be more vital than "dry sticks."

Through his elaborate, seemingly perverse, prefatory fictions, then, Yeats gestures toward the antithetical realm: these fables certainly implicitly affirm Yeats's personality, the imagination, and the realm of concrete human particularity. They showcase the poet's ability and right to create, to provide a kind of *sprezzatura*—richly, recklessly apart from what Yeats regards as a primary "general surrender of the will."⁵⁵ With these fictions, Yeats posits a contrary to the geometry of *A Vision*, and in so doing, in one sense, disobeys the Instructors. The geometry thus seems to be displayed prominently in *A Vision* in part to give Yeats something against which to fling the spectacle of his disobedience. And given the Instructors' role as analogue to that of his volatile, learned father, his defiance here also reads as the defiance of a poetic son toward a father unreceptive to mysticism, a defiance that accompanies the series of painstaking gestures with which he has sought to prove himself to that father on that father's terms. Yeats has established geometry not only so that he can show himself able to master and explain it, and thus display his active skills as intellect, student, and interpreter, but also so that he can, in other conspicuous ways, avert himself from it.

As Yeats asserts his love for the antithetical, however, there is still another way that he responds to the intellectual demands impressed upon him by JBY, meeting them in his fashion. On one level, sedimented with meaning as it has become in this context, geometry and all that has gone into explaining and transmitting it represents the intellectual labor that his father demanded of him: he has indicated both his ability to fulfill that demand and to surpass it. However, Yeats also remembered in his memoirs that JBY had insisted on combating abstraction with vivid portrayals of individual personality (*Autobiography* 39–40)—had insisted, in fact, on the assertion of personality (Coote, *Yeats: A Life* 45), an effort that Yeats associates with the antithetical realm. Even in rejecting geometry, then, in asserting the "antithetical" tincture and all that accompanies it, Yeats is in fact abiding by one of his father's desiderata, the countering of abstraction with dramatic particulars and vigorous personality. Occupying a realm of the mystical to which his father objected, Yeats can demonstrate both the intellectual rigor and the dramatic vividness that JBY prized, and thus at once both rebel against the father's directives in one sense while obeying them in another.

Geometry, then, not only provides the occasion for "much laboring" within the text of *A Vision*, but because Yeats associates it with the "primary" tendency, it also symbolizes the force against which he must rebel and provides a chance to prove himself on his father's rigorous intellectual terms and then dance away from those terms on a wave of fancy. And that dance, in turn, demonstrates to JBY that not only can Yeats display a rational and active intellect through the process of grappling with a "geometrical conception," but he can also advance a gesture of artistic bravura through the madcap fictions with which he festoons the geometry. He can meet JBY's demands for assiduously performed philosophic maneuvers and those for artistic brio, and do so in a realm of his own, one that indicates his hard-won independence, his desire for which was never quite extinguished, but always coexisted alongside the impulse to impress and satisfy JBY.

H.D. AND THE GEOMETRY OF THE MAGNIFYING GLASS

Likewise, the fashion in which H.D. presents her geometry in *Tribute to Freud* indicates that the use of geometry is informed by needs born out of her effort toward intellectual and epistemological authority, which arises, in part, from her desire to reply to the intellectual standards established by her father. Before H.D. presents her geometric visions in *Tribute to Freud*—"It is a circle or two circles, the base the larger of the two; it is joined by three lines" (45)—she has already introduced this shape and its significance in the narrative through a story from childhood of her brother's once having stolen a magnifying glass from their father's desk. Her brother uses the glass to set a leaf on fire. H.D. is complicit in the transgression, but not an active participant. As she reminisces about the event, she assigns the form of the magnifying glass a symbolic significance:

> I do not know, he does not know that this, besides being the magnifying glass from our father's table, is a sacred symbol. It is a circle and the stem of the circle. (25)

Later in the narrative, when we hear of H.D.'s visionary experiences, which likewise involve such "circles" and "stems" ("It is a circle or two circles.... [I]t is joined by three lines" [*TF* 45]), we are reminded of this magnifying glass episode and of her brother's transgressive gesture. Furthermore, H.D. then equates her father's objects with Freud's, suggesting that they are both "sacred" (25). Attributing to both the magnifying glass and the geometric images of her visions the position of "sacred symbol," H.D. lifts them out of their immediate context and confers upon them a transcendent status.

The ultimate effect of these linkages is to code H.D.'s interactions with Freud about the geometric visions as repeating, in a different form, her brother's defiance of their father's command through the theft of the magnifying glass. By narrating her geometric visions to Freud, H.D. can, like her brother, like Prometheus, steal fire and engage in a primal disobedience of paternal law. In "Advent," she again directly juxtaposes a short paragraph about her visionary "jelly-fish" experiences with a brief mention of her brother's stealing the magnifying glass, further confirming the link between the gesture of "stealing fire" against her father's wishes and visionary consciousness—both the experience and the narration thereof (*TF* 116). Clearly, geometric visions occupy a space in H.D.'s imagination proximate to the scene of the magnifying glass: the geometric shapes of her visions recall the shape of the magnifying glass. The implication, then, is that the gesture of having and transmitting the visions, the most significant of which involve geometric figures, parallels her brother's courageous violation. In this context, geometry thus comes to signify a Promethean effort at rebellion in the name of the attainment of greater knowledge.

Within H.D.'s oeuvre, geometry has come to be associated with her father and brother in other ways as well. In *HERmione*, her eponymous protagonist associates her scientific father and brother with a world of "biological-mathematical definition" from which she feels barred. Because one of Hermione's greatest downfalls has been her course in conic sections, she associates images of cones and other geometric figures with the trauma of failure. As the novel unfolds, however, we see that Hermione links geometric figures not only with her own academic shortcomings, but also with the clarity of mind to which she aspires (see Chapter 3). When, breaking away from the constraints and expectations of her home environment, Hermione begins an intense erotic relationship with a woman, Fayne, she describes Fayne's power over her in geometric terms. As indicated by this pattern of geometric images, then, Hermione seeks to meet those standards that she has hitherto failed to achieve, but now by an alternative route of her own. Her use of geometry to describe Fayne thus functions as a kind of subversive repetition, a summoning of the criteria according to which she has failed in order to reappropriate them for her own purposes: in a gesture of subversive mimicry, she both pays tribute to these standards and opposes them. As she has not in the past, this time she is able to meet them, now in her own way. Because, as HERmione indicates, geometry is so clearly linked in H.D.'s imagination to her father and brother and the scientific epistemology she associates with them, as well as to transgressive acts of disobedience in the name of gaining knowledge, her use of geometry in *Tribute*, I would offer, inscribes a desire to engage in a similar subversive repetition.

CONCLUSION

Previous chapters have made the case that the campaign against the "wandering and slack" was characteristic of Vorticism, initially impelled its efforts, and was repeated with a difference in late modernist writing of the 1930s—in Pound's writings on Mussolini's Italy and in H.D.'s *Nights*. I would argue, further, that these late modernist reappearances of geometric vocabulary enlisted in an effort toward rigor and intensity were significantly influenced by the *avant-guerre* Vorticist example, and that they continued the Vorticist impulse in transmuted form.

In Pound's case, the way geometric streamlining continued to dominate his imagination throughout the 1920s and 1930s in fact issued from his ongoing celebration of Vorticist values and his persistent desire to facilitate their revival. The heady atmosphere of Mussolini's Italy, abounding in cues that recalled for Pound the drive, intensity, and dynamism of Vorticism—for him, a pinnacle of avant-garde achievement—persuaded him that his longstanding wish for a Vorticist renaissance might at last be fulfilled, and his writing of the early 1930s was governed once again by the ideal of Vorticist geometry.

In H.D.'s case, the negative impact exerted by Vorticism on her imagination during the Great War resurfaced in the 1930s as she confronted a set of circumstances, personal and public, akin to those she had faced during the Great War. The Vorticist geometry scored on her consciousness during that last traumatic period surged up again, now permuted and enlisted in a strategy of response to crisis, one that coded aggressive geometry no longer as a sign of the bellicose enemy, but rather now as a welcome source of defense or desirable intensity. That she transformed what was once an enemy into something she could use for her own purposes, toward a project of resistance, was typical of H.D. Moreover, it indicated H.D.'s strenuous effort, in the face of escalating tensions in the 1930s, to meet this crisis more effectively than she had the last, this time to stand up to it rather than allow it to defeat her.

Like Pound's advocacy of a streamlined and dynamic aesthetic for the Italian Fascist regime and like H.D.'s enshrinement of a geometric visionary body charged to maximum intensity, H.D.'s and Yeats's visionary projects likewise converged with the Vorticist campaign against the "wandering and slack." On the one hand, they did so through the way that both H.D. and Yeats strove to make active intellectual contributions through an epistemological mode conventionally associated with passivity. In their efforts to frame their visionary experiences as involving more than merely passive reception, they were actuated by a desire for vigorous activity and rigorous work akin to that celebrated by Vorticism. More specifically, their conspicuous unease with "amorphous" visionary experience aligned them with the rejection enacted in *Blast* of that which is "medium-like" and "Blavatskyish." Like Lewis, in their visionary projects H.D. and Yeats edged close to Kandinsky's position, attracted to the spiritual wisdom it afforded, and then veered away from it, striving to ensure that their approach to it involved not only passive mediumship, but also active quest. And like Lewis, they enlisted geometric figures to enact the disassociative maneuver that aligned them with dynamic action.

To reply adequately to the ghosts of their fathers, who inspired their distrust of passivity of intellect and mystical knowledge, they offered aggressive gestures: aggressive insofar as they were intellectually active and rigorous, and insofar as they were defiant of paternal expectations. Cued in part by the Vorticist example, they enlisted a geometric lexicon for this expression of aggression. H.D. and Yeats resembled the Vorticists, then, not only in their use of geometry, nor only in their likely being influenced toward the use of geometry by contact with Vorticist values, but also in the way that they used the language of geometry.

Ultimately, both Yeats and H.D. employed geometry to develop adequate responses to confusion about the political crises of the 1930s as well as to inscribe complex personal responses to paternal expectations surfaced by these public crises, responses involving both the fulfillment of and resistance to these expectations. They couched their geometric gestures to signal that they had risen to the level of ability their fathers demanded of them: Yeats through the active intellectual labor he displays as having been necessary to understanding the mystic geometry, as well as the links he stresses between his geometric figures and those of prominent predecessors; H.D. by implicitly equating, as marked through geometry, her visionary endeavors with her father's rigorous scientific pursuits. Importantly, they also demonstrated that they had turned aside from their fathers' paths: Yeats created an array of fables whose vibrancy is highlighted by the geometry of *A Vision*, which foils them; H.D. connected her geometric visionary experiences with a forceful gesture of disobedience. The personal needs driving the course of their visionary narrations, spurred by the demand to respond to public crises and generating their anxieties about mysticism, significantly reactivated, in their imaginations and writing, a current of Vorticist geometry.

At the outset of this study, I addressed the ways in which chronicles of modernism's history have repeatedly displayed an investment in a caricature of the periodical *Blast* as pugnacious, antic, larger than life. This confined, easily transmissible image—still widely circulated in stories about the genesis of Anglo-American literary modernism—has obscured other, equally important facets of both *Blast* and the Vorticist project it at once announced and helped usher into being. Designed and led by Lewis, extended and strengthened by the participation of his comrades, Vorticism engaged in a sustained, phobic campaign against effeminacy, as the category was understood in its post-Aestheticist cultural milieu, that necessitated its commitment to qualities that would counter that effeminacy: "sternness and severity" and "mastered, vivid vitality." Of course the zeal with which Lewis refused a connection with Aestheticist effeminacy emerged from his own ambivalent attraction to many of the values and beliefs of his Aestheticist predecessors, including the male-male homoeroticism the Vorticists associated with Aestheticism; in Vorticism, his anxieties and ambivalent desires are writ large.

In the homophobic Vorticist view, because Aestheticism had been rendered shameful through its links with male homosexuality, ties with Aestheticism had to be disavowed, at least publicly. Influenced by the era's crisis in masculinity, which in turn gave rise to a surge of homophobia, the Vorticists were driven by an anxiety about exhibiting overtly any connections with Aestheticism—which, especially through the impact of the scandal of the Wilde trials, had come to be connected in the public mind with

Epilogue

forms of male-male eroticism and male homosexuality, both believed to be perverse.

Accordingly, Vorticism enlisted its geometric forms to figure those qualities it would celebrate as part of its publicly staged denial of effeminacy. In the early twentieth-century moment from which the Vorticists emerged, geometric forms were widely circulated in discourse about contemporary life (as I have discussed, they came to be increasingly associated with nonrepresentational work in the visual arts, machines, scientific and technological discovery, even study of the occult), so they formed a set of signifiers ripe for use in the Vorticists' phobic campaign. Given theorizations such as Hulme's, and the proliferation of geometric images in machine-age urban life, the language of geometry in the early twentieth century in many quarters became increasingly connected with the qualities of severity and starkness, mastery and detachment, to which the Vorticists wanted to announce their allegiance—in order to stave off the assumption that, given their interest in artifice and their concomitant disdain for Nature, they were allies of their Aestheticist forerunners in all respects. They would accept certain carefully chosen aspects of the Aestheticist artistic program, while simultaneously devoting themselves to denials of the linkage with male homoeroticism that, given their homophobia, they could not (in either sense) admit. Their work thus endowed geometric signifiers with the qualities they needed to celebrate in order to achieve this combination of acceptance and refusal; and it was this Vorticist coding of geometry that informed the work of many later modernist writers between the wars.

This vortex of summons and repulsion created out of Vorticism's radically ambivalent responses to Aestheticism was, I argue, both the driving force behind the formation of Vorticism and a manifestation of the crucial formative influence of the *fin de siècle* on early modernist work. This pattern fundamental to Vorticism's development, and thus also to the development of early modernism, becomes visible if we move beyond the reductive accounts of *Blast* to what these have occluded. Of course, much scholarship in modernist studies has made abundantly clear that the moderns' rhetorical rejections of their various nineteenth-century predecessors in fact belied a radical debt to, and affinity with, some of the work of those predecessors. We now know about modernism's many ties to the Romantics and the Victorians; Eliot and Stevens were steeped in the Symbolist poets of the *fin de siècle*; H.D. compelled by the *fin-de-siècle* figures of the male Aesthete and the femme fatale. But until now, the precise nature of Vorticism's relationship to Aestheticism has not yet been adequately defined.

I have brought this relationship forward, first, in order to enrich our understanding of what the moderns owe the *fin de siècle*: how the mischievous but nonetheless zealous, phobic investments of the Vorticists were significantly conditioned by their responses to the Aesthetes. I have also advanced it, however, because if we are to understand the geometric language that figures so prominently in the visual arts and written texts of the period, we need to understand how the Vorticists' relationship to Aestheticism gave rise to a sustained quarrel with effeminacy, which in turn governed the significance of its geometric vocabulary. Modernist criticism has loosely understood a semantic linkage among "hardness," "maleness," and "geometry," but no study to date has looked into how this coding of geometry, this semiosis so influential upon later modernist work, actually came about during the *avant-guerre* years.

Geometric images—used as metaphors, verbal images, and visual diagrams—appeared with startling frequency in modernist work after Vorticism; and the associations with which writers using them were working often derived from that formative *avant-guerre* moment. Most striking, as I have suggested, is the upsurge of geometric vocabulary in texts of late modernism that responded to the climate of anxiety of the years between the wars. The moderns, of course, were always searching for a new vocabulary, "new words," as H.D. said (*TF* 145), to supersede "existing categories of language," as Pound said (*G-B* 88). But in the 1930s, as social, economic, and political tensions heated to the boiling point, this need took a particularly acute form. Moreover, in an environment increasingly demanding decisive action and forceful responses to the brewing social and political crises, the values that these writers, influenced by the Vorticist example, had come to associate with geometric language seemed to them appropriate to the needs of the day.

Confronted with the political and economic crises of the 1930s, Pound returned to the aesthetic and philosophical values to which he had committed himself during his work with the Vorticists—such that Vorticism, in his mind, became their chief locus: in his view, these were expressed most eloquently in sleek material forms with geometrically clean lines. As I have argued, his attraction to Italian Fascism was clearly guided by a multiplicity of factors: his reverence for Renaissance Italy, especially its warriors, princes, artists, and rich culture of patronage; his propensity for hero worship; his belief that Italy could engineer the kind of economic regeneration for which he militated. Another major factor that demands recognition, however, was Pound's desire to reawaken Vorticist values in a new context in order to answer the needs of the 1930s. Based on what he observed in the visual culture of Italy, he believed that the Vorticist values of "sternness" and "severity," strength and efficiency, dynamism and precision, had already taken root in the new Fascist regime.

This desire and belief, in turn, significantly guided the routes he took in casting his arguments for Mussolini's regime; they also spurred him to include in his support of Mussolini's government a campaign to revive Vorticism in Italy, and through such a revival, to help foster a renewal of Italy.

At the same moment, H.D. was facing a number of crises, both external and internal. In 1931 she began an intensive engagement with psychoanalysis, lasting until 1934, which resurfaced a collection of anguished memories of her experiences from nearly twenty years before. At the same time, prompted especially by her observations as she traveled to Vienna to work with Freud, she became increasingly attuned to the political upheavals of Europe and began searching for adequate ways to respond to a climate that she read as leading once again toward war. Her novella *Nights*, clearly, offers no direct response to either crisis, but I would argue that its fantasy of a geometric body constitutes an oblique response insofar as it forms part of a defensive maneuver: an effort to find an image of invulnerability and transcendence that would help her face this war, the war she feared was coming, more effectively than she had the last, and that would help her surmount, especially, the memory of bodily exposure and fragility so painfully involved with her recollections of the First World War. The urgency of the environment of the 1930s conditioned the generation of such fantasy images.

And the way H.D. employs geometry in *Nights* to construct the geometric body, which in turn illuminates similar ways that she enlisted geometry in other prose fictions of the 1920s and 1930s, is deeply indebted to the example of Vorticism. It is the link H.D. forges in her imagination between geometry and violence in the 1910s, just after her first encounter with Vorticist movement, that remains active in how she directs her geometric vocabulary in the 1930s; the values of severity, intensity, strength, and austerity that she uses geometry to express reflect the influence of the Vorticist semiosis. The Vorticist movement was clearly not the only source for H.D.'s bent for geometric terms, yet it was nonetheless a crucial one—and her articulation of a rhetoric of violence by way of geometric figures of the 1930s suggests that her memory of the aggression she associated with Vorticist geometry exerted a lasting impact on her thought.

In the third chapter, I have concentrated on the greater implications of H.D.'s fantasy of the ideal geometric body, which has much in common with the phantasmic bodies produced by Pound and Lewis. I have underscored H.D.'s affinities with the male moderns, from whose work hers is usually said to diverge. This prevalent news (one might say, with H.D., "not always right") about H.D.'s departure from "male modernism" emerges from the assumption that her writing is, and the desire for her writing to be, feminist. I would argue in response that we may rightfully call H.D. a feminist writer, but only if our images of her are not formed at the expense of a sound understanding of her work, and particularly of the many connections between her aesthetic and philosophical commitments and those of her male contemporaries. Our descriptions of H.D.'s feminism must include such connections to remain both accurate to what H.D. actually did—and, moreover, to take full advantage of the forms of feminism H.D.'s work can suggest to us, some of them potentially helpful in developing new models of feminist practice for the future.

H.D.'s and Yeats's clear fascination with the occult was intensified, I have argued, by their need to find adequate responses to the political, social—and for them, spiritual—crises of the interwar years. Conspicuously, geometric forms became a language both employed to express the visions through which they hoped to bring to a world in trouble something that would help others make sense of the welter of events. H.D. sought to relay ancient wisdom, transmitted through her visions, as well as a transcendental language, articulated through geometric forms, that would help people to understand one another and work toward peace. Yeats, through the System he gleaned from his spiritual Instructors, hoped to convey a way of reading history that would help others to recognize more fully how the current course of events related to larger historical cycles, as well as to the cycles governing individual lives.

Pressing in on these efforts to respond to the climate of crisis with visionary texts, however—and interfering with their confidence—was the ambivalence that both Yeats and H.D. felt about visionary knowledge, which involved doubt about its validity and worth. And for both, as I have argued, this ambivalence derived in part, and significantly, from examples impressed upon them by their skeptical, rationalist fathers, whose educational and intellectual standards continued to hold sway in their imaginations, especially just after their fathers' deaths. Their fathers had dismissed visionary epistemology because of the passivity of the receipt of such knowledge, as well as because of the lack of verifiability, by rational or empirical means, of the truth of its findings. Accordingly, the geometric language H.D. and Yeats used in their writings on the occult, evident in the way it is framed, came to be enlisted by both in an ulterior project of replying to the ghosts of these disapproving fathers. For both, geometry came to be coded as connoting rigor, precision, and activity, which in turn helped them reassure themselves and others (including the fathers they remembered) that the visionary work they were engaged in was neither lax nor merely passive, but was, rather, a legitimate endeavor whose rigor equaled that of their fathers' rationalist and scientific work. Thus both H.D. and Yeats came to use geometry, albeit unwittingly, in a way that reads as Vorticist: to suggest their rejection of laxity and mere passivity and their refusal, moreover, of the kind of "Blavatsky-ish" visionary work that Lewis's manifestoes in *Blast* disdained.

I will not contend here that their use of geometry in this manner was deliberately Vorticist. I will offer that both H.D. and Yeats showed signs of guiding their use of geometric vocabulary according to what they remembered geometric forms to have been associated with in the Vorticist context. H.D. makes quite clear in her work, especially in her review of Yeats's *Responsibilities*, that the linkage between geometry and qualities such as aggression and strength stems in part from her exposure to the Vorticist example. And Yeats's letters of the late 1920s, together with comments dispersed throughout *A Vision*, indicate that he was still steering his use of geometry to a great extent according to what he recalled of Lewis's early Vorticist work—his geometric "cubes." Moreover, whatever the impact of the Vorticist example on H.D. and Yeats, their use of geometry as part of a project to combat "amorphous" mysticism rhymes notably with Vorticist uses of geometry.

What I hope to have shown here is not simply the surprising persistence of the Vorticist example long after the movement of the *avant-guerre* had faded from the scene. I have also hoped to enhance understanding of several major figures within modernist literature. If we are to understand Pound's attraction to Mussolini's Fascism, we need to include his responses to Italy's visual culture, engendered by his commitment to a Vorticist aesthetic, in our accounts of how his infatuation for Italian Fascism developed. With this case study I seek to model the kinds of specifics that are needed in any examination of how writers of this period responded to the allure of fascism, specifics that I hope will help scholarship to avoid the temptations of a priori assumptions about how an attraction to fascism evolves. Such assumptions are always as readily available as they are facile and damaging to rich historical understanding. With the study of H.D., I hope not only to have shed further light on modernist discourse about the body, but more generally to have challenged a set of critical misconceptions, still widespread in modernist scholarship, about H.D.'s attitudes toward the female body; about the supposed gynopoetics of her work; and about the relationship between her work and that of her male modernist contemporaries. I also hope to have illuminated more brightly both the dissident erotic that H.D. adumbrates for us with the fantasy, at once disturbing and compelling, of the geometric body—as well as the forms of feminism that this erotic might help to develop and sustain.

With my study of H.D.'s and Yeats's relationship to visionary epistemology, I have sought to add to modernist scholarship on the impact of occult thought on modernist work. Crucial here is the realization that if H.D. and Yeats were intensely drawn to the occult, and most forcefully so in the interwar context, they were also constantly haunted by a fear that their visionary knowledge was both illegitimate and ill-gotten. I have sought to highlight their struggle with visionary epistemology, one in which both were deeply invested for both public and personal reasons. On the one hand, both pressed forward with the creation of their visionary texts, despite the difficulty of articulating what they had experienced, because they felt that they had vital healing wisdom to impart to readers at a critical historical juncture. On the other hand, they were also resolved to continue with their projects because the realm of visionary knowledge had always, for both, represented that which would allow them to defy the exacting demands of their skeptical fathers. The formidable intellectual expectations of their fathers continued to command H.D. and Yeats, even as they sought to refuse them and even though neither ever felt fully able to meet them. The way they deploy and contextualize geometric language in their texts—not *that* they use geometric vocabulary, but rather *how*—indicated their desire at once to complete that gesture of defiance and to assuage the anxieties that dogged them—about occupying a sphere of knowledge their fathers had disdained.

■

In 1915, Lewis, outlining Vorticism's distinctive characteristics, recognizes the contingency of the value of a name "tag":

> Because VORTICISM is a word first used here, that is no reason why it should be used rather than another, unless there are a group of painters who are so distinctive that they need a distinctive tag, and to whom this especial tag may aptly apply. I consider that there are.
>
> (B2 38)

With Lewis, I maintain that there was indeed a group—of both painters and writers—to whom this "especial tag" applied and, furthermore, that Vorticism, as defined by its original struggle, can help us to identify a "distinctive" strain within modernist rhetorical practice. It can illuminate affinities among Lewis, Pound, H.D., and Yeats that would usually go unobserved, and help us acknowledge the compelling power of Vorticism's memory long after its heyday in 1914. It can bring into finer focus the contours of Pound's infatuation with Mussolini's Italy, and enhance understanding of the sources of H.D.'s images, seemingly anomalous, of the body under pressure in *Nights*. It can help us gain a better purchase on the impulse behind H.D.'s and Yeats's use of geometry in their late work that focused on occult experiences, and their reluctance to adopt a "passive," "medium-like" stance in their visionary work.

Moreover, it can augment understanding of the logic of the phenomenon we have come to regard as characteristic of the modernist milieu—the "movement." The propensity of artists and writers during these modernist decades to assemble into groups and to devise and announce programs of action unquestionably forms one of the more marked signatures of the era. As this study of the Vorticist geometric idiom, its attendant values, and its translations reveals, although a name and a movement may initially be forged out of expediency—out of a need to, as Lewis suggests, create and name a group strategically for promotional purposes—it can nonetheless later accrue other significances: it can accrete power, and a momentum of its own, as its initial meaning is transformed and superseded, even after the "movement" itself dies. It changes as artists use it, inhabit it, remember it, strive to recover it, reject it, remain haunted by it, and evoke it once again.

When critics invoke the concept of a movement, we usually employ it for purposes of classification. To ascertain whether a text belongs in a "movement," we ask how much the characteristics of a certain text resemble those of the texts circulating at the movement's inception. We ask if the artist responsible for the text interacted with those originally involved in the movement. Such a treatment of the concept of a "movement," however, remains too limited: it accords too little attention to the lived reality of a movement, to the way it can possess the minds of writers, even after the movement's demise, and compel them later to form an attachment to a new movement in a certain way or conduct their work in ways that seem to have little to do with conditions of their immediate environment. As scholars of modernism, we need to recognize the influence of movements on writers long after those movements have supposedly had their funeral. To understand more fully the collection of years, projects, commitments, and environments we have come to call modernism, we need to recognize the potential for time travel, for translation, that exists in all movements, whatever their provenance. We need to recognize the capacity of movements for resurrection at propitious, perhaps unexpected, junctures—to borrow a phrase from Walter Benjamin, their ability to "flash up" at "moments of danger."

Vorticism, and the potent geometrics it carries, was unquestionably revived at moments of crisis and need for Pound, Yeats, and H.D. and was enlisted to articulate their responses to the exigencies of the supposed bankruptcy of liberal capitalist democracy; their sense of helplessness in the face of escalating political tensions and impending violence; their personal psychic needs during (as well as partly in response to) this period of public crisis; and their urgent doubts about the authority of visionary epistemology. When Wyndham Lewis comments wryly in a retrospective essay of 1956 that Vorticism was what he "personally, did, and said, at a certain period" (*WLOA* 451), he introduces a red herring that keeps us from perceiving accurately the trajectories of these things we talk about when we talk about movements. No movement, Vorticism or any other, is merely what one artist, even a group of artists, do and say for a certain span of time. Nor does it end, neatly, with a span of time; nor does it even simply continue past a designated temporal boundary: it may disappear and reappear, in fitful bursts and gusts. As it lives in the minds of those who participate in it or encounter it, it shifts, emerges, and manifests itself later, transformed, translated: it reappears in impulses, trends, moments, and images, geometric or otherwise.

It is these traces of memory, unexpected generative moments of remembrance, that can help us to understand certain otherwise inexplicable moments in the late work of the moderns, moments that seem, given the immediate conditions out of which the artists were working, to emerge from nowhere. They emerge not from nowhere, but instead from elsewhere, from memory, from the sometimes still vivid—in this case still vividly Vorticist—past.

PREFACE

1. This study focuses on the late modernist work of Ezra Pound, H.D., and W. B. Yeats, which, I contend, draws significantly on a Vorticist geometric idiom. Beyond those on which this study focuses, there are myriad other cases in which writers of the modern period make use of geometric figures: Joyce in *Finnegans Wake*, for instance, uses a geometric figure, tongue in cheek, to diagram Anna Livia Plurabelle; Woolf draws a geometric figure of three fused rectangles in her notebooks to capture the structure of her novel *To the Lighthouse*; in "Six Significant Landscapes," Wallace Stevens's speaker complains of "Rationalists" who "confine themselves" to "right-angled triangles" and recommends instead "rhomboids, cones, waving lines, ellipses." The examples addressed in this study, however, belong to a specific category: they are cases in which the writers concerned developed their geometrical idiom, which they used in a sustained fashion, in part out of memories of how the geometric figure accumulated significance within the Vorticist movement.

2. Lewis uses the term "geometrics" to capture the Vorticist visual idiom in *Rude Assignment* 129.

3. As Ronald Schuchard notes, "[W]e are now at the threshold of a new age for the study of all modernist literature": "there is no richer time to be a modernist teacher and scholar," as "many of the riches are yet to be found in untapped archives and in the unexamined histories of modernist texts" (*Eliot's Dark Angel* 216). Robert Spoo comments likewise that "it is impossible to predict the future of a literary period that has yet to step forth fully from the archives" ("H.D. Prosed" 201).

4. *Oxford English Dictionary*, s.v. "geometry."

INTRODUCTION

1. The essay in which Pound asserted this, "The Wisdom of Poetry," was first published in *Forum*, April 1912.

2. The essay in which this claim appears, "Vorticism," was first published in the *Fortnightly Review* 96 (1914): 461–471.

3. Although a number of critics have addressed how geometric terms and figures function in the work of Pound, Lewis, and Yeats, no one, to my knowledge, has yet concentrated on the significance of geometric language in the work of H.D. More importantly, no critical work has yet argued that the geometric idiom serves similar purposes in the work of all these writers. In my effort to do so, I draw from a collection of illuminating critical discussions about geometry as it functions in the texts of individual writers, including Ian Bell's treatment of Pound's geometric analogies in *Critic as Scientist*, and remarks in Reed Way Dasenbrock's *Literary Vorticism of Wyndham Lewis and Ezra Pound*, Vincent Sherry's *Ezra Pound, Wyndham Lewis, and Radical Modernism*, Michael Wutz's "Energetics of *Tarr*," Timothy Materer's *Modernist Alchemy*, and Hazard Adams's *Book of Yeats's Vision*.

4. In "Canon, Gender, Text: The Case of H.D.," Lawrence Rainey notes the central place such theoretical work occupies within modernism: "It is a commonplace that literary modernism is distinguished by an unprecedented production of critical-theoretical writings that articulated the historical, formal, or ideological grounds for the modernist experiment, that sought to create or shape an audience receptive to modernist artworks" (106).

5. She draws Kenner's phrase, "Poets at the Blackboard" from his article of the same name.

6. See Cork on the debates about "pure form" and the "viability of abstraction" circulating in *avant-guerre* London (*Vorticism and Its Allies* 18), as well as Dasenbrock on how the Vorticist position on abstraction related to those of other artists and movements of this moment (*Literary Vorticism* 61–77). Dasenbrock emphasizes the differences between his reading of Vorticist abstraction and the interpretations of Cork, Wees, and Materer; I feature his account here because of my respect for his interrogation of the widespread view, promulgated by the above commentators, that Vorticist art was "abstract or nonrepresentational." As Dasenbrock maintains, Vorticism never "committed itself programmatically to abstraction" (64)—here he agrees with Kenner (see *Pound Era* 241)—but rather employed a geometric language usually read as abstract as a "means" to a kind of representation distinctive to Vorticism (61): the Vorticists sought to represent the underlying "essence" of their subjects (71) through a geometric visual idiom. See also Introduction, note 19, and Chapter 1, note 35.

7. Dasenbrock regards the Vorticist commitment to creating a movement both traversing and linking the arts as one of the attributes distinguishing it from Cubism and Futurism, two contemporary movements to which it was clearly indebted and with which it was in dialogue (*Literary Vorticism* 14). Pound pointed to Vorticism's effort to encompass several arts in his manifesto, "Vortex Pound," explaining that Vorticism in art involved discovering the "primary form" to which a "concept" or "emotion" "belongs" and using the "art of this form" to express it (*B1* 154). This process of ascertaining the medium in which an idea could be best expressed, he would note in 1916, is "the fundamental tenet of vorticism" (*G-B* 81). Pound provides a thorough inventory of the possibilities available to the Vorticist artist: if a concept or emotion "presents itself to the vivid consciousness" in sound, it is most properly expressed through music; if in words, it should be expressed through literature; if in images, through poetry; if in form, through design; if in an arrangement of colors, through painting; if in form or design in three dimensions, through sculpture; if in movement, through dance (*B1* 154). In his explanatory essay "Vorticism," published in the *Fortnightly Review* in 1914, Pound likewise emphasized that Vorticism included several arts—he mentioned painting, sculpture, music, and poetry—and similarly called for Vorticist artists to make full use of the "primary pigment" associated with their particular art, i.e., the medium distinctive to that art, and to concentrate

on employing that medium to present that which could best, or only, be conveyed by way of it (*G-B* 81–94, especially 87–92).

8. The artists named here had relationships to the Vorticist movement of diverse kinds and degrees. Some even deliberately dissociated themselves from it: Dasenbrock, for instance, notes that whereas Bomberg and Epstein had many connections with the Vorticists, and exhibited with them, they rejected official affiliation with Vorticism (*Literary Vorticism* 56, 245). Even Etchells, Cork observes, although part of the original cluster of proto-Vorticists around Lewis, refused to sign the Vorticist manifesto (*Vorticism and Its Allies* 23–24). Here, however, rather than distinguish between those artists who self-identified as official members of the movement and those who merely traveled in Vorticist circles and exhibited with the Vorticists, I simply mention artists who, in critical hindsight, have frequently come to be associated with the Vorticist geometric idiom. As Cork puts it, despite their efforts to distance themselves from Vorticism, Bomberg, Etchells, and Epstein are all "inextricably bound up with the movement" they sought to evade (*Vorticism and Its Allies* 23–24).

9. Hulme identifies the work of the artists who will soon be identified as Vorticists as a "new constructive geometric art" in "Modern Art—I. The Grafton Group," *New Age* 14.11 (January 15, 1914): 341–342. See also the other articles in the same series: "Modern Art—II. A Preface Note and Neo-Realism," *New Age* 14.15 (February 12, 1914): 467–469, and "Modern Art—III. The London Group," *New Age* 14.21 (March 26, 1914): 661–662.

10. Paul G. Konody, "Art and Artists: The London Group," *Observer*, March 8, 1914: 6. Quoted in Wees, *Vorticism and the English Avant-Garde* 141.

11. Pound refers here to "The Red Rag," a section in Whistler's *Gentle Art of Making Enemies*, in which Whistler comments,

> The vast majority of English folk cannot and will not consider a picture as a picture, apart from any story which it may be supposed to tell. My picture of a "Harmony in Grey and Gold" is an illustration of my meaning—a snow scene with a single black figure and a lighted tavern. I care nothing for the past, present, or future of the black figure.... All that I know is that my combination of grey and gold is the basis of the picture. Now this is precisely what my friends cannot grasp. They say, "Why not call it 'Trotty Veck,' and sell it for a round harmony of golden guineas?"—naively acknowledging that, without baptism, there is no ... market! (126; ellipses Whistler's)

Pound here no doubt accepts and takes pleasure in Whistler's alignment between an appreciation for pure form and a lack of commercial success, which Pound and his Vorticist cohort can wear as a badge of avant-garde honor.

12. See Eysteinsson, *The Concept of Modernism*; Benstock, *Women of the Left Bank*; and Rado, *Re-reading Modernism*.

13. Like Dasenbrock, I would maintain that Vorticism "is admittedly not a very conspicuous object in the landscape of modernism" (*Literary Vorticism* 11).

14. See Orage, writing under R.H.C. in "Readers and Writers," *New Age* 15.19 (September 10, 1914): 449. Orage notes, "In the 'Fortnightly Review,' Mr. Ezra Pound writes on 'Vorticism.' Whether he knows it or not, Vorticism is dead. It was, at best, only a big name for a little thing, that in the simmering of the pre-war period suddenly became a bubble, and is now burst. Of the magazine 'Blast,' which was devoted to the propaganda of Vorticism, I doubt whether another issue will appear. Compared with the war it is incomparably feeble."

For the phrase "snuffed out by the Great War," see "The Skeleton in the Cupboard Speaks" (*WLOA* 335). In his introduction to the catalogue for Wyndham Lewis and Vorticism, the 1956 retrospective about Vorticism at London's Tate Gallery, Lewis noted that "in general," he "repudiated" Vorticism "after the experiences" of the First World War (*WLOA* 452).

15. Peppis, "Surrounded by a Multitude of Other Blasts: Vorticism and the Great War," *Modernism/Modernity* 4.2 (April 1997): 39–66. I am responding especially to what Peppis observes at the outset of his article on the inadequacy of the current critical "stories" disseminated about Vorticism.

16. Kenner has most famously promulgated the view of Vorticism as short-lived, disappearing shortly after the war (*The Pound Era* 247, 553), and chroniclers of Vorticism such as Wees have followed suit. Benstock nicely summarizes the dominant view of Vorticism as an evanescent phenomenon: "Like many other of the 'isms' that collectively comprised Modernism, Vorticism was particularly short-lived and, except as a continuing metaphor for a certain narrowly defined literary practice around which Kenner plots *The Pound Era*, the literary effects of this movement died with the second—and last—issue of Wyndham Lewis's *Blast*" (*Women of the Left Bank* 24).

17. See H.D.'s review of Yeats's *Responsibilities*, thought to have been written about 1916. Here she uses comments about "cubes and angles" and "triangles and broken arcs" (52–53) to characterize the art of her generation, which has, she believes, glorified violence and thereby contributed to the onset of war. Gary Burnett argues convincingly for the linkage in this essay between these geometric figures and the projects of Vorticism ("A Poetics out of War: H.D.'s Responses to the First World War").

18. Marjorie Perloff quotes this phrase from Marinetti's letter to Belgian painter Henry Maassen, written between 1909 and 1910 (*Futurist Moment* 81).

19. I am not interested in continuing the debate Dasenbrock features about the degree to which Vorticist geometrics should be considered "abstract," but I agree with his contention that "abstraction" should not be attributed to the Vorticists if it obscures their interest in engaging with the world around them, both including and transforming its forms in their work. Indeed despite critical efforts to place the Vorticists in the "abstractionist" camp of modern artists, and notwithstanding Lewis's claims in "The Cubist Room" (one of the earliest descriptions of Vorticist goals) that his group of artists celebrated "the value of colour and form as such independently of what recognizable form it covers and encloses" (9), the geometrics of the Vorticists were not, strictly speaking, as purely abstract as those of say, Kandinsky. As Dasenbrock suggests, it may be fruitful to regard the apparently abstract forms of the Vorticists as employed in an effort toward nontraditional representation—a diagramming of a subject's essential qualities (*Literary Vorticism* 61–75). See also Chapter 1, note 35.

20. See Auden, "The Public v. the Late William Butler Yeats." Auden called this "failure" the "most obvious social fact of the last forty years."

21. Cued by Daniel Albright's work on the uses of scientific terminology in the work of Eliot, Pound, and Yeats, I should emphasize that this study focuses not on the discipline of geometry

per se, but rather on literary appropriations of geometric figures—both in the form of geometric visual images and geometric metaphors. Moreover, the significance accorded geometric figures in the works addressed here derives not from their role in the domain of mathematics, but instead mostly from the associations accrued by geometric figures in early twentieth-century abstract visual art. This study considers how geometry came to be enlisted as part of an effort toward expressing a value system shared by many modernist writers—one central to Vorticism, and one for which Vorticism was widely regarded among the moderns as a locus classicus—which celebrated analytic detachment of attitude, clarity of outline, and vigorous force. This study addresses what geometric language enabled them to accomplish between the wars, the conflicts to which it helped them respond, and the needs that it helped meet with appropriate form.

22. *Oxford English Dictionary*, s.v. "geometry."
23. Plato, *Republic* VII, 758–759.
24. Patke, *Long Poems of Wallace Stevens* 72.
25. For Pound's account of this lecture, see "The New Sculpture" (*Egoist* 1.4 [February 16, 1914]): 67–68. "Some nights ago," he comments wryly, "Mr. T. E. Hulme delivered to the Quest Society an almost wholly unintelligible lecture on cubism and the new art at large. He was followed by two other speakers [i.e., Lewis and Pound] equally unintelligible." With the bravura of high mischief, he describes these "unintelligible" lectures, his own included:

> Mr. Hulme told us that there was *vital* art and *geometric* art. Mr. Lewis compared the soul to a bullet. I gathered from his speech that you could set a loaf of bread in an engine shop and that this would *not* cause said loaf to produce cubist paintings. A third speaker got himself disliked by saying that one might regard the body either as a sensitized receiver of sensations, or as an instrument for carrying out the decrees of the will. (67; Pound's italics)

26. Of note here is that the Quest Society, founded by G. R. S. Mead in 1909, was an outgrowth of the Theosophical movement. Mead served as secretary to Madame Helena Blavatsky, founder of the Theosophical movement, before breaking away from the Theosophical Society after her death in 1908 (his departure was spurred by a scandal within the society about the sexual teachings of prominent Theosophist C. W. Leadbeater) to found his own society. By the time he founded the Quest Society, Theosophy was associated with the belief that the vibrations of thoughts would affect what the Theosophists theorized as the "mental body" (part of an individual's "aura"), which was "composed of innumerable combinations of the subtle matter of the mental plane" (Besant and Leadbeater, *Thought-Forms* 8), so as to prompt it to radiate certain geometric forms of certain colors. Annie Besant, coauthor with Leadbeater of *Thought-Forms* (1901), became president of one branch of the Theosophists when, in the wake of Blavatsky's death, the movement split in two. In 1914, the Theosophists in the audience at the Quest Society would thus likely have been primed to listen attentively to Hulme's comments on the "geometrical character" of the new art, though they would probably have assigned a different significance to the geometric forms than he did.

27. In "Modern Art I," Hulme notes, "I am attempting in this series of articles to define the characteristics of a new constructive geometric art which seems to me to be emerging at the present moment" (341).

28. Vincent Sherry notes that Ortega y Gasset "studied in Germany the same years that saw the emergence of Worringer" (*Radical Modernism* 18). For other examples of this theorization of the "geometrical trend" in modern art, see Worringer's *Abstraction and Empathy* and Ortega y Gasset's "Dehumanization of Art."

29. For a carefully nuanced account of Hulme's use of Worringer's ideas in the essays on the "geometrical character" of the new art, see Levenson, *Genealogy of Modernism*, Chapter 6, "Hulme: The Progress of a Reaction," especially 94–102.

30. Wees notes that "Hulme put Worringer's method to narrower and more polemic uses" (*Vorticism and the English Avant-Garde* 80) than those for which Worringer had intended it; indeed Hulme, clearly partisan, endorsed the new geometric art. Dasenbrock, meanwhile, rightly notes that Worringer's treatise does not recognize any appearance of the "tendency to abstraction" he identifies in modern art per se, though the appearance of the geometric in contemporary art is Hulme's chief focus (*Literary Vorticism* 54–55).

31. Materer notes that Kandinsky's theories were influenced by *Thought-Forms* by Besant and Leadbeater (*Modernist Alchemy* 34). Kandinsky, in fact, declared himself a Theosophist.

32. See Hulme, "Modern Art" (*Speculations* 94–103). In his articles in the *New Age* during the spring of 1914, Hulme likewise distinguishes the new "geometrical art" he associates with the coalescing Vorticists from other art—both realistic and abstract. Hulme remains guarded in his approval of Lewis and Epstein, however, crediting them with being en route to important discoveries, but not yet at the point of producing coherent paintings. Eventually, as Richard Cork points out, just as the Vorticists launched themselves publicly in the summer of 1914, Hulme dissociated himself from them, disapproving of what he perceived as the extremeness of their turn to abstraction (*Vorticism and Its Allies* 14, 17).

33. In "Modern Art—III," Hulme notes that what makes the new geometric art "important" is that "behind it" is "the re-emergence of a sensibility akin to that behind geometrical arts of the past" (661). In Michael Bullock's English translation of *Abstraktion und Einfühlung*, the phrase used is "urge to abstraction."

34. In *H.D. and the Victorian Fin-de-Siècle*, Cassandra Laity notes the way in which the threat posed by both the Decadent androgynous male Aesthete and the Decadent femme fatale crucially shapes the formation of the modernist poetic. Delimiting my scope more narrowly, I focus here on how the male Aesthete in particular guides the early modernist Vorticist program—how the influence of the figure of the male Aesthete manifests itself in the way a geometric idiom is enlisted within Vorticism and in the repeated emphasis placed within *Blast* on the figure of Oscar Wilde, as well as on related signifiers. See also Chapter 1, note 30.

35. In a later essay, "The Skeleton in the Cupboard Speaks," Lewis characterizes the Vorticist relationship to the machine world by noting, "'Vorticism' accepted the machine world.... It sought out machine-forms.... In the case of Vorticism ... the 'inner world of the imagination' was not an asylum from the brutality of mechanical life. On the contrary it identified itself with that brutality" (340–341).

36. Wutz elaborates on the series of concepts with which he suggests Lewis was familiar:

> In 1867, Lord Kelvin advanced a theory of "vortex atoms," whose rotary motions in a plenum, prop-

> agated through the mediation of an ether, provided a basis for his theory of matter and thus for a physical theory of the field. Building on Kelvin's rotation of molecular vortices, James Clerk Maxwell formulated in mathematical terms the physical nature of what Michael Faraday, the pioneer of field theory, had two decades earlier called magnetic "lines of force." He supposed that a magnetic field could be represented as an ethereal fluid filled with rotating vortex tubes, whose geometrical arrangement corresponded to these force-lines and in which the vortical velocities corresponded to the intensity of the field.
>
> ("ENERGETICS OF *TARR*" 848)

Wutz draws his information here from Peter Harman's *Energy, Force, and Matter: The Conceptual Development of Nineteenth-Century Physics* (Cambridge: Cambridge Univ. Press, 1982).

37. Many critical texts of the last ten years have addressed this tendency within modernism, interpreting it in slightly different ways. In *War of the Words* (volume 1 of *No Man's Land*), for instance, Sandra M. Gilbert and Susan Gubar construe the "hard" aesthetic that developed within modernism as a defense against what is perceived as the increasing "feminization" of art. Male moderns greeted the influx of women writers into the avant-garde scene, Gilbert and Gubar argue, not only by belittling these women writers but also by developing, as they comment of Eliot, "an implicitly masculine aesthetic of hard, abstract, learned verse that is opposed to the aesthetic of soft, effusive, personal verse supposedly written by women and Romantics" (154; see Chapter 3, "Tradition and the Female Talent," 125–162). In *Dedication to Hunger*, Leslie Heywood characterizes this aesthetic of hardness as part of what she terms the "anorexic logic" of modernism—the tendency of many modern writers, like Eliot, Pound, Williams, Conrad, and Rhys, to display, through the phantasmatics of their texts, a horror of the fleshly, the flabby, the fat and, accordingly, to seek to purge their texts of the heavy materiality traditionally associated with women. And in *H.D. and the Victorian Fin-de-Siècle*, Laity addresses what she terms the "hypermasculine" and "anti-Romantic" rhetoric characterizing much of the "modernist poetic enterprise" (1–2) as a reaction against the threat of two figures associated with Decadence: the femme fatale and the male Aesthete androgyne (ix–x).

38. See Laity, *H.D. and the Victorian Fin-de-Siècle*, Chapter 1, "The Rhetoric of Anti-Romanticism," in which, pointing to the work of Elizabeth Cullingford on Yeats's love poetry, she acknowledges both how Yeats's rhetoric sometimes "lapses into misogynistic posturings" and how Yeats's poetry in fact demonstrates many of the characteristics he repudiates in his public pronouncements (6).

39. In *Penelope's Web*, for example, Friedman construes the "crystalline" hardness of H.D.'s early poetry as indicating the

> phallocentric poetics with which H.D.-as-poet had to establish herself . . . . [H]er poetic discourse was . . . 'hard,' its vulnerabilities as a female voice deeply encoded beneath its crystalline sur-

face .... Her prose discourse, in contrast[,] ... unveiled the woman and directly narrated the story of her social relations in the world. (6)

CHAPTER 1. WYNDHAM LEWIS, VORTICISM, AND THE CAMPAIGN AGAINST WILDEAN EFFEMINACY

1. I take the phrase from Marshall McLuhan's later project, *Counterblast* (1969), which tributed Lewis's magazine, using it as a model and point of departure for its own cultural commentary on the effects of the "electric information environment" (5).

2. As Pound once put it, we might view *Blast* as a merely an "eccentrically printed volume issued by half a dozen aimless men" (*G-B* 107).

3. Marjorie Perloff, in "Modernist Studies," provides useful commentary on how modernism has been regarded over the past few decades:

> Surely no literary term has raised more controversy and misunderstanding than the modest little word *modernism* .... Once the site of all that was radical, exciting, and above all new ... by the early 1970s modernism found itself under attack as a retrograde, elitist movement—at best, the final phase of the great Romantic revolution and, at worst, the aestheticist reaction formation to an alienated social life that had close links to fascism. (154)

Since then, with the advent of many new scholarly approaches in modernist studies, modernism has been recuperated as a critical category. The attitude of the newly formed Modernist Studies Association, designed to mark and foster a new era in modernist scholarship, accords with that of many contemporary scholars in the field. What was once regarded as modernism may no longer be useful—but the idea of modernism can nonetheless still be used to discover and illuminate a wealth of experimental work produced between the nineteenth-century *fin de siècle* and the Second World War; "modernism" is a concept waiting to be redefined, rendered more capacious; and the assumptions driving modernist canon formation await further interrogation.

4. In my phrasing here, I take a cue from "What Was Modernism?"—Harry Levin's important discussion of modernism from 1960, which assumed modernism to be a cultural phenomenon that belonged to a past era. See Levin, "What Was Modernism?" in *Refractions: Essays in Comparative Literature* (New York: Oxford Univ. Press, 1966), 271–295.

5. Useful also are Witemeyer's remarks in the introduction's opening paragraph, which efficiently compiles opinions from a range of notable commentators on modernism: Julian Symons from *Makers of the New: The Revolution in Literature 1912–1939* (London: Andre Deutsch, 1987) observes that "modernism" is a "word often used but rarely defined" (9); and Bradbury and McFarlane (in *Modernism: A Guide to European Literature, 1880–1930*) register the intense confusion usually engendered by the term (Chapter 1: "The Name and Nature of Modernism"

19–55). Witemeyer also stresses that modernism is "construed differently by scholars trained in different countries and disciplines" (1). Like Witemeyer, I focus on Anglo-American modernism as it has been defined and debated among scholars of British, Irish, and American literature.

6. This is reflected in recent surveys such as Peter Nicholls's *Modernisms* (1995); as Peter Childs observes, however, the practice was in evidence as early as the 1960s (*Modernism* 12).

7. With this phrase I echo the title of Astradur Eysteinsson's useful survey of the evolution of critical discourse on modernism over the decades, *The Concept of Modernism*.

8. Wees provides an inventory of common descriptors for the color of *Blast*'s cover (*Vorticism and the English Avant-Garde* 165).

9. Pound notes that *Blast*'s "large type and the flaring cover are . . . bright plumage" (*G-B* 107).

10. *Poetry* 5 (October 1914): 44. The context for this comment reads:

> 'Vorticism' is the latest official title of the latest literary and artistic revolution in England, and *Blast*, a quarterly published by John Lane, with a bright cerise cover that makes one feel as if the outer cuticle had been removed, is its official organ. There is much entertainment to be had from the various Manifestoes, tables of Curses, and equally profane benedictions included, and no small food for thought—if thought is the product of such pre-digested nutriment.

11. "The men of 1914" is Lewis's phrase from his 1937 memoir, *Blasting and Bombardiering* (252).

12. McGann uses "bibliographical code" (*Textual Condition* 13)—alternately referred to as "bibliographic code" by theorists such as George Bornstein—to refer to the physical features of a book, such as "paper, ink, typefaces, layouts" (12), which, he argues, constitute a mode of signification associated with a text in its physical instantiation that is distinct from its linguistic codes. (See also Chapter 2, note 29.)

13. Morrisson places *Blast* in the context of other little magazines of its time, noting that its rise and fall paralleled that of many other such publications: "[B]y and large, the flurry of avant-garde little magazines and activity was not successfully reenergized in London after the war" (*Public Face of Modernism* 115).

14. For Bechhöfer's parodies of *Blast*, arguably some of the funniest on record, see *New Age* 15.13 (July 30, 1914): 308. For A. R. Orage's remarks, see the "Readers and Writers" column by "R.H.C.," *New Age* 15.10 (July 9, 1914): 229; and *New Age* 15.11 (July 16, 1914): 253. For an able summary of the critical response to *Blast 1* in 1914, see Wees, *Vorticism and the English Avant-Garde* 193–197. As Wees attests here, with the exception of praise from Ford, Aldington, and a few other reviewers such as Eunice Tjietjens and R. A. Scott-James, *Blast* was dismissed by critics as "the reductio ad absurdum of mad modernity" (*New York Times*); a "strange mixture of seriousness and facetiousness, common sense and absurdity" (*Observer*); and the misguided project of a "heterogeneous mob suffering from juvenile decay" (*New Statesman*). Again, as above, Lawrence Rainey suggests that even these reactions were spicier than most.

15. The *Pall Mall Gazette* and the *New York Times* likewise criticized *Blast* as derivative,

reading Vorticism as merely a degraded version of Italian Futurism: the first noted that the Vorticists had far less "snap" than their models; and the *New York Times* simply called *Blast* a "rather dull imitation of Signor Marinetti and his Futurists" (Wees, *Vorticism and the English Avant-Garde* 193).

16. Aside from studies by Kenner (1954 and 1971), Wees (1972), Cork (1976), Perloff (1986), and Morrisson (2001), accounts that have granted *Blast* a prominent place over the past few decades include Materer, *Vortex* (1979); Dasenbrock, *Literary Vorticism* (1985); and Lyon, *Manifestoes* (1999).

17. In 1914, even Richard Aldington, one of the few critics to praise *Blast*, called Ezra Pound's poems in the first issue "quite unworthy of their author" ("Blast" 273). Many contemporary critics have followed Aldington's lead: Rainey, for instance, damns the poems Pound published here as "among the dreariest he ever produced" ("Creation of the Avant-Garde" 210). Dasenbrock agrees, saying that although a few critics who are, like him, "deeply involved" in Vorticism may praise some of Pound's work from *Blast*, he believes Pound's contributions to be failures (*Literary Vorticism* 88–89). Perloff chimes in: "No one would argue that [Pound's] *Blast* poems have a central place in the Pound canon" (*Futurist Moment* 163).

18. *Blast* is much more frequently included in accounts of modernism, for instance, than Alfred Kreymborg's long-running *Others* (1915–1919), which, as a showcase for the work of writers such as Pound, H.D., Marianne Moore, Eliot, and Stevens, would seem to merit more attention than *Blast*.

19. In fact, as Cork points out, much of the Vorticist work generated 1914–1915 has been lost: "Incredible as it may seem, thirty-eight out of the forty-nine works displayed by the full members of the movement at the 1915 Vorticist exhibition are now missing" (*Vorticism and Its Allies* 26).

20. Monroe's pungent comments here, more fully, read:

> At the end of June, 1914, Wyndham Lewis and Ezra Pound had issued the first number of their cyclonic *Blast*, which was to blow away, in thick black capitals half an inch high, the Victorian Vampire; the Britannic Aesthete; Cream of the Snobbish Earth; Humor, and its First Cousin and Accomplice, Sport; and many other props of British civilization; including the Climate; also, crossing the Channel, Sentimental Gallic Gush, Sensationalism, and Fussiness. In fact, the list of Blasts and Curses covered eleven twelve-by-nine pages of a sizzling Manifesto.
>
> (POET'S LIFE 355)

21. I draw both phrases from Morrow ("Blueprint to the Vortex" v).

22. For detailed commentary on the relationship between *Blast* and other contemporary avant-garde manifestoes and projects of this moment, see Perloff, *Futurist Moment*, especially Chapter 5, "Ezra Pound and the Prose Tradition in Verse."

23. See Reynolds, "'Chaos Invading Concept.'"

24. Rainey stresses that it was *Blast*'s similarity to many manifesto-laden documents of its time that made it so wearisome to contemporary critics: it seemed, he says, "all too familiar" ("Creation of the Avant-Garde" 210).

25. I think here of Jameson's comment from *The Political Unconscious*: "Indeed, since by definition the cultural monuments and masterworks that have survived tend necessarily to perpetuate only a single voice . . . they cannot be properly assigned their relational place in a dialogical system without the restoration or artificial reconstruction of the voice to which they were initially opposed" (85). In this passage, Jameson refers to the necessity of reconstructing voices of the class dialogue so as adequately to contextualize individual texts for the kind of Marxist analysis he recommends; here, I expropriate this notion of the reconstruction of voices to capture the necessity of repositioning Vorticism in relation to the Aestheticist voices with which it was originally in dialogue.

26. See Orage, writing as R.H.C. in the "Readers and Writers" column of the *New Age* 15.11 (9 July 9, 1914): 229. Orage notes here that the comparison is "no great credit" to *Blast*—as, though Beardsley's weird genius gave *The Yellow Book* some luster, there was little "philosophy" in it, and nothing in it, aside from Beardsley's work, of "importance."

27. *Spectator*, May 19, 1894: 695.

28. For a letter of Lewis's indicating this tendency, prevalent since the 1890s, to associate *The Yellow Book* and Aestheticism with forms of corruption and disease, see his April 2, 1914, letter to the editor of the *New Age* (*Letters of Wyndham Lewis* 58–59). Lewis uncharitably connects the painter Walter Sickert, linked with the *fin de siècle*, to the "Yellow Plague-spot edited by Arthur Symons," by which he means *The Yellow Book* (58). (Henry Harland was actually literary editor of *The Yellow Book*; Symons served as editor of the short-lived journal that attempted to become *The Yellow Book*'s successor, *The Savoy*.) Sickert himself is referred to as "the Bohemian plague-spot on clean English life" (58).

29. Huyssen, "Mass Culture as Woman," in *After the Great Divide*, especially 47–53.

30. See Laity's *H.D. and the Victorian Fin-de-Siècle* for an insightful discussion about how an abjection of the figure of the male Aesthete underpins modernist poetics. Drawing upon Judith Butler's notion of the "two figures of abjection" that uphold the hegemony of heterosexuality—"the masculinized female" and the "feminized male" (Butler, *Bodies That Matter* 103–104)—Laity argues that equally crucial to the development of the modernist poetic was the rejection of a figure that acted as the Aesthete's spectral twin: the Romantic femme fatale. "[T]he figures of the Decadent femme fatale and the male androgyne," she maintains, "were almost always discernible behind male modernist denouncements of Romantic personality in favor of modernist 'impersonality.'" Such "denouncements" issued from "male theorizers of modernism such as Eliot, Yeats, and Pound," who "violently" rejected "these twin emblems of Romantic linguistic and sexual 'morbidity'" (ix–x). Here, in contrast to Laity, I focus on the formation of the Vorticist program, rather than on the development of modernism more generally; and accordingly, I concentrate on the role of the figure of the male Aesthete, which is far more integral to the development of Vorticism than the femme fatale.

31. I draw the term "geometric bias" from Dasenbrock, *Literary Vorticism*. Dasenbrock maintains that

> no matter what the subject, even in the absence
> of recognizable subject matter, Vorticist painting

is marked by its geometric bias. Lines demarcate angular shapes, which are manipulated for compositional reasons, not out of any fidelity to optical perceptions. However, these forms are not static, but are highly dynamic, as a sense of motion is produced by the diagonal lines and color contrasts. (41)

32. For lucid discussions of the crisis in masculinity fuelling much early modernist work, see Lisa Tickner, "Men's Work?" and Laity, *H.D. and the Victorian Fin-de-Siècle*, especially Chapter 1.

33. For a more detailed description of the Rebel Art Centre, see Wees, *Vorticism and the English Avant-Garde* 68–72, and Cork, *Vorticism and Abstract Art in the First Machine Age* 146–148.

34. For useful commentary on the Vorticist "concern with essence," see Dasenbrock, *Literary Vorticism* 71.

35. As Lewis notes in *Blast 2*, Vorticism does not reject representationalism, simply slavish "imitation": "imitation, and inherently unselective registering of impressions, is an absurdity," but "to attempt to avoid all representative element is an equal absurdity" (*B2* 45). The way Vorticist geometrics at once remain defiantly distinct from, yet point to, worldly forms is captured nicely in a segment of Dasenbrock's discussion: "[T]he forms Lewis used are *abstracted*, not *abstract*, and they betray their place of origin, the modern city. The shapes on the canvas ineluctably suggest modern buildings and the formal organization of these shapes . . . reflects the activity or dynamism of the city" (*Literary Vorticism* 71; my italics). I would go further to suggest that Lewis's forms, and Vorticist forms more generally, at times suggest life forms even other than those of the modern city. As a result, Vorticist geometrics exist in a complicated relationship to what Oliver Botar, drawing upon a term from Geoffrey Grigson, has called "biomorphic modernism," in which geometric figures are meant to evoke organic forms ("Prolegomena"; I am indebted to Cynthia Messenger for the reference). Although Vorticist geometrics in most respects and in most instances stand distinct from, and even opposed to, such biomorphic geometric shapes—the Vorticists generally champion the artificial over the organic—their shapes do at times refer obliquely to the forms of the natural world.

36. Fry's comment on the "spirit of fun" appears in the *Daily Leader* for August 7, 1913; his remark on "free play" comes from one of the Omega Workshop brochures.

37. For details of the schism, see Wees, *Vorticism and the English Avant-Garde* 62–68, and Meyers, *The Enemy* 39–54.

38. The term "greenery-yallery" came into cultural currency in response to the décor of the Grosvenor Gallery in London, which opened in 1877. The aesthetic scheme of the gallery, especially its gold and green color scheme, became fashionable in late-Victorian Aestheticist circles; as a result, "greenery-yallery," the term used to refer to colors of the gallery, came to be linked to Aestheticism more generally. W. S. Gilbert alluded to this cultural use of the term in 1881 in *Patience* when he referred satirically to the character of Bunthorne, an Aesthete, as a "greenery-yallery, Grosvenor Gallery / Foot-in-the grave young man." See David Cliffe, "A Companion to Evelyn Waugh's *Brideshead Revisited*" (Waugh's novel also invokes the term "greenery-yallery"): www.abbotshill.freeserve.co.uk/Book%201%20Chapter%202.html. Cliffe also suggests that "There is no doubt that in circles which knew about such things the term became synonymous with *homosexual*."

39. As Wyndham Lewis remarks in an essay of the 1930s, "The Skeleton in the Cupboard Speaks," the "'sensitivity' that was such a striking feature of the aesthete known as 'the Bloomsbury' was greatly deplored at the headquarters of the Great London Vortex; indeed it was incessantly ridiculed by Vorticist No. I"—that is, by Lewis himself (*WLOA* 342).

40. As addressed in the Introduction, Bell, with his famous term, "significant form," brought into sharp focus the assumption, animating the work of contemporary artists ranging from Kandinsky to Picasso to the Vorticists, that "lines and colours combined in a particular way, certain forms and relations of forms, stir our aesthetic emotions" (*Art* 8).

41. Lewis's letter is directed to the editor of the *New Age* for April 2, 1914. Lewis is defending himself against charges brought against him by painter Walter Sickert in his article "On Swiftness" (*New Age* 14.21 [March 26, 1914]): 655–656). See note 28 to this chapter.

42. See Foucault, *History of Sexuality* 43; Sinfield, *Wilde Century* 12. Foucault thus summarizes his constructionist argument about how the category of homosexuality came to be invented in the late nineteenth century (and Foucault focuses here on male homosexuality):

> As defined by the ancient civil or canonical codes, sodomy was a category of forbidden acts; their perpetrator was nothing more than the juridical subject of them. The nineteenth-century homosexual [in contrast] became a personage, a past, a case history, and a childhood, in addition to being a type of life, a life form, and a morphology, with an indiscreet anatomy and possibly a mysterious physiology. (43)

The assumption was, Foucault suggests, that "Nothing that went into his total composition was unaffected by his sexuality" (43).

43. I draw the phrase "sexual panic" from Laity. The defensive Vorticist response I describe here forms part of what Laity terms the "sexual panic on the part of the successors of Oscar Wilde, whose guilty verdict had unmasked the feminine, aristocratic, and insouciant pose of the Aesthete poet as sexually deviant" (*H.D. and the Victorian Fin-de-Siècle* 2). I would amend Laity's claim slightly by saying instead that the verdict had contributed significantly to the *belief* that the common persona of the Aesthete poet correlated with male-male sexual interaction widely regarded sexually deviant, and vice versa.

44. Lewis's text dates from 1919. Although there is no consensus about when the word "queer" came to be used as definitely signifying "homosexual," most accounts place the earliest of such usages in the early twentieth century; and whereas the *OED* dates the first usage of "queer" as an adjective meaning "homosexual" to 1922, the term seems to have had an underground currency somewhat before this. Wayne Koestenbaum suggests that even in the late nineteenth century, "queer" "nearly meant 'homosexual'" (*Double Talk* 147), as, for example, when the Marquess of Queensberry, in 1894, accused a group of prominent men of being "Snob Queers" (Ellmann, *Oscar Wilde* 402). The "uncertainty of the word's meaning" at the *fin de siècle*, Koestenbaum suggests, "helps it designate incomplete knowledge," refer to that which is difficult to explain, and, thus, often indicate a secret that would titillate, such as "sexual ambiguity": a realm of suspect sexuality apt to inspire unease in mainstream contexts (*Double Talk* 147–148). The "manic" use of the word with which Koestenbaum credits Robert

Louis Stevenson also applies to Lewis, though Lewis's repetition of the word, both nervous and vicious, clearly indicates not only fascination with same-sex male erotic desire (with which Koestenbaum credits Stevenson) but also homophobia.

45. As Jameson notes, such remarks are typical of Lewis: his texts display "an obsessive phobia against [male] homosexuals" (*Fables of Aggression* 4). For Lewis's later extensive commentary on the phenomenon of the "male invert," see *The Art of Being Ruled*, Part IX, "Man and Shaman," Chapters 1–3 (269–284). For purposes of this discussion, since I focus on Vorticism, I concentrate on Lewis's early texts of the Vorticist period.

46. As Anne Quéma notes, Lewis's "obsession with the homosexual question becomes an oblique expression of an obscure, anxious desire" (*Agon of Modernism* 114). For Quéma's lucid claims about what she regards as Lewis's repressed homosexuality, see Chapter 4, "Man and Woman," 82–120. Whereas Quéma focuses on Lewis's oeuvre broadly, I concentrate here on the implications of his early Vorticist work. And whereas Quéma's study ascribes to Lewis a general attraction to male homosexuality, I focus on the ambivalent attraction to a specific form of male homoerotic interchange that appears in the textual patterns of his Vorticist period. Quéma's survey of the various modes of "psychological analysis" is useful; here, I read signals of texts for the psychological dynamics they persistently reveal and refrain from making any larger claims about the writer's psyche. I am interested in the psychological impulses inscribed in Lewis's texts, regardless of the relationship between these and the impulses of his psyche more generally.

47. See Nordau, *Degeneration* (1895). In his dedication to the book, Nordau, a professor of psychiatry and forensic medicine, explains that he means to investigate "the tendencies of the fashions in art and literature" for signs of the "degeneracy of the authors" (viii). He goes on to provide copious descriptions of the "symptoms" of such degeneracy, to address the "etiology" of the disease, and to provide a "prognosis" and "therapeutics." In *The Eighteen Nineties* (1913), Holbrook Jackson prominently features passages quoted from *Degeneration*, indicating the important place Nordau's baleful commentary held in commentary about the *fin de siècle*.

48. See Tickner, "Men's Work?" especially 7.

49. For an insightful survey of this turn of events, see Showalter, *Sexual Anarchy*, especially Chapter 1, "Borderlines," 1–18.

50. The need to demean a figure such as Wilde in order to found masculine identity is a function of the social discourses of this moment that construct male-male sexual passion as a threat to masculine identity to begin with. As Sinfield notes, Lewis's period witnessed a radical change from the many epochs that have coded male-male erotic attachments as strengthening masculinity rather than weakening it (*The Wilde Century*; see especially Chapter 2, "The Uses of Effeminacy").

51. Lewis's Vorticist texts, I would argue, clearly manifest the structure of paranoia Loewenstein recognizes.

52. In this I agree with Quéma, who maintains that when reading the psychological "idiom" displayed by Lewis's texts, we must take into account the "social, political, and cultural language out of which his own vocabulary evolved" (*Agon of Modernism* 87). I agree further that "the obvious starting-point is the sociocultural discourse of the *fin de siècle* in Britain as analyzed and documented by Elaine Showalter" (87).

53. For Wilde's claim that "Life imitates Art," see "The Decay of Lying" (*Complete Works of Oscar Wilde* 981–982).

54. Materer also notes that in Lewis's play "Enemy of the Stars," which I read as illuminating Vorticist doctrine, the ultimate fate of Lewis's protagonist, Arghol, "illustrates Wilde's epigram, 'Nature hates Mind'" (*Wyndham Lewis the Novelist* 50).

55. See Materer, *Wyndham Lewis the Novelist* 98–99.

56. This is not to say that Wilde is the only representative of such self-conscious dandyism, but in the aftermath of the 1890s, given the publicity surrounding Wilde's trials, he is the best known. Neither Max Beerbohm nor Aubrey Beardsley, for instance, also famous exemplars of the dandy, had been branded into the public consciousness as indelibly as had Wilde.

57. For this claim, see Materer, *Wyndham Lewis the Novelist* 99. Lewis is actually best known for taking on the pose of the Spanish caballero—he swept about mysteriously in a cape and a Cordoba hat (Meyers, *The Enemy* 14)—so this costume differs in sartorial detail from the silk, satin, lace, and brightly colored accouterments generally associated with the dandy. Nonetheless, in spirit, it is clearly dandyish: Lewis did strike a self-conscious pose, expressing what Jackson called (though not in connection with Lewis) the dandy's commitment to artifice, the "revolt against Nature" that was "in reality a revolt against conventions which . . . acted as checks upon the free movements of personalities and ideas" (*Eighteen Nineties* 111).

58. For Lewis's introduction to Rothenstein, see Meyers, *The Enemy* 11.

59. In Augustus John's memoir, *Finishing Touches*, as he pays tribute to Wilde, he describes Wilde's death scene with a gruesome image of Wilde's body having exploded into a shower of bodily fluids (145, also 106). Of this, Ellmann remarks: "John says he heard about it from [Robert] Ross and [Reginald] Turner" (*Oscar Wilde* 549).

60. In 1913, Jackson notes the dearth of commentary on Wilde in the years after his public disgrace, calling it "the great silence which immediately followed his trial and imprisonment" (*Eighteen Nineties* 72).

61. See Ransome, *Wilde: A Critical Study* 219; Ellmann, *Oscar Wilde* 553. Ellmann features a photo of the monument on 498. A photo of the monument was also included in the exhibit "Vorticism and Its Allies" at the Hayward Gallery in London, March 27–June 2, 1974 (see Cork, *Vorticism and Its Allies* 43).

62. Cork notes the importance of Epstein to Vorticism: "Even though [David] Bomberg, [Jacob] Epstein, and [Frederick] Etchells all refused to sign the Vorticist manifesto, each of them is inextricably bound up with the movement he evaded" (*Vorticism and Its Allies* 23–24).

63. The expression "violent and explosive" is Rebecca West's, who describes one of Lewis's paintings this way (Cork, *Vorticism and Abstract Art in the First Machine Age* 270).

64. The literary selections of *Blast* are not entirely confined to such aggressive pieces; also included in the magazine is Ford Madox Ford's "Saddest Story"—later to evolve into his novel *The Good Soldier*—whose wistful tone contrasts markedly with the pugnacity of the manifestoes. The anomalous status of Ford's piece, however, only reinforces the impression of the aggressiveness of the journal as a whole.

65. Quéma agrees, using Jameson's arguments about Lewis to suggest that "[f]rom the start, Lewis's phallocentrcity was undermined by a relentless satire of the representation of the male body and culture" (*Agon of Modernism* 94–95). She comments further that although "feminist criticism responds to the undeniable misogyny of some of Lewis's writing, which seems to indicate the presence of a patriarchal author," as both Jameson and LaFourcade suggest, Lewis is not, ultimately, to be labeled neatly as a "patriarchal author": this is evidenced by "Lewis's repeated attack on the fetishistic rituals of a phallocentric culture" (95).

66. This comment originally appears in Gaudier-Brzeska's "Allied Artists' Association Ltd, Holland Park Hall," first published in the *Egoist* (June 15, 1914): 227–229, the same issue that features Pound's appreciative assessment of Wyndham Lewis (233–234). Pound reprints the review in *G-B* 30–35.

67. For Lewis's later denigration of the demands placed on men by conventional masculinity, see *The Art of Being Ruled*:

> Men were only made into 'men' with great difficulty even in primitive society: the male is not naturally 'a man' any more than the woman.... A man ... is made, not born: and he is made, of course, with very great difficulty. From the time he yells and kicks in his cradle, to the time he receives his last kick at school, he is recalcitrant. (279–280)

68. For a discussion of the relationship between the male homosexual and the male homosocial, see Sedgwick, *Between Men* 1–20.

69. Reminiscing in 1953 in a letter to Hugh Kenner, Lewis notes that *Tarr* was also such an attempt to create a literary equivalent to his Vorticist canvasses:

> In *Tarr* (1914–15) I was an extremist. In editing *Blast* I regarded the contributions of Ezra as compromisingly passéiste, and wished I could find two or three literary extremists. In writing *Tarr* I wanted at the same time for it to be a novel, and to do a piece of writing worthy of the hand of the abstractist innovator (which was an impossible combination).
>
> (*LETTERS OF WYNDHAM LEWIS* 552)

70. Wendy Flory, for instance, maintains that *Enemy of the Stars* "has not been taken as seriously as [Lewis] hoped it would"—"as seriously," in her estimation, as "it deserves" ("Enemy of the Stars" 92).

71. Graver regrets that although critics like Kenner and Materer often carefully analyze the London Vortex surrounding the play, they fail to attend closely to its formal maneuvers ("Vorticist Performance" 483).

72. Klein notes that "[a]ttention to 'Enemy of the Stars' has tended to diminish the theoretical problems raised by its overt assumption of a form it only problematically occupies, scanting issues of its narrative in favor of analyzing the audacity of its style" ("Vorticist Drama" 225–226).

73. Foshay comments: "It is instructive to chart the critical reception of *Enemy* in its uniform concern with form and style and its rejection of the work's thematic significance" (*Politics of Intellect* 23). Foshay laments Materer's slight discussion of the text's characters and action; Dasenbrock's contention that those who focus on the text's action and characters "miss Lewis's point," which is that the play should be read as a "gesture" (*Literary Vorticism* 135); and

Flory's dismissive view of the play's content, which leads her to "dispens[e]" — unfortunately, in Foshay's view — with Lewis's message to his audience" ("Enemy of the Stars" 23–24).

74. In 1950 Lewis remarked, "It became evident to me ... that words and syntax were not susceptible of transformation into abstract terms" (*Rude Assignment* 129). Klein agrees with Lewis's admission of defeat by maintaining that Lewis's effort to revolutionize language is "hopeless," echoing the "failure" staged by the play's narrative ("Vorticist Drama" 234). Beatty likewise deems the play an "unsuccessful experiment" ("Experimental Play" 42).

75. Perhaps it was in response to Lewis's efforts to translate the play into another idiom that Ezra Pound wrote to Lewis in 1936, "WD/ B/B/C/ broadcast Enemy of the Stars if you did a radio version ... Wd/ you bother with doing an AIR version of it.?" (*P/L* 188).

76. For insightful discussions of the linguistic strategies of *Enemy of the Stars*, see Dasenbrock, *Literary Vorticism*, especially Chapter 4; and Graver, "Vorticist Performance."

77. Given its structure, *Enemy of the Stars* does not comfortably occupy the usual dramatic categories: although perhaps best classified as a one-act play, even this appellation does not seem quite accurate. Its introductory matter announces that "THERE ARE TWO SCENES," but the "SCENES" differ markedly in length: the first, named "ARGOL" (the spelling of the character's name changes as the text develops) continues for only four pages, divided into four sections, the last three of which are headed by titles: "The Yard," "The Super," and "The Night." The second scene, "HANP," continues for twenty pages, consisting of untitled sections in some cases headed by Roman numerals at the top of pages and in some cases by thick horizontal lines across the page.

78. For a discussion of *Enemy of the Stars* as a "closet drama," see Graver, "Vorticist Performance" 485. For a comparison to Byron's *Manfred*, see Klein, "Vorticist Drama" 236.

79. P. K. Page, "Suffering," ll. 29–31.

80. In the explanatory essay Lewis includes with the 1932 *Enemy of the Stars*, he comments that a figure like Arghol is an "enemy of the stars," and hence punishable, because he cultivates too much of the principle of the "not self" seated in a human's intellect, which makes him an "enemy" of life, Nature, and his fellow humans: "The man who has formed the habit of consulting and adhering to the principle of the *not-self* ... is not ... *more like* other people. He is *less like* them .... [His] ultra-human activity is really inhuman .... It is an enemy principle. It is heartily disliked" ("Physics of the Not-Self" 53–54; Lewis's italics). Such a man's hubristic activity, then, is as much disapproved of by the "Universe" as by his fellow humans.

81. For another battle found in Lewis's work of the Vorticist period that displays similar eroticized violence between men, see the duel between Kreisler and Soltyk in *Tarr* (272–273). I describe the episode in greater detail in Chapter 3.

82. All this, of course, presumes that *Enemy of the Stars* illuminates the Vorticist perspective, that its implicit value judgments about problems and triumphs correspond to those of Vorticism. I would argue that they do because the context in which the play appears, in which *Blast* is establishing Vorticism by way of its manifestic work, invites readers to relate its values to those of Vorticism, and also because Lewis draws explicit links between this text and his Vorticist program. He suggests that it is the style of the text that reflects his desire to create a verbal equivalent to his Vorticist work in painting. Moreover, given the moment out of which this was written, the conflicts driving Lewis's creation of Vorticism are uppermost in his mind, such that the phantasms that play out their conflicts here reveal the guiding problems and anxieties of Vorticism more broadly.

83. See Loewenstein's comment on how Lewis, in *The Art of Being Ruled*, accompanies his

denunciation of the effeminate male "invert" with a surprising hospitality to the "male-pole type of invert" (*Art of Being Ruled* 238; Loewenstein, *Loathsome Jews and Engulfing Women* 147). I find such receptivity to the "male-pole type of invert" in the male homoeroticism of texts of the Vorticist period such as *Enemy of the Stars* and *Tarr*, a receptivity that displays both the phobic rejection of effeminacy and the concomitant latent desire for erotically charged relations between men.

84. In a similar vein, Leo Bersani even claims that gay-macho enactments of such bonds between men is an effect of gay males' internalization of the patriarchal condemnation of the feminine ("Rectum" 207).

85. These signs of Vorticist effeminization resonate with what Donald Pease asserts about masculinity more generally when, drawing upon an argument by Frank Lentricchia, he discusses the process of effeminization men must undergo under patriarchy in order to attain full masculinity. As Pease paraphrases Lentricchia's position:

> Before the patriarch can dominate others he is divided from within into two figures, the dominant or "masculinized" and the submissive or "feminized" male . . . . In the patriarchal unconscious, the figure who demands conformity to certain imposed standards of masculinity is in a necessary relation to another figure who must conform to these standards . . . . As the figure who should do the conforming he is what Lentricchia describes as the feminized male cohabiting the identity of the masculine patriarch. In submitting (or more pointedly in failing to submit) to the patriarchal demand to be masculine, this male experiences "becoming masculine" as cultural feminization.
>
> ("MALE FEMINIZATION" 379)

Vorticism's feminized postures, even as they serve to indicate Vorticism's celebration of Nature's ferocity and suggest a latent desire for eroticized sadomasochistic bonds between men, also resonate with what Pease describes as this necessary stage of the process of becoming "masculine" according to the demands of patriarchal society. The violent rites of passage en route to purity displayed here suggest that the Vorticist model of masculinity participates in such a logic.

CHAPTER 2. A VORTICIST RENAISSANCE? EZRA POUND, THE GEOMETRIC "CLEAN LINE," AND FASCIST ITALY

1. Dorothy Shakespear contributed drawings to *Blast 2*, and though she is not generally counted among the Vorticists, Cork includes her among the artists "adhering" to Vorticism in 1914 (*Vorticism and Its Allies* 17). Drawing upon information from Shakespear's *Etruscan Gate:*

A Notebook with Drawings and Watercolours, Ann Saddlemyer confirms that Vorticism exerted a significant influence on Dorothy Shakespear's artwork (*Becoming George* 39).

2. McGann notes that Pound "carefully oversaw" the production of the deluxe editions of 1925 and 1928 (*Textual Condition* 130), and Nancy Cunard confirms that he did much the same with the Hours Press book: "It was Pound himself," she notes, "who found Maître-Imprimeur Bernouard, in Paris, and told him exactly how he wanted the volume to look" (*Those Were the Hours* 131). Cunard's letter to Pound of March 16, 1930, sent as *A Draft of xxx Cantos* was in process, likewise indicates Pound's close involvement in planning for the Hours Press edition. Addressing details of the edition's physical format such as typeface, comparing her choices to those of William Bird at the Three Mountains Press, and alluding to the initials to be drawn by Dorothy Shakespear ("D"), Cunard writes: "How about this size (see over)? It is a format of paper — Proposed size of type: 11 pt. (same as Bill Bird's series of 6) D's capitals size of HOURS PRESS . . . Which justification do you prefer, 25 or 22?" (Yale Collection of American Literature, Beinecke Rare Book and Manuscript Library, Ezra Pound Papers, YCAL MSS 43 — hereinafter referred to as the "Yale Collection" — Series IV, Box 54, Folder 1930).

3. See Noel Stock, *Life of Pound* 304. Donald Gallup notes the particulars of the translation in *Ezra Pound: A Bibliography* 395–396. As early as 1919, five years before his move to Italy, Pound appears to have anticipated his later task of translating Vorticism into Italian terms by referring to the Vorticists as "i Vorticisti" (*P&P* 3:280). In 1919 this was likely just Pound's tongue-in-cheek, implicit acknowledgment of the affinities between the Vorticists and the Italian Futurists; Pound's readiness to conceptualize Vorticism through the Italian language may have prepared the way psychologically for his later belief in the suitability of Vorticism for Italy.

4. See Cork, *Vorticism and Its Allies* 107.

5. See Rainey, *Institutions of Modernism*, Chapter 4, "From the Patron to *il Duce*: Ezra Pound's Odyssey," and Redman, *Pound and Fascism*, especially Chapter 4, "The Turn to Fascism."

6. Rainey sheds new light on Pound's interest in Mussolini in 1923–1924, claiming that Pound's attunement to Mussolini's rise played an important role in inspiring his move to Italy (see *Institutions of Modernism*, Chapter 4, especially 142). Rainey thereby counters claims, such as Leon Surette's, that Pound's relocation to Italy had nothing to do with his attitude toward Mussolini, that Pound's earliest known acknowledgment of admiration for Mussolini appears in 1926 (*Pound in Purgatory* 70), and that Pound did not develop a full-fledged celebration of Mussolini's "genius" until 1931 (5). Rainey discounts motives for Pound's turn to Mussolini other than those having to do with "faith" in Mussolini's ability to resurrect the glory of Sigismondo Malatesta (all others are "rationalizations"), but I would argue instead that Pound's investment in Mussolini was significantly and "genuinely" conditioned by multiple factors: a desire for a Malatesta figure to rise again, certainly, but also a desire for economic reforms Pound wished to see implemented and a principled opposition to liberal democracy as he saw it practiced. For a lucid and thorough discussion of a range of reasons for Pound's attachment to Mussolini's Italy, including hero worship and respect for what he believed to be Mussolini's economic policies, see Redman, *Pound and Fascism*, especially Chapter 4. Surette's *Pound in Purgatory* provides a rich explanation of the relationships among Pound's attachments to fascism, Social Credit, and anti-Semitism, though Surette suggests that anti-Semitism was not a factor in Pound's admiration for Mussolini in the early 1930s (6) and maintains that Pound knew that Mussolini's policies were not consonant with those associated with Social Credit (83). My study of the influence of Pound's Vorticist commitments on his sympathy for Fascist

Italy is not meant to challenge or replace such other accounts of factors guiding Pound's "turn to fascism," but rather to add to them.

7. For Lewis's comment on the grand scale of Vorticist ambitions, see his "Plain Home-Builder: Where Is Your Vorticist?" (1934), reprinted in *WLOA* 276–285. Lewis's remark in full reads: "[I]n the early stages of this [i.e., Vorticist] movement, we undoubtedly did sacrifice ourselves as painters to this necessity to reform *de fond en comble* the world in which a picture must exist . . . . In the heat of this pioneer action we were even inclined to forget *the picture* altogether in favour of *the frame*" (278; Lewis's italics). In *Rude Assignment* (1950), Lewis later noted that with Vorticism, "It was, after all, a new civilization that I—and a few other people—was making the blueprints for . . . . At the time I was unaware of the full implications of my work, but that was what I was doing . . . . It was more than just picture-making: one was manufacturing fresh eyes for people, and fresh souls to go with the eyes" (125).

8. Arguably the last public event associated with Vorticism was an exhibit held March–April 1920 at the Mansard Galleries in London, in which several members of the Vorticist circle participated (Lewis, Dismorr, Etchells, Hamilton, Roberts, Wadsworth) and which featured several paintings in the geometric Vorticist idiom. The group no longer exhibited as "Vorticists," however: recognizing that the banner of Vorticism no longer possessed the cultural clout necessary to attract audiences and gain critical attention, they instead joined with a cluster of other artists under the name "Group X" (Wees, *Vorticism and the English Avant-Garde* 210–211).

9. Pound to Arthur Kitson, n.d. (ca. December 1933), Rapallo.

10. In his discussion of the underconsumptionist economist Arthur Kitson, David Kadlec glosses "underconsumptionism" as a "loosely knit movement" of unorthodox economic thinkers of the late nineteenth and early twentieth centuries, explaining that "'Underconsumptionist' economists . . . believed that shortages and crises could be averted by gearing currency and credit not toward the interests of producers and financiers but rather toward the consumptive needs of consumers. In England and America . . . these 'heretical' economists often traveled in anarchist circles" (*Mosaic Modernism* 243). The name of the movement is, he notes, "misleading": "'Underconsumption' is the condition to be remedied by making currency and credit more available to those who need it" (243).

11. See Kadlec, *Mosaic Modernism*, Chapter 2, especially 61, for detailed commentary on how the influence of Arthur Kitson and Dora Marsden contributed to Pound's early interest in underconsumptionist economics, several years before the pivotal meeting with C. H. Douglas in 1918 that kindled his allegiance to Social Credit and that is usually regarded as the prime catalyst for Pound's intense commitment to the study of economics. Redman (*Pound and Fascism*, especially Chapter 1, 17–50) and Surette (*Pound in Purgatory*, especially 20–29) both address how Pound's work for A. R. Orage's *New Age* in 1911–1921 fostered and shaped his economic thought.

12. For further commentary on Pound's shift in the early 1930s to a focus on economic and overtly political concerns, see Redman, *Pound and Fascism*, especially Chapter 4. Surette likewise maintains that while Pound had certainly been exposed to much economic thought during the 1910s and 1920s, it was not until 1931 that he committed himself seriously to the study of economics and that his writing on economics and politics began to take precedence over other dimensions of his work. Surette notes of *The Cantos* that, after 1931, the poem "began to serve Pound's economic and political agenda rather than merely being informed by it" (*Pound in Purgatory* 2).

13. Pound, letter to Ronald Duncan, October 25, 1936, quoted in Redman, *Pound and Fascism* 172.

14. Quoted in Schulze, *Web of Friendship* 132.

15. I take "suffice" from Wallace Stevens's "Of Modern Poetry" (1940), which twice emphasizes the word, using it to connote the responsibility of modern poetry to "the time" (*Collected Poems* 239–240). For astute accounts of Stevens's response to pressures of the climate of the 1930s, see James Longenbach, *The Plain Sense of Things*, especially Chapter 11, "Ideas of Ambiguity," 148–175, as well as A. Walton Litz's "Wallace Stevens's Defense of Pure Poetry." For detailed commentary on Moore's reactions to the 1930s, see Schulze, *Web of Friendship*, especially Chapter 5, "Pressure Within, Pressures Without: Marianne Moore, Wallace Stevens, and Pangolin Poetry," 127–155, and her article, "The Frigate Pelican's Progress." Sue Laver's doctoral dissertation, "Poets, Philosophers, and Priests: T. S. Eliot, Postmodernism, and the Social Authority of Art," offers a valuably detailed and thoughtful discussion of how Eliot in the 1930s faced the question of how poets should reply to public affairs; see especially Chapter 5, "From Moralism to Aestheticism."

16. For Williams's interest in Social Credit, see Alec Marsh, *Money and Modernity: Pound, Williams, and the Spirit of Jefferson*. For T. S. Eliot's interest, see Bonamy Dobrée, "T. S. Eliot: A Personal Reminiscence," 82.

17. For a discussion of the attacks on Stevens and Moore, see Schulze, *Web of Friendship*, 127–153.

18. As Surette points out, Pound's way of thinking about the role of the poet, although opposed to that of many of his modernist contemporaries, in fact has an illustrious lineage; we err in deeming it anomalous or unquestionably out of line. "[Pound] imagined that sound aesthetic perceptions could be mapped straightforwardly onto the practical world of politics and economics. Such a belief has a long provenance in literary culture. Certainly, Pound's early mentor, William Butler Yeats, held such a view and derived it explicitly from Blake and Shelley" (*Pound in Purgatory* 10).

19. Quoted in Surette, *Pound in Purgatory* 46; the letter to Por dates from May 1936.

20. See the letter from Pound to MacLeish dated September 27, 1933; quoted in Carpenter, *Serious Character* 509.

21. I take the phrase "clean line" from Pound's essay "Cavalcanti" (*LE* 150).

22. I draw my information about the exhibit from Schnapp, "Epic Demonstrations"; Stone, "Staging Fascism," "Politics of Cultural Production," and *Patron State*; Ghirardo, "Architects, Exhibitions, and Politics"; and Andreotti, "The Aesthetics of War." Schnapp reports that the exhibit received more than five thousand visitors daily (5); Stone describes how the artifacts for the exhibit were arranged ("Staging Fascism" 216–218).

23. Sherry provides an elegant formulation of this "riddle" in *Radical Modernism*:

> Archly experimental, the artistic temperament of the modernists promised to be progressive, forward-looking, liberal in a conventional sense, but this aesthetic intelligence colluded with social attitudes manifestly backward, reactionary, indeed atavistic.... Avant-garde and retro-grade: the disparity between the aesthet-

ics and the sociology of the modernists continues to define a riddle central to their problematic achievement. (3)

In 1967 Frank Kermode was one of the first commentators to observe the "correlation between early modernist literature and authoritarian politics which is more often noticed than explained" (*Sense of an Ending* 108). Since then, scholars such as Chace (*Political Identities of Pound and Eliot* [1973]), Cullingford (*Yeats, Ireland, and Fascism* [1981]), Craig (*Yeats, Eliot, Pound* [1982]), North (*Political Aesthetic* [1991]), and Redman (*Pound and Fascism* [1991]), have usefully explored the relationship between modernist literature and fascism.

24. This question has been valuably addressed by such scholars as Kristeva, Bacigalupo, and Kenner.

25. Robert Spoo and Omar Pound have pointed to the radical discrepancies between what Mussolini was actually doing and what Pound believed he was doing: "Ezra believed that Italian fascism was committed to breaking the stranglehold of international banking . . . . In reality, Mussolini, despite occasional flashes of early socialism, was far from doing away with the system of capitalism that underpinned his regime" (Pound, *Letters in Captivity* 1–2). For further discussion of Pound's misunderstandings of what was happening within the Italian government, many of them fueled by his correspondence with Hungarian economist Odon Por, see Redman, *Pound and Fascism*, Chapter 6, "The Wizard in General Practice."

26. As Auden put it in 1939, "The most obvious social fact of the last forty years is the failure of liberal capitalist democracy" ("William Butler Yeats" 50).

27. See, for instance, Chace, North, Craig, and Sherry.

28. As Surette suggests, because of our "perception of fascism and Nazism as self-evidently evil," we tend wrongly to assume that only "depraved individuals participated in, approved, or silently endorsed the brutalities of the period" (*Pound in Purgatory* 19, 18).

29. In both *Textual Condition* and *Black Riders*, McGann stresses the importance of the physical features of an edition, which constitute what he terms its "bibliographical code" (*Textual Condition* 13), to the significance of a text. As he puts it, literary critics need to break "the spell of romantic hermeneutics" by "considering much more than the formal and linguistic features of . . . imaginative fictions." "We must attend," he insists, "to typefaces, bindings, book prices, page format, and all those textual phenomena usually regarded as (at best) peripheral to 'poetry' or 'the text as such'" (*Textual Condition* 12–13). Resonating with McGann's values are those of Rainey, who likewise urges awareness of the material aspects of the books through which texts are transmitted. Rainey maintains that because "readers encounter only works that are presented to them in specific material forms," we would do well to develop "extended acquaintance with the sociomaterial instance of every work, with each 'inscripture' of it" (*Pound and Culture* 7).

30. Nelson argues that we need to examine the original settings of texts—to examine the periodicals that house them, the illustrations that accompany them, the typefaces and bindings that embody them—in order to recover the ideological valences a text possessed at the time that a particular edition was published. Nelson wants to reawaken our awareness of the cultural work these texts as books did at their historical moment and "to give them another opportunity to do productive work in our culture" today (*Repression and Recovery* xii).

31. In an article of 1933, Pound showed his tendency to regard books as artifacts when he declared that it was "[o]bviously a disgrace to our pretended civilization that it cannot produce

books which are, AS MATERIAL OBJECTS, paper, printing, etc. equal to those produced several centuries ago" (*P&P* 6:106).

32. When reading the way in which features of Pound's bibliographic code during the late 1920s and 1930s strongly imply arguments he employed when articulating sympathy for Mussolini's Italy, we should also attend to the ways in which these physical features may have other implications—unexpected, diverse, even seemingly at odds with one another. Pound's involvement in fine bookmaking during the 1920s, for instance, as McGann notes, signals his alliance with his Pre-Raphaelite predecessors. Rainey, meanwhile, observes that Pound's scruples about the design of the deluxe edition of *A Draft of XVI. Cantos* (1925) demonstrate his devotion to the legend of Malatesta. And Nelson remarks that the illustrations of Pound's *Draft of the Cantos 17–27* (1928), even as they invoke an atmosphere of "medieval romance," also dramatize the conflict between the individual worker and the "military-industrial complex" in a way that resonates with the gestures of many leftist writers of the late 1920s (*Repression and Recovery* 194).

33. In *Vorticism and the English Avant-Garde*, Wees indicates the vigor of Pound's desire to promote Vorticism at its moment of inception with a list of Pound's essays on the movement published in quick succession 1914–1915: "an appreciation of Edward Wadsworth in the *Egoist* (15 August 1914); an elaboration of a talk on Vorticism given at the Rebel Art Centre published in the *Fortnightly Review* (1 September 1914); an explanation of Vorticism for the *New Age* (14 January 1915); and a discussion of Gaudier-Brzeska for the same journal (4 February 1915)" (206).

34. For this letter of September 9, 1916, see *Pound and the Visual Arts* 292. Pound's letter to Saunders reads, more fully: "Dear Miss Saunders: If you deign to accept £18 of Quinn's money for your three drawings . . . I shall be pleased to hand over the said £ as you may direct . . . . Will you write to Miss Dissmorrrrrrrr [*sic*] that Q. offers her £12 for her painting" (292). As Wees notes, in tandem with wealthy lawyer and patron of the arts John Quinn, whom Pound was urging to buy Vorticist work, Pound assembled an exhibit of Vorticist work in New York in 1916–1917 at the Penguin, an artists' club (*Vorticism and the English Avant-Garde* 207).

35. See letter to John Quinn dated January 24, 1917, quoted in *Pound and the Visual Arts* 281.

36. Wees notes that Lewis had "talked of bringing out a third *Blast* in November 1919" and continued to consider bringing out another issue of *Blast* as late as 1920 (*Vorticism and the English Avant-Garde* 210). He may have been encouraged by Pound's zeal to continue the Vorticist project: during the war, Pound had asked Lewis if he should try to approach John Quinn for money "to bring out another issue of *Blast*—possibly an American number." See the letter from Pound to Lewis [n.d.], Wyndham Lewis Collection, 1877–1974, Number 4612, Courtesy of the Division of Rare and Manuscript Collections, Cornell University Library (hereinafter cited as "Cornell Collection"); quoted in Wees, *Vorticism and the English Avant-Garde* 210.

37. See "The Death of Vorticism," reprinted in *P&P* 3:279.

38. A letter from Pound to William Carlos Williams from February 1935 indicates Pound's acceptance by noting flatly, "Blast is dead" (*Pound/Williams* 162).

39. See "Epstein, Belgion, and Meaning," reprinted in *P&P* 5:217–220; these comments appear on page 217.

40. See "Anno nuovo (mirabilis?)," *L'Indice* 2.20/21 (December 25, 1931): 5; reprinted in *P&P* 5:332–333. Pound's remark in Italian reads "Non è mai stata fatta in Italia un [*sic*] mostra decente di Wyndham Lewis" (*P&P* 5:333).

41. Stock reports that "Pound's high regard for the Fascist government . . . prompted him in 1932 to join with F. Ferruccio Cerio in preparing a film scenario on the history of Fascism." Though the scenario was "privately printed in Rapallo on 21 December 1932," the film was never made (*Life of Pound* 305). For a more detailed description of the project, see Gallup, *Pound Bibliography* 156.

42. For an account of Pound's meeting with Mussolini, see Redman, *Pound and Fascism* 95–96. In 1935, as *Jefferson and/or Mussolini* was about to be published, Pound requested that a copy be sent to Mussolini for his birthday, attesting to his desire to influence il Duce (see Pound to Stanley Nott, July 29, 1935, Yale Collection, Series I, Box 34). Redman notes that in 1935 Pound sought unsuccessfully for another interview with Mussolini, "apparently on the strength of the recent appearance of . . . *Jefferson and/or Mussolini*" (163).

43. As Gallup reports, the four installments of Edmondo Dodsworth's translation appear in *Il Mare* between February 18, 1933, and May 6, 1933 (*Pound Bibliography* 395–396). For Pound's comment suggesting that Italy's climate had helped him better understand Vorticist principles, see "Riflessione nell'anno XI," the note appended to the first installment of Dodsworth's translation. Pound's comment in Italian reads, "Questa discussione artistica è divenuta quasi preistorica dopo vent'anni, sebenne ci siano dentro alcuni principii ch'io ho rischiarito meglio nell'intervallo. (È curioso per me stesso trovar questo saggio in lingua non mia)."

44. Perloff critiques the tendency among scholars of Vorticism to "take at face value" the Vorticists' own "hostile statements" about Marinetti and the Futurists, which has left the relation between Vorticism and Italian Futurism "imperfectly understood." Such statements, she suggests, should not blind us to the abundant similarities between the two movements: "To study *Blast* . . . is to see that, whatever the protests lodged by Lewis, Pound, and their artist friends, Vorticism would not have come into being without the Futurist model" (*Futurist Moment* 171).

45. For a chronology of lectures and exhibits by Marinetti and the other Futurists in London 1910–1914, see Perloff, *Futurist Moment* 172–173; she in turn draws upon Giovanni Cianci, "Futurism and the Englsh Avant-Garde: The Early Pound between Imagism and Vorticism," *Arbeiten aus Anglistik und Amerikanistik* 1 (1981): 17–27; Patrizia Ardizzone, "Il Futurismo in Inghilterra: Bibliografia (1910–1915)," *Quadermo* 9 (May 1979, special issue on *Futurismo/Vorticismo*): 91–115; and Wees, *Vorticism and the English Avant-Garde*. For a more detailed chronological account and extensive commentary on the impact of these lectures and exhibits on London during this *avant-guerre* moment, see Rainey, "Creation of the Avant-Garde," especially 198–199 and 204–209.

46. For evidence of the friendly relations between the Vorticists and Futurists, see, for instance, tickets presented to Pound, signed in pen, "Compliments of Signor Marinetti," to an exhibit in 1913; these attest to the traffic and even cordiality between the Vorticists and the Futurists despite the Vorticists' public denials of them (Cornell Collection, Box 167. Corbel now held by the Herbert F. Johnson Museum of Art, Cornell University).

47. The card from Marinetti to Pound, dashed off in haste as Marinetti hurries to Rome for the birth of his third child, reads, "Grazie. Accetto in linea di massima. Sperava venire a Rapallo ma . . . sono tornato a Roma dove aspetto una terza marinettina o un terzo marinettino." ("Thank you. I accept to the fullest extent. I hope to visit Rapallo but . . . I have returned to Rome where I await a third little girl or little boy"; my translation.) See the letter from Marinetti to Pound dated August 17, 1932, Yale Collection, Series I, Box 30.

48. Marinetti appears in Canto 72, one of the two "Lost Cantos" just recently included in the

1987 New Directions edition of the *Cantos*. In this Canto, written as Pound was stung by Marinetti's death in 1944, Pound creates a Dantescan world of shades, which features Marinetti as a fierce, admirably unrelenting warrior. "After his death Filippo Tommaso came to me, saying: 'Well, I'm dead, / But I do not want to go to Paradise. I want to keep fighting." A few lines later, Pound gently critiques both Marinetti and himself by making Marinetti's specter confess, "'In much I followed empty vanity, / I loved spectacle more than wisdom / Nor did I know the wise ancients and I never read / The words of Confucius or Mencius. / I sang of war, you wanted peace, / Both blind!'" (English translation provided by Casillo in "Fascists of the Final Hour").

49. Mussolini's statement praising Marinetti, a fragment quoted in 1934 in *Stile Futurista* (Turin), reads as follows: "Marinetti è il poeta innovatore che mi ha dato la sensazione dell'oceano e della macchina, il mio caro vecchio amico delle prime battaglie fasciste, il soldato intrepido che ha offerto alla Patria una passione indomita consacrata dal sangue." ("Marinetti is a poetic innovator who has given me the sensation of the ocean and of the machine, my old dear friend of the first fascist battles, the intrepid soldier who has offered to the nation an indomitable passion consecrated with blood.") Quoted in *P&P* 5:334; my translation.

50. In "Appunti," published in *L' Indice* for April 10, 1931, Pound states, "Ogni giorno che resto in Italia vengo piu vicino alla posizione di Marinetti. In Inghilterra resistevo al futurismo ... Mah!! per l'Italia." ("Every day I stay in Italy I move closer to Marinetti's position. In England I resisted Futurism ... But for Italy!") Reprinted in *P&P* 5:283; my translation. Presumably he is suggesting here that while Futurism may not be suitable for England, it is indeed appropriate for Italy.

51. Pound's comment reads, more fully, "Marinetti e il Futurismo hanno dato una gran spinta a tutta la letteratura europea. Il movimento che io, Eliot, Joyce, e altri abbiamo iniziatio a Londra non sarebbe stato, senza il Futurismo." ("Marinetti and Futurism gave a big push to all the literature of Europe. The movement that I, Eliot, Joyce, and others began in London could not have come into being without Futurism.") Reprinted in *P&P* 5:334; my translation.

52. Pound's statement appeared in several issues of *Stile Futurista*, 1934–1935. It was also quoted in Luigi Colombo Fillia's *Il Futurismo: Ideologie, realizzazione e polemiche del movimento futurista italiano* and in a 1936 issue of the *Listener* (here in English translation); see *P&P* 5:334.

53. Pound made a similar gesture in a letter to the *Listener* in 1936, this time repeating the critical claim from 1914 that Futurism in 1910 had been a sort of "accelerated impressionism," but mitigating the criticism by saying "[n]ot that this was bad, but emphasis on structure [was] needed"—a corrective, in other words, that the Vorticists had supplied. More importantly, he noted that whatever the differences between his group and Marinetti's in 1910, "Marinetti's force and significance are demonstrated in his keeping hold of the root of the matter for a quarter of a century.... Marinetti has got something done because he did not worry about the differences in detail, and has never lost sight of the basic need: renewal" (*Pound and the Visual Arts* 310).

54. See "Appunti," *Il Mare* 25.1235 (November 12, 1932): 3; the article is reprinted in *P&P* 5:379–381. As Stone notes, Futurism's suitability for the role of the official aesthetic of the new regime was widely contested, given that the Fascist regime involved in the creation of the Mostra not only Futurist-affiliated artists but also representatives from many other contemporary Italian artistic movements as well, such as the Rationalists, the Novecento, and the Strapaese ("Politics of Cultural Production" 262). Despite the actual hybridity of the aesthetic of the esposizione, however, Marinetti insisted on reading its ultimate design as evidence of the hegemony of the Futurist style (281). Stone remarks that historians differ widely about the degree to which the

mostra was actually influenced by the Futurist aesthetic. She does allow that Mario Sironi, a designer who had begun his career as a Futurist, signing the first Futurist manifesto, designed the exhibition's most "emotionally potent rooms" ("Staging Fascism" 224).

55. Marinetti argued that when Alfieri, organizer of the exhibit, called the major artists of Italy to execute the difficult task of expressing in a grand exhibition the glories and triumphs of the fascist revolution, they "felt themselves naturally carried toward a Futurist style." ("I maggiori artisti d'Italia . . . chiamati da S. E. Alfieri al difficile compito di esprimere in una grande mostra tutta la eroica e gloriosa Rivoluzione Fascista, si sentirono naturalmente portati ad uno stile futurista.") He continued: "Così crearono la magnifica facciata della mostra, metallica, guerriera e policroma, tipicamente ispirata dal genio futurista di Antonio Sant'Elia; e delle sale con architteture . . . soffitti, pannelli . . . tutti direttamente or indirettamente influenzati dal futurismo italiano." ("Therefore they created the magnificent achievement of the show, metallic, warlike, and polychrome, typically inspired by the Futurist genius of Antonio Sant'Elia; and of the rooms with architecture . . . ceilings, panels . . . all directly or indirectly influenced by Italian Futurism.") Quoted in *P&P* 5:380–381; my translation.

56. In his article, Marinetti demands "La presenza di un autentico futurista, poeta, pittore, architetto e musicista in tutte le commissioni." ("The presence of an authentic Futurist—poet, painter, architect, and musician—in all the commissions.") Quoted in *P&P* 5:381; my translation.

57. Pound's commentary reads, "All'EZPOSIZIONE del decennio io, come studioso della storia, ho appreso cose che non sapevo al tempo dell'ultimo numero di questo *Supplemento*." ("At the Eposizione I, as a scholar of history, learned things that I did not know as of the last number of this *Supplement*.") And further, "Mi pare che la maggior parte dei miei concittadini non comprenda la portata del decennio." ("It seems to me that the majority of my fellow citizens do not understand the importance of the decennio.") These comments appear in an article titled "Ave Roma" in 1933; the article is reprinted in *P&P* 6:8–9. All translations here are mine.

58. For an insightful account of the journeys people made to see the exhibit, as well as the many incentives provided by the Italian government for attendance, see Stone, *Politics of Production*, Chapter 5, "Fascist Self-Representation," especially Section 7, "The Orchestration of Consent I," and Section 8, "The Orchestration of Consent II," 298–319.

59. See Ghirardo, "Architects, Exhibitions, and Politics." Ghirardo describes all three versions of the Mostra della Rivoluzione Fascista.

60. Pound's comment appears in "Ave Roma." The remark in full reads, "La prima impressione dell'esposizione è confusione, ma una confusione salutare" ("The first impression of the exposition is confusion, but a salutary confusion"). Reprinted in *P&P* 6:9; my translation.

61. Negri, "Madri di martiri," *Corriere della Sera* (March 11, 1933): 3; quoted in Schnapp, "Epic Demonstrations" 22.

62. *Blast*'s pronouncements present an ostensibly paradoxical combination of turbulent whirling and stasis: "Our Vortex desires the immobile rhythm of its swiftness"; "Our Vortex is white and abstract with its red-hot swiftness"; "The Vorticist is at his maximum point of energy when stillest" (*B1* 148–149).

63. Schnapp notes that the exhibit was parsed into two units: one covering the years 1914–1922, and one addressing 1922–1932. The first unit provided a historical account of Italian Fascism's genesis, constructing a narrative that built to the "climax" of the March on Rome ("Epic Demonstrations" 11).

64. Pound would have been especially sensitized to the coincidence of modernist and

Fascist triumphs of 1922, since he had been travelling through Italy doing research that year. And although he had left Italy in the summer of 1922, before the October March on Rome, he nonetheless experienced some of the effects of Mussolini's rise to power at close range; see also note 6 to this chapter. For Pound's itinerary through Italy in 1922, see Rainey, *Pound and Culture*, "Appendix Two: Pound's Travels in Italy, 1922," 234–242. For an account of Pound's positive, almost reverential, reaction to the way that, in 1923, a Fascist official in Rimini was able to cut red tape for him and allow him access to the library he needed for his research, see Rainey, *Institutions of Modernism*, Chapter 4, "From the Patron to *il Duce*." Initially impressed by this gesture, and also guided toward interest in and admiration of Mussolini by a friend, the sculptor Nancy Cox-McCormack, Pound afterward firmly associated Mussolini with a powerful efficiency he intensely admired.

65. Pound commented of Mussolini, "I don't believe any estimate of Mussolini will be valid unless it *starts* from his passion for construction. Treat him as *artifex* and all the details fall into place.... Take him as anything save the artist and you will get muddled with contradictions" (J/M 33–34). Later, in a section in which he describes Picabia's and Gaudier-Brzeska's genius, Pound provides a remark that resonates with this one: "Transpose such sense of plasticity or transpose your criteria to ten years of fascismo in Italy. And to the artifex" (92).

66. As Casillo notes, Pound shared with Marinetti a belief that under fascism there could be developed a fruitful "alliance between the aesthetic and the political avant-garde, whereby art would become an instrument of politics and politics an instrument of art" ("Fascists of the Final Hour" 102–103).

67. Stone notes that in the spring of 1932 a team organized by Dino Alfieri, director of the exhibit, began to gather a "collection of the most important and significant relics, photographs, pamphlets, autographs, artifacts, newspapers, and publications" ("Staging Fascism" 216). Stone draws her information from the catalogue for the exhibit by Alfieri and Luigi Freddi.

68. Margherita Sarfatti, "Architettura, arte e simbolo alla Mostra del Fascismo," quoted in Schnapp, "Epic Demonstrations" 4. Sarfatti was also Mussolini's biographer and mistress.

69. Quoted in Stone, *Patron State* 168, from "Mostra della rivoluzione—La ceremonia inaugurale," *Il Popolo d' Italia*, October 30, 1932.

70. As Redman notes, it was Frobenius's notion that a culture's *paideuma*, or "spiritual essence"—defined by Léopold Senghor as the culture's "own peculiar capacity for and manner of being moved" by the phenomena of the surrounding world (Haberland, *Frobenius Anthology* ix)—was best expressed by its everyday artifacts that underwrote Pound's strategy of reading at this time (*Pound and Fascism* 84–85). "[I]f we search," for the "true nature or soul" of cultures, Frobenius notes in *Paideuma—Umrisse einer Kultur- und Seelenlehre* (1921), we find that it "pervades their every manifestation.... The shape of a hut or other dwelling-place," he says, for example, "has a pronounced symbolic importance, as is shown by the relationship of the simplest architectural forms to other manifestations of cultural development and decline." The "spiritual basis" of a culture—its paideuma—is "more clearly expressed in objects of everyday life than in any conscious intellectual process" (Haberland, *Frobenius Anthology* 23).

71. Pound's comments originally appear in "Gaudier: A Postscript."

72. Elsewhere in *Guide to Kulchur*, Pound likewise noted, "I suggest that finer and future critics of art will be able to tell from the quality of a painting the degree of tolerance or intolerance of usury extant in the age and milieu that produced it" (27).

73. As attested by the photos and diagrams included in Frobenius's scholarship on Africa, he tended to use as his exhibits for a culture its pottery, paintings, carvings, sculpture, weap-

ons, utensils, walls, and buildings (see Haberland, *Frobenius Anthology*, plates following 233, and Frobenius, *The Voice of Africa*).

74. Canto 46 likewise notes that once usurious conditions were in place, "Thereafter art thickened. Thereafter design went to hell, / Thereafter barocco, thereafter stone-cutting desisted" (*c* 234). The term "barocco" is generally Pound's shorthand for aesthetic excesses, "wilfully [*sic*] ornate" art (*SP* 225) that was in his view generated by a climate of economic malaise that was in turn born out of, and marked by, usurious practice.

75. Sarfatti, "Architettura, arte, e simbolo"; quoted in Stone, *Patron State* 144.

76. Dworkin notes that

> [i]n the early twentieth century, the "functionalism and quiet line" associated with the unadorned and hard-edged sanserif made it de rigueur for those who wanted to signify a futuristic modernity in line with the streamlined look of an industrial machine age. "Futura," the name of Paul Renner's famous sanserif, was not incidental. Indeed, sanserif was so strongly established as the textual look of the Bauhaus that in 1928 Jan Tschichold could write ... "to proclaim sanserif as the typeface of our time is not a question of being fashionable; it really does express the same tendencies to be seen in our architecture."
>
> (*READING THE ILLEGIBLE* XX)

Dworkin valuably underscores the need to historicize our understanding of the implications of typefaces: for instance, the sanserif font that signified modernity in the 1930s instead connoted classical antiquity in eighteenth-century Germany; here he points to James Mosley's "Nymph and the Grot: The revival of the sanserif letter," *Typographica* 12, 1965. Dworkin takes his quoted phrases from Tschichold's *New Typography* from 1928 (*Reading the Illegible* xx). I would press back only somewhat against Tschichold here in his assessment of the "clean line" as necessarily suggesting a "*quiet* line" (my italics), given that "quiet" can imply not only "lacking in volume," but also "passive" and "gentle": my point here is that clean lines for Pound, for the Vorticists, and for the observers in Fascist Italy were coded to signify an aggressive, strong, and active, though not necessarily loud, modernity. My thanks to Robin Feenstra for pointing out Dworkin's argument to me.

77. Worth registering here is that some aspects of the MRF were inspired by the notably geometric work of Le Corbusier: his 1928 Nestlé Pavilion, for instance, and designs from *L'art Decorative d'aujourd'hui* (1925). See Andreotti, "Aesthetics of War." Le Corbusier arises in the discussion of "Sala O," designed by Giuseppe Terragni (81–82). Stone also notes that the artists belonging to the Rationalist group were influenced by Le Corbusier as well as Gropius (*Politics of Production* 266).

78. For Pound's explication of the "New Method in Scholarship," developed during the early days of his career, see "I Gather the Limbs of Osiris" (1911–1912), *SP* 21–43.

79. One further significant difference between Pound's methods of interpretation from 1918 and the 1930s: in 1918 he implied that physical features can deceive the observer about what

went into making them; by the 1930s, determined to read the landscape of a culture quickly and accurately for signs of danger, he will not allow for the possibility of a misreading born out of deception.

80. See Gallup, *Pound Bibliography* 150: A cordial note from Pound appears in a volume brought out by Otto Loos for Adolf Loos's sixtieth birthday (1930).

81. Quoted in Kenner, *Wyndham Lewis* 28.

82. See Kenner, *Pound Era* 258. As Kenner suggests, in this belief in the eloquence of shapes, Pound was significantly influenced by Gaudier-Brzeska, whose manifesto of artistic principles, "Vortex, Gaudier Brzeska" first appeared in *Blast 2*; Pound then reprinted it in his 1916 tribute to the sculptor. In the manifesto, Gaudier declares, "I SHALL DERIVE MY EMOTIONS SOLELY FROM THE ARRANGEMENT OF SURFACES, I shall present my emotions by the ARRANGEMENT OF MY SURFACES, THE PLANES AND LINES BY WHICH THEY ARE DEFINED." Shapes, for him, directly connoted moods: "Two days ago I pinched from an enemy a mauser rifle. Its heavy unwieldy shape swamped me with a powerful IMAGE of brutality" (*B2* 34). As Kenner emphasizes, the "effect" of brutality was "derived . . . not from his knowledge of what the Mauser was for," but instead, as Gaudier puts it, "'FROM A VERY SIMPLE COMPOSITION OF LINES AND PLANES'" (*Pound Era* 258; Gaudier's assertion appears in *B2* 34).

83. Pound first read Fenollosa's essay when with Yeats at Stone Cottage in 1914; Longenbach notes that he was editing it during 1914–1915 (*Stone Cottage* 41, 142). In 1915, Pound wrote a letter to Felix Schelling attesting to his involvement with the Fenollosa manuscripts: "Fenollosa has left a most enlightening essay on the written character (a whole basis of aesthetic, in reality)" (*LEP* 61). Pound finally published Fenollosa's essay in four installments in the *Little Review* in 1919; in 1920, he released it as part of *Instigations*; and in 1936, it was published as an independent book through Stanley Nott Ltd.

84. Pound's comment originally appeared in "Wyndham Lewis."

85. Kenner suggests that during this period Pound increasingly displayed a preoccupation with "patterned integrit[ies] accessible to the mind," made accessible and "visible," that is, by shapes that registered currents of rushing energy (*Pound Era* 145–146). During the 1910s, Pound conceived of the universe as being composed of "fluid force" (*Spirit of Romance* 92). As Ian Bell notes, Pound's conception is notably akin to Descartes's idea of space as discussed in Oliver Lodge's *Pioneers of Science* (1893), which was reprinted in 1913, as Pound was working with the Vorticists (*Critic as Scientist* 12–13). Descartes, Lodge notes, "regarded space as a plenum full of an all-pervading fluid. Certain portions of the fluid were in a state of whirling motion, as in a whirlpool or eddy of water" (*Pioneers of Science* 152).

86. Pound names *bonifica*, or land reclamation by drainage of the swamps, as one of the undeniably successful effects of Mussolini's efforts (*J/M* 73).

87. Rainey carefully documents Pound's fascination with Malatesta's Tempio in Rimini, its architecture, sculptures, and objects, all of which Pound read as emblems of Malatesta's glory. Rainey notes that Pound collected more than 700 pages of material for the project, approximately two-thirds of which consisted of "nonliterary documentation," including drawings and photographs of epistolary seals (*Pound and Culture* 8).

88. As Rainey notes, during the 1930s Pound often compared himself to Malatesta and his own work to Malatesta's Tempio (*Pound and Culture* 4).

89. Eliot's *The Waste Land*, published in 1922, had so goaded Pound to achieve in the Malatesta Cantos the kind of "outline" Eliot had attained that he opened the Malatesta Cantos with a allusion to it: "These fragments you have shelved (shored)," which clearly refers to

Eliot's line from *The Waste Land*: "These fragments I have shored against my ruins." As he wrote to Eliot in 1921, when *The Waste Land* was being completed, "Complimenti, you bitch. I am wracked by the seven jealousies, and cogitating an excuse for always exuding my deformative secretions in my own stuff, and never getting an outline. I go into nacre and objets d'art" (*LEP* 169).

90. For discussions of the influence of the Tempio Malatestiano on how Pound conceived of *The Cantos*, see Rainey, *Pound and Culture*, as well as Chapter 4 of Rainey, *Institutions of Modernism*.

91. *Eleven New Cantos* was published by Farrar and Rinehart in 1934 and by Faber and Faber in 1935; the same firms published *The Fifth Decad of Cantos* in 1937.

92. At this point, Random House became the distributor for small private presses, including the Nonesuch, the Golden Cockerel, and the Spiral Press. "All of these private presses," Bennett Cerf writes in *At Random*, "came begging us to take them on, since they would then be basking in the reflected glory of the Nonesuch Press, which was the established name in limited editions. By 1929 we had a catalogue of about thirty limited-edition books each season" (77). That Random House sponsored these private presses may have angered Pound not only because these presses fell under the sway of Random House's standards of taste and because they would be more likely to succeed than the presses with which he affiliated, but also because these presses, rather than publishing the work of the moderns, tended instead to publish work of already canonized or contemporary mainstream authors.

93. Pound angrily accused Random House of creating a "trust": in the letter to Caresse Crosby he had noted that "the luxe was made into a trust (Random Louse etc.)." Accordingly, he exploded to Louis Zukofsky in 1931: "*Random House* ought to be attacked . . . [for] trying to make a de luxe book trust and stifle even the faint flicker of independednt [*sic*] selection that before functioned in the separate printers" (*P/Z* 88).

94. As Pound wrote to Zukofsky in 1931, at this point he definitely sought "wider distribution" of his work (*P/Z* 125).

95. See Pound's letter to Nott, January 23, 1935, Yale Collection, Series I, Box 34.

96. Pound to Nott, July 29, 1935, Yale Collection, Series I, Box 34.

97. Given this overriding imperative, several different aspects of Pound's thought align as homologous: his early celebration of the whirling vortex from his days with *Blast* in 1914; his admiration for Mussolini's ability to make the trains run on time; his insistence that money must circulate and that the root of all troubles is not shortage but blocked distribution; and his push to unstop the publishing industry. As early as 1925 his characterization of the role of the state clearly indicates that he made such analogies about the role of circulation in these different realms: "The function of the state is to facilitate the traffic, i.e. the circulation of goods, air, water, heat, coal . . . power, and even thought" (*SP* 213).

98. Because of his broadcasts over Rome Radio during the Second World War, in 1943 Pound was indicted for treason by the U.S. government; he was reindicted in 1945. Returned to Washington D.C. from Italy for trial, Pound was examined by a psychiatrist, deemed medically unfit to stand trial, and sent instead to St. Elizabeths Hospital for the Criminally Insane in Washington, where he spent the next twelve and a half years.

99. For Pound, the two concepts—"simplicity" and "influence"—were intimately related, as, in his view, the visual simplicity of books evidenced the existence of an infrastructure for the effectual distribution of writing, which in turn enabled readers to be influenced.

100. In the 1950s, Pound published a few fine press editions through James Laughlin's publishing firm, New Directions, which by this point was publishing trade editions of his *Cantos* and other work; through Vanni Scheiwiller, the son of a publisher friend in Milan; and through another Italian firm in Rome. As Gallup notes, *Section: Rock Drill* of the *Cantos* (1955) was brought out through Scheiwiller's All'Insegna del Pesce d'Oro in a limited edition of 506 copies; "three de luxe copies and one proof copy were bound in beige silk stamped in red" and "issued in a tan paper-covered box" (*Pound Bibliography* 92). Scheiwiller's other editions of Pound's work in the 1950s—*Enrico Pea. Moscardino* (1956), *Gaudier-Brzeska* (1957), *A Lume Spento* (1958), . . . *Canto 98* (1958), and *Thrones* (1959)—were all limited numbered editions, but they were neither so ornate nor so limited as the deluxe editions of the 1920s. In 1958, New Directions published a special hand-press edition of *Diptych Rome-London*, consisting of 200 copies of Pound's "Homage to Sextus Propertius" and *Hugh Selwyn Mauberley*.

101. Gallup's bibliography lists five items published by the Square Dollar Series: *The Chinese Written Character as a Medium for Poetry* (1951); *Confucian Analects* (1951); *Gists from Agassiz* (1953); *Thomas Hart Benton. Bank of the United States* (1954); and *Alexander Del Mar: Roman and Moslem Moneys* (1956).

102. For information on John Kasper, see Carpenter, *Serious Character* 827–831.

103. His phrase is quoted in Perloff, *Futurist Moment* xvii.

CHAPTER 3. "EMBODIED . . . IN
SQUARE AND CUBE AND RECTANGLE":
H.D. AND THE VORTICIST BODY

1. *Nights* was one of five novellas which, along with a sketch, comprised what H.D. called her "Dijon" series, four of whose texts were issued through the Dijon firm of Maurice Darantière. Donna Hollenberg notes that the books were actually brought out through the press of "Pool," established by H.D.'s companion Winifred (Bryher) Ellerman and Ellerman's then husband Kenneth Macpherson (*Between History and Poetry* 62). The other novellas in the series were *Narthex* (1928), *The Usual Star* (1934), *Kora and Ka* (1934), and *Mira-Mare* (1934). In *Compassionate Friendship*, H.D. remarks that these "booklets," all featuring narratives à clef funded by details of her domestic life of the 1930s, were written during a period framed on one side by her mother's death in 1927 and on the other by her analysis with Freud 1933–1934 (Friedman, *Penelope's Web* 216). As noted on the flyleaves of those texts brought out through Darantière, each was issued in a tiny edition of 100 copies—in three cases, "privately printed for the author's friends," and in the case of *Nights*, "by friends of the author for private circulation." Bryher funded the privately circulated editions (Friedman, *Penelope's Web* 21). For further information about when texts in the "Dijon Series" were written and published, see "Chronology: Dating H.D.'s Writing," in Friedman, *Penelope's Web* 362–363.

Regarding the house in *Nights*, Barbara Guest notes that H.D. modeled it after Kenwin, her companion Bryher's house, built 1930–1931 in a "late Bauhaus, or Lac Leman international" style (*Herself Defined* 204–205).

2. In *Nights*, H.D. provides only one actual description of Natalia's visions when she reaches an altered state of consciousness, but many other signals in the text suggest that Natalia has often achieved such a condition that transcends both ordinary bodily existence and ordinary

consciousness—a higher plane of existence that allows her to commune with a realm of "deity." Alicia Ostriker suggests that Natalia uses her young lover "to get into a visionary state"; she "sees his kisses as a . . . sexual (mystical) technique which she uses to get herself out of time . . . to another space-time" (quoted in Friedman, *Penelope's Web* 400). I would liken Natalia's experiences to those of the initiate, or *mystes*, who participated in the Eleusinian mysteries: through witnessing a sexual coupling between the priestess of Demeter and the Hierophant (who symbolized Demeter and Zeus), the *mystes* would attain a greater knowledge of the mystery of Demeter. Here, of course, Natalia takes on the role not only of initiate but also of priestess, actually herself involved in the ritual of sexual coupling; this is consonant with the way that H.D. elsewhere likens her protagonists to priestesses (see, for instance, HERmione). For a description of the Eleusinian mysteries, see Tryphonopoulos, *Celestial Tradition*, Chapter 2, "The Occult Tradition." I'm also reminded by the state that Natalia achieves of the mystical concept of the "subtle body," thought to derive from Neoplatonic and Gnostic sources and summarized in the early twentieth century by theosophist G. R. S. Mead, which Tryphonopoulos has related to Pound's *Cantos* (*Celestial Tradition* 380–381).

3. Guest suggests that although H.D. did not comment directly on Vorticist ideas, she felt eclipsed by the Vorticist movement: "H.D. has never noted what she thought about the Vorticist program, but what she felt about it was another matter. What she felt was deserted. The little clan of Imagists who had been foremost on the stage, the most modern of all poets, were now pushed aside by a movement that was primarily for art and architecture" (*Herself Defined* 65).

4. See, for instance, Friedman's *Penelope's Web*, which refers to Burnett's discussion in "A Poetics out of War," and Kathleen Crown's "H.D.'s Jellyfish Manifesto and the Visible Body of Modernism," which alludes to Burnett's similar discussion in *Between Image and Epic*.

5. Friedman uses "gynopoetic" to describe the way that H.D.'s poetic is "anchored in the maternal" (*Penelope's Web* 11), in the "specifically female body that gives birth" (9). As a result, Friedman maintains, H.D.'s poetic opposes that of what Friedman calls "male modernism" (23): i.e., mainstream modernism, which was conditioned by a specifically male perspective. Recent poststructuralist readings of H.D.'s work, influenced by Lacan and Kristeva, have questioned the feminist perspective on H.D. offered by Friedman and other critics such as DuPlessis and Ostriker, interrogating the way such "liberal humanist" feminism regards writing as the production of an autonomous unified subject (Chisholm, "H.D.'s Auto*hetero*graphy" 79) and challenging the related contention that H.D., in particular, achieves an "authentic female voice" (Friedman, *Psyche Reborn* x). Instead, they read H.D. as demonstrating, through the fissures and divisions in her texts, the riven condition of a woman within the realm of the symbolic. Nonetheless, as Susan Edmunds remarks of Deborah Kloepfer's poststructuralist work, many such readings still characterize H.D.'s texts as "maternally connoted" (*Out of Line* 3).

6. Edmunds suggests the need to modify many feminist critical constructions of H.D. to better accommodate the diversity of H.D.'s attitudes and practices. Edmunds surveys the variety of feminist responses to H.D.'s work, moving from Friedman's, DuPlessis's, and Ostriker's liberal-feminist arguments to poststructuralist readings such as those of Hirsch, Kloepfer, Chisholm, and Buck. The differences among all these readings notwithstanding, Edmunds notes that "they are uniformly committed to recuperating H.D. according to the preferred terms [of a] chosen approach. Even when feminists have located areas in H.D.'s work that could not be assimilated to the positive poles of their respective evaluative frameworks, they have tended to position those areas as temporary nadirs in larger narratives of ascent" (*Out of Line* 3–4). Like Edmunds, I am committed to readings that admit H.D.'s ambivalences and acknowledge

that elements of her attitudes and work not easily assimilable within earlier critical pictures may not be dismissible aberrations but rather indications that the frames of those critical pictures need to be expanded.

7. Previously unpublished texts by H.D. now published since the advent of an intense wave of H.D. scholarship in the 1980s include HERmione (1981), *Notes on Thought and Vision* (1982), *The Gift* (1982; new edition, 1998); *Paint It Today* (1992), *Asphodel* (1992), and *Pilate's Wife* (2000).

8. Works that do address *Nights* include Friedman, *Penelope's Web*; Collecott, *H.D. and Sapphic Modernism* (especially 74–75); Chisholm, *H.D.'s Freudian Poetics* (especially 82–87); and Young, "Between Science and 'The New Psychology': An Examination of H.D.'s Sociohistorical Consciousness" (which concentrates primarily on *Nights*). Although DuPlessis refers in general to the group H.D. called the "Dijon Series" (see note 1 to this chapter) in "Romantic Thralldom in H.D." and *H.D.: The Career of that Struggle*, she conspicuously omits *Nights*.

9. In "Romantic Thralldom," DuPlessis again mentions novellas of the "Dijon Series" only briefly, only in an endnote, and omits *Nights* from the group. Of these novellas, she says, "[h]owever positively the works end, their tone is quite uneasy" (437), suggesting her own uneasiness with them.

10. Critics who credit H.D.'s work with an inscription of the Kristevan semiotic include Kloepfer ("Flesh Made Word: Maternal Inscription in H.D." and *The Unspeakable Mother: Forbidden Discourse in Jean Rhys and H.D.*), DuPlessis (*H.D.: The Career*), Collecott (*Sapphic Modernism*), and Spoo ("H.D. Prosed").

11. In the introduction to her 1998 edition of *The Gift*, for instance, Jane Augustine accepts Friedman's arguments about H.D.'s gynopoetic with no indication of such claims having been complicated by more recent scholarship. Augustine notes that *The Gift* is "particularly important as a *locus classicus* of [H.D.'s] visionary and revisionary woman-centered poetics, her 'Moravian gynopoetics.'" The phrase "Moravian gynopoetics" Augustine draws from Friedman, *Penelope's Web* 352.

12. Ostriker suggests persuasively that with the poetics of her late long poems such as *Trilogy*, H.D. sought both to match the status of, and to break away from the poetic strategies of, masterwork epic poems by male contemporaries such as Pound's *Cantos*, Eliot's *Four Quartets*, and Williams's *Paterson* ("No Rule of Procedure," 339, 345). And as Friedman notes, H.D. called *Helen in Egypt* her "Cantos," suggesting her effort to supersede Pound's example (Friedman, "Creating a Women's Mythology," 374). Certainly H.D. often wished to part ways with, even to take issue with, the work of her male contemporaries: but it oversimplifies H.D.'s diverse oeuvre to suggest—as do Friedman, DuPlessis, and Ostriker—that her writing of the 1920s and onward generally provides an alternative to, and thus emerges from values that differ considerably from, those of her male contemporaries. Although some strands of her work indeed do lead away from the projects and principles of such "men of 1914" as Pound, Eliot, and Lewis, a significant number of other strands, like the one revealed by the example of the geometric body, in fact coincide with or intersect with those in their work. In this chapter I focus particularly on the affinities between the geometric body fantasized through her work and similar bodies constructed in the work of Pound and Lewis.

13. Kaufmann also notes that recently the critical construct termed "female modernism" has "been defined primarily *against* male modernism rather than *in relation* to it" ("Gendering Modernism" 69). Although I agree with Kaufmann's statements about the need to supersede the critical habit of assuming that the work of women modernists necessarily differs from, and

usually opposes, that of male modernists—in both style and motivating values—I diverge from him in my degree of receptivity to the category of "male modernism" or "masculinist modernism," which he seems to accept, suggesting that H.D.'s early poetry belongs within it, and even contributed to its making. The constellation of values animating H.D.'s early work, though these values also drive much of the work of her male peers, is only problematically deemed "masculinist" and, I would argue, is more productively understood without applying a descriptive adjective that reaffirms the Manichean divide between male and female and implies that certain poetic strategies and projects are inherently more "male" or "female" than others. For such designations to be productive, much more careful historicization of how these categories of "male" and "female" were used from 1910 to 1950 would be needed than Kaufmann supplies. Moreover, whereas Kaufmann sees H.D.'s early Imagist work, whose valences accord with those of male contemporaries such as Pound and Eliot, as contrasting with her later work, which he reads as turning away from the projects of Pound and Eliot (she moved on, he suggests, to "forge her own epic strain" [69]), I would offer that we need to consider the ways that her later work, such as her prose of the 1930s, also resonates with that of her male contemporaries.

14. For a detailed account of Hulme's engagement with the Vorticists, see Wees, *Vorticism and the English Avant-Garde*, 77–85.

15. Strikingly, in 1925 Ortega y Gasset posited a similar opposition between the bodily and the geometric: "It is not an exaggeration," he writes, "to assert that modern paintings and sculptures betray a real loathing of living forms or forms of living beings" ("Dehumanization of Art" 40). Like Hulme, he expresses wonderment that so many contemporary artists, using a geometric vocabulary, will depict bodies presumably to transform them and supplant them with something radically different. Calling that transformation "dehumanization," he asks, "Why is it that round and soft forms of living bodies are repulsive to the present-day artist? Why does he replace them with geometric patterns?" (40). He goes on to place the current phenomenon in a larger cyclical pattern: "[C]razes of this kind have periodically recurred in history. Even in the evolution of prehistoric art we observe that artistic sensibility begins with seeking the living form and then drops it, as though affrighted and nauseated, and resorts to abstract signs" (40–41).

16. Ortega y Gasset similarly justifies involving the human or organic form in the geometric design, though he presents the rationale in slightly more macabre terms: "For the modern artist, aesthetic pleasure derives from such a triumph over human matter. That is why he has to drive home the victory by presenting in each case the strangled victim" ("Dehumanization of Art" 23).

17. In *Dedication to Hunger*, for example, Leslie Heywood has argued for what she construes as a modernist contempt for the body, an "anorexic logic" central to the work of modernists such as Eliot and Pound. Although Heywood is right to note the "agonized relation to the body in literary modernism" and, specifically, "the ambivalent, even hostile relationship to that body as feminine and maternal" (64), she goes too far when she suggests that such modernist writers consistently inscribe in their texts a desire to repudiate the body. Her effort to demonstrate the "anorexia" of modernist literary texts leads her to emphasize the textual moments that display disgust with the fleshly body at the expense of moments, equally prevalent in modernist work, of hospitality to the vitality of the body and a desire to elevate the body into what Pound calls, in a discussion that admires the aesthetic of medieval Tuscan poets, a "perfect instrument of the increasing intelligence" ("Cavalcanti" 152). Again, Heywood is right that the image of the fleshly female body is usually vilified in modernist texts as exces-

sive and stupid (and simultaneously endorsed as the necessary abject to the idealized, more streamlined male body), but she overstates the case when she suggests that the ideal for male modernists like Eliot and Pound involves a rejection of flesh and physicality altogether. Pound, in the work with which I engage here, advocates not transcendence and refusal, but rather command and use, of the physical body. Pound would reject the view that Heywood attributes to him as unfortunate asceticism—as "dogmatic," "monastic," and part of an "idiotic asceticism and a belief that the body is evil" ("Cavalcanti" 150, 152). Lewis, too, at times explicitly refuses the asceticism Heywood ascribes to modernists, regretting that the English, driven by a puritanical asceticism, try to "tame" and "drown" the body, in what he terms a "vast Anglo-Saxon conspiracy against the body" ("Our Wild Body" 8).

18. In a brief 1914 commentary on Futurism, "Futurism and the Flesh," Lewis indirectly suggests that the Vorticist aesthetic, despite its pronouncements against Nature, does not reject the body (*Creatures of Habit* 35–36). In "Our Wild Body" (1910), Lewis has noted that a man's body should be recognized as a "vessel of his life" and a desirable "symbol of his recklessness" (10). In "Futurism and the Flesh," Lewis weighs in on the body at the moment of Vorticism's coalescence, as he leads the movement into public view. Although at this point Lewis is publicly scornful of the Futurists (though impressed by their impact), in this piece, responding to a critique of Futurism by G. K. Chesterton, he seeks to clarify an aspect of the Futurist program for a readership that may misunderstand it. Because Chesterton includes under his rubric "Futurist" all modern artists, not just Marinetti and his group, Lewis implies that he counts himself among those accused. In the piece, Lewis responds to Chesterton's critique of the Futurists for their "fierce contempt for the body." Lewis's fundamental point here is that the absence of human bodies in an artist's work does not necessarily mean, as Chesterton seems to think it does, that the artist repudiates the flesh. Although Lewis never mentions Vorticism explicitly, the date of his essay's publication coincides almost exactly with that of *Blast 1*. It appeared on July 11, 1914 in *T. P.'s Weekly*; *Blast* appeared on July 2 (Wees, *Vorticism and the English Avant-Garde* 162). We can assume, then, that Vorticist issues were uppermost in Lewis's mind as he wrote it—and suppose that the attitude toward the body he ascribes to the Futurists here may well also indicate the views on the body he associates with Vorticism. The piece is entitled "A Futurist's Reply," and though Lewis may not have endorsed this title, he does suggest that what he says about "Futurism" he means to pertain to his own art as well, the art that will soon be known as Vorticist. Accordingly, we are to understand, Vorticism does not hold a "fierce contempt for the body."

19. For a helpful discussion of the Aristotelian view of the process of redeeming matter by impressing upon it a *schema*, see Butler, *Bodies that Matter* 31–33. Butler stresses that, for Aristotle, matter is "potentiality"; form, "actuality": that matter, or *hule*, is by definition something that awaits transformation and actuation by the imposition of a stamp or a shape. Through the imposition of a shape or schema, matter is given form, usefulness, and intelligibility in human terms, much as when raw wood is made into a table. That the desire of the Vorticists to act upon the body often reveals itself in geometric forms rhymes nicely with the Aristotelian concept of schema. Pound, in fact, actually uses the Aristotelian term *hule* in his work: in the *Cantos*, for instance, he employs it to accuse the figure of Lucrezia Borgia of gross materialism. But the Vorticist geometric transformation of the body differs from the Aristotelian in that it entails appreciation for the body as a valuable origin rather than denigration of it as merely an inferior state of being awaiting supersession.

20. Again, for my understanding of the "subtle body" I am indebted to Tryphonopoulos, *Celestial Tradition*, especially Chapter 5, "The Subtle Body: Cantos 90 and 91."

21. Curiously, although "Cavalcanti" was first published in 1934, T. S. Eliot, the editor of Pound's *Literary Essays*, in which the essay appears, dated it "1910–31" (*LE* 149), implying that even if Pound had not been writing the piece for twenty years, he had at least been considering the issues addressed in it for that long. Indeed, much of Pound's praise of the troubadours here resembles that which he offers in an essay of 1912, "Psychology and Troubadours."

22. As Kevin Oderman notes in *Ezra Pound and the Erotic Medium*, Pound, "from very early on, was preoccupied with the 'mediumistic' potentiality of sexuality, its ability to stimulate visions" (xi). Pound drew many of his ideas about what Oderman calls "mediumistic sexuality" from his understanding of the Eleusinian mysteries of ancient Greece, which is thought by some scholars to have involved ritual sexual coupling—an *hieros gamos*—as an element of the process toward revelation. (Although there is much scholarly controversy on this point, Pound was convinced that the Eleusinian rites involved the *hieros gamos*.) On how Pound's understanding of the Eleusinian mysteries informs *The Cantos*, see Tryphonopoulos, *The Celestial Tradition*; for comments on Pound's belief in the *hieros gamos*, see especially 30–31.

23. See Tryphonopoulos, *Celestial Tradition* 178–179, for a discussion of how this passage and the concept of the "radiant world" captures Pound's conception of a "divine or permanent world" through to which the mystic initiate, ideally, is able to break. Most relevant for the discussion here is that Pound associates such an ideal state with geometry and the ability to perceive forms, as well as with the dominance of the subtle body. If the mystic initiate is able to achieve the condition of the subtle body through *palingenesis*, he will renew contact with the "radiant world" of forms that most have lost.

24. In this section of "Cavalcanti," Pound celebrates the "medieval clean line" as distinct from, and countervailing, the "medieval niggle" (*LE* 150).

25. Materer notes that in his use of the "spherical triangle" as the "central life-form" of the Vorticists, Pound was inspired by the thought of Kandinsky in *On the Spiritual in Art* (*Modernist Alchemy* 35).

26. For Lewis's theory of comedy, see his essay, "The Meaning of the Wild Body." For a perceptive account of how Lewis's views on the "wild body" fluctuated between 1910 and 1927, see Sherry, "Anatomy of Folly."

27. In *Rude Assignment*, his memoir of 1950, Lewis further links abstraction with violence in his reminiscences about the First World War:

> War . . . presented me with a subject matter so consonant with the austerity of that "abstract" vision I had developed, that it was an easy transition . . . . [W]hen Mars with his mailed finger showed me a shell-crater and a skeleton, with a couple of shivered tree-stumps behind it, I was still in my "abstract" element. (128)

Lewis thus links his "abstract" perspective, which has led his audiences to expect of him geometric "conundrums in paint," not only with the violence of war but also with the attenuated, skeletal figures and shapes, denuded of substance and flesh, to which that violence gave rise. More importantly, he suggests that at the front in 1916–1917, shortly after the heyday of the Vorticist movement, he was making such linkages between geometry and violence.

28. For insightful commentary on the sadomasochism displayed in Lewis's texts, see Quéma, *Agon of Modernism* 107–108.

29. Burnett mentions that the review is bound together in the same volume as "heavily revised drafts of *Notes on Thought and Vision*" (*Between Image and Epic* 8).

30. In her commentary, Crown draws from Scott's essay "Jellyfish and Treacle: Lewis, Joyce, Gender, and Modernism," noting that Scott "demonstrates that the question of sexuality and gender in 'male modernism' was played out over the jellyfish metaphor in the work of Wyndham Lewis and James Joyce, with Joyce falling into the 'jellyfish realm' that Lewis rejected" ("Visible Body" 229). Crown suggests that with her jellyfish imagery, H.D. was quite likely responding to the way jellyfish had been employed in Lewis's *Tarr* (serialized in the *Egoist* in 1916–1917). In the novel, Lewis has the eponymous Frederick Tarr note,

> A woman was a lower form of life. Everything was female to begin with. A jellyfish diffuseness spread itself and gaped on the beds and in the bas-fonds of everything. Above a certain level of life sex disappeared, just as in highly organised sensualism sex vanishes. And, on the other hand, *everything* beneath that line was female. (313–314; Lewis's italics)

Although this statement expresses only Tarr's view, and its relationship to Lewis's own views is problematic, it nonetheless contributes to a discourse that uses jellyfish-like qualities to capture qualities constructed as distinctively female, and in this context, consequently undesirable.

31. Even Friedman concedes that although, in *Notes*, H.D. calls for artistry that arises from the knowledge of the "specifically female body," she doesn't always bear out such principles in her work. But Friedman nonetheless seems prepared to associate the ideals of *Notes* with H.D.'s prose more generally, to define "gynopoetic" from the claims of *Notes*, and to privilege this notion of the gynopoetic as registering what is most fundamental to H.D.'s work.

32. See Crown, for instance, for a perceptive discussion of the ways that *Notes* is "rife with contradictions" ("Visible Body" 219) and how H.D.'s speaker's attitude toward the body, specifically the female body, is not as uncomplicated as it might at first seem. DuPlessis also recognizes the ways that the attitude evinced by the speaker toward the female at the beginning of *Notes* is not sustained to the end: early textual focus on the female body later gives way to sections that consider the two sexes with equal attention and that present a utopian image of a child beyond gender. DuPlessis finesses this nicely by remarking that, nonetheless, *Notes* "passes through a serious consideration of the knowledge to be achieved from the female body, from female difference" (*H.D.: The Career* 41). Although DuPlessis's statement here is accurate, I would resist her implication that the textual moments concentrating on female difference therefore hold an elevated status in the text. Other moments in the text that trouble the notion of the woman's possessing "privileged access" to vision, some of which appear later in the text than those that DuPlessis highlights but some of which even occur directly around them, should be accorded equal "seriousness."

33. Although Natalia has used Christian discourse here, elsewhere in *Nights* she uses

terminology from other religious systems: Egyptian, Greek, Aztec, or Navajo (as H.D. puts it, "Navaho" [87]). Like *Notes*, *Nights* moves so flexibly among references to different religious systems that the text ultimately privileges no one religious system but instead implies that these different references to religion function interchangeably. In keeping with H.D.'s signature syncretism, we are meant to forget the specificity of the religions mentioned and subsume them all within the general category of the sacred, reading them all as similarly indicating a domain of the divine. Tryphonopoulos has suggested that "radical syncretism" and "eclecticism" of the kind that H.D. displays in this narrative is typical of those working with occultism, as H.D. was at this time ("Fragments of Faith" 231, 236).

34. For a moment, H.D. evokes an atmosphere through Neil similar to that associated with Fayne Rabb, a character in her autobiographical novel HERmione, who is also associated with a lens.

35. In this reading I differ from Chisholm, who suggests that the figure of the woman appears in *Nights* as a goddess whom Natalia worships (*H.D.'s Freudian Poetics* 86). What reverence Natalia evinces here, I would offer, is much more notably directed toward the geometric figures of the text.

36. Gregory suggests that although Walter Pater's Hellenism, which deeply influenced H.D., avoids the material body and physical matter, indicating a yearning for "consummation beyond the debris of the body and a longing for light far removed from its shadows" and an uneasiness with the "material ground" from which the etherealized state of ascesis is achieved, H.D. both "comprehends" and engages with that "material ground," which Gregory associates with the matrix, or maternal realm (*H.D. and Hellenism* 87–89). In contrast, I would argue that H.D.'s texts such as *Nights* and *Notes* in fact do signal a discomfort with the matrix, or at least a desire to value it only insofar as it can be disciplined into something purer.

37. In my interpretation of the ending of HERmione as inscrutable, I agree with Friedman and DuPlessis, who read the last lines of the novel as presenting an "enigma" ("I Had Two Loves" 214); I agree with their reading, too, of "Fayne's trances" as dominating Hermione "just as George's kisses had earlier" (212). Alternatively, in "A Crack in the Ice" S. Travis reads the ending of HERmione as "a positive statement of Hermione's new identification with woman, the new stage in her process of gaining identity by finding that identity through a social connection to a greater context" (139). Hermione's state of mind at the end, however, is too numb, and the status of Fayne within the novel too ambiguous, to make this reading cogent.

38. For H.D., as she indicates in *Notes*, the "daemon" is equivalent to the "highest in ourselves" (37).

39. Friedman places the composition of the prologue in summer and December 1934 ("Chronology: Dating H.D.'s Writing" in *Penelope's Web* 363).

40. Like Young, I read Helforth as a target of critique, even satire. Admittedly, the text presents a mixed view of him: he is "dull," as Friedman notes, but is also the "survivor" of *Nights* (*Penelope's Web* 280), and he might articulate, as Chisholm offers, "a critical dissatisfaction of the author herself" (*H.D.'s Freudian Poetics* 87). But given the way that H.D. creates the character of Natalia so clearly to outrace him, he is equally held up as a figure of fun.

41. In fact, given H.D.'s accord with Pound and Lewis here, both of whom are often associated with masculinist and misogynistic thought, she would seem at first glance to be colluding with the patriarchal enemy, which she may be. But Pound's remarks about the "sanity" of the body in essays such as "Cavalcanti" are not necessarily fuelled by masculinism or misogyny,

nor are Lewis's scenes of homoerotic combat. Pound's unforgettable valorization of the penis as a source of thought and inspiration in "Postscript to *The Natural Philosophy of Love*" is unquestionably masculinist, but his thought about the body here many not be. This case is a welcome reminder that we cannot assume all of Pound's thought about the body, sexuality, and gender to be monolithic, but rather need to consider the significance of his claims case by case. The same holds true of Lewis, eminently capable, in *Blast*, *Time and Western Man*, and many other texts, of homophobic and misogynistic tirades against effeminacy, but not necessarily expressing such a condemnation of effeminacy in his gestures about the body. In all, we cannot assume that an alliance with Pound and Lewis necessarily indicates H.D.'s complicity with forms of antifeminist thought. To determine this, we need to ask instead if H.D.'s turn from the childbearing body is antifeminist and if a turn to the geometric is necessarily antifeminist.

42. As Altman notes,

> The particular applicability of the maternal metaphor to H.D. continues to elude me. To my mind, she was among the least "motherly" of writers .... I cannot understand why critics find it important to search for buried or metaphorized images (or "structures") of motherhood (or "maternal discourse") when the manifest content of the texts contains so much else that is of interest to feminists. In fact, H.D.'s biography ... shows her to have been intensely preoccupied with sexuality as distinct from reproduction or the family—with both lesbian and heterosexual sex as visionary experience and as personal history.
>
> ("PRISONER OF BIOGRAPHY" 39)

43. Gregory and Collecott have also noted how H.D.'s emphasis on "whiteness," "white light," "ice," and shades of "blue" can be read as encoding homoerotic attraction: on the one hand, through the way that such references recall the palette that Victorian writers such as Pater associated with Dorian Hellenic male homoeroticism (see Gregory, *H.D. and Hellenism* 85–107); and on the other, through the way that they recall a palette associated with the poetry of Sappho (see Collecott, *Sapphic Modernism* 5).

44. I am thinking particularly of the claims about ascesis Bersani offers toward the end of his essay "Is the Rectum a Grave?"

45. For a full account of Haraway's argument, see "A Cyborg Manifesto."

46. Critical debate has arisen about whether we are to celebrate Hermione's current of feeling for Fayne or regard it as a form of entrapment, but whatever the case, Hermione's desire very much resonates with Natalia's. Fayne's "blue-white face" is described as bathed in "cold steel light" (*HERmione* 164); in the descriptions of interaction between Fayne and Hermione, the palette and the invocation of metal, light, and cold recall the environment Natalia in *Nights* associates with sexual ecstasy. Moreover, Fayne is also aligned with geometry when she is first introduced in *HERmione*, with "diagonals," "parallels," "long lines of pure blue," "people bisected by long lines of blue curtain" (52), and later with "parallelograms" (128). In the novel's

climactic kiss between Hermione and Fayne, Hermione perceives "rings on rings that made a geometric circle toward a ceiling" (164). As Hermione presses her fingers against Fayne's "swallow-blue" eyes, Fayne marvels that Hermione's hands, which she compares to "white stars" and "snowdrops," have "dynamic white power" (180). We hear that "[f]ire and electric white spark pulsed" in Hermione's "thin wrists" (180). The power summoned by Hermione's desire for Fayne, then, electric and white, intertwined with images of geometry, closely resembles the erotic force in *Nights*, where David says to Natalia: "Your fingers are full ... of the most terrific electricity" (86). Fayne's and Hermione's intimacy culminates when Hermione hypnotizes Fayne into a state in which she seems to die, recalling Natalia's longing for obliteration: "she had felt under hypnotizing fingers the temples in that other head cease ... and the eyelids ... flutter and stay silent" (181). H.D. further signals the sadomasochistic dynamic of their encounter here by invoking "Faustine," A. C. Swinburne's poem about a femme fatale. (For discussion of how Swinburne's "Faustine" suggests a sadomasochistic dynamic, see Laity, "H.D. and Swinburne: Decadence and Sapphic Modernism.")

47. Under Rico's influence, Julia's writing is said to be like "[b]lue lightning"; she associates Rico with "blue-flame licked out of the paper" (55) and opposes the "cerebral" intensity of the passionate relationship she has with Rico to the desire of the "firm-fleshed bodies" and "over-physical sensuality" of Rafe and Bella (58–59). As in *Nights*, then, electric blue passion is aligned with bodilessness and visionary consciousness. And because throughout the novel Julia is haunted by the anguishing memory of a stillbirth, seeking to erase that memory through Rico and artistic vision, Julia's ardor for Rico is also associated with a turn away from childbearing.

CHAPTER 4. "MYSTIC GEOMETRY": THE VISIONARY TEXTS OF YEATS AND H.D.

1. For my definition of "the occult" here, I am indebted to Materer (*Modernist Alchemy*), Surette (*Birth of Modernism*) and Tryphonopoulos (*Celestial Tradition*). As Tryphonopoulos notes, the term "occult" is "[d]erived from the Latin root *occulere* (to cover over, hide, conceal)," and thus "signifies anything hidden or secret, in the sense of being mysterious to ordinary understanding or scientific reason" (24–25). The generative premise of occultism is that there exists a secret reality (a noumenal realm), not accessible by ordinary modes of understanding or scientific reason, that can be accessed and understood only by a privileged, enlightened few: those gifted with special talents for direct knowledge of the transcendent realm through mystical revelation (gnosis), those willing to undertake a rite of initiation or a course of instruction to gain knowledge of this noumenal domain, or adepts versed in arts of divination such as astrology. According to Mircea Eliade, the term "occultism" was first used in English to describe this set of beliefs and attendant practices in 1881 by Theosophist A. P. Sinnett, a disciple of Madame Blavatsky and author of the book thought to have inspired Yeats's interest in the occult (*Occultism, Witchcraft* 49). Nineteenth- and twentieth-century occultists have generally claimed descent from a host of ancient mystery religions and schools of thought dating from the late classical period: as Surette notes, "Occultism sees itself as the heir of an ancient wisdom" (*Birth of Modernism* 7). According to Tryphonopoulos, the category of the occult encompasses "the whole body of speculative, heterodox religious thought which lies outside all religious orthodoxies and includes such movements as Gnosticism, Hermeticism,

Neoplatonism, Cabalism, and Theosophy" (*Celestial Tradition* xii). As Materer points out, drawing upon an argument by French scholar and occultist Denis Saurat, occult doctrines are by definition heretical: it is in part their characteristic heterodoxy, their stance of "rebelliousness" toward mainstream scientific thought and institutionalized religion (*Modernist Alchemy* xiii), that grants them their "glamour" and "authority" (28–29).

2. Cued by Surette, I differentiate here between "mysticism" and the "occult." Addressing Yeats's and H.D.'s work, I use "mystical revelation" to refer to the epistemological mode by which both access occult wisdom: "mysticism," "mystical revelation," or "visionary experience" refers to the process of knowing that involves direct revelation of secret wisdom; "the occult," "occult knowledge," or "wisdom," that which is accessed through such revelation. As discussed in note 1 immediately above, according to occult thought, occult wisdom can, but need not, be obtained through mystical illumination.

3. *A Vision* has traditionally inspired critical unease: at best, it has been regarded as a Blakean cosmology or an index that can be used to "shed light on Yeats's poetry and plays" (Vendler, *Yeats's "Vision"* 2); at worst, lamented, as Bette London notes, as "an embarrassing lapse in the otherwise stunning career of a man of genius" (*Writing Double* 186). George Harper characterizes it as the "most maligned and misunderstood *tour de force* in the history of modern literature" (*Automatic Script* 1:xiv). For an able summary of the critical reception of *A Vision*, see Croft, *"Stylistic Arrangements"* 18–25.

4. For recent work on Yeats and the occult, see Surette, *Birth of Modernism* (1993) and Materer, *Modernist Alchemy* (1995). Older studies include Harbans Bachchan, *W. B. Yeats and Occultism* (1965); George Mills Harper, *Yeats and the Golden Dawn* (1974); *Yeats and the Occult*, a collection of essays edited by George Harper (1975), M. C. Flannery, *Yeats and Magic* (1977); James Olney, *The Rhizome and the Flower* (1980); Graham Hough, *The Mystery Religion of W. B. Yeats* (1984); Kathleen Raine, *Yeats the Initiate* (1986); Frank Kinahan, *Yeats, Folklore, Occultism* (1988). Extensive monographs on H.D. and the occult are not yet as plentiful: see Friedman, *Psyche Reborn* (1981) and Sword, *Engendering Inspiration* (1995), both of which include sections on H.D.'s relationship to occult thought.

5. For a detailed account of the centrality of Yeats's work with the occult to his thought and verse, see Surette, *Birth of Modernism*. Surette considers his work part of an effort to counter much traditional Yeats scholarship by critics such as Ellmann and Hough, who claim that Yeats's extensive work with the occult had little impact on his verse. Surette's study, which also addresses the place of occult thought in the work of Ezra Pound and T. S. Eliot, aims more generally to combat "scholarship's longstanding avoidance" of the topic of the occult (8), a general reluctance stemming, he suggests, from a "largely justifiable contempt for the beliefs it represents" (11). In 1993 Surette insisted that, although many scholars may still harbor both a fear of the occult and an accompanying desire to believe art by beloved masters such as Yeats free of its contamination, "Scholarship has now reached a point where the question of the relevance of occultism to Yeats, Pound, Lawrence, and even Eliot is no longer open" (10). Ten years later, Tryphonopoulos maintained that, thanks in large part of Surette's efforts, the battle to accord serious attention to the occult dimensions of the thought of the moderns had been won: "[H]appily, there is no need any longer for ... defending one's interest in the topic .... [T]he tendency by Modernist scholars who have long been loath to give any serious consideration to even the acknowledged occult provenance in the work of such writers as W. B. Yeats seems to be no longer widespread" ("Fragments of Faith" 230).

6. Mead's article, "The Rising Psychic Tide," appears in *Quest* 3 (1911–1912): 401–402. For a

helpful discussion of the intense period of interest in occultism during the late nineteenth and early twentieth centuries, see Bachchan, *Yeats and Occultism* 4–7, and Tryphonopoulos, *Celestial Tradition*, Chapter 2, "The Occult Tradition," especially 23–27. Tryphonopoulos, drawing upon the work of Robert Galbreath, Ellmann, Samuel Hynes, and Eliade, notes that the surge of interest in the occult during the Victorian and Edwardian years was prompted by a dissatisfaction with materialist thought, with its insistence that the world could be known only through empirical scientific means, as well as disappointment with traditional Christianity's ability to help people toward renewal and a sense of the sacred.

7. See Foster, *Apprentice Mage* 45–52, 101–102. For Yeats's commentary on his relationships with Blavatsky and Mathers, see his *Autobiography* 106–115. For an account of Yeats's break in 1890 with Blavatsky and the London Theosophical Society because of what Blavatsky and the other Theosophists perceived as Yeats's excessively empirical approach to magic—which Blavatsky thought might harm the reputation of the Society—see Yeats, *Autobiography* (111–112). In *Modernist Alchemy*, Materer notes that Yeats also quarreled with Mathers in 1900 (27). What seems apparent here is that, far from being a passive or slavish follower of these groups, Yeats was actively critical, even skeptical, of some of their tendencies—he objected especially to what he read as their undue emphasis on abstraction and their dogmatism, as well as the gullibility of many of their followers—even as he respected their philosophy. As he wrote telegraphically to O'Leary of his response to Blavatsky's demand for loyalty and of the promise the members of the Theosophical Society tried to exact from him never again to criticize the society again as he had in an article in the *Weekly Review*: "I refused because I looked upon request as undue claim to control right of individual to think as best pleased him" (*LWBY* 160). Yeats took seriously the import of the oath each of the Theosophists had taken vowing to obey the directives of the society according to his "own conscience" (Coote, *Yeats: A Life* 83). But as Ellmann notes, despite the severance from the Theosophical Society in 1890, "five or six years of Theosophy, three of them years of active membership under the organization's founder, had left their mark on Yeats" (*Man and Masks* 69). Yeats may have broken formally with the organizations associated with the occult, but he took to heart many of their founding assumptions and teachings, appropriating and transforming them for his own purposes.

8. Yeats evidently made this assertion in response to O'Leary's expressed criticism of his occult studies. The entire quotation reads as follows:

> It is surely absurd to hold me 'weak' or otherwise because I chose to persist in a study which I decided deliberately four or five years ago to make, next to my poetry, the most important pursuit of my life. Whether it be, or be not, bad for my health can only be decided by one who knows what magic is and not at all by any amateur.
>
> (*LWBY* 210)

9. Thereafter followed two major essays on the occult, "Magic" (1901) and "Swedenborg, Mediums, and the Desolate Places" (1914). *Per Amica Silentia Lunae*, completed in 1917 just as he was beginning *A Vision*, introduced many of the major ideas that would later be elaborated upon in *A Vision*. For a detailed account of Yeats's early occult essays, see Croft, "Stylistic Ar-

rangements" 40–56. In *Yeats and the Occult*, George Harper surveys the unpublished papers of Yeats related to his occult interests (1–10), which indicate the importance Yeats placed upon preserving a record of his occult studies.

10. H.D. was Moravian on her mother's side; her grandfather, a Moravian minister, was principal of the Moravian Seminary for Young Ladies in Bethlehem.

11. H.D.'s memoirs from later in life suggest that when young she was not consciously aware that her religious upbringing had sensitized her to mysticism. In the 1940s, when the circumstances of the Second World War prompted her to revisit memories of her childhood and especially her connection to Moravianism, she discovered aspects of the home environment in which she had been raised, and the religious tradition that had surrounded her, that evidently had not registered with her before. I would argue, however, that her lack of conscious understanding notwithstanding, her early conversations with her mother, who spoke of a spiritual "gift" of second sight, and with her grandmother Elizabeth Seidel, who claimed to have "second sight," primed her to be receptive later in life to the authority of mystical knowledge. For H.D.'s account of her upbringing in a Moravian community, see her memoir, *The Gift*; also useful for understanding this dimension of H.D.'s thought is Augustine's introduction to her 1998 edition of *The Gift*.

12. Although the Moravian Christian tradition in which H.D. was raised was arguably influenced by seventeenth-century forms of what has been called "theosophy," here I use the term "Theosophy" to refer strictly to the late nineteenth-century esotericism associated with Madame Blavatsky and her disciples. For this distinction, see Antoine Faivre, *Theosophy, Imagination, Tradition*: Faivre notes that whereas earlier esoteric thought classified as "theosophist" belongs to the Judeo-Christian tradition, Blavatsky's thought, in contrast, relies heavily on sources within Eastern thought, especially Hinduism and Buddhism (4). Augustine observes that later in H.D.'s work with the occult, in the 1930s, she was touched by Blavatsky's Theosophy through her acquaintance with the work of Harriette Augusta and F. Homer Curtiss, American students of Madame Blavatsky, who wrote extensively on their combination of Christianity and Theosophy. H.D. owned copies of their books; she was especially impressed by their claim in *The Message of Aquaria* that 1910, the year of the appearance of Halley's comet, had ushered in a new "Woman's Age" (Augustine, *Gift Complete* 11). However, H.D. was clearly not as deeply immersed in Theosophy as Yeats had been during his early work with the occult in the 1880s and 1890s, nor was she as influenced by Blavatsky's example.

13. I take the phrase from a portion of H.D.'s narrative in *The Gift* in which she notes that she "did not altogether understand" a story that her grandmother told her upon first hearing it, but "pieced" it "together afterwards" (Augustine, *Gift Complete* 166).

14. Several recent studies have made available admirably detailed accounts of both Yeats's process of writing *A Vision* and H.D.'s work with Freud. Yeats's work is attentively chronicled by George Mills Harper in the two volumes of *The Making of Yeats's "A Vision": A Study of the Automatic Script*. Records of the automatic writing and "sleeps" of Yeats's wife from which he gathered his material are now collected in the three volumes of *Yeats's "Vision" Papers* (1992; George Mills Harper, general editor). The genesis of H.D.'s visions and her collaboration with Freud have likewise been carefully reconstructed by Friedman in *Psyche Reborn*. Useful detailed commentary on H.D.'s visionary experiences can be found in Adalaide Morris's "Concept of Projection: H.D.'s Visionary Powers."

15. The phrase is from Pound's *Hugh Selwyn Mauberley*.

16. Materer claims that unlike Yeats, H.D. never doubted the legitimacy or reliability of occult epistemologies nor of the findings she derived through visions.

> Similar as Yeats and H.D. appear as occult poets, there is a major difference: H.D. did not weave doubts about the validity of the "dreaming wisdom" or "daemonic images" into the fabric of her poetry. Of all the poets of the occult, and despite her psychoanalytic insights into it, H.D. seems the least self-conscious about occultism ... The countertradition represented by occultism seemed to her a native heritage she need never doubt.
>
> (*MODERNIST ALCHEMY* 87–88)

H.D. did usually seem confident in the wisdom that she received, but unlike Materer, I am not willing to concede that "H.D.'s belief in astrological predictions and invocations of the dead seemed unqualified and unshakeable. She felt no need to argue for the reality of what was so deeply real to her, even when her occult beliefs were challenged by Sigmund Freud himself" (2). This attributes to H.D., I think, too uncritical a view of occultism. On the one hand, as Friedman points out, H.D. did doubt the truth of visions, both hers and others', and sought reassurance that those from whom she was learning about the occult were reliable and were enlisting "critical intelligence" and "intellect" as much as faith (Friedman, *Psyche Reborn* 200). Friedman concludes, "Unlike many occultists, H.D. did not accept the authenticity or significance of all psychic phenomena produced by supernormal states of mind" (198). She also asserts, quite rightly, "Her attitude toward authority, whether mystic or scientific, was never passive or receptive" (198).

17. Sword, for instance, itemizes H.D.'s many images for her role as a visionary in a paratactic sequence that suggests that any one may be substituted for another: H.D. "figures her own visionary capacity through a remarkable array of metaphors: a womb ... a jellyfish, a radio, a telegraph receiving station, an Aeolian harp, a switchboard, a battery, an opera glass, a film projector, a magic lantern, a kaleidoscope" (*Engendering Inspiration* 120–121). H.D. herself sometimes implies the interchangeability of her metaphors for vision: in *Notes on Thought and Vision*, for instance, after adhering to a jellyfish metaphor for most of the text, apparently quite invested in it, she then has her narrator remark, "I saw that the state of mind I had before symbolised as a jelly-fish was just as well symbolised differently" (51). Despite what this implies, however, H.D.'s geometry, as it is used here metaphorically to articulate visionary experience, in fact bears a distinctive and important significance in her imagination.

18. Worth noting here is that Blavatsky herself, according to Yeats, frowned upon mediumship: Yeats reports in his *Autobiography* that Blavatsky had said to him, "Beware of mediumship; it is a kind of madness; I know for I have been through it" (108). Lewis's characterization clearly bespeaks an ignorance of the fine points of Theosophy and Blavatsky's teachings—Lewis was never familiar with them—but he does portray a popular understanding of what the work of figures like Blavatsky and her followers entailed.

19. Letter from H.D. to Bryher, May 28, 1933. As Friedman suggests, H.D. sometimes had to

assuage Bryher's uneasiness at her work with the occult ("My friend Bryher is like a bull with a red rage when I mention any thing supernatural," she noted in a letter to Viola Jordan from July 30, 1941), so her defensive assertion here may have stemmed in part from an effort to placate what Friedman terms Bryher's "distress about H.D.'s fascination with the supernatural" (*Psyche Reborn* 201).

20. See "Swedenborg, Mediums, and the Desolate Places," *Collected Works of W. B. Yeats* 5:60.

21. See Sword, *Engendering Inspiration*, Chapter 3, for H.D.'s efforts to cultivate models of visionary inspiration that would enable her conscious effort and assertion as well as her passive receptivity.

22. Most notable here is not that both H.D. and Yeats experienced their visionary knowledge by way of geometric figures, but rather the ways that, in their reports of visionary experience, they emphasized these geometric figures. My argument here is not about why their visionary information manifested in geometric terms—here, I don't wish to judge whether they invented or received these visions—but instead about how they featured and framed the geometric figures in their narratives, about the role these figures came to play in expressing H. D's and Yeats's relationship to visionary consciousness. I want to consider, on the one hand, the significance of the degree of pressure they placed upon geometric figures in their descriptions and, on the other, the ways in which they coded the figures rhetorically. Again, I would suggest that the work enabled by geometric figures in their narratives served a project akin to those served by geometric figures within the context of Vorticism.

23. For Yeats's emphatic remarks to Olivia Shakespear and Lady Gregory about how favorably impressed he has been by Lewis's *Time and Western Man* between 1927 and 1928, see especially *LWBY* 723, 734, and 739. In the letter of March 1927 (723), Yeats specifically mentions Lewis's commentary on Bergson.

24. Much ink has been spilled about the similarities between Yeats's and H.D.'s thought and that of C. G. Jung, but Jung seems not to have exercised a major influence on either. Yeats was certainly familiar with Jung through his work with the Society for Psychical Research in London; H.D. is thought to have read Jung in the 1920s and 1930s. But Olney, who remarks extensively on the likenesses between Jung's thought and Yeats's (underscoring especially the affinities between *A Vision* and Jung's "Red Book") claims that Yeats "apparently" was not "aware" of the similarities between his occult work and Jung's ("Esoteric Flower" 27). H.D., meanwhile, did accept some of Jung's ideas, but as Materer and Friedman note, remained chiefly indebted—and loyal—to the ideas of Freud. In *Compassionate Friendship*, H.D. acknowledges that Jung is "redoubtable," but emphasizes that she has not engaged much with his thought: "I have read very little of Jung and not everything of Freud. But Jung left as they say, medicine for mysticism and as I have said, I studied my mysticism or magic from the French writers Ambelain and Chaboseau" (*Compassionate Friendship* 20; quoted in Friedman, *Psyche Reborn* 192).

25. In 1901, for instance, the Theosophists Annie Besant and C. W. Leadbeater published the study called *Thought-Forms*, filled with diagrams of brilliantly colorful geometric shapes corresponding to thoughts and feelings such as anger, affection, greed, jealousy, or devotion. Their three general principles for the way emotions gave rise to particular geometrical shapes were that "1. Quality of thought determines color. 2. Nature of thought determines form. 3. Definiteness of thought determines clearness of outline" (*Thought-Forms* 21). Materer reproduces images from *Thought-Forms* in *Modernist Alchemy* (35).

26. H.D. acknowledged that she "read and re-read" this text (*Compassionate Friendship* 10), and her copious notes at the back of her copy, housed at Yale's Beinecke Rare Book and Manuscript Library, attest to her careful attention of it. The book is a study of hermetic symbolism, secret doctrines, astrology, magic, and alchemy. For the note from *Compassionate Friendship*, see Yale Collection of American Literature, Beinecke Rare Book and Manuscript Library, H.D. Papers, YCAL MSS 24, Box 38, Folder 1102.

27. Having begun work on *A Vision* in 1917, Yeats continued to revise the text for the rest of his life, producing an abundance of drafts and published versions in 1925 and 1937; as Connie Hood notes, he persisted in revising the book even after the 1937 edition was published ("Remaking *A Vision*" 35). The first version of *A Vision* was published through T. Werner Laurie on January 15, 1926, in a limited edition of 600 copies, "Privately printed for subscribers only"; the second appeared in a trade edition through Macmillan in 1937. For a richly detailed account of the many stages of development of *A Vision*, see Hood, "Remaking *A Vision*." A text much like the 1937 edition, reissued by Macmillan in 1956—the sources of whose slight improvements to the 1937 text, according to Richard Finneran, remain unverifiable, despite Macmillan's claim on the title page that it is "A Reissue with the Author's Final Revisions"—is the most widely available version of *A Vision*. Another version of *A Vision*, incorporating changes made to the text by George Yeats and Thomas Mark of Macmillan—and probably W. B. Yeats as well, though this is not certain—was issued in 1962. See Finneran, "A Preliminary Note on the Text of *A Vision* (1937)" for an analysis of the genesis of this 1956 text and how it compares with the less widely available 1962 edition, which Finneran deems the "best available text" (317, 320). The 1925 text is now available in *A Critical Edition of Yeats's "A Vision" (1925)*.

28. For a lucid account of H.D.'s four visions and the different texts in which she tried to recount them, see Morris, "Concept of Projection," especially 278–282.

29. H.D. remarks of the two texts: "'Writing on the Wall' . . . was written in London in the autumn of 1944, with no reference to the Vienna notebooks of spring 1933." "Writing on the Wall" was first published in *Life and Letters Today* (1945–1946), the journal of H.D.'s companion Bryher. Of "Advent," H.D. notes, "the continuation of 'Writing on the Wall,' or its prelude was taken direct from the old notebooks of 1933, though it was not assembled until December 1948, Lausanne" (*TF* xiv).

30. Harper and Hood quote from this typescript of *Dramatis Personae* in the editorial introduction to *A Critical Edition of Yeats's "A Vision" (1925)* xi.

31. As Morris notes, the first of H.D.'s visionary experiences, in 1919, involved H.D.'s feeling as though "two transparent half-globes" were "enclosing" her; the second, an "apparition of an ideal figure," whom she thought a fellow passenger, when she was on a ship bound for Greece in 1920; the third, the "writing on the wall" in a hotel room in Corfu in 1920; and the fourth, also in Corfu in 1920, a series of dance scenes that she suddenly received through inspiration and acted out for Bryher ("Concept of Projection" 279).

32. Further indication that geometric images were at the forefront of H.D.'s mind in 1944 is the appearance of references to geometry in a poem contemporaneous with the composition of "Writing on the Wall." As Morris notes, H.D. wrote "Writing on the Wall" during September 19–November 2, 1944, in between writing two sections of her long poem, *Trilogy*: "Tribute to the Angels" (May 17–31, 1944) and "The Flowering of the Rod" (December 18–31, 1944) ("Concept of Projection" 289). In "The Flowering of the Rod," H.D. notably uses geometric images, attesting to their important place at this juncture in her imagination. Her poetic speaker, invok-

ing the "geometric pattern" of a landscape, enjoins her reader not to be "beguiled / by the geometry of perfection" (*Collected Poems* 577) and celebrates instead a more dynamic form of geometry, "geometry on the wing" (585).

33. In a letter of 1934, Yeats notes that the diagrams are drawn by his wife, George (*LWBY* 819).

34. In the 1925 edition, diagrams most notably dominate "The Geometrical Foundation of the Wheel," Section 2 of Book II ("What The Caliph Refused to Learn"). This section of Book II of the 1925 version corresponds roughly, in the information it imparts, to the opening section of Book I in *A Vision* (1937). The diagram for "Dove or Swan," though in the 1925 edition it falls in Book III rather than V, appears in *A Vision* (1925) as well.

35. I draw this summary from information in *A Vision* (1937), especially Book I, and from Adams's *Book of Yeats's Vision*, particularly Chapter 5, "Book I: The Great Wheel."

36. Two letters written in January 1923, in the midst of the civil war, suggest how closely Yeats was affected by the strife: in both, he notes that he has two bullet holes in his windows (*LWBY* 696, January 4, 1923, and January 5, 1923).

37. For commentary on Yeats's feelings of unease as a senator, see Ellmann, *Man and Masks* 247, as well as Cullingford, *Yeats, Ireland, and Fascism* 165; see also Yeats's own later comments from "A Packet for Ezra Pound" at the beginning of *A Vision* (1937), in which he retrospects about his six years in the Senate. Especially helpful for characterizing Yeats's relationship to politics in the 1920s and 1930s are Cullingford, *Yeats, Ireland, and Fascism* (especially Chapter 10: "The Senate") and North, *Political Aesthetic*.

38. By the late 1930s, Yeats was sufficiently disappointed by O'Duffy's thuggery to give up his brief infatuation with Irish Fascism, but his willingness to publish these footnotes from Gentile and Croce in 1937 suggests that, even after becoming disenchanted with the Blueshirts per se, he was still ruminating seriously on ideas closely linked to Italian Fascism.

39. Letter to Viola Jordan, January 9, 1933, quoted in Friedman, *Psyche Reborn* 170. Friedman notes further that "World War II most likely renewed H.D.'s interest in the occult, raised it to a level of great intensity, and expanded it into a study of many different mystical traditions . . . . [T]he destruction of war made acute her need to find meaning embedded in the harsh realities of a nightmarish existence" (170).

40. Quoted in Friedman, *Psyche Reborn* 178. Whereas Friedman defends H.D.'s choice to contribute to the political efforts of her day by way of her work with psychoanalysis and the occult, Victoria Harrison takes a different perspective. Friedman contends that "H.D.'s esoteric and psychoanalytic explorations did not result from a desire to escape external reality" but rather from "an attempt to find a vision that would explain" that external reality; she maintains further that H.D. believed in "self-conscious alienation from political involvement as an effective way to usher in a new age" (*Psyche Reborn* 176–178). Harrison, on the other hand, laments that H.D.'s tendency during this period was in some ways escapist. She grants that H.D. registered her desire to engage as directly as possible with the terrors of the war by refusing to "escape" her London home during the war, convinced that if her host country's inhabitants had to suffer the raids, then so did she; she was persuaded also that her vocation as a writer required her to stay and record her experiences. Nonetheless, Harrison suggests, H.D. was escaping the realities of war during this period by disappearing into an intense period of reminiscence about her childhood and by searching for spiritual transcendence. "Both directions," Harrison observes, "avoid the present terrifying moment of bombing" ("When a Gift Is Poison"

72). H.D.'s writings, Harrison suggests, "overcome the world-erasing realities of bombed-out neighborhoods, incinerated Jews, and the terror of daily life under attack" (73). Thus H.D. participates in what Harrison reads as denial—albeit denial of a psychologically understandable kind—and as a regrettable erasure of the "material world" (74).

41. For H.D.'s belief that the visions she was receiving might offer a way of restoring peace to Europe, see Augustine's introduction to her edition of *The Gift*, especially 15. While writing *The Gift* and reflecting on her childhood within a Moravian Christian community, H.D. came to liken the visions she was receiving to those experienced by her maternal grandmother, Elizabeth Seidel; Seidel's visions, in turn, harked back to the Moravian community's successful attempts in the eighteenth century to promote harmony between white settlers and Native American tribes. Thus H.D. believed that the visions she was receiving might analogously provide clues about how to foster peace among European nations in conflict.

42. Significant here is that H.D.'s father died just before she began to experience the sequence of visions that would inspire her first text addressing the occult, *Notes on Thought and Vision* (1919), as well as her first period of concentrated study of esoteric thought. Similarly, Yeats was experiencing his father's death as he was hard at work on the first version of *A Vision* in 1922. Given H.D.'s and Yeats's consistent attention to their fathers before their passing (Yeats wrote to his father constantly; H.D., according to Bryher, mentioned her father daily), their fathers' deaths quite probably intensified memories of their conflicted relationships and their quarrels over intellectual principles, which had generated these conflicts. Such memories may have imbued their writing about visionary consciousness with an impulse to reply to the ghosts of their fathers.

43. For discussions of H.D.'s relationship to her father, see Guest, *Herself Defined*, especially Chapter 2, 9–21; and Janice Robinson, *H.D.: The Life and Work of an American Poet*, Chapter 1, "A Moravian Childhood in Bethlehem," 3–9. For Yeats's relationship to his father, see Ellmann, *Man and Masks*, especially 21–32.

44. As William Murphy notes, "John Butler Yeats's aversion to his son's dabblings with the occult began early and never ended" ("Psychic Daughter, Mystic Son, Sceptic Father" 11).

45. As Materer notes in *Modernist Alchemy* (25), "Occultism was so crucial to Yeats's resistance to his father's intellectual power that he dated his break from that influence from the time he began to study 'psychical research and mystical philosophy'" (*Autobiography* 54).

46. Murphy quotes a letter from John Butler Yeats to William Butler Yeats dated April 27, 1918.

47. Samples from Yeats's letters attest to his attentiveness to his father's letters and to his effort to show his father how valuable JBY's ideas were to him. Even if we allow for the possibility that the following remarks were not always altogether sincere, their volume and frequency nonetheless indicate an intense desire on Yeats's part to assure his father of his appreciation and his keen concern about his father's good opinion: "Your last letter came just in time to give me a most essential passage" (*LWBY* 586), he writes to JBY in January 1914 from Stone Cottage; his father's letters "interest" him "deeply," he emphasizes to JBY in December 1914 (589); and in January 1915, again, he insists that his father's letters "interest" him "very much" (590). In early 1916, he says, "I value the letters very much. I send them to be typed the moment they come" (606). And in June 1917, "Your letters are as interesting as ever—those of last November were I think especially good" (626). He mentions that, out of his admiration, he wants to assemble his father's letters into a book to be published by the Cuala Press, which was run by his

sisters. The edition of letters was published in 1917; Yeats had entrusted Ezra Pound with the task of selecting them.

48. Yeats here mentions his work with the Christian cabbala, noting that a fellow student of his had observed that "the cabbalistic tree has a green serpent winding through it which represents the winding path of nature or instinct," and that a path called "Samekh" is part of a "long straight line that goes up through the centre of the tree . . . interpreted as the path of 'deliberate effort'" (*Autobiography* 225).

49. Reading what she also believes to be H.D.'s generative ambivalence about visionary experience, Sword notes that

> throughout most of the thee decades preceding World War II . . . H.D. would portray visionary experience more often as a curse than as a source of power. Nonetheless, even her earliest poetry displays a deep-seated fascination with the tropes of inspiration and prophecy. . . . H.D.'s apparent terror of being overwhelmed by a frightening Other is frequently matched by a simultaneous desire for contact with some powerful external source of knowledge and vision.
>
> ("ENGENDERING INSPIRATION" 122)

50. As Allan Wade notes in his bibliography of Yeats's work, *Autobiographies: "Reveries over Childhood and Youth" and "The Trembling of the Veil"* appeared in 1926 and *Autobiography: Consisting of "Reveries over Childhood and Youth," "The Trembling of the Veil," and "Dramatis Personae"* appeared in 1938. Here I cite from the 1938 edition, but the same comments appear in the 1926 edition.

51. Frank Pearce Sturm (1879–1942) was a poet, mystic, and translator. In 1929, upon reading Yeats's improved introduction to *A Vision*, the one that was published separately along with *A Packet For Ezra Pound* (1929) and eventually included in *A Vision* (1937), Sturm chided Yeats (with mischief) for his lack of scholarly accuracy: "Do get some friend who knows Latin to read the proofs this time. I know that I am a pedant, but pedants read you. We cough in the ink till the worlds [sic] end, as you cruelly said, but the least of us would save you from the errors which spoil The Vision [sic] as it is now" (quoted in Jeffares, "Critical Heritage" 274).

52. Many valuable critical arguments have been made about the significance of these collaborations: the way in which, for instance, they serve usefully to trouble the now often challenged but still tenacious myth of single individual authorship (Margaret Harper, "Twilight Vision," on Yeats and George's work on *A Vision*); or the way in which they serve to show us feminist exemplars, for instance, in H.D.'s strong response to Freud (Friedman, "Against Discipleship") or in George Yeats's contribution to *A Vision* (Margaret Harper, "Medium as Creator"). Bette London also offers extensive and insightful commentary on Yeats and George's collaboration, advocating that we read *A Vision* as a "complex partnership production" (*Writing Double*, Chapter 6, "Romancing the Medium: The Silent Partnership of George Yeats" 181), although, thanks in large part to George's active efforts to hide her work, her role in the partnership has long been "trivialized" and "underrated," often even ignored altogether (183). And Holly

Laird takes up H.D.'s collaborations with both Freud and Bryher in *Women Coauthors* (Chapter 5, "Rewriting the Uncanny" 129–147), offering an incisive reading through the psychoanalytic concept of the uncanny. Here, by focusing on the relationship between these collaborations and the geometry of these texts, I draw forth an argument different from those offered in these accounts—in this case about the way in which the collaborations assuage H.D.'s and Yeats's anxieties about visionary knowledge.

53. In 1933 Yeats noted to Olivia Shakespear that he was reading T. E. Hulme's "Modern Art," which assigns geometry the significance of "abstraction" and opposes it to the "organic" and "vital"; he also commented that Hulme's essay helped him make sense of what he read as the opposition between such books as Wyndham Lewis's *Apes of God* and D. H. Lawrence's *Lady Chatterley's Lover*. When he suggests that Lawrence "is directed against modern abstraction," this suggests that Hulme's dichotomy between the categories of the "abstract" and the "organic" (which Lawrence also emphasizes, celebrating the latter) has compelled him. Moreover, he positions Lewis, whom he often associates with geometric figures, against Lawrence, suggesting that, for him, a geometric idiom represents abstraction (*LWBY* 810).

54. This allusion to "bundles" would seem to be a reference to fascism, but since Yeats uses nearly the same phrase about "sticks" and "bundles" in a 1936 letter to Ethel Mannin, in which he assigns it a different significance, it need not refer to fascism exclusively (*LWBY* 869). Explaining his growing indifference to contemporary politics and his continuing loyalty to the old Fenian convictions of his youth, Yeats observes, "[W]hy should I trouble about communism, fascism, liberalism, radicalism, when all . . . are going down stream with the artificial unity which ends every civilization? Only dead sticks can be tied into convenient bundles" (*LWBY* 869). The implication here is that any "live" political conviction, any one that has avoided the desiccation that occurs as conviction hardens into dogma, will elude attempts to classify and label it.

55. In using this term to describe Yeats's performance here, I borrow from Hazard Adams, who in turn draws it from Baldassare Castiglione's description of the attitude of a Renaissance courtier. Yeats, Adams notes, greatly admired Castiglione's *Book of the Courtier* (1528) (*Book of Yeats's Vision* 14).

Adams, Hazard. *The Book of Yeats's Vision: Romantic Modernism and Antithetical Tradition.* Ann Arbor: Univ. of Michigan Press, 1995.

Albright, Daniel. *Quantum Poetics: Yeats, Pound, Eliot, and the Science of Modernism.* Cambridge: Cambridge Univ. Press, 1997.

Aldington, Richard. "Blast." *Egoist* 1.14 (July 15, 1914): 272–273.

Alfieri, Dino, and Liuigi Freddi. *Mostra della Rivoluzione Fascista.* Milan: Industrie Grafiche Italiane IGIS, 1982 (orig. pub. 1933).

Allen, James Lovic. "'The Red and the Black': Understanding 'The Historical Cones.'" *Yeats Annual* 3 (1985): 209–212.

Altman, Meryl. "A Prisoner of Biography." *Women's Review of Books* 9.10–11 (July 1992): 39–40.

Andreotti, Libero. "The Aesthetics of War: The Exhibition of the Fascist Revolution." *Journal of Architectural Education* 45 (February 1992): 76–86.

Anspaugh, Kelly. "Blasting the Bombardier: Another Look at Lewis, Joyce, and Woolf." *Twentieth Century Literature* 40.3 (Fall 1994): 365–378.

Apollonio, Umbro, ed. *Futurist Manifestos.* Translated by Robert Brain, R. W. Flint, J. C. Higgitt, and Caroline Tisdall. London: Thames and Hudson, 1973.

Ardis, Ann. *Modernism and Cultural Conflict, 1880–1922.* Cambridge: Cambridge Univ. Press, 2002.

———. "Reading 'as a Modernist': Denaturalizing Modernist Reading Protocols: Wyndham Lewis's *Tarr*." In Rado, *Re-reading Modernism*, 373–390.

Auden, W. H. "The Public v. the Late William Butler Yeats." *Partisan Review* 6.3 (1939): 46–51.

Augustine, Jane. Introduction to *The Gift by H.D.: The Complete Text*, 1–28.

Bachchan, Harbans Rai. *W. B. Yeats and Occultism.* Delhi: Motilal Banarsidass, 1965.

Bauman, Zygmunt. *Modernity and Ambivalence.* Ithaca, N.Y.: Cornell Univ. Press, 1991.

Beatty, Michael. "'Enemy of the Stars': Vorticist Experimental Play." *Theoria* 46 (1976): 41–60.

Bechhöfer, C. E. "More Contemporaries." *New Age* 15.13 (July 30, 1914): 308.

Bell, Clive. *Art.* New York: Stokes, 1913.

Bell, Ian. *Critic as Scientist: The Modernist Poetics of Ezra Pound.* New York: Methuen, 1981.

Benjamin, Walter. *Illuminations: Essays and Reflections*. Ed. Hannah Arendt. Trans. Harry Zorn. New York: Schocken Books, 1968.

Benstock, Shari. *Women of the Left Bank: Paris, 1910–1940*. Austin: Univ. of Texas Press, 1986.

Bersani, Leo. "Is the Rectum a Grave?" *October* 43 (1987): 197–222.

Besant, Annie and C. W. Leadbeater. *Thought-Forms*. Wheaton, Ill.: Theosophical Publishing House, 1971 (orig. pub. 1901).

Blavatsky, H. P. *The Secret Doctrine*. Vol. 1, *Cosmogenesis*. Madras, India: Theosophical Publishing House, 1978 (orig. pub. 1888).

Bloom, Harold. *Yeats*. New York: Oxford Univ. Press, 1970.

Boone, Joseph A., and Michael Cadden, eds. *Engendering Men: The Question of Male Feminist Criticism*. New York: Routledge, 1990.

Bornstein, George, ed. *Representing Modernist Texts: Editing as Interpretation*. Ann Arbor: Univ. of Michigan Press, 1991.

———. "What Is the Text of a Poem by Yeats?" In *Palimpsest: Editorial Theory in the Humanities*, edited by George Bornstein and Ralph G. Williams, 167–193. Ann Arbor: Univ. of Michigan Press, 1991.

Botar, Oliver. "Prolegomena to the Study of Biomorphic Modernism: Biocentrism, Lázló Moholy-Nagy's 'New Vision' and Erno Kállai's Bioromantik." PhD diss., University of Toronto, 1998.

Boughn, Michael. *H.D.: A Bibliography, 1905–1990*. Charlottesville: Univ. Press of Virginia, 1993.

Bourdieu, Pierre. *The Field of Cultural Production: Essays on Art and Literature*. Edited by Randall Johnson. New York: Columbia Univ. Press, 1993.

Bradbury, Malcolm, and James McFarlane, eds. *Modernism: A Guide to European Literature, 1890–1930*. London: Penguin, 1976.

Brooks, Cleanth. *The Hidden God: Studies in Hemingway, Faulkner, Yeats, Eliot, and Warren*. New Haven, Conn.: Yale Univ. Press, 1963.

Brooks, Peter. *Reading for the Plot: Design and Intention in Narrative*. Cambridge, Mass.: Harvard Univ. Press, 1992.

Bruzzi, Zara. "H.D. and the Eleusinian Landscape of English Modernism." *Agenda* 25.3–4 (Autumn/Winter 1987–1988): 97–112.

Burnett, Gary. *H.D. between Image and Epic: The Mysteries of Her Poetics*. Ann Arbor: UMI Research Press, 1990.

———. "A Poetics out of War: H.D.'s Responses to the First World War." *Agenda* 25.3–4 (Autumn/Winter 1987/1988): 54–63.

Bush, Ronald. *The Genesis of Ezra Pound's Cantos*. Princeton, N.J.: Princeton Univ. Press, 1985.

Butler, Judith. *Bodies That Matter: On the Discursive Limits of "Sex."* New York: Routledge, 1993.

Bynum, Caroline Walker. "Why All the Fuss about the Body? A Medievalist's Perspective." *Critical Inquiry* 22 (Autumn 1995): 1–33.

Carpenter, Humphrey. *A Serious Character: The Life of Ezra Pound*. London: Faber and Faber, 1988.

Carswell, John. *Lives and Letters: A. R. Orage, Beatrice Hastings, Katherine Mansfield, John Middleton Murray, and S. S. Koteliansky, 1906–1957*. New York: New Directions, 1978.

Casillo, Robert. "Fascists of the Final Hour: Pound's Italian Cantos." In Golsan, *Fascism*, 98–127.

Cerf, Bennett. *At Random*. New York: Random House, 1977.

Cézanne, Paul. *Correspondance*. Edited by John Rewald. Paris: Bernard Grasset, 1978.

Chace, William. *The Political Identities of Ezra Pound and T. S. Eliot*. Stanford, Calif.: Stanford Univ. Press, 1973.

Childs, Peter. *Modernism*. New York: Routledge, 2000.

Chisholm, Dianne. *H.D.'s Freudian Poetics: Psychoanalysis in Translation*. Ithaca, N.Y.: Cornell Univ. Press, 1992.

———. "H.D.'s Auto*heter*ography." *Tulsa Studies in Women's Literature* 9.1 (Spring 1990): 79–106.

———. "Pornopoeia, the Modernist Canon, and the Cultural Capital of Sexual Literacy: The Case of H.D." In *Gendered Modernisms*, edited by Maragret Dickie and Thomas Travisano, 69–94. Philadelphia: Univ. of Pennsylvania Press, 1996.

Cohen, Ed. *Talk on the Wilde Side*. New York: Routledge, 1993.

Collecott, Diana. *H.D. and Sapphic Modernism, 1910–1950*. Cambridge: Cambridge Univ. Press, 1999.

Conover, Anne. "Ezra Pound and the Crosby Continental Editions." In *Ezra Pound and Europe*, edited by Richard Taylor and Claus Melchior, 105–118. Atlanta: Rodopi, 1993.

Cooney, Seamus, Bradford Morrow, Bernard Lafourcade, and Hugh Kenner, eds. *Blast 3*. Santa Barbara, Calif.: Black Sparrow Press, 1984.

Coote, Stephen. *W. B. Yeats: A Life*. London: Hodder and Stoughton, 1997.

Cork, Richard. *Vorticism and Abstract Art in the First Machine Age*. Berkeley and Los Angeles: Univ. of California Press, 1976.

———. *Vorticism and Its Allies: A Catalogue of an Exhibition Organised by Richard Cork in Collaboration with the Arts Council of Great Britain, Held at the Hayward Gallery, London, 27 March–2 June 1974*. London: Arts Council of Great Britain, 1974.

Craig, Cairns. *Yeats, Eliot, Pound, and the Politics of Poetry*. Pittsburgh: Univ. of Pittsburgh Press, 1982.

Cranston, Sylvia. HPB: *The Extraordinary Life and Influence of Helena Blavatsky, Founder of the Modern Theosophical Movement*. New York: Putnam, 1993.

Croft, Barbara L. *"Stylistic Arrangements": A Study of William Butler Yeats's "A Vision."* Lewisburg, Pa.: Bucknell Univ. Press, 1987.

Crown, Kathleen. "H.D.'s Jellyfish Manifesto and the Visible Body of Modernism." *Sagetrieb* 14.1–2 (Spring-Fall 1995): 217–241.

Cullingford, Elizabeth Butler. *Gender and History in Yeats's Love Poetry*. Cambridge: Cambridge Univ. Press, 1993.

———. *Yeats, Ireland, and Fascism*. New York: New York Univ. Press, 1981.

Culver, Michael. "The Art of Henry Strater: An Examination of the Illustrations for Pound's *A Draft of XVI. Cantos*." *Paideuma: A Journal Devoted to Ezra Pound Scholarship* 12 (1983): 447–478.

Cunard, Nancy. *These Were the Hours: Memories of My Hours Press, Reanville, and Paris, 1928–1931*. Carbondale: Southern Illinois Univ. Press, 1969.

Dasenbrock, Reed Way. *The Literary Vorticism of Ezra Pound and Wyndham Lewis*. Baltimore: Johns Hopkins Univ. Press, 1985.

———. "Metaphysics of the Not-Self." *Enemy News* 29 (Winter 1989): 11–14.

———. "Vorticism among the Isms." In Cooney et al., *Blast 3*, 40–46.

———. "Wyndham Lewis's Fascist Imagination and the Fiction of Paranoia." In Golsan, *Fascism*, 81–97.

DeKoven, Marianne. *Rich and Strange: Gender, History, Modernism*. Princeton, N.J.: Princeton Univ. Press, 1991.

Dettmar, Kevin J. H., and Stephen Watt, eds. *Marketing Modernisms: Self-Promotion, Canonization, and Rereading*. Ann Arbor: Univ. of Michigan Press, 1996.

Diepeveen, Leonard. *The Difficulties of Modernism*. New York: Routledge, 2003.

DuPlessis, Rachel Blau. *H.D.: The Career of That Struggle*. Bloomington: Indiana Univ. Press, 1986.

———. "Romantic Thralldom in H.D." In Friedman and DuPlessis, *Signets*, 406–429.

———. *Writing beyond the Ending: Narrative Strategies of Twentieth-Century Women Writers*. Bloomington: Indiana Univ. Press, 1985.

DuPlessis, Rachel Blau, and Susan Stanford Friedman. "'Woman Is Perfect': H.D.'s Debate with Freud." *Feminist Studies* 7.3 (Fall 1981): 417–430.

Dworkin, Craig. *Reading the Illegible*. Evanston, Ill.: Northwestern Univ. Press, 2003.

Edelman, Lee. "Redeeming the Phallus: Wallace Stevens, Frank Lentricchia, and the Politics of (Hetero) Sexuality." In Boone and Cadden, *Engendering Men*, 36–52.

Edmunds, Susan. *Out of Line: History, Psychoanalysis, and Montage in H.D.'s Long Poems*. Stanford, Calif.: Stanford Univ. Press, 1994.

Eliade, Mircea. *Occultism, Witchcraft, and Cultural Fashions: Essays in Comparative Religion*. Chicago: Univ. of Chicago Press, 1976.

Ellmann, Richard. *Oscar Wilde*. New York: Knopf, 1988.

———. *Yeats: The Man and the Masks*. New York: Dutton, 1958.

Epstein, Jacob. *Let There Be Sculpture*. New York: Putnam, 1940.

Eysteinsson, Astradur. *The Concept of Modernism*. Ithaca, N.Y.: Cornell Univ. Press, 1990.

Faivre, Antoine. *Theosophy, Imagination, Tradition: Studies in Western Esotericism*. Translated by Christine Rhone. Albany: State Univ. of New York Press, 2000.

Fenollosa, Ernest. *The Chinese Written Character as a Medium for Poetry*. Edited by Ezra Pound. San Francisco: City Lights.

Finlay, John. *Social Credit: The English Origins*. Montréal: McGill-Queen's Univ. Press, 1972.

Finneran, Richard J. "A Preliminary Note on the Text of *A Vision* (1937)." In G. Harper, *Yeats and the Occult*, 317–320.

Flory, Wendy Stallord. "Enemy of the Stars." In Meyers, *Wyndham Lewis*, 92–106.

Ford, Hugh. *Published in Paris: American and British Writers, Printers, and Publishers in Paris, 1920–1939*. London: Garnstone Press, 1975.

Forster, E. M. *Maurice*. London: Edward Arnold, 1971.

Foshay, Toby. *Wyndham Lewis and the Avant-Garde: The Politics of the Intellect*. Montréal: McGill-Queen's Univ. Press, 1992.

Foster, R. F. *W. B. Yeats: A Life*. Vol. 1: *The Apprentice Mage, 1865–1914*. New York: Oxford Univ. Press, 1997.

———. *W. B. Yeats: A Life*. Vol. 2: *The Arch-Poet, 1915–1939*. New York: Oxford Univ. Press, 2003.

Foucault, Michel. *History of Sexuality*. Vol. 1: *An Introduction*. New York: Vintage, 1990.

Frank, Joseph. "Spatial Form in Modern Literature." In *The Idea of Spatial Form*, 31–66. New Brunswick, N.J.: Rutgers Univ. Press, 1991 (orig. pub. 1945).

Friedman, Susan Stanford. "Against Discipleship: Collaboration and Intimacy in the Relationship of H.D. and Freud." *Literature and Psychology* 33.3 (1987): 89–108.

———, ed. *Analyzing Freud: Letters of H.D., Bryher, and Their Circle*. New York: New Directions, 2002.

———. *Penelope's Web: Gender, Modernity, H.D.'s Fiction*. Cambridge: Cambridge Univ. Press, 1990.

———. *Psyche Reborn: The Emergence of H.D.* Bloomington: Indiana Univ. Press, 1981.

Friedman, Susan Stanford, and Rachel Blau DuPlessis. "'I had two loves separate': The Sexualities of H.D.'s HER." In Friedman and DuPlessis, *Signets*, 205–232.

———, eds. *Signets: Reading H.D.* Madison: Univ. of Wisconsin Press, 1990.

Frobenius, Leo. *The Voice of Africa*. New York: Benjamin Blom, 1968 (orig. pub. 1913).

Fry, Roger. "Post-Impressionism." *Fortnightly Review* (May 1, 1911): 856–867.

Frye, Northrop. *Spiritus Mundi: Essays on Literature, Myth, and Society*. Bloomington: Indiana Univ. Press, 1976.

Gagnier, Regenia. *Idylls of the Marketplace: Oscar Wilde and the Victorian Public*. Stanford, Calif.: Stanford Univ. Press, 1986.

Gallup, Donald. *Ezra Pound: A Bibliography*. Charlottesville: Univ. Press of Virginia, 1983.

Gaudier-Brzeska, Henri. "Allied Artists' Association Ltd, Holland Park Hall." *Egoist* (June 15, 1914): 227–229.

Ghirardo, Diane. "Architects, Exhibitions, and the Politics of Culture in Fascist Italy." *Journal of Architectural Education* 45.2 (February 1992): 67–75.

Gilbert, Sandra, and Susan Gubar. *No Man's Land: The Place of the Woman Writer in the Twentieth Century*. 3 vols. New Haven, Conn.: Yale Univ. Press, 1988–1994.

Golsan, Richard J., ed. *Fascism, Aesthetics, and Culture*. Hanover, N.H.: Univ. Press of New England, 1992.

Graver, David. "Vorticist Performance and Aesthetic Turbulence in *Enemy of the Stars*." PMLA 107.3 (May 1992): 482–496.

Gregory, Eileen. *H.D. and Hellenism: Classic Lines*. Cambridge: Cambridge Univ. Press, 1997.

Guest, Barbara. *Herself Defined: The Poet H.D. and Her World*. New York: Doubleday, 1984.

Haberland, Eike, ed. *Leo Frobenius, 1873–1973: An Anthology*. Translated by Patricia Crampton. Wiesbaden, Germany: Franz Steiner Verlag, 1973.

Hanscombe, Gillian, and Virginia L. Smyers. *Writing for Their Lives: The Modernist Women, 1910–1940*. London: Women's Press, 1987.

Haraway, Donna J. "A Cyborg Manifesto: Science, Technology, and Socialist-Feminism in the Late Twentieth Century." Chapter 8 of *Simians, Cyborgs, and Women: The Reinvention of Nature*. New York: Routledge, 1991.

Harper, George Mills. *The Making of Yeats's "A Vision": A Study of the Automatic Script*. Vols. 1 and 2. Carbondale: Southern Illinois Univ. Press, 1987.

———. "'Out of a Medium's Mouth': Yeats's Theory of 'Transference' and Keats's 'Ode to a Nightingale.'" *Yeats Annual* 1 (1983): 17–32.

———, ed. *Yeats and the Occult*. Toronto: Macmillan of Canada, 1975.

Harper, Margaret Mills. "The Medium as Creator: George Yeats's Role in the Automatic Script." *Yeats Annual* 6 (1988): 49–71.

———. "Twilight to Vision: Yeats's Collaborative Modernity." *Bucknell Review* 38.1 (1994): 61–83.

Harrison, Victoria. "When a Gift Is Poison: H.D., the Moravian, the Jew, and World War II." *Sagetrieb* 15.1–2 (1996): 69–93.

H.D. *Bid Me to Live*. London: Virago, 1984 (orig. pub. 1960).

———. "The Borderline Pamphlet." *Sagetrieb* 7 (Fall 1987): 29–50.

———. *Collected Poems, 1912–1944*. Edited by Louis Martz. New York: New Directions, 1983.

———. *End to Torment: A Memoir of Ezra Pound*. Edited by Norman Holmes Pearson and Michael King. New York: New Directions, 1979.

———. *The Gift*. New York: New Directions, 1982.

———. *The Gift by H.D.: The Complete Text*. Edited by Jane Augustine. Gainesville: Univ. of Florida Press, 1998.

———. "H.D. by Delia Alton [Notes on Recent Writing]." *Iowa Review* 16.3 (Fall 1986): 174–221.

———. *Hermione*. New York: New Directions, 1981.

———. *Kora and Ka (with Mira-Mare)*. New York: New Directions, 1996.

———. *Nights*. New York: New Directions, 1986.

———. *Notes on Thought and Vision and The Wise Sappho*. San Francisco: City Lights. 1982.

———. "Responsibilities." *Agenda* 25.3–4 (Autumn–Winter 1987–1988): 51–53.

———. *Tribute to Freud*. New York: New Directions, 1974 (orig. pub. 1956).

Heywood, Leslie. *Dedication to Hunger: The Anorexic Aesthetic in Modern Culture*. Berkeley and Los Angeles: Univ. of California Press, 1996.

Hoffman, Frederick, Charles Allen, and Carolyn Ulrich, eds. *The Little Magazine: A History and a Bibliography*. Princeton, N.J.: Princeton Univ. Press, 1946.

Hollenberg, Donna, ed. *Between History and Poetry: The Letters of H.D. and Norman Holmes Pearson*. Iowa City: Univ. of Iowa Press, 1997.

———. *H.D.: The Poetics of Childbirth and Creativity*. Boston: Northeastern Univ. Press, 1991.

Hood, Connie. "The Remaking of *A Vision*." *Yeats: An Annual* 1 (1983): 33–67.

Hulme, T. E. "Modern Art—I. The Grafton Group." *New Age* 14.11 (January 15, 1914): 341–342.

———. "Modern Art—II. A Preface Note and Neo-Realism." *New Age* 14.15 (February 12, 1914): 467–469.

———. "Modern Art—III. The London Group." *New Age* 14.21 (March 26, 1914): 661–662.

———. *Speculations*. Edited by Herbert Read. New York: Harcourt, Brace, 1961 (orig. pub. 1924).

Huyssen, Andreas. *After the Great Divide*. Bloomington: Indiana Univ. Press, 1986.

Jackson, Holbrook. *The Eighteen Nineties*. New ed. London: Jonathan Cape, 1927 (orig. pub. 1913).

Jaffe, Norma Crow. "'She Herself Is the Writing': Language and Sexual Identity in H.D." *Literature and Medicine* 4 (1985): 86–111.

Jameson, Fredric. *Fables of Aggression: Wyndham Lewis, the Modernist as Fascist*. Berkeley and Los Angeles: Univ. of California Press, 1979.

———. *The Political Unconscious*. Ithaca, N.Y.: Cornell Univ. Press, 1981.

Jeffares, Norman, ed. *W. B. Yeats: The Critical Heritage*. London: Routledge and Kegan Paul, 1977.

John, Augustus. *Finishing Touches*. Edited by Daniel George. London: Jonathan Cape, 1964.

Kadlec, David. *Mosaic Modernism: Anarchism, Pragmatism, Culture*. Baltimore: Johns Hopkins Univ. Press, 2000.

Kaufmann, Michael. "Gendering Modernism: H.D., Imagism, and Masculinist Aesthetics." In *Unmanning Modernism: Gendered Re-readings*, edited by Elizabeth Jane Harrison and Shirley Peterson, 59–72. Knoxville: Univ. of Tennessee Press, 1997.

Kenner, Hugh. *The Pound Era*. Berkeley and Los Angeles: Univ. of California Press, 1971.

———. "Self-Similarity, Fractals, Cantos." *ELH: A Journal of English Literary History* 55.3 (Fall 1988): 721–730.

———. *Wyndham Lewis*. Norfolk, Conn.: New Directions, 1954.

Kermode, Frank. *The Sense of an Ending: Studies in the Theory of Fiction*. New York: Oxford Univ. Press, 1967.

Klein, Scott. "The Experiment of Vorticist Drama: Wyndham Lewis and 'Enemy of the Stars.'" *Twentieth Century Literature* 37.2 (Summer 1991): 225–239.

———. *The Fictions of James Joyce and Wyndham Lewis: Monsters of Nature and Design*. Cambridge: Cambridge Univ. Press, 1994.

Kloepfer, Deborah Kelly. "Flesh Made Word: Maternal Inscription in H.D." *Sagetrieb* 3.1 (Spring 1984): 27–48.

———. *The Unspeakable Mother: Forbidden Discourse in Jean Rhys and H.D.* Ithaca: Cornell Univ. Press, 1989.

Knapp, Peggy A. "Women's Freud(e): H.D.'s *Tribute to Freud* and Gladys Schmitt's *Sonnets for an Analyst*." *Massachusetts Review* 24.2 (Summer 1983): 338–352.

Koestenbaum, Wayne. *Double Talk: The Erotics of Male Literary Collaboration*. New York: Routledge, 1989.

———. "Wilde's Hard Labor and the Birth of Gay Reading." In Boone and Cadden, *Engendering Men*, 176–189.

Kristeva, Julia. *Powers of Horror: An Essay on Abjection*. Translated by Leon Roudiez. New York: Columbia Univ. Press, 1982.

———. "Women's Time." In *The Kristeva Reader*, edited by Toril Moi, 187–213. New York: Columbia Univ. Press, 1986.

LaFourcade, Bernard. "The Taming of the Wild Body." In Meyers, *Wyndham Lewis*, 68–84.

Laird, Holly. *Women Coauthors*. Chicago: Univ. of Illinois Press, 2000.

Laity, Cassandra. "H.D. and Swinburne: Decadence and Sapphic Modernism." In *Lesbian Texts and Contexts*, edited by Karla Jay and Joanne Glasgow, 217–240. New York: New York Univ. Press, 1996.

———. *H.D. and the Victorian Fin-de-Siècle*. Cambridge: Cambridge Univ. Press, 1996.

Langeteig, Kendra. "Visions in the Crystal Ball: Ezra Pound, H.D., and the Form of the Mystical." *Paideuma: A Journal Devoted to Ezra Pound Scholarship* 25.1–2 (Spring–Fall 1996): 55–81.

Laver, Sue. "Poets, Philosophers, and Priests: T. S. Eliot, Postmodernism, and the Social Authority of Art." PhD diss., McGill University, 2000.

Le Corbusier. *The City of To-Morrow and Its Planning*. Translated and with an introduction by Frederick Etchells. London: John Rodker, 1929.

———. *Towards a New Architecture*. Translated and with an introduction by Frederick Etchells. London: John Rodker, 1927.

Lentricchia, Frank. "Patriarchy against Itself—The Young Manhood of Wallace Stevens." *Critical Inquiry* 13 (Summer 1987): 742–786.

Levenson, Michael. "Form's Body: Wyndham Lewis's *Tarr*." *Modern Language Quarterly* 45.3 (September 1984): 241–262.

———. *A Genealogy of Modernism: A Study of English Literary Doctrine, 1908–1922*. Cambridge: Cambridge Univ. Press, 1984.

Levin, Harry. "What Was Modernism?" In *Refractions: Essays in Comparative Literature*, 271–295. New York: Oxford Univ. Press, 1966.

Lewis, Wyndham. *The Apes of God*. Santa Barbara, Calif.: Black Sparrow Press, 1981.

———. *The Art of Being Ruled*. London: Chatto and Windus, 1926.
———, ed. *Blast 1*. Santa Rosa, Calif.: Black Sparrow Press, 1992.
———, ed. *Blast 2*. Santa Rosa, Calif.: Black Sparrow Press, 1993.
———. *Blasting and Bombardiering*. London: Calder and Boyars, 1967 (orig. pub. 1937).
———. *The Caliph's Design: Architects! Where Is Your Vortex?* In *WLOA*, 129–183.
———. "Code of a Herdsman." *Little Review* 4.3 (July 1917): 3–7.
———. *Creatures of Habit and Creatures of Change: Essays on Art, Literature, and Society, 1914–1956*. Edited by Paul Edwards. Santa Rosa, Calif.: Black Sparrow Press, 1989.
———. "The Cubist Room." *Egoist* 1 (January 1914): 8–9.
———. *Enemy of the Stars*. London: Desmond Harmsworth, 1932.
———. "Futurism and the Flesh." In *Creatures of Habit and Creatures of Change*, 35–36.
———. *The Letters of Wyndham Lewis*. Edited by W. K. Rose. London: Methuen, 1963.
———. "A Man of the Week: Marinetti." In *Creatures of Habit and Creatures of Change*, 29–32.
———. "Our Wild Body." *New Age* 7.1 (May 5, 1910): 8–10.
———. "Physics of the Not Self." In *Enemy of the Stars*, 51–59.
———. "Prevalent Design." In *WLOA*, 117–128.
———. *Rude Assignment*. London: Hutchison, 1950.
———. *Self-Condemned*. Santa Barbara, Calif.: Black Sparrow Press, 1983.
———. "The Skeleton in the Cupboard Speaks." In *WLOA*, 334–345.
———. "Super-nature vs. Super-real." In *WLOA*, 303–333.
———. *Tarr: The 1918 Version*. Edited by Paul O'Keeffe. Santa Rosa, Calif.: Black Sparrow Press, 1990.
———. *Time and Western Man*. Santa Rosa, Calif.: Black Sparrow Press, 1993 (orig. pub. 1926).
———. "The Vorticists." In *WLOA*, 454–458.
———. *The Vulgar Streak*. Santa Barbara, Calif.: Black Sparrow Press, 1985 (orig. pub. 1941).
———. *The Wild Body*. London: Chatto and Windus, 1927.
———. *Wyndham Lewis on Art: Collected Writings, 1913–1956*. Introduced and with notes by Walter Michel and C. J. Fox. New York: Funk and Wagnalls, 1969.
Lidderdale, Jane, and Mary Nicholson. *Dear Miss Weaver*. New York: Viking Press, 1970.
Lipke, William C., and Bernard W. Rozran. "Ezra Pound and the Vorticists: A Polite Blast." *Wisconsin Studies in Contemporary Literature* 7 (1966): 201–210.
Lodge, Sir Oliver. *Pioneers of Science*. London: Macmillan, 1893.
Loewenstein, Andrea Freud. *Loathsome Jews and Engulfing Women: Metaphors of Projection in the Works of Wyndham Lewis, Charles Williams, and Graham Greene*. New York: New York Univ. Press, 1993.
London, Bette. *Writing Double: Women's Literary Partnerships*. Ithaca, N.Y.: Cornell Univ. Press, 1999.
Longenbach, James. *Stone Cottage: Pound, Yeats, and Modernism*. New York: Oxford Univ. Press, 1988.
Lyon, Janet. *Manifestoes: Provocations of the Modern*. Ithaca, N.Y.: Cornell Univ. Press, 1999.
———. "Militant Discourse, Strange Bedfellows: Suffragettes and Vorticists before the War." *differences: A Journal of Feminist Cultural Studies* 4.2 (1992): 100–133.
Marek, Jayne. *Women Editing Modernism: "Little" Magazines and Literary History*. Lexington: Univ. Press of Kentucky, 1995.
Marsh, Alec. *Money and Modernity: Pound, Williams, and the Spirit of Jefferson*. Tuscaloosa: Univ. of Alabama Press, 1998.

Materer, Timothy. "Make It Sell! Ezra Pound Advertises Modernism." In Dettmar and Watt, *Marketing Modernisms*, 17–36.

———. *Modernist Alchemy: Poetry and the Occult*. Ithaca, N.Y.: Cornell Univ. Press, 1995.

———. *Pound/Lewis*. New York: New Directions, 1985.

———. *Vortex: Pound, Eliot, and Lewis*. Ithaca, N.Y.: Cornell Univ. Press, 1979.

———. *Wyndham Lewis the Novelist*. Detroit: Wayne State Univ. Press, 1976.

Maxim, Hudson. *The Science of Poetry and the Philosophy of Language*. New York: Funk and Wagnalls, 1910.

McDonald, Gail. *Learning to Be Modern: Pound, Eliot, and the American University*. Oxford: Clarendon Press, 1993.

McDowell, Colin. "'The Completed Symbol': *Daimonic* Existence and the Great Wheel in *A Vision* (1937)." *Yeats Annual* 6 (1988): 193–208.

———. "The Six Disincarnate States of *A Vision* (1937)." *Yeats Annual* 4 (1986): 87–98.

———. "To 'Beat upon the Wall': Reading *A Vision*." *Yeats Annual* 4 (1986): 219–227.

McGann, Jerome. *Black Riders: The Visible Language of Modernism*. Princeton, N.J.: Princeton Univ. Press, 1993.

———. *The Textual Condition*. Princeton, N.J.: Princeton Univ. Press, 1991.

McLuhan, Marshall. *Counterblast*. New York: Harcourt, Brace, and World, 1969.

Meyers, Jeffrey. *The Enemy*. London: Routledge and Kegan Paul, 1980.

———, ed. *Wyndham Lewis: A Revaluation*. London: Athlone Press, 1980.

Michel, Walter. "Vorticism and the Early Wyndham Lewis." *Apollo* 77 (January 1963): 5–9.

Moi, Toril. *Sexual/Textual Politics*. New York: Routledge, 1985.

Monroe, Harriet. *A Poet's Life*. New York: Macmillan, 1938.

Morris, Adalaide. "The Concept of Projection: H.D.'s Visionary Powers." In Friedman and DuPlessis, *Signets*, 273–296.

Morrisson, Mark S. *The Public Face of Modernism: Little Magazines, Audiences, and Reception, 1905–1920*. Madison: Univ. of Wisconsin Press, 2001.

Morrow, Bradford. "Blueprint to the Vortex." Foreword to Lewis, *Blast 1*, v–viii.

Munton, Alan. "Fredric Jameson: *Fables of Aggression*" (review). In Cooney et al., *Blast 3*, 345–351.

Murphy, William. *Family Secrets: William Butler Yeats and His Relatives*. Syracuse, N.Y.: Syracuse Univ. Press, 1995.

———. "Psychic Daughter, Mystic Son, Sceptic Father." In G. Harper, *Yeats and the Occult*, 11–26.

Nelson, Cary. *Repression and Recovery: Modern American Poetry and the Politics of Cultural Memory, 1910–1945*. Madison: Univ. of Wisconsin Press, 1989.

Nevinson, C. R. W. *Paint and Prejudice*. London: Methuen Publishers, 1937.

Nicholls, Peter. *Ezra Pound: Politics, Economics, and Writing*. London: Macmillan, 1984.

———. *Modernisms: A Literary Guide*. Berkeley and Los Angeles: Univ. of California Press, 1995.

Nordau, Max. *Degeneration*. New York: Appleton, 1895.

Norman, Charles. *Ezra Pound*. New York: Funk and Wagnalls, 1969.

North, Michael. *The Political Aesthetic of Yeats, Eliot, and Pound*. New York: Cambridge Univ. Press, 1991.

Nott, Charles Stanley. *Teachings of Gurdjieff: The Journal of a Pupil: An Account of Some Years with G. I. Gurdjieff and A. R. Orage in New York and at Fontainebleau-Avon*. London: Routledge and Kegan Paul, 1961.

Oderman, Kevin. "'Cavalcanti': That the Body Is Not Evil." *Paideuma: A Journal Devoted to Ezra Pound Scholarship* 11.2 (Fall 1982): 257–279.

———. *Ezra Pound and the Erotic Medium*. Durham, N.C.: Duke Univ. Press, 1986.

O'Keeffe, Paul. *Some Sort of Genius: A Life of Wyndham Lewis*. London: Jonathan Cape, 2000.

Olney, James. "The Esoteric Flower: Yeats and Jung." In G. Harper, *Yeats and the Occult*, 27–54.

Orage, A. R. (writing as "R.H.C."). "Readers and Writers." *New Age* 15.10 (July 9, 1914): 229.

———. "Readers and Writers." *New Age* 15.11 (July 16, 1914): 253.

———. "Readers and Writers." *New Age* 15.19 (September 10, 1914): 449.

Ortega y Gasset, José. "The Dehumanization of Art." In *The Dehumanization of Art*, 3–54. Princeton, N.J.: Princeton Univ. Press, 1968.

Ostriker, Alicia. "No Rule of Procedure: The Open Poetics of H.D." In Friedman and DuPlessis, *Signets*, 336–351.

"Our Contemporaries." *Poetry* 5.1 (October 1914): 42–48.

Oxford English Dictionary. New ed. Vol. 6. Oxford: Clarendon Press, 1989.

Page, P. K. "Suffering." In *The Glass Air: Selected Poems*, 173, New York: Oxford Univ. Press, 1985.

Parker, Andrew. "Ezra Pound and the 'Economy' of Anti-Semitism." *Boundary 2* 11.1–2 (Fall–Winter 1982–1983): 103–128.

Parkinson, Thomas. "This Extraordinary Book." *Yeats Annual* 1 (1982): 195–206.

Patke, Rajeev S. *The Long Poems of Wallace Stevens: An Interpretive Study*. Cambridge: Cambridge Univ. Press, 1985.

Pearce, Donald R. "The Systematic Rose." *Yeats Annual* 4 (1986): 195–200.

Pease, Donald. "Patriarchy, Lentricchia, and Male Feminization." *Critical Inquiry* 14 (Winter 1988): 379–385.

Peppis, Paul. "Surrounded by a Multitude of Other Blasts: Vorticism and the Great War." *Modernism/Modernity* 4.2 (April 1997): 39–66.

Perloff, Marjorie. *The Futurist Moment: Avant-Garde, Avant-Guerre, and the Language of Rupture*. Chicago: Univ. of Chicago Press, 1986.

———. "Modernist Studies." In *Redrawing the Boundaries*, edited by Stephen Greenblatt and Giles Gunn, 154–178. New York: Modern Language Association of America, 1992.

———. *Twenty-first Century Modernism: The "New" Poetics*. Malden, Mass.: Blackwell, 2002.

Plato. *The Collected Dialogues of Plato*. Edited by Edith Hamilton and Huntington Cairns. Princeton, N.J.: Princeton Univ. Press, 1961.

Poggioli, Renato. *Theory of the Avant-Garde*. Translated by Gerald Fitzgerald. Cambridge, Mass.: Harvard Univ. Press, 1968.

Pound, Ezra. *ABC of Reading*. New York: New Directions, 1960 (orig. pub. 1934).

———. "Affirmations II: Vorticism." *New Age* 16.11 (January 14, 1915): 277–278.

———. "Anno nuovo (mirabilis?)." *L'Indice* 2.20/21 (December 25, 1931): 5.

———. "Art Notes: Building: Ornamentation!" *New Age* 23.20 (September 12, 1918): 320 (signed "B. H. Dias").

———. "Ave Roma." *Il Mare* 7 (January 1933): 3–4.

———. "Brancusi." *Little Review* 8 (Autumn 1921): 3–7.

———. *The Cantos*. New York: New Directions, 1986.

———. "Cavalcanti." In *LE*, 149–200.

———. "The Death of Vorticism." *Little Review* 5.10–11 (February–March 1919): 45, 48.

———. *DK/Some Letters of Ezra Pound*. Edited by Louis Dudek. Montréal: DC Books, 1974.

———. "Epstein, Belgion, and Meaning." *Criterion* 9.36 (April 1930): 470–475.
———. *Ezra and Dorothy Pound: Letters in Captivity, 1945–1946*. Edited by Omar Pound and Robert Spoo. New York: Oxford Univ. Press, 1999.
———. *Ezra Pound and Dorothy Shakespear: Their Letters, 1909–1914*. Edited by Omar Pound and A. Walton Litz. New York: New Directions, 1984.
———. *Ezra Pound and James Laughlin: Selected Letters*. Edited by David Gordon. New York: Norton, 1994.
———. *Ezra Pound and the Visual Arts*. Edited by Harriet Zinnes. New York: New Directions, 1980.
———. *Ezra Pound's Poetry and Prose: Contributions to Periodicals*. Edited by Lea Baechler, A. Walton Litz, and James Longenbach. 10 vols. New York: Garland, 1991.
———. "Gaudier: A Postscript." *Esquire*, August 1934, 72–75.
———. *Gaudier-Brzeska*. New York: New Directions, 1970 (orig. pub. 1916).
———. *Guide to Kulchur*. New York: New Directions, 1970 (orig. pub. 1938).
———. "*I Cease Not to Yowl*": Ezra Pound's Letters to Olivia Rossetti Agresti. Edited by Demetres Tryphonopoulos and Leon Surette. Chicago: Univ. of Illinois Press, 1998.
———. Interview published in *La Stampa*, Turin (between January and April 1932). Reprinted in *P&P* 5:334.
———. *Jefferson and/or Mussolini*. New York: Liveright, 1970 (orig. pub. 1935).
———. *Letters of Ezra Pound*. Edited by D. D. Paige. New York: Harcourt, Brace, 1950.
———. *Literary Essays*. Edited by T. S. Eliot. Norfolk, Conn.: New Directions, 1954.
———. *Personae*. Edited by Lea Baechler and A. Walton Litz. New York: New Directions, 1990.
———. "Postscript to *The Natural Philosophy of Love* by Remy de Gourmont." In *Pavannes and Divagations* by Ezra Pound, 203–214. Norfolk, Conn.: New Directions, 1958.
———. *Pound/Lewis: The Letters of Ezra Pound and Wyndham Lewis*. Edited by Timothy Materer. New York: New Directions, 1985.
———. *Pound/Williams: Selected Letters of Ezra Pound and William Carlos Williams*. Edited by Hugh Witemeyer. New York: New Directions, 1996.
———. *Pound/Zukofsky: Selected Letters of Ezra Pound and Louis Zukofsky*. Edited by Barry Ahearn. New York: New Directions, 1987.
———. *Selected Prose, 1909–1965*. Edited by William Cookson. New York: New Directions, 1973.
———. "The Serious Artist." *The New Freewoman* 1.9 (October 15, 1913): 161–163.
———. *The Spirit of Romance*. New York: New Directions, 1952 (orig. pub. 1910).
———. "Terra Italica." In *SP*, 54–60.
———. *The Translations of Ezra Pound*. London: Faber and Faber, 1953 (orig. pub. 1910).
———. "The Wisdom of Poetry." In *SP*, 359–362 (orig. pub. 1912).
———. "Wyndham Lewis." *Egoist* (June 15, 1914): 233–234.
Quéma, Anne. *The Agon of Modernism: Wyndham Lewis's Allegories, Aesthetics, and Politics*. Lewisburg, Penn.: Bucknell Univ. Press, 1999.
Rabaté, Jean-Michel. *Language, Sexuality, and Ideology in Pound's Cantos*. New York: Macmillan, 1986.
Rado, Lisa, ed. *Re-reading Modernism: New Directions in Feminist Criticism*. New York: Garland, 1994.
Rae, Patricia. "From Mystical Gaze to Pragmatic Game: Representations of Truth in Vorticist Art." *ELH: A Journal of English Literary History* 56.3 (Fall 1989): 689–720.

Rainey, Lawrence. "Canon, Gender, Text: The Case of H.D." In Bornstein, *Representing Modernist Texts*, 99–123.

———. "The Creation of the Avant-Garde: F. T. Marinetti and Ezra Pound." *Modernism/Modernity* 1.3 (September 1994): 195–219.

———. *Ezra Pound and the Monument of Culture: Text, History, and the Malatesta Cantos*. Chicago: Univ. of Chicago Press, 1991.

———. *Institutions of Modernism: Literary Elites and Public Culture*. New Haven, Conn.: Yale Univ. Press, 1998.

Ransom, Will. *Private Presses and Their Books*. New York: Bowker, 1929.

Ransome, Arthur. *Oscar Wilde: A Critical Study*. New York: Haskell House, 1971 (orig. pub. 1912).

Redman, Tim. *Ezra Pound and Italian Fascism*. New York: Cambridge Univ. Press, 1991.

Reynolds, Paige. "'Chaos Invading Concept': *Blast* as a Native Theory of Promotional Culture." *Twentieth Century Literature* 46.2 (Summer 2000): 238–268.

Robinson, Janice S. *H.D.: The Life and Work of an American Poet*. Boston: Houghton Mifflin, 1982.

Ruskin, John. *The Stones of Venice*. Vol. 2. London: Dent, 1907.

Saddlemyer, Ann. *Becoming George: The Life of Mrs. W. B. Yeats*. London: Oxford Univ. Press, 2002.

Schnapp, Jeffrey. "Epic Demonstrations: Fascist Modernity and the 1932 Exhibition of the Fascist Revolution." In Golsan, *Fascism*, 1–32.

———. "Propeller Talk." *Modernism/Modernity* 1.3 (September 1994): 153–178.

Schneidau, Herbert N. "Vorticism and the Career of Ezra Pound." *Modern Philology* 65 (February 1968): 214–227.

Schuchard, Ronald. *Eliot's Dark Angel: Intersections of Life and Art*. New York: Oxford Univ. Press, 1999.

Schulze, Robin. "The Frigate Pelican's Progress: Marianne Moore's Multiple Versions and Modernist Practice." In *Gendered Modernisms: American Women Poets and Their Readers*, edited by Margaret Dickie and Thomas Travisano, 117–139. Philadelphia: Univ. of Pennsylvania Press, 1996.

———. *The Web of Friendship: Marianne Moore and Wallace Stevens*. Ann Arbor: Univ. of Michigan Press, 1995.

Scott, Bonnie Kime, ed. *The Gender of Modernism*. Bloomington: Indiana Univ. Press, 1990.

———. "Jellyfish and Treacle: Lewis, Joyce, Gender, and Modernism." In *Coping with Joyce*, edited by Morris Beja and Shari Benstock, 168–179. Columbus: Ohio State Univ. Press, 1989.

Sedgwick, Eve Kosofsky. *Between Men: English Literature and Homosocial Desire*. New York: Columbia Univ. Press, 1985.

———. *Epistemology of the Closet*. Berkeley and Los Angeles: Univ. of California Press, 1990.

Seltzer, Mark. "The Love Master." In Boone and Cadden, *Engendering Men*, 140–160.

Sheppard, Richard W. "Wyndham Lewis's *Tarr*: An (Anti-)Vorticist Novel?" *Journal of English and Germanic Philology* 88.4 (October 1989): 510–530.

Sherry, Vincent. "Anatomy of Folly: Wyndham Lewis, the Body Politic, and Comedy." *Modernism/Modernity* 4.2 (April 1997): 121–138.

———. *Ezra Pound, Wyndham Lewis, and Radical Modernism*. New York: Oxford Univ. Press, 1993.

Showalter, Elaine. *Sexual Anarchy: Gender and Culture at the Fin de Siècle*. New York: Viking, 1990.

Shugar, Dana. "Faustine Re-membered: H.D.'s Use of Swinburne's Poetry in *Hermione*." *Sagetrieb* 9.1–2 (Spring–Fall 1990): 79–94.

Sickert, Walter. "On Swiftness." *New Age* 14.21 (March 26, 1914): 655–656.

Sieburth, Richard. "In Pound We Trust: The Economy of Poetry/The Poetry of Economics." *Critical Inquiry* 14.1 (Autumn 1987): 142–172.

Sinfield, Alan. *The Wilde Century: Effeminacy, Oscar Wilde, and the Queer Moment*. New York: Columbia Univ. Press, 1994.

Slatin, Myles. "A History of Pound's *Cantos* I–XVI, 1915–1925." *American Literature* 35 (1963): 183–195.

Smith, Paul. "H.D.'s Flaws." *Iowa Review* 16.3 (Fall 1986): 77–86.

Spackman, Barbara. "Mafarka and Son: Marinetti's Homophobic Economics." *Modernism/Modernity* 1.3 (September 1994): 89–107.

Spoo, Robert. "H.D. Prosed: The Future of an Imagist Poet." In Witemeyer, *The Future of Modernism*, 201–221.

Starr, Alan. "*Tarr* and Wyndham Lewis." *ELH: A Journal of English Literary History* 49 (1982): 179–189.

Stock, Noel. *The Life of Ezra Pound*. New York: Pantheon, 1970.

Stone, Marla. *The Patron State: Culture and Politics in Fascist Italy*. Princeton, N.J.: Princeton Univ. Press, 1998.

———. "The Politics of Cultural Production: The Exhibition in Fascist Italy, 1928–1942." PhD diss., Princeton University, 1990.

———. "Staging Fascism: The Exhibition of the Fascist Revolution." *Journal of Contemporary History* 28.2 (April 1993): 215–243.

Stoppard, Tom. *Arcadia*. London: Faber and Faber, 1993.

Surette, Leon. *The Birth of Modernism: Ezra Pound, T. S. Eliot, and the Occult*. Montréal: McGill Queen's Univ. Press, 1993.

———. *A Light from Eleusis*. Oxford: Clarendon Press, 1979.

———. *Pound in Purgatory: From Economic Radicalism to Anti-Semitism*. Chicago: Univ. of Illinois Press, 1999.

Sword, Helen. *Engendering Inspiration: Visionary Strategies in Rilke, Lawrence, and H.D.* Ann Arbor: Univ. of Michigan Press, 1995.

Terrell, Carroll. "Mang Tze, Thomas Taylor, and Madam YLH." *Paideuma: A Journal Devoted to Ezra Pound Scholarship* 7.1–2 (Spring/Fall 1978): 141–175.

Thacker, Andrew. "Dora Marsden and *The Egoist*: 'Our War Is with Words.'" *English Literature in Transition, 1880–1920* 36.2 (1993): 179–196.

Tickner, Lisa. "Men's Work? Masculinity and Modernism." *differences: A Journal of Feminist Cultural Studies* 4.3 (1992): 1–37.

Travis, S. "A Crack in the Ice: Subjectivity and the Mirror in H.D.'s *Her*." *Sagetrieb* 6.2 (Fall 1987): 123–140.

Tryphonopoulos, Demetres. *The Celestial Tradition: A Study of Ezra Pound's* The Cantos. Waterloo, Ontario: Wilfrid Laurier Univ. Press, 1992.

———. "'Fragments of a Faith Forgotten': Ezra Pound, H.D., and the Occult Tradition." *Paid-*

euma: Studies in American and British Modernist Poetry 32.1–3 (Spring, Fall, and Winter 2003): 229–244.

Vendler, Helen. *Yeats's "Vision" and the Later Plays*. Cambridge, Mass.: Harvard Univ. Press, 1963.

Verstl, Ina. "*Tarr*—A Joke Too Deep for Laughter? The Comic, the Body, and Gender." *Enemy News: Newsletter of the Wyndham Lewis Society* 33 (Winter 1991): 4–9.

Wade, Allan. *A Bibliography of the Writings of William Butler Yeats*. 3rd ed. Revised and edited by Russell K. Alspach. London: Hart-Davis, 1968.

Wees, William C. "Pound's Vorticism: Some New Evidence and Further Comments." *Wisconsin Studies in Contemporary Literature* 7 (1966): 211–216.

———. *Vorticism and the English Avant-Garde*. Toronto: Univ. of Toronto Press, 1972.

———. "Wyndham Lewis and Vorticism." In Cooney et al., *Blast 3*, 47–50.

Whistler, James Abbott McNeill. *The Gentle Art of Making Enemies*. London: William Heinemann, 1929.

Whittier-Ferguson, John. *Framing Pieces: Designs of the Gloss in Joyce, Woolf, and Pound*. New York: Oxford Univ. Press, 1996.

Wilde, Oscar. *Complete Works of Oscar Wilde*. New York: Harper and Row, 1989.

Willison, Ian, Warwick Gould, and Warren Chernaik, eds. *Modernist Writers and the Marketplace*. London: Macmillan Press, 1996.

Witemeyer, Hugh, ed. *The Future of Modernism*. Ann Arbor: Univ. of Michigan Press, 1997.

Worringer, Wilhelm. *Abstraction and Empathy*. Translated by Michael Bullock. New York: International Universities Press, 1953.

Wutz, Michael. "The Energetics of *Tarr*: The Vortex Machine Kreisler." *Modern Fiction Studies* 38.4 (Winter 1992): 845–869.

Yeats, William Butler. *The Collected Works of W. B. Yeats*. Vol. 5: *Later Essays*. Edited by William H. O'Donnell with assistance from Elizabeth Bergmann Loizeaux. New York: Scribner's, 1994.

———. *A Critical Edition of Yeats's "A Vision" (1925)*. Edited by George Mills Harper and Walter Kelly Hood. New York: Macmillan, 1978.

———. *Essays and Introductions*. New York: Macmillan, 1961.

———. *Explorations*. New York: Macmillan, 1962.

———. *The Letters of William Butler Yeats*. Edited by Allan Wade. London: Hart-Davis, 1954.

———. *Per Amica Silentia Lunae*. London: Macmillan, 1918.

———. *The Variorum Edition of the Poems of W. B. Yeats*. Edited by Peter Allt and Robert K. Alspach. New York: Macmillan, 1965.

———. *A Vision*. Rev. ed. New York: Macmillan, 1956.

———. *Yeats's "Vision" Papers*. Edited by George Mills Harper, with the assistance of Mary Jane Harper. Vol. 1, *The Automatic Script: 5 November 1917–18 June 1919*, edited by Steve L. Adams, Barbara J. Freiling, and Sandra L. Sprayberry. Vol. 2, *The Automatic Script: 25 June 1918–29 March 1920*, edited by Steve L. Adams, Barbara J. Freiling, and Sandra L. Sprayberry. Vol. 3, *Sleep and Dream Notebooks 1 and 2, Card File*, edited by Robert Anthony Martinich and Margaret Mills Harper. Iowa City: Univ. of Iowa Press, 1992.

Young, Suzanne. "Between Science and the 'New Psychology': An Examination of H.D.'s Sociohistorical Consciousness." *Tulsa Studies in Women's Literature* 14.2 (Fall 1995): 325–345.

The ABC of Economics (Pound), 95
ABC of Reading (Pound), 101
abstraction, 45, 118, 141–144, 258n.19, 290n.27, 304n.53
Abstraction and Empathy (Worringer), 15–18, 143
Adams, Hazard, 236–237, 256n.3, 304n.55
"Advent" (H.D.), 188, 199, 300n.29
Aestheticism and Aesthetes: and "effeminacy," xviii, 14, 19, 41, 47–48, 50–51; male Aesthete androgyne, 19, 41, 260n.34, 261n.37, 265n.30; and Nature, 58–59, 61, 85; and Omega Workshops, 47–48, 50, 69; relationship of *Blast* with, 37–42; Vorticism and Wildean Aestheticism, 50–61, 72–75, 88, 245–247; and *The Yellow Book*, 38, 39–41, 65, 69–70, 265n.28. *See also* "effeminacy"
Agassiz, Louis, 128, 285n.101
aggression. *See* violence
Albright, Daniel, 213, 258n.21
Aldington, Richard, 33, 75, 76, 137–138, 263n.14, 264n.17
Alfieri, Dino, 281n.67
Altman, Meryl, 181, 293n.42
Ambelain, Robert, 190, 200, 300n.26
anti-Semitism, 128, 130, 273n.6
Apes of God (Lewis), 304n.53
Apollinaire, Guillaume, 36
Aquinas, Thomas, 227, 236
Arbuthnot, Malcolm, 3
Arcadia (Stoppard), xiii–xiv
architecture, 116–117, 121–122, 283n.87

Aristotle, 71, 78, 144, 289n.19
The Art of Being Ruled (Lewis), 270n.67, 271–272n.83
Asphodel (H.D.), 139, 287n.7
Auden, W. H., xvi, 11–12, 129, 258n.20, 276n.26
Augustine, Jane, 287n.11, 297n.12, 302n.41
Autobiographies (Yeats), 226, 303n.50
Autobiography (Yeats), 214–215, 223, 226, 303n.50

Balla, Giacomo, 27, 68, 151
Balzac, Honoré de, 190
Barnes, Djuna, 179
Baudelaire, Charles, 50
Bauman, Zygmunt, 13–14
Beardsley, Aubrey, 40, 62, 70, 265n.26, 269n.56
Beatty, Michael, 77, 82, 271n.74
Bechhöfer, C. E., 33
Beerbohm, Max, 58, 62, 269n.56
Bell, Clive, 4, 48, 53, 54
Bell, Ian, 22, 45, 118, 256n.3, 267n.40, 283n.85
Bell, Vanessa, 47
Benstock, Shari, 7, 258n.16
Benton, Thomas Hart, 128, 285n.101
Bergson, Henri, 197–198, 299n.23
Bersani, Leo, 183, 272n.84, 293n.44
Besant, Annie, 22–23, 259n.26, 260n.31, 299n.25
bibliographic/al code, 30, 99, 263n.12, 276n.29, 277n.32
Bid Me to Live (H.D.), 136, 183, 294n.47

Index

Bird, William, 89, 121–122, 123, 124
Black Sparrow Press, 27, 33
Blackstone, William, 128
Black Sun Press, 125
Blake, William, xiv, 190, 227, 230
Blast: and Aestheticist precursors, 37–42; artwork in, 34, 66–68, 272n.1; on Balla and Marinetti, 27; campaign against effeminacy by, 46–51; compared with other little magazines, 263n.13, 265n.24; compared with *The Yellow Book*, 39–42, 265n.26; covers of, 29, 30, 67–68; and *fin de siècle*, 36–42, 57–58; Gaudier-Brzeska's manifesto in, 283n.82; geometrics of, 21, 42, 66–68, 151; as "history book," 27–28, 36; and Kandinsky, 5, 16, 193–194; literary selections of, 68, 135, 264n.17, 269n.64; on machinery, 21; and monstrosity, 29, 32; and myths of origin, 34–36; on occult, 193–194, 250; on Omega Workshops, 48; Orage on demise of, 258n.14; physical appearance of, 29–32, 35–38, 41–42, 68, 263nn.9–10; possibility of publishing third issue of, 100, 277n.36; publication dates of, xiv, 3, 7, 27, 32–33, 109, 258n.16; reprint of, 27, 33–34; reviews of, 33, 263–264nn.14–15, 265n.24; significance of, 33–36; on Vortex, 280n.62; and Vorticist/geometric body, 143–144, 151; Vorticist manifestoes in, 43–44, 48, 49, 53, 58, 59, 68, 80, 82, 84–85, 250; on Vorticist painting, 4–5; and Wildean Aestheticism, 42, 50–51, 57–58, 59, 260n.34; and Yeats, 9. *See also Enemy of the Stars* (Lewis)
Blavatsky, Madame Helena, 12, 22, 189, 190, 193–194, 199, 259n.26, 294n.1, 296n.7, 297n.12, 298n.18
Bloom, Harold, 193
Bloomsbury group, 4, 5, 47–48, 54, 69, 267n.39
body: ascetic attitude toward, 147; childbearing body, 145, 157–159, 167–169, 171, 293n.41; and Hellenism, 292n.36; Heywood on alleged modernist contempt for, 288–289n.17; mystical "subtle body," 145, 165, 171, 286n.2, 290n.23; in *Notes on Thought and Vision*, 157–159, 167–171, 291n.32; Ortega y Gasset on, 288n.15; and Pater, 144; in Pound's "Cavalcanti," 146–148, 169, 288–289n.17, 292–293n.41. *See also* Vorticist/geometric body
Boehme, Jakob, 199, 227
Bomberg, David, 3, 6, 17, 47, 257n.8, 269n.62
books: as artifacts, 121–122, 276–277n.31; bibliographic/al code of, 30, 99, 263n.12, 276n.29, 277n.32; deluxe editions of, 89–92, 97, 99, 121–125, 127, 273n.2, 277n.32; format of Pound's books, 90–92, 97–99, 121–128, 273n.2, 285n.100; and publishing industry, 124–126, 284nn.92–93; and typefaces, 282n.76
Borgia, Lucrezia, 289n.19
Bornstein, George, 99, 263n.12
Botar, Oliver, 266n.35
Bradbury, Malcolm, 262n.5
Brancusi, Constantin, 16, 194, 237–238
Brown, Capability, xiii
Bryher: attitude of, on occult, 298–299n.19; and collaborations with H.D., 232, 304n.52; on H.D.'s father, 217, 302n.42; and H.D.'s visions, 167, 187–188, 229, 230, 232–233; and H.D.'s work in mysticism, 195, 219–220, 298–299n.19; house of, 285n.1
Burke, Edmund, 207, 209, 210
Burnett, Gary, 135–136, 155, 156, 258n.17, 291n.29
Burnshaw, Stanley, 95
Buss, Kate, 122
Butler, Judith, 61, 265n.30, 289n.19
Bynum, Caroline Walker, 144

The Caliph's Design (Lewis), 21, 53–55, 73
The Cantos (Pound): deluxe editions of, 89–92, 99, 121–124, 127, 273n.2, 277n.32; economic and political themes in, 95, 111, 126, 274n.12, 282n.74; on Eleusinian mysteries, 290n.22; and Eliot's *Waste Land*, 283–284n.89; and H.D.'s poetry,

287n.12; illustrated pages of, 90–91; on Lucrezia Borgia, 289n.19; Malatesta Cantos, 92, 283–284n.89; on Marinetti, 102, 278–279n.48; McLuhan on, 130; on Mostra della Rivoluzione Fascista (MRF) exhibition, 105; publication of, in 1930s and 1950s, 284n.91, 285n.100; on Yeats, 9
Carpenter, Edward, 52
Carson, Sir Edward, 53
Casillo, Robert, 102, 281n.66
Castiglione, Baldassare, 304n.55
"Cavalcanti" (Pound), 146–148, 169, 288–289n.17, 290n.21, 290n.24, 292–293n.41
Cendrars, Blaise, 129–130
Cerf, Bennett, 284n.92
Cerio, F. Ferruccio, 101, 278n.41
Cézanne, Paul, 14, 16
Chaboseau, Jean, 190
Chace, William, xvi, 276n.23
Chadwick, Mary, 137
Chesterton, G. K., 289n.18
childbearing, 145, 157–159, 167–169, 171, 184, 293n.41
Childs, Peter, 263n.6
Chisholm, Dianne, 160, 181–182, 286n.6, 292n.35, 292n.40
"The City" (Pound), 116
Cixous, Hélène, 140
Coburn, Alvin, 3, 100
"Code of a Herdsman" (Lewis), 73
Colbourne, Maurice, 126
Collecott, Diana, 293n.43
Compassionate Friendship (H.D.), 285n.1, 299n.24
Confucius, 127, 129, 285n.101
Conrad, Joseph, 261n.37
Coote, Stephen, 192
Cork, Richard, xvii, 6, 7, 31, 32, 69, 256n.6, 257n.8, 260n.32, 264n.19, 269n.62, 272–273n.1
Counterblast (McLuhan), 262n.1
Cox-McCormack, Nancy, 281n.64
Craig, Cairns, xvi, 276n.23
"Creation" (Lewis), 69
Croce, Benedetto, 209
Crosby, Caresse, 125, 284n.93

Crown, Kathleen, 156, 158, 291n.30, 291n.32
Cubism, xviii, 2, 5–6, 10, 16, 17, 18, 43, 48, 193, 256n.7
Cullingford, Elizabeth Butler, xvi, 208–209, 261n.38, 276n.23
culture, 110–111, 113–115, 130–131, 281n.70, 281–282n.73, 282–283n.79
Cunard, Nancy, 89, 124, 273n.2

dandyism, 52, 53, 57–58, 87, 269n.56. *See also* "effeminacy"
Dante, xiv, 121
Darantière, Maurice, 285n.1
Dasenbrock, Reed Way, xvii, xviii, 5–7, 14, 15, 66, 75, 256n.3, 256–257nn.6–8, 257n.13, 258n.19, 260n.30, 264n.17, 265–266n.31, 266n.35, 270n.73
Davidson, Eugene, 95
decadents, 40, 55, 260n.34, 261n.37, 265n.30
"The Decay of Lying" (Wilde), 58–60
"The Dehumanization of Art" (Ortega y Gasset), 142–143, 288nn.15–16
Del Mar, Alexander, 128, 285n.101
Descartes, René, xiv, 22, 283n.85
"Desert Geometry or the Gift of Harun Al-Raschid" (Yeats), 223
Diepeveen, Leonard, 12
"Dijon Series" (H.D.), 285n.1, 287nn.8–9
Dismorr, Jessica, 3, 68, 274n.8
Dodsworth, Edmondo, 278n.43
Doolittle, Charles Leander, 217–222
Douglas, C. H., 94, 274n.11
Douglas, Lord Alfred, 52, 62
Dramatis Personae (Yeats), 201
Drogheda, Countess of, 79
Duchamp, Marcel, 2
Dudek, Louis, 128
DuPlessis, Rachel Blau, 137–140, 156, 157, 176, 178, 183, 286nn.5–6, 287n.9, 291n.32, 292n.37
Dworkin, Craig, 112, 282n.76

Ede, H. S., 197
Edelman, Lee, 85
Edmunds, Susan, 140, 286nn.5–6
"effeminacy": and Aestheticism, xviii, 14, 19,

321

Index

41, 47–48; associated with Wilde, 19, 25; characteristics and mannerisms associated with, 18, 19, 20, 53–54; and *Enemy of the Stars*, 74–75, 77–87, 272n.83; and male homosexuality, 19, 20, 41, 52–55; of Omega Workshop artists, 47–48; and sentimentality and romanticism, 49–50; and sodomy and dandyism, 52, 53, 56, 87; and *Tarr*, 272n.83; Vorticist campaign against, xvi, 10, 18–20, 41, 46–51, 70, 73, 87–88, 245–247

Egoist, 94, 270n.66, 277n.33

Eliade, Mircea, 294n.1, 296n.6

Eliot, T. S.: compared with H.D., 287; and Dorothy Shakespear's artwork, 92; *Four Quartets* by, 287; on Marianne Moore's poetry, 94; masculine aesthetic of, 261n.37; and occult, 187, 295n.5; on Pound's "Cavalcanti," 147, 290n.21; and Social Credit, 95; and Symbolist poets, 246; *The Waste Land* by, 109, 283–284n.89; writings by, in *Others* magazines, 264n.18

Ellerman, Winifred Bryher. *See* Bryher

Ellis, Edwin, 190

Ellmann, Richard, 208, 213, 269n.59, 269n.61, 295–296nn.5–6

Empedocles, xiv, 199, 228, 230, 236

Enemy of the Stars (Lewis): beginning of, 78–79; compared with *Nights*, 175–176; critics on, 33, 75, 270–271nn.70–74; different versions of, 11, 76, 77–78; and effeminacy, 74–75, 77–87, 272n.83; eroticism in, 150, 151–153; as failure, 75–77, 271n.74; geometric idiom in, xvi; Lewis's commentary on, 59, 271n.80; linguistic strategies of, 75, 76–78, 270n.72, 271n.74, 271n.82; masculinity in, 69, 70; and Nature, 74–75, 77, 79–82, 84–87, 269n.54, 271n.80; radio version of, 271n.75; structure of, 271n.77; violence in, 68, 74–75, 78, 79–85, 149, 150, 151–152; Vorticist/geometric body in, 149, 150, 151–152; Vorticist perspective of, 75, 271n.82; and Wildean Aestheticism, 61

Epstein, Jacob: and Hulme, 16, 17, 141, 143–144, 167; monument for Wilde's tomb by, 64, 65; Pound on, 101, 149; Sickert on, 70; and Vorticism, 3, 141, 257n.8, 269n.62

eroticism: and electricity, 165, 175–176, 183; in *Enemy of the Stars*, 150, 151–152; in *HERmione*, 173, 174–175, 183, 241–242, 293–294n.46; in *Nights*, 159–162, 163–168, 172, 174–178, 181–184, 294n.46; in Pound's writing, 145, 150, 290n.22; and sadomasochism, 12, 85, 86, 176, 184, 272n.84; in *Tarr*, 150, 152–154

Esposizione del Decennio. *See* Mostra della Rivoluzione Fascista (MRF) exhibition

Etchells, Frederick: art of, in *Blast*, 34; Hulme on, 17; Mansard Gallery exhibit (1920) of, 274n.8; and Omega Workshops, 4, 5, 46–48; translations of Le Corbusier's writings by, 3; and Vorticist manifesto, 257n.8, 269n.62

Euclid, xiii, xiv, 236

Expressionism, 2, 5, 43, 48–49, 151, 193–194

Eysteinsson, Astradur, 263n.7

Fascism: documentary on Mussolini's regime, 101, 278n.41; and Futurism, 279–280n.54; historicization of Pound's relationship to, 98–99; Irish Fascism, 208, 301n.38; Mostra della Rivoluzione Fascista exhibition on, xviii, 89, 96–97, 104–112, 279–280nn.54–60, 280n.63, 281n.67, 282n.77; and Pound's attempted revival of Vorticism, 12, 25, 95–98, 100–104, 242, 247–248; Pound's meeting with Mussolini, 101; Pound's sympathy for, xv, xvi–xvii, xviii, 12, 25, 93, 98–99, 130, 207, 247–248; and Yeats, 207–210, 301n.38, 304n.54

femininity. *See* "effeminacy"

feminism of H.D., 24, 156–157, 179–180, 183–184, 248–249

femme fatale, 246, 260n.34, 261n.37, 265n.30, 294n.46

Fenollosa, Ernest, 117, 118–119, 283n.83

fin de siècle, 27–28, 36–42, 55–58, 65, 69–70, 246–247

Finneran, Richard, 300n.27
Flaubert, Gustave, 228, 230
Flory, Wendy, 77, 270n.70, 271n.73
Ford, Ford Madox, 33, 263n.14, 269n.64
Forster, E. M., 52–53
Foshay, Toby, 75, 77, 270n.73
Foucault, Michel, 52, 267n.42
Freddi, Luigi, 281n.67
Freud, Sigmund: compared with H.D.'s father, 222; dog of, 234; and H.D.'s interest in astrology, 220; H.D.'s sessions with, xvi, 12–13, 137, 178, 188, 198, 200, 201, 202, 211–212, 213, 230, 233–234, 248, 285n.1, 301n.40; and melancholia, 163. *See also Tribute to Freud* (H.D.)
Friedman, Susan Stanford, 24, 137, 139–141, 156–158, 176–177, 178–180, 192, 220, 261–262n.39, 286nn.5–6, 287nn.11–12, 291n.31, 292n.37, 292n.40, 297n.14, 298n.16, 298–299n.19, 299n.24, 301n.39
Frobenius, Leo, 110, 111, 114, 115, 281n.70, 281–282n.73
Fry, Roger, 2, 4, 16, 46–49, 54–55
Frye, Northrop, 196
Futurism, Italian: and automobiles and airplanes, 68, 86–87, 151; *Blast* on, 16, 49; and geometric art, 2, 16, 18, 68; and Italian Fascism, 279–280n.54; and machinery, 21, 155–156; Pound on, 103–104; and Theosophy, 194; and violence, 68, 151–152, 155–156; and Vorticism, xviii, 5–6, 10, 21, 43, 86, 102, 104, 151, 193, 264n.15, 273n.3, 278n.44, 278n.46, 289n.18; and Wilde, 50

Gallup, Donald, 273n.3
Gaudier-Brzeska, Henri: biography of, 197; death of, 100; and geometric line, 118; Hulme on, 17; manifesto of artistic principles by, 283n.82; Pound on, 100, 147–148, 149, 277n.33, 281n.65; "Red Stone Dancer" by, 147–148; Sickert on, 70; studio of, 111; and Vorticism, 3, 45–46, 92, 101; on Vorticism's manliness, 71
Gelpi, Albert, 139, 158, 180
Gentile, Giovanni, 209

geometric body. *See* Vorticist/geometric body
geometry/geometrics: Bauman on, 13–14; and *Blast*, 41–42, 66–68; definition of, xiv, 14; diagonal lines in Vorticist art, 66–68; geometric bias, 41, 265–266n.31; and H.D., 2, 137, 154–171, 191, 193, 196–202, 204–205, 212, 234–235, 239–244, 248; Hulme on, 15–21, 45, 119, 197, 246, 259n.25, 260n.30, 260nn.32–33; Le Corbusier on, 2, 3, 13; Lewis on, 4, 37, 44–45, 255n.2; lines in architecture, 116–117; and machinery, 20–21, 23, 45, 155–156, 260n.35; and mystical revelation/visionary knowledge, xv, 9, 191, 192–193, 196–205, 212–213, 235–244, 299n.22, 301n.34; Nature versus, 43–44; and occult, xvii, 22–23; and Pound generally, 1–2, 10, 26, 146–149, 242, 283n.85; Pound on the geometric "clean line," 11, 25, 92, 96, 97–98, 111–112, 115–121, 123–124, 129, 146, 147, 290n.24; and science, 21–22; significance of and associations with, xiii, xiv, 13–20, 22; and Theosophy, 194; and violence, 66–68, 151, 155–157, 165–167, 172, 174, 198, 248; and vortices, 2, 22, 109, 280n.62, 284n.97; of Vorticism, xiv, xv, xviii, 4–6, 14, 18–20, 41–46, 88, 118–120, 193, 194, 196–197, 246–247, 249–250, 266n.35; and Yeats, xv, 2, 9, 12, 191–193, 196–204, 212–213, 228, 235–240, 243–244, 250, 301n.34. *See also* Vorticist/geometric body
Gertler, Mark, 47
The Gift (H.D.), 214, 217, 229, 287n.7, 287n.11, 297n.11, 297n.13, 302n.41
Gilbert, Sandra M., 261n.37
Gilbert, W. S., 266n.38
Gill, Winifred, 47
Grant, Duncan, 47
Graver, David, xvii, 7, 270n.71
Gray, Cecil, 138
Gregg, Frances, 190
Gregory, Eileen, 144, 182, 292n.36, 293n.43
Gregory, Lady Augusta, 198, 201, 227, 299n.23

Grierson, H. J. C., 207
Grigson, Geoffrey, 266n.35
Gropius, Walter, 2, 282n.77
Grosvenor Gallery, 266n.38
Group X, 274n.8
Gubar, Susan, 261n.37
Guest, Barbara, 8, 218, 285n.1, 286n.3
Guide to Kulchur (Pound), xvi, 101, 111, 114–115, 126, 191, 281n.72
Gynopoetics of H.D., 137, 140–141, 156–159, 183, 286n.5, 287n.11, 291n.31

Hamilton, Cuthbert, 3, 4, 5, 17, 46–47, 274n.8
Hamnet, Nina, 47
Harland, Henry, 265n.28
Harper, George, 295n.3, 297n.9, 297n.14
Harrison, Victoria, 301–302n.40
H.D.: ambivalence of, about the occult and visionary consciousness, 191–192, 195, 212–214, 222–225, 242–244, 249–251; and anxiety about vagueness and passivity, 195–197; attitude of, toward Vorticism, 135–136, 137, 155–156, 242–243, 286n.3; and childbearing body, 145, 157–159, 167–169, 171, 293n.41; and collaborations on visionary narratives, 229, 230, 233–234; compared with male contemporaries, 24–25, 141, 179–180, 248–249, 287n.12, 292–293n.41; criticism on gynopoetics of, 137, 140–141, 156–159, 183, 286n.5, 287n.11, 291n.31; critics on, 136–137, 139–141, 156–158, 180–182; death of, 139; education of, 217–219; and eroticism, 145, 159–162, 163–167, 172–178, 181–185, 293nn.42–43; father of, 192, 202, 214, 217–220, 222, 224, 234–235, 240–241, 243, 249, 251, 302n.42; feminism of, 24, 156–157, 179–180, 183–184, 248–249; feminist criticism of, 140–141, 156–158, 181–182, 286n.5, 286nn.5–6; and geometrics, 2, 137, 154–171, 191, 193, 196–202, 204–205, 212–213, 234–235, 240–244, 248; and Hellenism, 144, 181–182, 292n.36; home of, 134; and jellyfish imagery, 157, 158, 161, 169–171, 241, 298n.17; and Jung, 299n.24; and Lewis, 8; metaphors in works by, 298n.17; and Moravianism, 190, 297nn.10–12, 302n.41; on need for "new words," 9, 247; and occult, 12, 187–194, 196–197, 199–200, 211, 212, 219–220, 249–251, 298n.16, 298–299n.19, 300n.26; poetry by, 135, 139, 140, 181, 185, 212, 261–262n.39, 287n.12, 288n.13, 300–301n.32, 303n.49; and politics, 206, 211–212, 242–243, 248; and Pound, 8, 135, 140, 190; prose style of, 179; review of Yeats's *Responsibilities* by, 8, 135–136, 154–157, 165, 172, 198, 250, 258n.17; and scientific developments, 21; self-doubt of, 213, 217–219, 228–229; siblings of, 217, 219, 240–241; and Theosophy, 190, 297n.12; traumatic experiences of, during 1910s, 137–138, 176–178, 184; and visions/mystical revelation, 12, 26, 156–159, 187–188, 190–192, 195–197, 200, 224–225, 228–229, 232–234, 240–241, 249–251, 295n.2, 299nn.21–22, 300n.31, 302nn.41–42, 303n.49; Vorticist influences on, xv, 20, 24–25, 26, 137, 193, 197, 198, 242–244, 250, 252–253; work with Freud (as Freud's student and analysand), xvi, 12–13, 137–138, 178, 188, 198, 200, 201–202, 211–212, 213, 230, 233–234, 248, 285n.1, 301n.40; and World War I, 177, 198, 242, 248; and World War II, 190, 212, 301–302nn.39–40; and Yeats, 8–9. *See also* Vorticist/geometric body; and specific works
"H.D. by Delia Alton" (H.D.), 212, 222
Helen in Egypt (H.D.), 287n.12
Hellenism, 144, 181–182, 292n.36
Hemingway, Ernest, 70, 72, 85
Heraclitus, 204, 209
HERmione (H.D.): compared with *Nights*, 292n.34; on educational failure, 217–218; ending of, 292n.37; eroticism in, 173, 174–175, 183, 241, 293–294n.46; geometric idiom in, xvi, 21, 241–242; protagonist compared with priestess in, 286n.2; publication of, 287n.7; on relationship with

father, 214, 241–242; Vorticist/geometric body in, 136, 172–175
Heywood, Leslie, 261n.37, 288–289n.17
Hollenberg, Donna, 156, 285n.1
homosexuality: and dandyism, 52, 53, 87; and "effeminacy," 19, 20, 41, 52–55, 245–246; fiction on, 52–53; Foucault on, 52, 267n.42; Lewis on, 53–55, 70, 73–74, 268nn.45–46; and Lewis's use of word "queer," 54–55, 70, 267–268n.44; sexological studies of, 52; and sodomy, 52, 53, 56, 73; Vorticism's covert attraction to eroticized male dyad, 72–75; of Wilde, 19, 52, 62, 73
Hood, Connie, 188, 300n.27
Horton, David, 127
Hours Press, 89, 92, 124, 273n.2
Hugh Selwyn Mauberley (Pound), 177, 297n.15
Hulme, T. E., 4, 15–21, 45, 119, 167, 197, 246, 259n.25, 260n.27, 260n.30, 260nn.32–33, 304n.53
Huyssen, Andreas, 41
Hynes, Gladys, 47

Ibsen, Henrik, 55
Imagism, 139, 162, 190, 286n.3, 288n.13
Impressionism, 43
Irigaray, Luce, 140, 160
Irish politics, 206–210, 301n.36
Italian Fascism. *See* Fascism
Italian Futurism. *See* Futurism, Italian
Izzo, Carlo, 111

Jackson, Holbrook, 62, 268n.47, 269n.60
Jameson, Fredric, 69, 70, 74, 265n.25, 268n.45, 269n.65
Jefferson, Thomas, 12, 114
Jefferson and/or Mussolini (Pound), xvi, 12, 95, 103, 105, 123, 278n.42
jellyfish imagery, 157, 158, 161, 169–171, 241, 291n.30, 298n.17
John, Augustus, 27, 54, 62, 73, 269n.59
Jordan, Viola, 299n.19
Joyce, James, 51, 109, 255n.1, 291n.30
Jung, C. G., 299n.24

Kadlec, David, 93, 274nn.10–11
Kandinsky, Wassily, 2, 5, 16, 43, 48–49, 193, 243, 258n.19, 260n.31, 290n.25
Kasper, John, 127, 128–129, 130
Kaufmann, Michael, 25, 141, 287–288n.13
Kenner, Hugh, xvii, 2, 7, 29–30, 34, 118, 256n.5, 258n.16, 270n.69, 270n.71, 283n.82, 283n.85
Kermode, Frank, xviii, 276n.23
Kitson, Arthur, 94, 274nn.10–11
Klein, Scott, 51–52, 75, 270n.72, 271n.73
Kloepfer, Deborah, 286n.5–6
Koestenbaum, Wayne, 267n.44
Konody, Paul, 4
Kora and Ka (H.D.), 285n.1
Kreymborg, Alfred, 264n.18
Kristeva, Julia, 72, 140, 286n.5, 287n.10

Lacan, Jacques, 286n.5
LaFourcade, Bernard, 269n.65
Laird, Holly, 303–304n.52
Laity, Cassandra, 41, 260n.34, 265n.30, 267n.43
Lane, John, 39
Langeteig, Kendra, 180
Laughlin, James, 285n.100
Laurie, T. Werner, 300n.27
Lawrence, D. H., 138, 140, 158, 179–180, 295n.5, 304n.53
Leadbeater, C. W., 22–23, 259n.26, 260n.31, 299n.25
Lechmere, Kate, 43
Le Corbusier, 2, 3, 13, 116, 282n.77
Lentricchia, Frank, 272n.85
Levenson, Michael, xvii
Levin, Harry, 262n.4
Lewis, Wyndham: and anti-collaborations, 51–56; on artist's role, 59; artwork of, 2, 4, 5, 22, 34, 66–67, 69, 79, 119, 148, 269n.63, 274n.8; on *Blast* as "history book," 27–28, 36; on *fin de siècle*, 27–28, 57–58, 69–70; as founder of Vorticism, xiv, 3, 7; on geometrics, 4, 37, 44–45, 255n.2; and H.D., 8; on homosexuality and "effeminacy," 53–55, 70, 73–74, 268nn.45–46, 293n.41; and Hulme, 15,

16, 17, 141; and jellyfish imagery, 158, 291n.30; on machinery, 21, 260n.35; and masculinity, 69–72, 270n.67, 271–272n.83; on occult and Theosophy, 12, 193–194, 242, 250, 298n.18; and Omega Workshops, 4, 5, 46–48; personae used by, 43, 269n.57; and possibility of publishing a third issue of *Blast*, 100, 277n.36; revisiting of Vorticism by, in later years, 11, 253; and scientific developments, 22, 260–261n.36; on Vorticist art, 4–5, 48, 112, 274n.7; and Vorticist/geometric body, 141, 143–145, 149–154, 289n.18; and Vorticist headquarters, 43; and Wildean Aestheticism, 51–66, 72–75; on World War I, 290n.27; writing style of, 60; and Yeats, xv, 9, 197–198, 237–238, 250, 299n.23. *See also Blast*; *Enemy of the Stars* (Lewis); *Tarr* (Lewis); Vorticism; and other works

lines. *See* geometry/geometrics

Little Review, 60

Lodge, Sir Oliver, 22, 283n.85

Loewenstein, Andrea Freud, 56, 268n.51, 271–272n.83

London, Bette, 188, 295n.3, 303n.52

Longenbach, James, 9

Lyon, Janet, xviii, 37

machinery, 20–21, 23, 45, 155–156, 260n.35

MacLeish, Archibald, 95

Macmillan, 300n.27

Macpherson, Kenneth, 285n.1

"Magic" (Yeats), 296n.9

Malatesta, Sigismondo, 92, 121, 273n.6, 277n.32, 283nn.87–88

male homosexuality. *See* homosexuality

Marinetti, F. T.: on airplanes and automobiles, 86–87, 151; death of, 279n.48; and fascism, 281n.66; and Mostra della Rivoluzione Fascista (MRF) exhibition, 280n.55; Mussolini's praise of, 279n.49; and Pound, 102–104, 278n.44, 278–279nn.46–48, 279n.53, 279nn.50–51; on violence and precision, 10; Vorticists on, 27, 36, 43, 49, 68, 193

Marsden, Dora, 94, 274n.11

masculinity: and effeminization under patriarchy, 272n.85; in *Enemy of the Stars*, 69, 70; and *fin-de-siècle* culture, 56, 268n.50; Lewis's ambivalent relationship to, 69–72, 270n.67, 271–272n.83; and Phallic aesthetics, 69–71, 85, 269n.65, 293n.41; and Vorticism, 20, 24, 43, 47–48, 56, 70–72. *See also* misogyny

Materer, Timothy, xvii, 7, 22, 34, 58, 60–61, 187, 192, 199, 256n.3, 256n.6, 260n.31, 269n.54, 270n.71, 270n.73, 290n.25, 294–295n.1, 298n.16, 299n.24, 302n.45

Mathers, MacGregor, 189, 194, 199, 296n.7

Maurice (Forster), 52–53

McAlmon, Robert, 178

McDonald, Gail, 2

McFarlane, James, 262n.5

McGann, Jerome, 30, 99, 263n.12, 273n.2, 276n.29, 277n.32

McLuhan, Marshall, 113, 130, 262n.1

Mead, G. R. S., 145, 165, 189, 259n.26, 286n.2

Messenger, Cynthia, 266n.35

Meyers, Jeffrey, 22, 66

Michel, Walter, 5

Mira-Mare (H.D.), 285n.1

Misogyny: alleged misogyny in Pound's writings, 158, 179–180, 293n.41; in Lewis's writings, 69, 73, 269n.65, 291n.30, 293n.41; and Vorticism, 24, 43, 69; in Yeats's love poetry, 261n.38. *See also* masculinity

"Modern Art and Its Philosophy" (Hulme), 15–21, 119, 141–144, 167, 197, 259n.25

modernism: and aesthetic of hardness, 261n.37; and asceticism, 288–289n.17; biomorphic modernism, 266n.35; concept of, 28–29, 262–263nn.3–5; and critical-theoretical writings, 256n.4; female versus male modernism, 141, 287–288n.13; and skepticism, 192; and threat of feminized Other, 41; Vorticism's influence on, xv–xvi, xviii, 6, 7–13, 23–24, 26, 251–253. *See also* specific artists and authors

Modernist Studies Association, 28–29, 262n.3
Monroe, Harriet, 35, 264n.20
Moore, Marianne, 94, 95, 264n.18
Moravianism, 190, 297nn.10–12, 302n.41
Morris, Adalaide, 297n.14
Morris, William, 47, 122
Morrisson, Mark, 32, 34, 40, 60–61, 263n.13
Morrow, Bradford, 27
Mostra della Rivoluzione Fascista (MRF) exhibition, xviii, 89, 96–97, 104–112, 279–280nn.54–60, 280n.63, 281n.67, 282n.77
"Murder by Capital" (Pound), 110
Murphy, William, 302n.44
Mussolini, Benito: gift of *Jefferson and/or Mussolini* to, 278n.42; *Il Popolo* newspaper founded by, 105; and Marinetti, 102, 103; Pound's admiration of, 12, 25, 93, 101, 120–121, 207, 247–248, 273n.6, 280–281n.64, 283n.86, 284n.97; Pound's meeting with, 101; Pound's misunderstandings of policies of, 276n.25; Pound's view of, as artist, 109, 281n.65; praise of Marinetti by, 279n.49; violence of regime of, 97; Yeats's interest in, 207–210. *See also* Fascism; *Jefferson and/or Mussolini* (Pound)
mystical revelation/visionary knowledge: ambivalence of H.D. and Yeats about, 191–192, 195, 213–216, 222–225, 242–244, 249–251; and collaborations by Yeats and H.D., 230–235; definition of, 295n.2; and geometrics, xv, 9, 191, 192–193, 196–205, 212–213, 234–244, 299n.22; and H.D., 187–188, 190–192, 195–197, 219–220, 224–225, 228–229, 232–234, 235, 239–242, 249–251, 295n.2, 299nn.21–22, 300n.31, 302nn.41–42, 303n.49; and politics, 206–213; relationship of, to the occult, 295n.2; and Yeats, 188–189, 191–192, 195–197, 224–228, 230–232, 234–240, 249–251, 299n.22. *See also* occult; *Vision* (Yeats)

Narthex (H.D.), 285n.1
Nature: Vorticist view of, 43–44, 46, 58–59, 74–75, 77, 79–82, 84–87, 246, 269n.54, 271n.80, 272n.85, 289n.18; and Wildean Aestheticism, 58–59, 61, 85, 269n.54
Negri, Ada, 89, 108, 109, 110
Nelson, Cary, 99, 276n.30, 277n.32
New Age, 4, 15, 33, 40, 94, 149, 260n.32, 265n.28, 267n.41, 274n.11, 277n.33
New Directions publisher, 139, 285n.100
"New Method in Scholarship" (Pound), 113
Nicholls, Peter, xvii, 263n.6
Nights (H.D.): as autobiographical text, 176–178; childbearing in, 167–169; compared with *Enemy of the Stars*, 175–176; compared with *Notes on Thought and Vision*, 159–161, 167–171; compared with "Responsibilities," 172; critical neglect of, 139–141; electricity in, 165, 175–176, 183; eroticism in, 159–162, 163–167, 172, 174–178, 181–184, 294n.46; geometrics in, xvii, 137, 156, 198, 248; Helforth in, 161, 175, 178–179, 292n.40; house in, 133–134; narrative frames in, 175–179; Natalia's suicide in, xvi, 12, 159, 161, 176, 177–178, 184; Natalia's visions in, 285–286n.2; Neil in, 159, 160, 162–167, 292n.34; Prologue of, 161, 175, 292n.39; prose style of, 179; publication and reissue of, 139, 285n.1; religious terminology in, 291–292n.33; theme and plot summary of, xvi, xvii, 12, 159; violence in, 165–167, 172, 175–177, 181, 184, 198, 248; Vorticist/geometric body in, 133–135, 138, 140, 158–169, 172, 175–184, 248, 292n.35
Nordau, Max, 55, 268n.47
North, Michael, xvi, 207, 208, 276n.23
Notes on Thought and Vision (H.D.): body in, 157–159, 167–171, 291nn.31–32; compared with *Nights*, 159–161, 167–171; on "daemon," 292n.38; and father's death, 302n.42; Gelpi on, 180; and geometric idiom, xvi; and gynopoetics, 156–159, 291n.31; jellyfish imagery in, 157, 158, 161, 169–171, 298n.17; publication of,

287n.7; and "Responsibilities," 156–157, 291n.29; as visionary writing, 188, 302n.42

Nott, Stanley, 126

occult: ambivalence of H.D. and Yeats about, 191–192, 195, 213–216, 223–225, 242–244, 249–250; definition of, 294–295nn.1–2; and Eliot, 295n.5; and geometry, xvii, 22–23; and H.D., 12, 187–193, 196–197, 199–200, 211, 219–220, 249–251, 298n.16, 298–299n.19, 300n.26, 301n.39; in late nineteenth and early twentieth centuries, 199, 296n.6; and mediumship, 195, 298n.18; and Pound, 22, 295n.5; and psychoanalysis, 212; relationship of, to mysticism, 295n.2; scholarship's avoidance and fear of, 295n.5; scientific study of, 192; and Yeats, xvi, 12, 13, 22, 187–193, 195, 195–197, 199, 214, 215–216, 249–251, 294n.1, 295n.5, 296–297nn.7–9, 302nn.44–45. *See also* mystical revelation/visionary knowledge; *A Vision* (Yeats)

Oderman, Kevin, 290n.22

O'Duffy, Eoin, 208, 301n.38

O'Leary, John, 190, 215, 226, 296nn.7–8

Olney, James, 299n.24

Omega Workshops, 4, 5, 47–50, 69

Orage, A. R., 7, 33, 40, 94, 258n.14, 265n.26, 274n.11

Order of the Golden Dawn, 189, 194, 199

"Oread" (H.D.), 135

organic versus abstract, 141–144, 304n.53

Ortega y Gasset, José, 15, 142–143, 260n.28, 288nn.15–16

Orwell, George, 129

Ostriker, Alicia, 139, 165–166, 286nn.5–6, 287n.12

Others magazine, 264n.18

"Our Wild Body" (Lewis), 149–150, 153, 289n.17

Ovid Press, 124

Page, P. K., 78

Paint It Today (H.D.), 139, 287n.7

Paracelsus, 199

Pater, Walter, 144, 182, 183, 292n.36, 293n.43

Patke, Rajeev, 14

Pearson, Norman Holmes, 178, 188

Pease, Donald, 272n.85

Peppis, Paul, xvii, 7, 8, 258n.15

Per Amica Silentia Lunae (Yeats), 195, 216, 226, 296n.9

Perloff, Marjorie, xviii, 25, 31–32, 34, 258n.18, 262n.3, 278n.44

Phallic aesthetics, 69–71, 85, 269n.65, 293n.41. *See also* masculinity; misogyny

Phrases and Philosophies for the Use of the Young (Wilde), 60

Picabia, Francis, 2, 281n.65

Picasso, Pablo, 43, 48, 193

The Picture of Dorian Gray (Wilde), 59, 60

Pilate's Wife (H.D.), 287n.7

Plan of War (Lewis), 67, 68, 79

Plato, xiii, xiv, 1, 14, 201, 226, 236

Plotinus, 199

Poetry magazine, 29, 33, 35, 263n.10

Poggioli, Renato, xv

politics: and H.D., 206, 211–213, 242–243, 248; and Pound, 93–96, 125–127, 130–131, 274n.12, 284n.97; and Yeats, 206–210, 301n.37, 304n.54

Pollexfen, George, 215

Por, Odon, 95, 276n.25

Portrait of an Englishwoman (Lewis), 67, 79

Post-Impressionism, 2, 16–18, 46, 48

"Postscript to *The Natural Philosophy of Love*" (Pound), 293n.41

Pound, Dorothy. *See* Shakespear, Dorothy

Pound, Ezra: on "accelerated grimace" of 1920s–1930s, 191; and aesthetic of hardness, 261n.37; and anti-Semitism, 130, 273n.6; on *Blast*, 29, 35–36, 262n.2, 263n.9; and the "clean line," 11, 25, 92, 96, 97–98, 111–112, 116–117, 119–121, 123–124, 129, 146, 147, 290n.24; on culture, 20, 110–111, 113–115, 130–131, 282–283n.79; deluxe editions of, 89–92, 97, 99, 121–124, 127, 273n.2, 277n.32; on "divine and permanent world," 290n.23;

economic and political views of, 93–96, 125–127, 130–131, 274n.12, 284n.97; format of books by, 90–92, 97–99, 121–128, 273n.2, 285n.100; on "form-sense" of Vorticist geometrics, 10, 26, 149, 169; on Futurism, 103–104; and geometrics, 1–2, 10, 26, 117–120, 146–149, 241–242, 283n.85, 284n.97; and H.D., 8, 135, 140, 190; and hermeneutic of the line, 115–120; historicization of Pound's relationship to Fascism, 98–99; and Hulme, 15, 16, 259n.25; *Il Mare* column by, 103–104, 105; and Italian Fascism, xv, xvi–xvii, xviii, 12, 25, 93, 98–99, 130, 207, 247–248; and Kasper's bookshop, 128–129; on language, xiii, 9, 247; and Marinetti, 102–104, 278n.44, 278–279nn.46–48, 279nn.50–51, 279n.53; misogyny of, 158, 179–180; and Mostra della Rivoluzione Fascista exhibition, 96–97, 104–112, 280n.57, 280n.60; move to Italy by, 273n.6; and Mussolini, 12, 25, 93, 101, 120–121, 207, 247–248, 273n.6, 280–281n.64, 283n.86, 284n.97; and occult, 22, 187, 295n.5; poetry by, in *Blast*, 264n.17; on poet's role, 117–118, 275n.18; radio broadcasts by, during World War II, 284n.98; on radio version of *Enemy of the Stars*, 271n.75; on relationship between geometry and art and poetry, 1, 22, 117; on "repeat in history," 230; and revival of Vorticism attempted by, 12, 25, 92–93, 95–98, 100–104, 242, 247–248, 252–253, 273n.3; at St. Elizabeths Hospital, 127–128, 130, 284n.98; and scientific developments, 22; and simplicity and influence in 1950s, 127–128, 130, 284–285nn.99–101; treason charges against, 130, 284n.98; on Vorticism, 46, 100–101, 148–149, 256–257n.7, 277n.33; and Vorticist/geometric body, 143–149, 157; on Whistler, 4, 257n.11; writings by, in *Others* magazine, 264n.18; and Yeats, 8–9. *See also Cantos* (Pound); and other specific works
Pound, Omar, 96, 276n.25

psychoanalysis of H.D., xvi, 12–13, 137–138, 178, 188, 198, 200, 201–202, 212, 213, 230, 233–234, 248, 285n.1, 301n.40
"Psychology and Troubadours" (Pound), 146
publishing industry, 124–126, 284nn.92–93. *See also* Books
Pythagoras, xiv, 1, 199, 230

Queensberry, Marquess, 52, 53, 73, 267n.44
"queer" as term, 54–55, 70, 267–268n.44
Quéma, Anne, 56, 268n.46, 268n.52, 269n.65
Quest Society, 15, 22, 119, 259n.25, 259n.26
Quinn, John, 100, 277n.36

Rainey, Lawrence, xvii, 33, 93, 98–99, 256n.4, 263n.14, 264n.17, 265n.24, 273n.6, 276n.29, 277n.32, 283nn.87–88
Ramacharaka, Yogi, 22
Random House, 124–125, 284nn.92–93
Ransome, Arthur, 62, 63
Rebel Art Centre, 43, 71
Redman, Tim, xvi–xvii, 93, 130, 274n.11, 276n.23, 278n.42, 281n.70
"Responsibilities" (H.D.'s review), 8, 135–136, 154–157, 165, 172, 198, 250, 258n.17
The Revenge for Love (Lewis), 69
Reynolds, Paige, xvii, 7, 36
Rhys, Jean, 261n.37
Roberts, William, 3, 17, 18, 68, 274n.8
Rodker, John, 89, 122, 124
Ross, Robert, 62, 65, 269n.59
Rothenstein, William, 62
Rougement, Denis de, 190
Rude Assignment (Lewis), 75, 274n.7, 290n.27

Sachs, Hans, 137
Saddlemyer, Ann, 273n.1
Sant'Elia, Antonio, 66, 280n.55
Sarfatti, Margherita, 110, 112
Saunders, Helen, 3, 68, 100, 277n.34
Saurat, Denis, 295n.1
Scheiwiller, Vanni, 285n.100
Schelling, Felix, 121, 283n.83

Schnapp, Jeffrey, 87, 89, 105, 112, 275n.22, 280n.63
Schuchard, Ronald, 255n.3
science, 21–22, 217–228, 260–261n.36
Scott, Bonnie Kime, 158, 291n.30
Scott-James, R. A., 263n.14
Sea Garden (H.D.), 181
Seidel, Elizabeth, 297n.11, 302n.41
sexuality. *See* eroticism; homosexuality
Shakespear, Dorothy, 68, 92, 272–273nn.1–2
Shakespear, Olivia, 187, 198, 227, 299n.23, 304n.53
Shaw, George Bernard, 62
Sherry, Vincent, xvii, 122, 256n.3, 260n.28, 275–276n.23
Showalter, Elaine, 55–56, 268n.52
Sickert, Walter, 51, 54–55, 63, 65, 69–70, 265n.28, 267n.41
Sieburth, Richard, 116
Sinfield, Alan, 19, 52, 71, 268n.50
Sinnett, A. P., 199, 294n.1
"The Skeleton in the Cupboard Speaks" (Lewis), 267n.39
Slow Attack (Lewis), 67, 79
Social Credit movement, 94, 95, 126, 273n.6, 274n.11
sodomy, 52, 53, 56, 70, 73
The Spirit of Romance (Pound), 117, 147
Spoo, Robert, 96, 255n.3, 276n.25
Square Dollar Series, 127–128, 285n.101
Stein, Gertrude, 170
Stevens, Wallace, 94, 95, 246, 264n.18, 275n.15
Stevenson, Robert Louis, 267–268n.44
Stock, Noel, 278n.41
Stone, Marla, 103, 108, 275n.22, 279–280n.54, 281n.67, 282n.77
Stoppard, Tom, xiii–xiv
Strater, Henry, 123
Strindberg, Frida, 8
Sturm, Frank Pearce, 227, 303n.51
Surette, Leon, xvii, 8, 95, 189, 273n.6, 274nn.11–12, 275n.18, 276n.28, 294n.1, 295n.5
Swedenborg, Emanuel, 22, 190, 199, 228, 230, 236

"Swedenborg, Mediums, and the Desolate Places" (Yeats), 296n.9, 299n.20
Swift, Jonathan, 209
Swinburne, A. C., 50, 294n.46
Sword, Helen, xvii, 192, 225, 298n.17, 299n.21, 303n.49
The Sword Went Out to Sea (H.D.), 196
Symbolists, 246
Symons, Arthur, 265n.28
Symons, Julian, 262n.5

Tarr (Lewis): and effeminacy, 272n.83; eroticism in, 150, 152–154; geometric idiom in, xvi; goal for, 270n.69; jellyfish imagery in, 291n.30; misogyny in, 69; revised editions of, 11; sexual ideology of, 54, 69; violence in, 69, 149, 150–151, 152–154, 271n.81; Vorticist/geometric body in, 149, 150, 152–154
Tempio Malatestiano, 121–122, 283n.87
Theosophy, 12, 22–23, 145, 190, 194, 195, 199, 259n.26, 260n.31, 286n.2, 294n.1, 296n.7, 297n.12, 298n.18, 299n.25
Three Mountains Press, 89, 124
Tickner, Lisa, 24, 55
Time and the Western Man (Lewis), 197–198, 293n.41, 299n.23
Timon of Athens (Lewis), 66–67, 79, 119
Travis, S., 292n.37
Tribute to Freud (H.D.): "Advent" and "Writing on the Wall" in, 188, 191; on father, 21–22, 214, 217, 222, 241; geometrics in, 21–22, 201–202, 204–205, 240, 241; on H.D.'s attitude toward Freud, xvi, 12–13, 233–234; on H.D.'s "gift," 229; on H.D.'s self-doubt, 167; on H.D.'s visions, 167, 201–202, 204–205, 233–234, 241; on magnifying glass, 240–241; on period between the world wars, 138; and politics, 211
Trilogy (H.D.), 184–185, 212, 287, 300–301n.32
Tryphonopoulos, Demetres, xvii, 145, 179–180, 190, 286n.2, 290n.23, 294–295n.1, 295nn.5–6
Tschichold, Jan, 282n.76
Turner, Reginald, 62, 269n.59

underconsumption, 94, 126, 274nn.10–11
The Usual Star (H.D.), 285n.1

Vico, Giambattista, 209, 230
violence: and abstraction, 290n.27; in *Enemy of the Stars*, 68, 74–75, 78, 79–85, 149, 150, 151–152; and Futurism, 68, 151, 155–156; and geometry/geometrics, 66–68, 151–152, 155–157, 172–173, 174, 248; of Mussolini's regime, 97; in *Nights*, 165–167, 172, 175–177, 181, 183–184, 198, 248; in *Tarr*, 69, 149, 150, 152–154, 271n.81; and Vorticism, 155–156; and Vorticist/geometric body, 149–154; of World War I, 177, 198, 290n.27
A Vision (Yeats): Bloom on, 193; critics on, 295n.3; difficulties in reading, 13; fictional account of origin of, 223–224, 236–238, 243; Frye on, 196; geometric idiom and diagrams in, xv, 9, 191, 192–193, 196–204, 205, 227–228, 235–240, 244, 250, 301nn.33–34; "Great Wheel" in, 204, 209; intersecting gyres in, 203; Introduction to, 9, 198, 236, 303n.51; and Irish politics, 206–210, 301n.37; and Lewis, 9; publication of, 300n.27; revisions and editions of, 188, 197–198, 226, 300n.27; on "revolt of the soul against the intellect," 226–228; themes of, xvi, 188; Vorticist influence on, 193, 197–198, 250; W. B. Yeats's relationship with his father, 221, 226–227, 235–236, 239–240, 302n.42; wife's collaboration on, 188–189, 191, 205, 223, 230–232, 233, 236, 301n.33, 303n.52; writing process for, 297n.14; on Yeats's avowed ignorance of philosophy, 226–227
visionary knowledge. *See* mystical revelation/visionary knowledge
vortices. *See* geometry/geometrics
Vorticism: and Aestheticism, xviii, 14, 37–42; artists associated with, 3, 4, 257n.8; beginning and end of, xiv, 3; campaign against "effeminacy" by, xvi, xviii, 10, 18–20, 41, 46–51, 70, 73, 87–88, 245–247; characteristics of, 4–7, 10–11, 19–20, 37, 88, 96, 245, 266n.35; covert attraction of, to eroticized male dyad, 72–75; and Cubism, xviii, 5–6, 10, 43, 48, 193, 256n.7; and double desire for precision and vigorous force, 10–11, 19–20, 23; and Futurism, xviii, 5–6, 10, 21, 43, 86, 102, 104, 151, 193, 264n.15, 273n.3, 278n.44, 278n.46, 289n.18; and geometry, xiv, xv, xviii, 4–6, 8–11, 14, 18–20, 37, 41–46, 118–120, 193, 194, 196–197, 246–247, 249–250; H.D.'s attitude toward, 135–136, 137, 155–156, 242–243, 286n.3; influence of, on modernism, xv–xvi, xviii, 6, 7–13, 23–24, 26, 251–253; loss of Vorticist work, 264n.19; and machinery, 21, 23, 45, 155–156, 260n.35; manifestoes of, 43–44, 48, 49, 53, 58, 59, 68, 80, 82, 84–85; Mansard Gallery exhibit (1920) of, 274n.8; and masculinism and misogyny, 20, 24, 43, 47–48, 56, 69–73, 158, 269n.65; and Nature, 43–44, 46, 58–59, 74–75, 79–82, 84–87, 246, 272n.85, 289n.18; original headquarters of movement, 43, 71; Pound on, 46, 100–101, 148–149, 256–257n.7, 277n.33; Pound's attempted revival of, 12, 25, 92–93, 95–98, 100–104, 242, 247–248, 273n.3; purpose of, xiv–xv, 3; scholarly studies of, xvii–xviii, 7–8; self-differentiation of, from other contemporary movements, 48–49; and Wildean Aestheticism, 50–66, 72–75, 88. *See also Blast*; Geometry/geometrics; Lewis, Wyndham; Vorticist/geometric body
"Vorticism" (Pound), 1, 16
Vorticist/geometric body: in *Bid Me to Live*, 136; characteristics of, 144–146, 154; *Enemy of the Stars*, 150, 151–152; and eroticism, 145, 150–154, 159–161, 163–167, 172–177, 181–184; and H.D., xv, 12, 25–26, 136, 145; in *HERmione*, 136, 172–175; and Hulme, 141–144; and Lewis, 143–145, 149–154, 289n.18; in *Nights*, 133–135, 138, 140, 158–169, 172, 175–184, 248, 292n.35; and Pound, 143–149, 157; related to Aristotelian concept of

schema, 289n.19; in *Tarr*, 150, 152–154; and Wilde's tomb, 64, 65–66

Wade, Allan, 303n.50
Wadsworth, Edward, 3, 4, 5, 17, 34, 46–48, 274n.8, 277n.33
Wagner, Richard, 55
Waugh, Evelyn, 266n.38
Wees, William, xvii, 6, 7, 15, 31, 32, 256n.6, 258n.16, 260n.30, 263n.8, 263n.14, 277n.33, 277n.36
West, Rebecca, 68, 269n.63
Whistler, James Abbott McNeill, 4, 12, 22, 257n.11
Whitman, Walt, 52, 55
Wilde, Oscar: on art, 59–60; *Blast* on, 42, 50–51, 260n.34; death of, 62, 269n.59; "effeminacy" of, 19, 52; and Futurism, 50; homosexuality of, 19, 52, 62, 73; influence of, on Vorticists, 58–66; Lewis on, 53–56; as male Aesthete, 19, 42, 50–61, 260n.34; after release from prison, 62, 269n.60; tomb of, 64, 65–66, 269n.61; trials and imprisonment of, 19, 52, 53, 62, 73, 245, 269n.56; Vorticism and Wildean aestheticism, 57–61, 72–73, 245–247, 269n.54
Williams, William Carlos, 94–95, 124, 261n.37, 287n.12
"The Wisdom of Poetry" (Pound), 117, 199
Witemeyer, Hugh, 262–263n.5
Woolf, Virginia, 3, 129, 137, 176–177, 255n.1
World War I, 177, 198, 242, 248
World War II, 190, 198, 212, 284n.98, 301–302nn.39–40
Worringer, Wilhelm, 15–18, 142, 260n.30
"Writing on the Wall" (H.D.), 188, 191, 198–199, 201–202, 300n.29, 300n.32
Wutz, Michael, 22, 256n.3, 260–261n.36

Yeats, George: and collaboration on *A Vision*, 188–189, 191, 205, 223, 230–232, 233, 236, 301n.33, 303n.52; diagrams in *The Vision* drawn by, 301n.33; and revisions of *A Vision*, 300n.27; on W. B. Yeats's father's relationship with Yeats, 215–217
Yeats, John Butler, 214–217, 221, 224, 226–227, 235–236, 239–240, 302n.42, 302–303nn.44–47
Yeats, William Butler: ambivalence of, about the occult and visionary consciousness, 191–192, 195, 212–217, 223–225, 243, 249–251; and anxiety about vagueness and passivity, 195–197; education of, 213, 215; and Fascism, 98, 130, 207–211, 301n.38; father of, 192, 214–217, 221, 224, 226–227, 234–236, 239–240, 243–244, 249, 251, 302n.42, 302–303nn.44–47; and Fenollosa, 283n.83; and geometrics, xv, 2, 9, 12, 191–193, 196–204, 212–213, 227–228, 234–240, 243–244, 250, 301n.34; H.D.'s review of *Responsibilities* by, 8, 135–136, 154–157, 165, 172, 198/-199, 250, 258n.17; and Hulme, 304n.53; and Irish politics, 206–211, 301n.36; and Jung, 299n.24; and Lewis, xv, 9, 197–198, 237–238, 250, 299n.23; love poetry by, 261n.37; marriage of, 188; and mystical revelation/visionary knowledge, 12, 13, 26, 188–189, 191–192, 195–197, 224–228, 230–233, 234–240, 249–251, 295n.2, 299n.22; and occult, xvi, 12, 13, 22, 187–194, 195–197, 199–200, 214, 215–216, 249–251, 294n.1, 295n.5, 296–297nn.7–9, 302nn.44–45; and poet's role, 275n.18; and politics, 206–211, 301n.37, 304n.54; and Pound, 8–9; as senator in Ireland, 206, 207, 209–210, 301n.37; and Theosophy, 189–190, 195, 199, 296n.7, 297n.12; Vorticist influences on, 20, 24, 26, 193, 197–199, 243–244, 250, 252–253. *See also* Vision (Yeats); and other specific works
The Yellow Book, 38, 39–41, 65, 69–70, 265n.26, 265n.28
Young, Suzanne, 176, 292n.40

Zola, Émile, 55
Zukofsky, Louis, 284nn.93–94

www.ingramcontent.com/pod-product-compliance
Lightning Source LLC
Chambersburg PA
CBHW060940230426
43665CB00015B/2007